MW00632390

R. Shiratori, K. Arai, F. Kato (Eds.)

Gaming, Simulations, and Society
Research Scope and Perspective

R. Shiratori, K. Arai, F. Kato (Eds.)

Gaming, Simulations, and Society

Research Scope and Perspective

With 89 Figures, Including 1 in Color

 Springer

Rei Shiratori
Professor, Faculty of Political Science and Economics, Tokai University;
President, The Institute for Political Studies in Japan (IPSJ)
1-35-15-304 Nishihara, Shibuya-ku, Tokyo 151-0066, Japan

Kiyoshi Arai, Dr. Eng.
Professor, Faculty of Social Systems Science, Chiba Institute of Technology
2-17-1 Tsudanuma, Narashino, Chiba 275-0016, Japan

Fumitoshi Kato, Ph.D.
Associate Professor, Faculty of Environmental Information, Keio University
5322 Endo, Fujisawa, Kanagawa 252-8520, Japan

This project has been executed with a grant from the Commemorative Organization for the Japan World Exposition '70.

Library of Congress Control Number: 2004108945

ISBN 4-431-22308-8 Springer-Verlag Tokyo Berlin Heidelberg New York

This work is subject to copyright. All rights are reserved, whether the whole or part of the material is concerned, specifically the rights of translation, reprinting, reuse of illustrations, recitation, broadcasting, reproduction on microfilms or in other ways, and storage in data banks.
The use of registered names, trademarks, etc. in this publication does not imply, even in the absence of a specific statement, that such names are exempt from the relevant protective laws and regulations and therefore free for general use.

Springer is a part of Springer Science+Business Media
springeronline.com
© Springer-Verlag Tokyo 2005
Printed in Japan

Typesetting: SNP Best-set Typesetter Ltd., Hong Kong
Printing and binding: Nikkei Printing Inc., Japan
SPIN: 11017615

Printed on acid-free paper

Preface

The Japan Association of Simulation & Gaming (JASAG) and the Science Council of Japan (SCJ) hosted ISAGA 2003, the 34th annual conference of the International Simulation and Gaming Association (ISAGA), at Kazusa Akademia Park in Kisarazu, Japan, August 25–29, 2003.

About 450 participants and guests attended, with 330 from Japan and 101 from 34 other countries. The number of submitted papers and reports exceeded 210, and in addition, many poster presentations and experiential sessions were held. This book is made up of 30 papers submitted to ISAGA 2003 and provides a good example of the diverse scope and standard of research achieved in simulation and gaming today. The theme of ISAGA 2003 was "Social Contributions and Responsibilities of Simulation and Gaming."

Looking back over the history of simulation and gaming research in Japan, in 1991 JASAG hosted ISAGA 1991 in Kyoto. However, even though there were only 12 years between ISAGA 1991 and ISAGA 2003, and both conferences were held in the same country, Japan, for Japanese researchers, the meaning of hosting these two international conferences of simulation and gaming research was very different.

Kyoto ISAGA 1991 was held in part to commemorate the establishment in 1989 of JASAG and aimed to introduce the cutting-edge work in simulation and gaming—research established from social scientific concepts quite different from engineering OR—to the academic community of Japan. However, in the case of ISAGA 2003 in Kisarazu, 14 years had passed since the establishment of JASAG, a large body of Japanese research had accumulated in the interim, and the standard of research was certainly now at least the equal of work from Europe and the United States. Against this more-established background, and in addition to the conventional simulation and gaming research developed mainly in Europe and the United States, the avowed intention of the organizers was to contribute to the future of simulation and gaming research in the world by demonstrating the unique scope of research in Japan, with its "softer" and more fluid Asian concepts; with its research into the social acceptance of entertainment games and the exploration of ethical issues; and with its wider application of new models and techniques such as agent-based modeling into the research of simulation and gaming.

JASAG had a clear awareness of the importance of a variety of practical and social issues and chose the overall theme of ISAGA 2003, "Social Contributions and Responsibilities of Simulation and Gaming," with the aim of providing a forum to focus on and explore the following subject areas:

(1) Attention to the practical nature of simulation and gaming and consideration of how best to incorporate the academic results of simulation and gaming into such areas as conflict resolution, decision making, environmental problems, education, and social welfare.
(2) Consideration of the possibility of holding the conference in Asia and helping eliminate the global digital divide by making use of the latest techniques and innovations of simulation and gaming to encourage social advances in developing countries. At present, the developed countries of the North possess the knowledge, technology, and techniques of simulation and gaming, but the majority of countries that would gain maximum benefit from such an approach are the developing countries of the South.
(3) Inclusion of the important and often-ignored issue of social influence and acceptance of entertainment games, with the raising of the ethical issue of practical study and the shedding of new light on the relation of knowledge and society, both opening new horizons for conventional simulation and gaming research.

The aim of making a contribution toward the elimination of the global digital divide became a guiding principle, resulting in the invitation of many researchers from developing countries, mainly in Asia. Moreover, as shown in the program in the Appendix at the end of this book, a special open session entitled "Open Day for the Public" was also planned for teachers from elementary to high schools, with the aim of demonstrating real-world applications of the very latest simulation and gaming techniques and innovations.

Concerning the academic examination of the theory of simulation and gaming, the conference focused on the exploration of the following subject areas.

(1) How do new academic frameworks (paradigms) of simulation and gaming contribute to the reframing and remodeling of the existing social sciences, such as political science, economics, business administration, and social psychology?
(2) How do we incorporate the newly developed methods and techniques, including agent-based modeling (ABM) and soft computing, into the present theories of simulation and gaming, and continue to establish simulation and gaming research as an academic discipline with its own separate identity?

The Organizing Committee thought the opportunity presented by ISAGA 2003 could be a turning point in the establishment and further development of a new academic discipline for simulation and gaming with a practical and interdisciplinary character, making full use of the new techniques of ABM and soft computing.

From an awareness of the above issues and purposes, the ISAGA 2003 conference program for August 26–29 was drawn up. First, in order to establish the identity of simulation and gaming research and with the aim of ensuring that all participants shared a common knowledge and awareness of the issues, all the morning programs were plenary sessions of the joint conference and the afternoon programs were for parallel specialized sessions, followed by after-dinner experiential sessions.

On August 26, the opening day of the conference, the chairperson (organizer) gave an opening address to the plenary session entitled "Toward a New Science of Simulation and Gaming: ISAGA and the Identity Problem of Simulation and Gaming as an Academic Discipline" and outlined the conference theme. On August 27, participants from abroad were able to visit the local sights, while an "Open Day for the Public" was held for Japanese schoolteachers and ordinary citizens.

The main subjects in the plenary sessions on the following days were all areas of current interest in simulation and gaming research: On August 28, "The Simulation and Gaming of Project and Program Management" and "Simulation and Gaming in the Classroom"; on August 29, "The Impact of Entertainment Games on Society" and "The Future of Online Games in Asia."

Nearly 30 afternoon parallel sessions were held including "Agent-Based Modeling Meets Gaming Simulation," "U-Mart: What We Have Learned from the Virtual Market," "Simulation and Gaming for Participatory Planning," "Peter F. Drucker's Thoughts and Gaming," "Policy Exercise for Transition and Change," and "Cross-cultural Communication and Foreign Language Education."

These sessions are shown in the contents: (1) Introduction; (2) Social Sciences and Simulation and Gaming; (3) Social Relevancies in Simulation and Gaming; (4) Strategies and Policy Exercise; (5) Designs and Tools of Simulation and Gaming; and (6) Paradigms in Simulation and Gaming, giving a true reflection of the issues and structure of ISAGA 2003.

In addition to these programs, at the opening ceremony, Mr. Tsutomu Hata, Prime Minister at the time of the establishment of the Japanese Government's IT Headquarters, gave a lecture entitled "Social Transformation and Politics in Japan." Before the opening of ISAGA 2003, JASAG commemorative symposiums "The Past, Present, and Future of JASAG" and "The Contribution of JASAG to Simulation and Gaming" were held.

ISAGA 2003 was the fruit of the efforts of many people, the following of whom served on the Organizing Committee:

Honorary Conference Chairperson	Jiro Kondo	The first President of JASAG and former Chairperson of the Science Council of Japan; Professor Emeritus, Tokyo University, Mathematics
Conference Chairperson (Organizer)	Rei Shiratori	Former President of JASAG; Tokai University, Political Science

ConferenceVice-chairperson and Program Department Chairperson	Kiyoshi Arai	President of JASAG; Chiba Institute of Technology, Social Systems Engineering
Secretary General and General Administration Department Chairperson	Fumitoshi Kato	Keio University, Sociology
Public Relations Department Chairperson	Arata Ichikawa	Ryutsu Keizai University, Business Administration
Finance Department Chairperson	Shigehisa Tsuchiya	Chiba Institute of Technology, Management System Science
Venue Department Chairperson	Hiroyuki Matsui	Kyoto University, Economics
Chairperson of Fund-raising	Yoichi Erikawa	Founder of Koei Co., Ltd.

Without these committee members' dedicated efforts, the support of the members of the ISAGA Steering Committee, including Dr. Jan Klabbers, the board members (including Mr. Taro Yuzawa, Secretary General), and ordinary members of JASAG, it would have been impossible to host the conference.

Furthermore, we received much-valued assistance from about 140 groups, including academic research associations of the Science Council of Japan, the city council of Kisarazu, Chiba, and financial support from 30 private enterprises. Without their invaluable assistance, the conference would have been much smaller and it would have been impossible to support the participants from developing countries, especially from other parts of Asia. We express our sincere gratitude and appreciation for the support and assistance of everyone who contributed to and participated in the success of ISAGA 2003.

In publishing this book, we are grateful for the helpful advice from the members of the Advisory Board. Mr. Yusuke Arai, a member of JASAG, took on the difficult task of collating manuscripts and indexes, while the staff of the Tokyo office of Springer-Verlag supported us with the overall editing and structuring of the book.

In conclusion, we will be very satisfied if this book can play a part, in however small a way, in the development of simulation and gaming research by inspiring scholars to further innovative and practical studies and research.

June 28, 2004

Rei Shiratori
Kiyoshi Arai
Fumitoshi Kato

Contents

Part V Paradigms in Simulation and Gaming

Authors

Nireka Adachi	Research Institute of Science and Technology for Society	(Chapter 16)
Kanji Akahori	Tokyo Institute of Technology	(Chapter 9)
Atsuko Arai	Jiji Press Ltd.	(Chapter 14)
Kiyoshi Arai	Chiba Institute of Technology	(Chapter 19, 27)
Norio Baba	Osaka-Kyoiku University	(Chapter 22)
Linda Carton	Delft University of Technology	(Chapter 5)
Jian Chen	Tsinghua University	(Chapter 30)
Ed Dammers	Netherlands Institute for Spatial Research	(Chapter 5)
Martin de Jong	Delft University of Technology	(Chapter 5)
Angelika Dufter-Weis	Ludwig-Maximilians-University Munich	(Chapter 23)
Minako Fujiie	Tokyo Electric Power Company	(Chapter 17)
Cathy S. Greenblat	Rutgers University	(Chapter 25)
Tadashi Hasebe	Tohoku University	(Chapter 19)
Fumihiko Hashimoto	Osaka City University	(Chapter 6)
Kazuo Hiraki	The University of Tokyo	(Chapter 11)
Koichi Hosoi	Ritsumeikan University	(Chapter 28)
Van Nam Huynh	Japan Advanced Institute of Science and Technology	(Chapter 30)
Arata Ichikawa	Ryutsu Keizai University	(Chapter 24)
Seiji Inokuchi	Hiroshima International University	(Chapter 21)
Kenichi Ishibashi	Keio University	(Chapter 4)
Masayori Ishikawa	The University of Tokyo/RISTEX	(Chapter 16)
Kouhei Iyori	Kyoto Sangyo University	(Chapter 7)
Hideki Kaji	Keio University	(Chapter 4)
Haruo Kamijo	Jugyou Zukuri Nettowaaku (the Quality Class Network)	(Chapter 13)
Toshiyuki Kaneda	Nagoya Institute of Technology	(Chapter 4)
Hidehiko Kanegae	Ritsumeikan University	(Chapter 4)
Juliane Karl	Ludwig-Maximilians-University, Munich	(Chapter 23)
Fumitoshi Kato	Keio University	(Chapter 8)
Satoshi Kimura	Tokai University	(Chapter 2)
Shinobu Kitani	Tohoku University	(Chapter 19)

Jan Klabbers	KMPC; University of Bergen	(Chapter 26)
Willy C. Kriz	Ludwig-Maximilians-University Munich	(Chapter 23)
Masayoshi Kuboya	Tokai University	(Chapter 2)
Elyssebeth Leigh	University of Technology, Sydney	(Chapter 20)
Martijn Leijten	Delft University of Technology	(Chapter 5)
Goh Matsuda	The University of Tokyo	(Chapter 11)
Toshiki Matsuda	Tokyo Institute of Technology	(Chapter 10)
Katumi Matsumura	System Kagaku Kenkyujo	(Chapter 4)
Igor Mayer	Delft University of Technology	(Chapter 5)
Jun Mihira	Keio University	(Chapter 4)
Noriko Nagata	Kwansei Gakuin University	(Chapter 21)
Yoshihiro Nakajima	Osaka City University	(Chapter 6)
Yoshiteru Nakamori	Japan Advanced Institute of Science and Technology	(Chapter 30)
Mieko Nakamura	Ryutsu Keizai University	(Chapter 24)
Fumihiro Nakano	Tohoku University	(Chapter 19)
Noriaki Nomura	Tohoku University	(Chapter 19)
Sobei H. Oda	Kyoto Sangyo University	(Chapter 7)
Kazuhito Ogawa	Kyoto University	(Chapter 7)
Shigenobu Ohara	PMCC Research Center; University of Technology, Sydney	(Chapter 27)
Susumu Ohnuma	Hokkaido University	(Chapter 3)
Mieko Ohsuga	Osaka Institute of Technology	(Chapter 21)
Koichi E. Okamoto	Toyo Eiwa University/RISTEX	(Chapter 16)
Matthias Puschert	Ludwig-Maximilians-University Munich	(Chapter 23)
Akira Sakamoto	Ochanomizu University	(Chapter 12)
Richard Scalzo	Erasmus University Rotterdam	(Chapter 5)
Koichi Sekimizu	Aitel Corporation	(Chapter 17)
Akiko Shibuya	Keio University	(Chapter 12)
Rei Shiratori	Tokai University; The Intitute for Political Studies in Japan	(Chapter 1)
Wang Shuqin	Northeast Normal University	(Chapter 22)
Laraine Spindler	University of Technology, Sydney	(Chapter 20)
Shigemasa Suganuma	Japan Advanced Institute of Science and Technology	(Chapter 30)
Akira Tanabe		(Chapter 17)
Kazuhisa Taniguchi	Kinki University	(Chapter 6)
Takao Terano	University of Tsukuba	(Chapter 14)
Sigehisa Tsuchiya	Chiba Institute of Technology	(Chapter 17)
Femke Verwest	Netherlands Institute for Spatial Research	(Chapter 5)
Sanae H. Wake	Doshisha Women's College of Liberal Arts	(Chapter 21)
Ivo Wenzler	Accenture; Technical University Delft	(Chapter 15)
Joseph Wolfe	Experiential Adventures LLC	(Chapter 18)
Mari Yahagi	Keio University	(Chapter 4)
Nagisa Yokoyama		(Chapter 29)

Introduction

1. Toward a New Science of Simulation and Gaming: ISAGA and the Identity Problem of Simulation and Gaming as an Academic Discipline[1]

Rei Shiratori[2]

What Are the Challenges Facing ISAGA?

On this occasion of opening the program of an academic meeting, the 34th Annual Conference of the International Simulation and Gaming Association (ISAGA), you may find it strange that I am beginning my speech by mentioning the organizational weakness of ISAGA and not by employing the more usual theoretical analysis of simulation and gaming.

Four years ago, in May 1999, I was late in attending the board meeting of the Japan Association of Simulation & Gaming (JASAG). When I arrived, I found that I had been elected to be the President of the association.

I felt it a great honor to be chosen as the President of JASAG and I was naturally pleased with the election and its result. I must also admit, however, that what has always concerned me since then were the organizational weakness and the ambiguity of the academic identity of the association.

It is these two issues that have been at the forefront of my mind as we organized our 34th annual conference, ISAGA 2003. In 1999 when I was elected to be President of JASAG, the membership of JASAG had reached slightly more than 400. The number of ISAGA members is completely unknown at this moment because the definitions and qualifications for membership of ISAGA are not clear.

In 1999, the most important goal for attaining stable management of JASAG as an organization was to improve the financial situation by increasing the number of members and membership fee income. ISAGA is in the same situation today.

I am deeply concerned with the future of ISAGA at this moment. It is very easy to claim, "Even if the academic association collapses, the academic disci-

---

[1] This article was originally "Introductory Speech" on the occasion of the 34th Annual Conference of International Simulation and Gaming Association "ISAGA 2003".
[2] Professor, Faculty of Political Science and Economics, Tokai University; and President, The Institute for Political Studies in Japan (IPSJ), Shibuya-ku, Tokyo 151-0066, Japan; rei@ipsj-tokyo.org.

pline will continue to develop." In reality, however, if this research organization named ISAGA were to disappear, it would be impossible for us to hold a conference like this. It would then be impossible for us to exchange the achievements of our research in simulation and gaming and to plan further research developments on the basis of this exchange of information. The collapse of ISAGA as an academic association would seriously hinder the academic development of simulation and gaming. There is a very close and direct relationship between the organizational situation of researchers and the academic development of related fields. This is why I proposed to the steering committee of ISAGA, 2 years ago at ISAGA 2001 in Bari, the establishment of a Subcommittee for Organizational and Financial Reform to create greater financial and organizational stability.

I believe that if ISAGA becomes a stronger organization in both its organizational and financial aspects, ISAGA can publish a history of the development of the theories and techniques of simulation and gaming in the form of a book, or it can open a library of simulations and games developed by researchers and make the library available to the public. These activities of ISAGA will, in turn, contribute to the development of the future of simulation and gaming research.

Simulation and Gaming: An Issue of Identity

Academic societies such as JASAG and ISAGA are voluntary associations of independent researchers. Even though such associations may attempt to offer a maximum amount of services to their membership, if the number of members is still small, it means that research in the academic field is not fully developed. An academic organization cannot be firmly and fully established unless the related science is fully developed. Unfortunately, this is the case of the research of "Simulation and Gaming," which ISAGA and JASAG are based on.

Of course there is a common understanding among all of us gathered here today that the simulation and gaming research that ISAGA and JASAG deal with has the special feature of an interdisciplinary awareness of the issues and approaches. All of us agree that both associations have interdisciplinary characteristics as research associations.

However, the interdisciplinary nature of simulation and gaming research does not mean that the comprehensive perceptual framework commonly used by academic researchers (the paradigm described by Thomas Kuhn) is not necessary. An awareness of the same problem consciousness and a mutual understanding of methodology are also necessary in simulation and gaming research. The interdisciplinary nature of simulation and gaming research can invigorate it as a new academic discipline. However, at the same time, it can be a fatal flaw and weakness as an academic discipline.

The present situation of simulation and gaming research is this: I know what I am researching, but I do not know anything about what others are researching. Everyone assumes and imagines the current situation of the science of simulation and gaming, but nobody knows with any certainty. Under such circumstances, it can be said that the establishment of both the identities of simulation and gaming as an academic discipline and the identities of ISAGA as an academic association are uncertain and unclear.

Over the last 2 years, at ISAGA 2001 in Italy, and 2002 in Edinburgh, I have been acutely aware of this weakness of simulation and gaming as a clearly defined independent academic discipline. ISAGA 2002 in Edinburgh was a very well organized conference, and the greater part of the conference reports were concerned with educational and business-related games. Throughout the conference I was still very concerned as to what degree simulation and gaming can be academically theorized and established as a field of academic study. It is beyond doubt that simulation and gaming is an effective tool in education and business, especially in vocational skill training. It is also invaluable to support policy formation. My great concern is, however, whether simulation and gaming will become more than just a tool in the hands of other disciplines.

As could clearly be seen at Napier University, most participants from Britain were researchers from universities for vocational education, many of them being newly raised to university status from polytechnic in the 1990s. There was a notable absence of participants from the older traditional universities such as Oxford and St Andrews in Scotland or even the newly established universities of Essex and Sussex.

I have no intention of undervaluing vocational education. I have always appreciated the true value of vocational education. We need to raise, however, the status of simulation and gaming research beyond being a "useful tool kit" in the field of vocational education to the level of a new paradigm of knowledge. It may be an opportune time for us now to step forward beyond our success in the vocational field and to lay down a new foundation and establish simulation and gaming research as an academic discipline in its own right. This endeavor may be an area where JASAG can make an extremely valuable contribution. I think JASAG with its researchers from many well-established universities is in a unique position to help contribute to the development of the science of simulation and gaming.

ISAGA 2003 contains many examples of simulation and gaming research in such traditional academic fields as pedagogy, psychology, economics, literature, business administration, political science, and sociology. At the same time, the program contains an impressive number of presentations using new techniques such as agent-based modeling (ABM) and soft computing. Some people will say the common perceptual framework of simulation and gaming research will gradually and naturally come into focus if we continue to build our research in many diverse fields. However, I do not think in that way. I think it is definitely necessary for ISAGA and JASAG to take a step further and consciously increase their efforts to establish a clear perceptual framework for the science of simulation and gaming.

I not only believe that ISAGA 2003 is a tremendous opportunity to solve such organizational problems as increasing membership and securing our finances;

I also feel that ISAGA 2003 is a great opportunity to construct a new academic perceptual framework for the simulation and gaming.

In response to social scientific concerns, or perhaps it might be better to say in response to "social" concerns, we have chosen a common theme for ISAGA 2003: the "Social Contributions and Responsibilities of Simulation and Gaming." Through exploring this theme in a variety of ways during our week at ISAGA 2003, I sincerely hope that we can develop a mutual understanding about a common framework of knowledge and methodology as researchers of simulation and gaming.

What Can Be Done? A Seven-Point Plan

What can we do specifically to establish the identity of "Simulation and Gaming Research" as an academic discipline? Of course we should all actively continue our individual research, but I think that ISAGA needs to collectively formulate a plan. I have identified seven key areas where I believe ISAGA would be best able to make an effective contribution to help the establishment of the science of simulation and gaming. No one field is more important than another and it would be best to work on all seven simultaneously.

1. Firstly, it is necessary for ISAGA to consolidate and archive our past with the creation of a comprehensive record of the books and theses published in the field of simulation and gaming. It is also necessary for ISAGA to create a catalogue of the games and an index of the important simulation results achieved to date. A clear evaluation and categorization of them within a single framework of the development of the science of simulation and gaming and promotion of the research is needed to achieve this. I would like to emphasize the importance of such "historical research" to the development of simulation and gaming.

2. Secondly, a comprehensive examination of how to evaluate and position the research of simulation and gaming in relation to the existing social sciences, art and humanities, and engineering, needs to be carried out. In other words, a systematic and orderly effort to position the science of simulation and gaming within the academic system is vitally necessary.

3. Thirdly, a mutual evaluation of the various tools used in Simulation and Gaming research and the establishment of a commonly accepted way of applying such tools within Simulation and Gaming research is needed. In relation to this point, it is also necessary to promote the invention and development of new tools and technology commonly used in the various fields of Simulation and Gaming research.

These tools not only include soft technology such as the theory for creating a game and communication techniques but also hard technology such as electronic display techniques and mathematical algorithms.

In the conference of "ISAGA 2003", examples of this evaluation can be found in a large number of papers submitted for the sessions titled "Agent-Based Modeling Meets Gaming Simulation" and "Utilization of Soft Computing Techniques in the Field of Simulation and Gaming."

4. The fourth point is very similar to the development and positioning of the tools of simulation and gaming, but rather than defining a tool, we need to categorize the research styles and approaches found in simulation and gaming.

The Organizing Committee of "ISAGA 2003" has planned two panels immediately after the first Plenary Session to explore this theme entitled "Actor-Oriented Approach to Simulation and Gaming" and "Structure-Oriented Approach to Simulation and Gaming."

5. The fifth point is a clear need to evaluate our performance in society by promoting research on the "social acceptance" of simulation and gaming, to assess how it is perceived, used, evaluated, and valued within real societies throughout the world. In some cases, this study will compare and contrast the different cultural perceptions of games.

For the Science of Simulation and Gaming to be established, it must have the special characteristic of being closely associated with real society and be appreciated for its ability to help solve social issues. I feel it is vital to make intentional and organizational efforts to strengthen the link between the research of simulation and gaming and real society. By establishing a new academic discipline to cooperate with and be valued by society, we will be able to reassess existing abstract studies that have lost their links with real society.

It can be said that in order to recognize the issue of social ethics underlying the science of simulation and gaming, research into the social acceptance of simulation and gaming is necessary. On the last day of "ISAGA 2003", many sessions on the social acceptance of entertainment games will be set up. Such research, although limited as a theme and peripheral as a topic, is actually very important from the viewpoint that it has a contribution to decisively define the basic attitudes of the science of simulation and gaming as a future academic discipline.

6. The sixth point is to examine the value structure, theory structure, and communication patterns inherent in the intellectual creation of simulation and gaming. This will naturally give rise to philosophical speculation and insight and become a very important research field in determining the future direction of simulation and gaming.

If simulation and gaming research transcends the level of a purely academic approach and analytical method and offers a new perceptual framework (paradigm) for the human exploration of knowledge, it will not only provide the foundation to develop the knowledge system that is specific to the science of simulation and gaming, but will also make a great contribution to the development of human intelligence.

I do not have enough time or knowledge to discuss the recent trends of knowledge science, but Michael Polanyi's theory and the dialogue over "personal" and "tacit knowledge" or Robert D. Putnam's definition of "social capital" in political science have all yielded very useful insights into the science of simulation and gaming. Unfortunately, up to this moment, only a few reports including a paper by Mr. Jan Klabbers given at ISAGA 2002 have been presented within ISAGA. I feel this is a matter of regret. Even in ISAGA 2003, apart from the session exploring a new direction for management science, the number of presentations in this field is very small.

7. Finally and certainly not least, in order to encourage use of the knowledge and techniques of simulation and gaming within educational institutions from the level of elementary school through to university, or in organizations including corporations and central and local governments, ISAGA and the researchers of simulation and gaming need to promote the practice of simulation and gaming throughout society.

I would like to emphasize here again, that if the science of simulation and gaming loses touch with real society, its foundation as a new science will be lost. The attitude of actually playing games and evaluating simulation practice will create the future of simulation and gaming, which will be quite different from the traditional academic disciplines.

On the second day, ISAGA 2003 will hold an Open Day for the public to share the latest results of simulation and gaming research with the local citizens and teachers. This shows how seriously the organizing committee views the importance of connecting our research and results with society.

Conclusion

I believe that for all the participants gathered here in "ISAGA 2003" it is our social responsibility to help raise simulation and gaming research from the level of tools and techniques to one of an established science and academic discipline. I hope that all of our guests for this week in Kazusa will both enjoy the atmosphere of a Japanese traditional farm village on the one hand and academic discussion on the other hand. Please relax with old friends, discuss with colleagues, and fully explore this gathering of knowledge.

Part I
Social Sciences and Simulation and Gaming

2. The Game of "Forming a Coalition Government"

Masayoshi Kuboya[1] and Satoshi Kimura[2]

Introduction

"Forming a Coalition Government" is a game that focuses on coalition making and bargaining in the world of contemporary Japanese politics. From the perspective of political science, this game successfully describes and simulates the characteristics of politics. From the view of gaming simulation studies, it is a valid game. In fact, most players thought that the game skillfully simulated real political situations. Through examining the game, we will demonstrate that the world of politics is quite familiar with the principles of gaming simulation. Before the case study this idea is presented from a methodological viewpoint.

Why Is Gaming Simulation a Good Way to Analyze Politics?

An important feature of politics is the interaction among actors (agents) who are free to decide their own behavior. Obviously, it is people who talk politics and are engaged in politics. Neither society nor politics can exist without people. Even though people can decide their behavior independently, they are not isolated. They live within a society and play out their roles. In a social context, their decisions are influenced by each other. *A*'s decision can be affected by *B*'s decision and vice versa.

Another essential feature of politics is the diversity of values. Political scientists, to some extent, agree that politics concerns the problem of values. For example, Easton (1965) pointed out that the political system concerns the "authoritative allocations of values." Crick (1962) claimed that politics is generated by accepting the fact that different groups, interests, and traditions simultaneously exist within some territory under a common rule. Consequently, politics

[1] Graduate School of Political Science, Tokai University, Hiratsuka, Kanagawa 259-1292, Japan; kuboya@white.plala.or.jp
[2] Graduate School of Political Science, Tokai University, Hiratsuka, Kanagawa 259-1292, Japan; rtkimura@ba3.so-net.ne.jp

includes conflicts concerning people's philosophy and sense of values, for example, some individuals are committed to power politics while others pursue the cause of justice. It is this diversity of values that yields such a wide variety of goals and it is this rich diversity that prevents us from defining the boundaries of politics. A good example is governmental intervention in the economy. Communist countries view the problem as a wholly political issue while capitalist countries treat it as a private issue and governmental intervention is restricted. Of course, "communism or capitalism" is a political choice and defining the boundary of politics is a central part of politics itself. In other words, a crucial characteristic of politics is its boundlessness (Shiratori 1993a).

Although these two features are critical elements of politics, they are hardly compatible with methodological sophistication. Shiratori (1993a) argued that modern political science has limited its boundaries and developed its methodology. The boundlessness of politics is not familiar with methodological sophistication. The statistical approach, a general method of modern political science, assumes that the values of variables are independent from both the values of dependent variables and those of other independent variables (Benoit 2000). As noted above, however, such assumptions do not always match real social phenomena and this approach is inflexible and incapable of describing the boundlessness of politics. On the other hand, traditional political science can describe the two characteristics of politics. Nevertheless, it is neither methodologically sophisticated nor operational. Consequently, existing political science has lacked appropriate methodologies to analyze these factors.

Even with relatively new approaches, it is still difficult to include such a diversity of values. For instance, game-theoretical and agent-based models can describe the interaction among actors (agents), but many of them cannot work unless an analyzer strictly defines an agent's goal. Although these models can generate agents that have different preferences, the range of the diversity of their preferences is limited by the analyzer's definitions. In game-theoretical models, all differentiating properties are defined by a game designer in advance (Shubik 1982). In agent-based models, agents are defined so as to have some characteristics and to conduct some range of behaviors by the researcher (Benoit 2000). In other words, these approaches cannot include all the diversity of values.

Gaming simulation with human players is a solution. Even though gaming is not popular in the discipline, it is one of the best methods to simulate the two characteristics of politics. According to Arai (1997), gaming simulation is the interaction among independent agents who play given roles in a specific environment. This feature is quite similar to that of politics. As noted above, politics is the interaction between independent actors (agents) and gaming may simulate the diversity of real humans, because they generate their own goals. Because of these resemblances, gaming simulation seems to be a useful way to analyze politics.

The superiority of gaming simulation in describing the diversity of values over game-theoretical and agent-based models is especially crucial. In these models, as noted above, the range of the diversity of values is not as broad as that of real human behavior. It follows that these models do not experiment on real humans.

Because it is only people who can talk politics and can be engaged in politics, this can be a serious methodological disadvantage; gaming does not have such a difficulty. Although gaming simulation cannot experiment on real humans in real society either, it is possible to experiment on real humans in a virtual world. If we succeed in constructing a virtual world which skillfully simulates real society, it must contribute to the development of the discipline to observe and examine how real people in a virtual world make decisions about politics. Because it is called "man simulation" (Inbar and Stoll 1972), gaming is one such type of experimentation that is carried out by humans. Although experimentation has not been popular in political science (McDermott 2002), it will come to be regarded as a useful method among political scientists (Lupia 2002).

The characteristics of politics, such as its boundlessness and high uncertainty, are compatible with gaming simulation and the approach allows experiments on real humans. At first, gaming can generate more diverse cases than these two models. Gaming simulation is an excellent tool to reveal hidden problems and to discover new hypotheses. Although game-theoretical and agent-based models also create an artificial society and allow agents to be diverse, these models hardly simulate the diversity of values that real humans have. The range of diversity is limited by the range of the researchers' assumptions or computer algorithms designed by the researchers. In contrast to these models, gaming often yields unpredictable and unexpected results. According to Gray and Borovits (1986), gaming can demonstrate not only how researchers assume people will respond, but "how people really respond." Gaming can also provide intellectual clues to both understand the current situation and to predict the future. In particular, when researchers focus on uncertain and complicated situations or matters in society, these clues must be quite useful. Gaming is suitable for "exploratory studies in which human responses or interactions are not predictable" (Gray and Borovits 1986). Gaming simulation is a good tool to analyze politics because it is highly uncertain in its nature.

An Overview of the Game

"Forming a Coalition Government" is a game of creating a coalition government in contemporary Japanese politics. This game focuses on political leaders and their negotiations with each other rather than the efficient creation of policies. Each player represents a political leader and commits to coalition-making bargaining. The most significant and striking point of the game is that neither the rule book nor the facilitator declares the goal of the game, as will be argued later in detail, these are the most distinctive features which make the game more realistically political.

The abstract of the rules of the game is below:

- Virtual political world
- Figure 1 is a draft map of the game. The figure shows the starting point, which simulates the situation just after the 2000 general election.

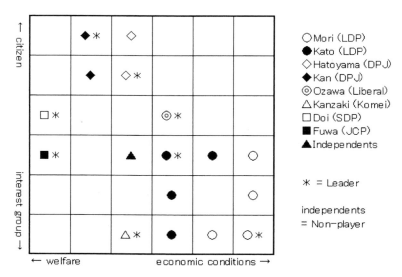

FIG. 1. Draft map of the game (starting point: June 2000)

- Each human player is in charge of one political leader in the game.
- One turn represents 1 year.
- There are two axes in a virtual political space: "welfare versus economic conditions," and "citizens versus interest groups."
- In the political space, there are 17 units which can move within the political space. Each unit represents a group of approximately 25 politicians. They are classified into two categories: "leader unit" or "follower unit."
- In each turn, players have 5 min of negotiation time.
- There are two facilitators. One is called the "Speaker" who keeps time for the players. The other is called the "Mass media" who facilitates players' discussions.
• Political funds
- In each turn, leaders can gain political funds from the governmental budget. The amount depends upon the number of units the leaders have.
- Political funds are used for maintaining group solidarity, inviting politicians from other groups, or for changing their own policy stance in the space.
- Leaders can freely give political funds to other political leaders.
• Distance in the political space (coexistence of cooperation and competition)
- If the distance between units is large, they are less likely to influence each other.
- If two or more units are located in close proximity, they are more likely to influence each other. The form of the influence can be either cooperation or competition.
- A follower unit located far from its leader unit easily rebels.
• General elections
- A general election has to be held at least every four turns. If units spread over the space, it is useful for getting votes from the various electorates.

– If the distance between one's unit and another unit which belongs to another leader is close, these two units compete strongly for votes within a narrow political space. As a result, they spoil each other's vote.
• Political group (faction)
– Each political leader has his/her political group (faction). Political groups (factions) are basic components of a political party or coalition government.
– Political leaders may scramble for unit(s). Leaders may control follower unit(s).
• Political parties
– Each player must establish a political party, either by himself/herself or with one or more other leaders.
– If two such units belong to the same party, they have an opportunity to make an electoral arrangement and to negotiate with each other. They may effectively allocate votes for the two units.
– Unless all the leaders who belong to the same party agree on electoral arrangements or on the Prime Minister, the party has to be dissolved.
• Prime Minister and government
– One of the leader units is in charge of the Prime Minister and the Prime Minister can always dissolve the Diet. Also, the Prime Minister declares an "annual governmental policy" in every turn. The Prime Minister designates a particular point on the space.
– Leaders who locate near the annual governmental policy gain extra funds.
– Everyone has the right to call for a vote of confidence or no confidence in the cabinet.

In the rest of this section, we briefly argue the validity of this game. We focus on three aspects of the game: players' perception and behavior, academic background, and similarity to real events.

Most players regarded this game as realistic. Such perceptions, of course, endorse the validity of the game. Moreover, the variation of their behavior in the game reinforces the validity. Through the results of the test plays, we found interesting differences in the players' characteristics. The more information or interest that players had, the more they became involved. Such differences may indicate that this game is well designed. According to Greenblat (1989), skilled players behave better than unskilled players in a well-designed game. Consequently, the validity and reality of the game are proved by both players' perception and behavior.

The accuracy of modeling influences the validity of a game. In this game, the way of modeling cooperation and competition among politicians reflects academic views. In political science, party competition is often described through two-dimensional spatial models. For example, Laver and Hunt (1992) introduced a two-dimensional model to analyze coalition bargaining. Some Japanese scholars also concluded that two-dimensional models are appropriate for describing contemporary Japanese politics (Kabashima and Takenaka 1996). However, even a pioneer of political gaming simulation, who has been engaged in studies of coalition government for a long time, has not effectively made a two-dimensional party competition model (Laver 1997). Thus, successful introduction of a two-dimensional model is a significant achievement of this game. Also, such an academic background increases the validity of the game.

A number of events that appeared in the test plays matched real political situations. For example, Kato, a leader of a faction of the Liberal Democratic Party (LDP), held the casting votes to form a coalition government at the first turn in the test plays. In real politics, Kato had been likely to rebel against the Mori cabinet in November 2000. In short, the game skillfully simulated Kato's rebellion. Moreover, this political event appeared in the test plays that were conducted in September 2000. In other words, this game not only simulated but also predicted the event. It also successfully simulated the fluctuation of the number of LDP seats and Komei Party's policy stance while in office. Even though this game models the boundlessness of politics, the chances of an unrealistic or fantastical outcome at the conclusion of the game were very low.

The Subject of the Game

The subject is one of several factors that get players involved in a game. It is said that setting appropriate goals is an effective way to motivate players (Inbar and Stoll 1972); however, as noted earlier, this game successfully encourages players without given goals. In this section, it is shown that some features concerning the subject increase the validity of the game and motivate players.

The fact that contemporary Japanese politics includes a high degree of uncertainty may affect player behavior. In the post cold war era, several long-lived political institutions disappeared. The LDP, which had been in office for 38 years, became the opposition in 1993. Since 1993 the usual form of government has been coalition governments, while before 1993 single government had been the norm. Moreover, the Japan Socialist Party (JSP), which until 1993 had severely criticized the LDP, made a coalition government with the LDP in 1994. All these political events were unimaginable and now people think that it is uncertain what will happen in the near future. Such feelings give players a broader range of behaviors. Because role playing is a key element of gaming simulation (Greenblat 1989), players' knowledge and prejudice about their roles may subconsciously restrict their options and behavior. In this game, however, players freely interpret the situations and are encouraged to behave as they like. The broad range of player behaviors leads to more plausible actions rather than unrealistic ones. In other words, players are less likely to suspect the validity and reality of the game and are more likely to be motivated.

The subject of the game emphasizes the interaction among political leaders and encourages and motivates the players. Among Western European democracies, coalition government is formed by political parties and the government is based on the party system. The causal arrow clearly flies from the party system to the coalition government. Therefore, the options and behaviors of political leaders are limited. On the other hand, in contemporary Japanese politics, the causal arrow may fly in both directions. Some political leaders had discussed the form of future coalition governments, then, dissolved existing political parties and created new parties which were more suitable for their plans for future coalition governments. In the 1990s, Japanese political leaders often brought about this kind of party system change. In the process of coalition bargaining, the roles of political leaders and their personalities are more influential in Japan than in Europe. Consequently, this game focuses on and emphasizes the interaction among political leaders in parliamentary politics. This encourages players to create their own goals and behaviors. As opposed to policy-exercise or international-conflict games, whose goals are more likely to be described as a single standard, such as policy efficacy or national power, players are more easily engaged in value judgments in this game. In "Forming a Coalition Government" each player is supposed to play the role of a political leader with a strongly defined personality. Also, the players' own feelings and prejudices about real politicians helps them to individualize their goals and behaviors. Moreover, many players interpret contemporary Japanese politicians as actors who behave in unpredictable ways. Thus, a far broader range of behaviors becomes possible.

As a whole, the subject and structure of the game influences both its validity and reality. The two characteristics, high uncertainty and interaction among political leaders in parliamentary politics, strongly motivate players to act freely. Thus, the validity and reality are, to some extent, explained by the peculiar characteristics of the game's subject and the subject makes it ideal for gaming.

Political Characteristics in the Game

The "Forming a Coalition Government" game is concerned with politics. As noted earlier, contemporary Japanese politics may present a more appropriate case for gaming simulation than other political systems in different times and places. However, this does not mean that only contemporary Japanese politics is suitable for gaming simulation. As presented earlier, the characteristics of politics are similar to those of gaming simulation. In this section, the characteristics of politics are compared with those of gaming simulation. In this game, political characteristics include the coexistence of cooperation and competition, the diversity of values, and simplification. After this comparison, these ideas will be examined in detail through comparing the political characteristics of this game and the features of gaming simulation.

First of all, this game represents the diversity of values in several ways. The goal of politics is not obvious. This is quite different from the economy, where the goal is far more obvious. Even if a facilitator forgets to declare the goal of an economy game, players will easily assume that the goal is to earn and amass as much money as is humanly possible, a commonly held assumption about the purpose of actors (agents) in the economic world. However, the goal a facilitator declares is crucial in the world of politics which contains such serious conflicts about values.

The goal of the game was revised several times. Along with the definition of politics by Dahl (1963), who says that power is one of the key concepts of politics, the goal in the first prototype was for each player to gain "power points." However, many players did not think that the game was realistic. In the second prototype, plural goals were introduced. There were three goals; "gaining power," "maintaining long-term government," and "increasing a party's number of seats." Players regarded these rules as more realistic. However, some players soon began to pursue other goals than the three mentioned. Finally, the rules were revised again. In the final version, facilitators declared neither the goal nor the winner. Players were free to decide their own goals by themselves.

This greater diversity of goals yields an increased diversity in player behavior. A player making little progress toward their goal may suddenly create a new goal. For example, a player may change his/her goal from becoming Prime Minister to promoting clean politics. Similar behavior can be found in an economic game. For example, a player who diligently earns and saves money over many moves may suddenly spend large amounts of money in a moment. However, such behavior in an economic game tends to be regarded as a meaningless action designed to attract public attention by a loser. In other words, player behavior is basically interpreted and appreciated from the standpoint of fund-raising activity in an economic game. On the other hand, this kind of spontaneous behavior is more natural and meaningful in a political game, where player behavior can be interpreted in a variety of ways.

Compared with other gaming simulations, this game may seem to be problematic. According to Inbar and Stoll (1972), setting the criteria for winning is a major part of designing gaming simulation. Greenblat (1989) pointed out that gaming simulation, as opposed to role playing, includes given goals. These assertions raise a serious question as to whether this game can be defined as gaming simulation. However, Inbar and Stoll (1972) referred to the criteria for winning because it influences participant motivation. Similarly, Greenblat (1989) mentioned given goals because they decide player behavior in a different way from role playing. It might be said that given goals are needed for involving players in a game. In other words, if players can find their own goals by themselves and absorb themselves in a game, a facilitator does not need to give them goals. It would seem that who decides the goals is not an essential problem of gaming.

In order to keep the diversity of values, the role of facilitators was regulated, as players' ideas or philosophies should not be held back by the facilitators. Facilitators should not be too restrictive, but they do need to have some influence on the game. Firstly, they must keep the game moving in a timely fashion, and secondly, they must act as a catalyst when discussion is stagnant. In this game, the facilitators' divinity was reduced by naming them the Speaker or the Mass media. The Speaker is in charge of timing and the Mass media's role is to encourage interaction among the players. By giving these two specific roles to facilitators, the game became more realistic and players were more easily involved.

The coexistence of cooperation and competition is skillfully and elegantly simulated in this game. Cooperation and competition simultaneously exist in the political world. Political scientists, especially in Europe, share this view (Shiratori 1993b). The coexistence of cooperation and competition, which is one of the most essential features of politics, may be found in party politics. Two parties whose policies or ideologies are nearly the same may cooperate in the House, while those same parties may furiously fight with each other during elections. This is because the parties probably attract the same voters who have specific political preferences. The rules of this game reflect such a feature of politics.

Furthermore, simplification is a common characteristic of politics and gaming simulations. We can find many simplifications in the political process. When someone makes political decisions, only three alternatives are usually given: for, against, or abstention. In other words, politics urges people to choose between two or very limited alternatives. According to Shiratori (1981), the essence of political decisions is "acceptance or refusal." Moreover, political changes are radical rather than incremental and people often simplify the information of complicated real political situations. Similarly, gaming simulations need simplification. As opposed to computer simulations, it is difficult to include complicated structures in gaming simulations because human players do not respond well to such restrictions. For example, the grid on the board was reduced from 20×20 in the first prototype to 6×6. The number of units was also reduced from 48 to 17. Unexpectedly, such simplifications did not affect the validity of the game significantly. As noted above, it follows that simplification is a feature common to both politics and gaming simulation. The simplifications, which enlarged the threshold or margin of changes in this virtual world, made the game more political. Interestingly, Laver (1997) reached a similar conclusion while designing several political games.

Above all, this game was very successful in expressing a political element and this case would suggest that gaming simulation is a useful method for describing political characteristics. It would seem that this game presents a good case for suggesting that gaming simulation, as noted earlier, is similar to politics.

Conclusions

Interaction and diversity of values are essential features of politics. Existing political science, however, has lacked appropriate methodologies to analyze these features. An advantage of gaming simulation is that this approach properly simulates these features.

The game demonstrates that the subject influences players' motivation and the validity of the game, as opposed to policy-exercise or international-conflict games, where players are easily engaged in value judgments. Each player is supposed to play the role of a political leader with a strong personality and many players interpreted contemporary Japanese politicians as actors who behave in ways which are unimaginable to most people. In short, the features of the subject, which contains a high uncertainty factor and interaction among political leaders in parliamentary politics, partly explain the validity and reality of the game. It could be concluded that the world of contemporary Japanese politics is a more appropriate case for gaming than other political arenas.

This does not, of course, mean that other political situations are not suitable for gaming simulation. As noted above, this is because politics is by its nature familiar with gaming. This game skillfully simulated the two essential features of politics. These characteristics are not peculiar to just this specific area, but are, more or less, common to all political activity. This game presents a good example of how the essential characteristics of gaming simulation and politics are similar and how gaming simulation lends itself to creating a virtual but realistic model of the political world.

References

Arai K (1997) What is gaming simulation? (in Japanese). In: Arai K, Deguchi H, Kaneda T, et al (eds) Gaming simulation. JUSE Press, Tokyo, pp 1–43

Benoit K (2000) Simulation methodologies for political scientists. The political methodologist 10:12–16

Crick BR (1962) In defence of politics. Weidenfeld and Nicolson, London

Dahl R (1963) Modern political analysis. Prentice Hall, Englewood Cliffs

Easton D (1965) A system analysis of political life. Wiley, New York

Gray P, Borovits I (1986) The contrasting roles of Monte Carlo simulation and gaming in decision support systems. Simulation 47:233–239

Greenblat CS (1989) Designing games and simulations: an illustrated handbook. Sage, London

Inbar M, Stoll CS (1972) Simulation and gaming in social science. Free, New York

Kabashima I, Takenaka Y (1996) Political ideology in Japan (in Japanese). Tokyo University Press, Tokyo

Laver M (1997) Playing politics: the nightmare continues. Oxford University Press, Oxford

Laver M, Hunt WB (1992) Policy and party competition. Routledge, New York

Lupia A (2002) New ideas in experimental political science. Political analysis 10:319–324

McDermott R (2002) Experimental methodology in political science. Political analysis 10:325–342

Shiratori R (1981) The theory of political development (in Japanese). Toyo Keizai, Tokyo

Shiratori R (1993a) Genealogy of theories of modern political science (in Japanese). In: Shiratori R (ed) Theories of modern political science: vol 2. 2nd edn. Waseda University Press, Tokyo, pp 254–274

Shiratori R (1993b) Tradition of Europe and modern political science (in Japanese). In: Shiratori R (ed) Theories of modern political science: vol 3. 2nd edn. Waseda University Press, Tokyo, pp 282–294

Shubik M (1982) Game theory in the social sciences: concepts and solutions. MIT Press, Cambridge

3. Environmental Commons Game: Is the Free Rider a "Bad Apple"?[1]

Susumu Ohnuma[2]

Outline of the Environmental Commons Game

The Environmental Commons Game simulates "The Tragedy of Commons" (Hardin 1968), in which gradual pollution of environment caused by egotistic behaviors reduces player profit. This game has been developed on the basis of Baba (1986).

Players are required to maximize their assets as a manager of a factory in the game. They have three choices in how to use their assets: investment, purification, and saving. The more assets they spend on investment, the more they get in the next phase, and the more polluted the environment becomes. On the other hand, the more assets they spend on purification, the more purified the environment becomes in the next phase, and the more their assets are reduced. As the environment gets polluted, the profit rate to investment becomes worse. Accordingly, players have to purify the environment to keep the high profit rate. However, the profit rate affects all players, which means that if a player expects other players to cooperate, he/she can benefit. Thus, the structure of the game complies with the traditional definition of the commons dilemma (Fig. 1).

This game enables us to analyze the processes of building a consensus for the benefit of each player, while at the same time maintaining the environment. The Environmental Commons Game should help players find a solution for daily environmental problems such as the illegal disposal of garbage. After experiencing the Environmental Commons Game, players should realize both the importance and difficulty of mutual cooperation, and thus should consider how to achieve mutual cooperation.

[1] This study was supported by a Grant-in-Aid for Science Research (no. 14710102), by the Foundation for the Fusion of Science and Technology, and by The Asahi Glass Foundation, to Susumu Ohnuma. The author thanks Professor Yukio Hirose for his helpful suggestions to the earlier draft of this paper, Junkichi Sugiura and Yumiko Taresawa for their collaboration in organizing the Environment Session at ISAGA 2003, and Masaki Yuki, Nobuyuki Takahashi, and Mark H.B. Radford for their editorial assistance.
[2] Department of Behavioral Science, Graduate School of Letters, Hokkaido University, Sapporo 060-0810, Japan; ohnuma@let.hokudai.ac.jp

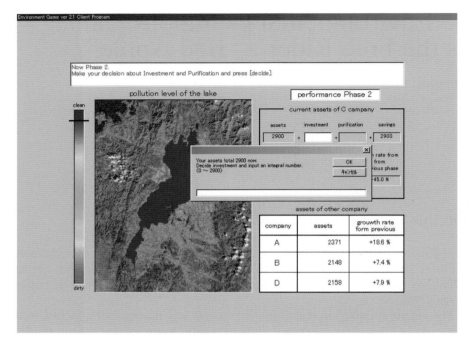

FIG. 1. Sample picture of the Environmental Commons Game

The Advantage of the Environmental Commons Game as a Research Tool

One of the main issues about the commons dilemma is the problem of the free rider, who exploits resources without contributing to them (Olson 1965). Within the game theory perspective, free riding has been regarded as rational behavior. However, it should be noted that many theoretical models that predict miserable consequences have assumed that players have only two choices: co-operation or defection, as in the prisoner's dilemma game. In such a situation, the free rider chooses defection because it brings more individual profit than cooperation. However, the choice between cooperation and defection is not always a dichotomous one in the real world and is often continuous. It is often difficult to define a particular behavior as exclusively cooperative or defective. For example, the discharge of polluted water is generally considered to be an example of the free rider problem. However, is the use of chemical detergents in households an absolute free-rider problem? It does not immediately cause a serious problem, although it does not mean that it is not a problem at all. Therefore, we need to take the degree of free riding into consideration with behavior treated as a continuous variable to capture people's cooperative/defective behavior in the real world.

There are at least two advantages of using the gaming simulation method to deal with the free-rider problem. First, it is easy to handle behavior as a continuous variable and to define the cooperation rate. This would make it possible for a more detailed analysis than in a zero-sum situation. Second, it is possible to objectively analyze irrational behaviors, by comparing them with optimal strategies calculated from the rational model.[3] There is much criticism of the rational choice model, stating that human beings do not always act in a rational manner. However, such criticisms have not been able to provide a means of analyzing irrational behavior. The Environmental Commons Game opens up the possibility of finding a way to analyze both rational and irrational behavior.

In the following, the usefulness of the Environmental Commons Game is demonstrated by reviewing two previous studies and an experiment conducted by the author and colleagues.

The Research Question: Bad Apple Effect

We have studied the free-rider problem using the Environmental Commons Game. In particular, we have focused on situations in which it is impossible to resolve the problem if all players are rational; however, because not all players are always rational, it may provide a way to resolve the free-rider problem.

The "bad apple effect" is known as the phenomenon in which the existence of free-riding behavior by a small number of people gradually spreads within a society, with the overall cooperation rate declining over time. People who were cooperative at first soon fail to cooperate if a free rider exits (Bonacich et al. 1976).

To resolve the social dilemma problem, a change in the incentive structure such as implementing a sanction system is not always the logical solution, because the rational choice model predicts that no one wants to pay for the cost of changing the incentive structure. This is called a second-order dilemma, which predicts the failure of change to the incentive structure because of rational choice.

However, looking at real situations, it seems that cooperative people sometimes try to punish a free rider. It seems that the free-rider problem and second-order dilemmas are sometimes resolved. We focus on cases when these problems might be resolved and attempt to analyze some possible psychological processes, although there may be many possible answers.

Some findings from our own work are introduced in the following series of experiments. In these studies, we examined what psychological processes of players inhibit the emergence of the bad apple effect.

---

[3] Some might claim that it is rational if a person acts according to his/her attitude or belief, even if it is cooperative behavior. However, the most limited definition is used in this article, that is, rational means a person seeks to maximize his/her benefit without regard to mutuality.

Previous Studies: Decline of the Bad Apple Effect!

We demonstrated through two experiments that the cooperation rate increased with gradual pollution of environment even if a free rider existed (Ohnuma 2001). The procedure of the experiments was as follows. Four players were in a game. Participants were told that they were playing with other university students connected via the Internet. However, only one player was the true participant and the other three players were controlled by previously programmed actions. Their behavior was programmed so that the reduction rate of environmental degradation was constant: that is, the profit rate decreased linearly. Because the environment level was influenced by all players' behavior, the three manipulated players had to modify their behavior depending on the behavior of the true participant. There were two sets of conditions imposed on the dummy players. One was the free-rider condition and the other was a social-loafing condition. In the free-rider condition, one of the dummy players behaved as a free rider, while the other two behaved rather cooperatively. In the social-loafing condition, all three players behaved in a weakly cooperative fashion, with some free riding. The ranges of cooperation rate were determined by a calculation, in which environmental degradation was kept constant in each phase even though a participant engaged in an extreme behavior.

Results showed that the cooperation rate of participants increased as the environment became polluted in both conditions. This finding is contrary to the previous theories of the bad apple effect, which state that the cooperation rate would be reduced if a free rider exists. It is thought that because environmental degradation, which directly determines the profit rate, has a stronger effect than the bad apple effect, and the cooperation rate increased to restore the environment even though a free rider existed.

Furthermore, we asked participants if they preferred introducing a sanction system. The results showed that a sanction system with a cost to put it into force was more preferred in the free-rider condition than in the social-loafing condition. Results suggest that it was more feasible to introduce a sanction system with a cost in the free-rider condition than in the social-loafing condition, although some previous theories state that it would be difficult because of a second-order dilemma.

This study observed that the cooperation rate increased as the environment became more polluted, which in turn suggest that the bad apple effect declined. A sanction system was more preferred when a free rider existed. Next, we clarified the determinants of preference for introducing a new rule (Ohnuma and Sakai 2002). The procedure of the experiments was essentially the same as the previous study. We again found that the cooperation rate increased as the environment became more polluted. Results also showed that the sanction system with high cost was more preferred in the free-rider condition than in the social-loafing condition. A multiple regression analysis indicated that intention to pay a cost to punish a free rider, including the loss of their assets, had a stronger effect on the preference for sanction than cost/benefit evaluation. Given that the cost/benefit evaluation represented rational thinking, and given that the intention to pay a cost is regarded as irrational, it would be reasonable to interpret the findings as irrational thinking being stronger than rational thinking. In summary, this study suggests that a free rider is not always the bad apple, but rather becomes the scapegoat and is made responsible for the environmental pollution.

Present Study: The Function of Emotions as a Key to Resolving Social Dilemma

To explore the reason why the free rider becomes the scapegoat, we conducted a new experiment. The role of emotion is the focus of an experiment in which a free rider gains assets without contributing, which in turn evokes anger against the free rider. In addition, cooperative people continue to exist, even though the environment becomes worse and the profit rate decreases. It is predicted that this situation evokes empathy toward the cooperative people. Furthermore, these emotions would be related to some cognitive aspect. For example, it would be supposed that anger is related to perceptions of unfairness, while empathy is related to a social norm.

The procedure of the experiments was similar to the previous studies. Participants were told that the game would be played by four persons and that they were students from different universities connected via the Internet, although once again, three of the players' behaviors were manipulated. It was emphasized that participants should seek to maximize their assets. In fact, they could get rewards according to their acquired assets. Participants were also instructed that if they used 15% of their assets for purification and 85% for investment, their assets increase by keeping the environment in the same state as the previous phase. Participants (81 students) were randomly assigned to two conditions: in the free-rider (FR) condition, there was one free rider (10% ± 3% of cooperation rate) and two cooperators (14.5% ± 3% of cooperation rate); and in the social-loafing (SL) condition, three players displayed the cooperation rates of 12.5% ± 3%. Participants were asked to answer a questionnaire after the phase 14. They were told that the game would continue after the questionnaire was completed and that the answers to their questionnaires would be reflected to the following phases: that is the results of participants' voting about introducing a sanction system would be executed in the following phase.

The results replicated the precious findings; cooperation rate increased as the environmental pollution became worse, despite the presence of a free rider (Fig. 2). A cooperation rate of over 15%, which was the reference point, was observed in the later half of the game, in spite of the continued existence of free riders.

Analysis of participant responses to other players showed that they were more angry with the free rider than the cooperator or loafing players. Furthermore there was a great empathy for the cooperator than the free rider or loafing players. In short, they felt anger toward the free rider, and felt empathy toward

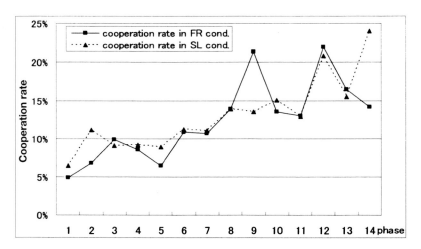

FIG. 2. Change of cooperation rate. *FR*, free rider; *SL*, social loafing

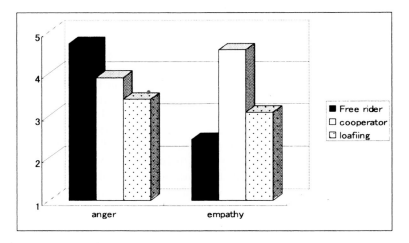

FIG. 3. Emotional evaluation of players (measures were reported on a 5-point scale)

the cooperator (Fig. 3). Furthermore, multiple regression analysis indicated that emotion, especially anger, had positive effects on the preference for introducing sanctions. It was also shown by multiple regression analysis that (1) anger against the free rider had a direct positive effect on the payment for the establishment of a sanction system, (2) anger toward a free rider affected feelings of unfairness, and (3) empathy toward the cooperator affected the social norm.

To summarize, the anger toward the free rider and the sympathy toward the cooperator directly determined the preference for sanctions. Moreover, the anger against the free rider was related to unfairness, which was also correlated with a preference for sanctions. The sympathy toward the cooperator was related to the social norm, which also had an effect on the preference for sanctions. These results suggest that both unfairness and social norm are important factors to induce cooperation. Emotions such as anger and sympathy might be the base of such a norm and fairness for resolving a social dilemma, as well as being directly responsible for initiating the preference for sanctions.

The results of this study are consistent with previous theories which argue that "emotion, which looks irrational, might promote resolving social dilemma" (Frank 1988) and "anger has a function of punishment" (Toda 1992). Because human beings have emotions, the free rider might become a scapegoat to promote cooperation and encourage a preference for sanctions. In summary, emotion might be a key to resolving the free-rider problem. The interactions between emotion and social system formation need further study.

Conclusion: Free Riders Are not Bad Apples but Scapegoats

The findings from our series of studies suggest that sometimes free riders are not bad apples, but rather are scapegoats who serve to promote cooperation and bring about a preference for sanctioning systems, making it possible to cause structural changes and avoid a second-order dilemma. These results suggest possible solutions for environmental problems such as illegal disposal of garbage.

Educational Effect of Environmental Commons Game

After participating in the game, participants reported that they realized two points. First, they understood the structure of a social dilemma and the free-rider problem. They learned why it was difficult to cooperate. Many students do not like mathematical explanations; however, they can intuitively understand the structure of social dilemmas and the free-rider problem through playing the game itself. Second, they realized the importance of mutual cooperation, because without it an environmental catastrophe can occur and cause further loss for every individual.

Many participants commented on the importance of mutual cooperation, for example:

"I knew I should use my assets for purification, but when I competed with another player (the free rider) I completely forgot about purification."

"It is easy to say that cooperation is important, but it is difficult to practice."

"We, including the free rider who is concerned only about his/her own benefit, must understand the consequence of egoistic behavior."

"A spirit of cooperation in the whole group must be emphasized because it will bring about welfare to all group members."

Moreover, it was observed that this realization could be transferred to the real world. Some participants reported that they were willing to cooperate in the real world if they were in a similar situation. Although it is merely a simulation game, it has the possibility to encourage mutual cooperation in the real world.

Finally, the Environment Commons Game is an effective tool in environmental education, by making participants realize through experience of tragedy of commons the importance of mutual cooperation and changing the structure so as not to bring about environmental catastrophe.

References

Baba N (1986) Personal computer gaming method (in Japanese). Nikkan Kogyo Shinbunsha, Tokyo

Bonacich P, Shure GH, Kahn JP et al (1976) Cooperation and group size in N-person prisoners' dilemma. Journal of Conflict Resolution 20:685–702

Frank RH (1988) Passions within reasons: the strategic role of the emotions. Norton, New York

Hardin G (1968) The tragedy of the commons. Science 162:1243–1248

Ohnuma S (2001) Effects of environment change and others' behavior on the cooperative behavior and solution preference in social dilemma (in Japanese). Japanese Journal of Psychology 72:369–377

Ohnuma S, Sakai T (2002) Psychological study in consensus building using Environmental Commons Game (in Japanese). Abstract Book of Annual Conference of JASAG 2002 Autumn. pp 16–21

Olson M (1965) The logic of collective action. Harvard University Press, Cambridge, MA

Toda M (1992) Emotion: the innate adaptive software system that drives human beings (in Japanese). University of Tokyo Press, Tokyo

Appendix: Basic Formulation of Environmental Commons Game

$$Ai_{t-1} = Ii_t + Pi_t + Si_t$$
$$E_{t+1} = E_t - a + b + c$$
$$Ai_t = E_t \times Ii_t - Ii_t - Pi_t + Si_t$$

E_t: Environment level at phase t
Ai_t: Asset of player i at phase t
Ii_t: Investment of player i at phase t
Pi_t: Purification of player i at phase t
Si_t: Savings of player i at phase t
a: Constant reduction rate of environment level by investment
b: Constant increase rate of environment level by purification ($b = \sqrt{17/13a}$)
c: Constant increase in quantity by self-purification of the lake

4. Use of Gaming for Training Emergency Headquarters in Responding to Earthquake Damage: VEQRES/SAITAI—Virtual Earthquake RESponses—[1]

Hideki Kaji[2], Katumi Matsumura[3], Toshiyuki Kaneda[4], Hidehiko Kanegae[5], Kenichi Ishibashi[6], Mari Yahagi[7], and Jun Mihira[8]

Introduction

When a large-scale earthquake occurs, disaster-related agencies such as police, fire services, medical services including the Red Cross, the Self-Defense Forces, and others rush to the scene of the damaged area and start rescue and relief operations. Utility companies that provide telephone, electricity, and gas and water services, and railway companies also immediately stop their operations to investigate damage and start recovery works.

The emergency response headquarters, which is supposed to be formed within about 1 h of the event, is expected to function as a control center to put all information together and coordinate the response activities of these agencies. According to the Basic Act for Disaster Countermeasure of Japan, the headquarters are to be formed at the national, prefectural, and local government level. This paper, however, focuses on the one at the local government level, because it is the most directly involved in the affected area.

The respective disaster-related agencies transmit the information of an ever-changing situation of the extent of damage in the affected area and the progress of response activities, to the emergency headquarters and requests assistance for coordination between the agencies. From judgments based on relayed information, the headquarters takes the necessary actions such as:

---

[1] This paper is a revised version of the paper presented at the Seventh US/Japan Workshop on Urban Earthquake Hazard Reduction, Maui, USA, 24–26 March, 2003.
[2] Keio University, Fujisawa, Kanagawa 252-8520, Japan; kaji@sfc.keio.ac.jp
[3] System Kagaku Kenkyujo; matumura@skk-jv.co.jp
[4] Nagoya Institute of Technology; kaneda@archi.ace.nitech.ac.jp
[5] Ritsumeikan University; hkanegae@sps.ritsumei.ac.jp
[6] Keio University; kishibas@sfc.keio.ac.jp
[7] Keio University; yahagi@sfc.keio.ac.jp
[8] Keio University; jmihira@sfc.keio.ac.jp

- To issue instructions to the respective agencies in its response operation
- To distribute the rescue materials, water, food, and other goods that are needed in the affected area
- To give evacuation warnings to people in areas affected by fires
- To request assistance from other municipalities and the central government
- To release progress reports to the media

As is obvious, the staff of the emergency headquarters do not work at the disaster scene but stay in the control center of city hall, and judge and issue appropriate instructions based on information transmitted by the disaster-related agencies at the scene. However, this work is very difficult in practice. Some of the main reasons for this difficulty lie in the facts that:

- The information transmitted from the agencies is very limited at the early stage of the event, and it may normally need at least 1 day for the staff to have overall picture of the damage. Therefore, they must make judgments and take actions based on partial information at the early stage.
- Information available in most cases is uncertain. Most decisions have to be made promptly without careful consideration of the situation. Few staff members involved in the task have experience in such situations because large-scale earthquakes seldom occur.

It is very obvious that the prompt and proper management of the emergency headquarters is vital to mitigate immediate and consequential damage in the affected area after the earthquake. Thus, the emergency response drills to train the local government officials, who are supposed to be involved in the emergency headquarters, are organized on September 1 every year in Japan. It mainly focuses on the smooth transmission of information between the disaster-related agencies. Recently, a scenario-based drill using a map has been tested for training coordination between headquarters at different levels.[9] These drills, however, only cover a 1-day response operation after the occurrence of an earthquake of given magnitude and intensity. Training in the response operation to unforeseen and consequent events over the following couple of the days, during which the daily living of the affected peoples recommences, is definitely needed. From this point of view, the authors launched a research project for the development of a computer-based gaming simulation model of an emergency headquarters. Figure 1 shows the structure of the game. As seen in the figure, the decision-making process of the headquarters staff is designed as a role-playing game, and the events in the affected area, including the immediate damage caused by the earthquake and its consequences, citizen behavior, and response operations by the disaster-related agencies, are modeled as a computer simulation. The result of the simulation model is transmitted to the players, who are given roles of headquarters staff.

---

[9]Map Exercise by the Seven Provinces (http://www.soumu.metro.tokyo.jp/04saigaitaisaku/nanato.html).

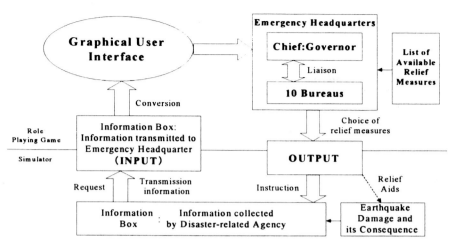

FIG. 1. Structure of role-playing gaming. Source: scenario-based mapping drill on response operation by central and seven governments, January 15, 2003

Players and Their Roles in Headquarters

Emergency headquarters at the local government level are the target of this game. The structure of the headquarters differs from local government to local government. However, in this research the Tokyo Metropolitan Office was used as a pilot model to select players.

According to the Tokyo Metropolitan Regional Disaster Plan[10] the present emergency headquarters consists of (1) a director's office that determines fundamental policies and (2) 15 departments that have authorities to give directions to each responsible organization.

Director's Office—Director (1 Player)

1. Ordering the emergency deployment and dissolving the emergency situation in the Tokyo Metropolitan Emergency Headquarters Office.
   – Deciding which emergency deployment level among the five levels should be ordered after grasping the intensity of the earthquake.
2. Gathering of significant disaster information and releasing it.
3. Ordering evacuation and its direction.
4. Applying the Disaster Rescue Law.
   – The action that must be first taken just after the disaster occurs.
5. Ordering mutual cooperation among local governments.
6. Transferring some responsibilities to heads of each department and mayors of local governments.

---

[10] Tokyo Metropolitan Office (1998) Tokyo Metropolitan Regional Disaster Plan.

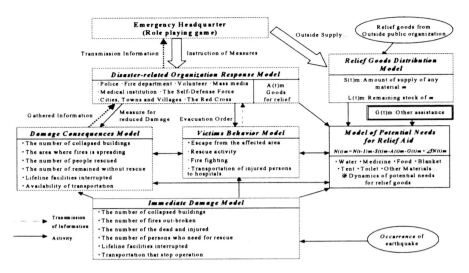

Fig. 2. Simulation diagram for damage and response

7. Requesting the Self-Defense Forces to deploy the emergency detachment.
8. Requesting the central government organizations, and other prefecture and public sector organizations to aid in its emergency activities.

The director's office settles the eight tasks mentioned above. If there are more players available, vice-directors or supplementary directors can be deployed.

Nine Departments Consisting of Two to Six Personnel

In a real situation, 15 departments are deployed under the emergency headquarters. In the gaming simulation, the departments are classified into 9 as follows:

1. Department of General Affairs
   - Information collecting and controlling.
   - Communication coordination among governments and other organizations. Information distributing to the media.
   - Investigation of damaged buildings, cliffs, etc. and judging the degree of damage.
   - Prevention of further disaster involving hazardous objects (e.g., high-tension gas).
2. Department of Finance
   - Allocating emergency automobiles
   - Ordering the signage for emergency roads to be issued.
3. Department of Citizens and Cultural Affairs
   - Distributing rice, hardtack, and other emergency supplies.
   - Providing the necessary people with disaster relief activities.
   - Asking foreign organizations and volunteer groups to help.

4. Department of Social Welfare
   - Distributing emergency supplies and transporting evacuees.
   - Setting up evacuation centers and managing them.
5. Department of Public Health
   - Directing the disposal of garbage, human waste, and disaster waste.
6. Department of Medical Services
   - Directing the activities of the medical sectors.
   - Making inspections of people killed in the disaster.
7. Department of Construction and Transportation
   - Keeping roads and bridges usable.
   - Removing obstacles.
   - Inspecting the Tokyo metropolitan transportation systems, and returning them to normal operation.
8. Department of Ports and Harbors
   - Preserving rivers and keeping harbor facilities working.
   - Allocating emergency ships and helicopters.
9. Department of Waterworks and Sewage
   - Inspecting and recovering waterworks and sewage.

Each department must select contingency actions necessary to rescue and relieve people as soon as possible, judging from information available. If necessary, the director's office and other departments may cooperate to take the policy actions.

The Structure of the Simulation Model

The game is designed to cover 3 days of response operations. The simulator applied to the game must have the following functions:

1. It must give the overall output information, on which the necessary relief actions for 3 days can be judged by the headquarters staff. It means that the outputs include, as mentioned earlier, not only the immediate damage caused by an earthquake and its consequences, but also citizen behavior and response operations of the disaster-related agencies. The living conditions of the affected citizens on the second and third days is also important information to be outputted.

2. The model must illustrate the interactive relation between changes of damage status and the response operations of the disaster-related agencies. For instance, the dead or injured remain untreated at the scene in the early stages, and will be transported to hospitals at a later stage. The model must describe the different aspects of the dead or injured in this example because the assistance needed for them is totally different.

3. As part of the response operations of disaster-related agencies, the process of damage information acquisition has to be modeled. Only through intensive investigation can the agencies gradually accumulate accurate damage information in time sequence.

4. The model must accept instructions issued by headquarters staff as an exogenous variable, and compute its impact.

5. The performance of the headquarters staff (the game players) can be evaluated on the basis of the balance between demand and supply of relief assistance to the affected people. In other words, good performance can be achieved only when timely supply of relief is given to satisfy the potential demand for help of the affected people. The model must cover this aspect.

A flow diagram of the overall structure of the model is illustrated in Fig. 3. The model consists of two parts. One part describes immediate damage caused by the earthquake and its consequence at the scene of the affected area. Another part models relief, rescue, and response operations at the scene performed by the disaster-related agencies, such as police, fire services, and medical services. The emergency headquarters staff then make proper decisions, issue instructions, and take appropriate actions based on the damage information and its consequences, and the progress of response operations reported by those agencies. The function of each submodel can be summarized as follows.

The four submodels are designed to illustrate the dynamic situation of the affected area, which changes with time and also by the response actions taken by various disaster-related agencies.

Immediate Damage Model

This model provides the outputs of immediate damage caused by the earthquake just after its occurrence, the given level of magnitude, and the given location of the epicenter. The outputs are:

– The number of buildings that are totally and partially collapsed,
– The number of dead, injured, and those that need rescue,

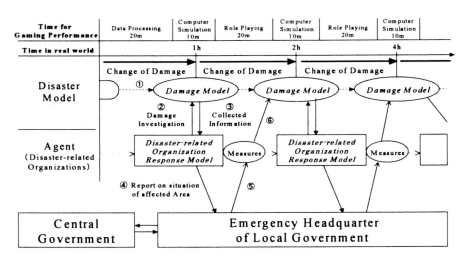

FIG. 3. Time sequences of the model operation

- The number of fires that have simultaneously broken out,
- The number of places where utility facilities are interrupted,
- The public transportation lines that have been halted.

Damage Consequences Model

As time passes, immediate damage changes its features. Buildings that are partially collapsed may totally collapse. Some fires may be extinguished but others may spread and become hazards to the greater city. Some injured citizens may be rescued but others may die. This model describes such consequential changes of immediate damage after the earthquake. The changes are also brought by the variety of response operation by disaster-related agencies and even by the victims themselves. The outputs of this model are:

- The number of buildings that are totally and partially collapsed,
- The number of people rescued and those that remain without rescue,
- The areas where fires are spreading,
- The places where utilities are interrupted without restoration,
- Availability of public transportation.

Victim Behavior Model

This model traces people's behavior in the affected area after the earthquake. The first action of the affected people is to save themselves by stepping outside of their houses. Then, if they are not injured, they may be involved in rescue activities or in fire fighting. Some may take injured people to hospitals. As is popularly known, the best human resources for rescue and relief in the affected area are the affected peoples themselves. Women, children, or aged people may evacuate to refuge sites. The others will also evacuate when fires come within the vicinity. The model computes the number of people evacuated in each refuge site on a time series basis.

Model of Potential Needs for Relief Aid

The affected citizens need water, foods, medicine, blankets, tents, and so on. The model computes such potential demand for things that are necessary for living for affected people in either damaged houses or refuge sites. These demands may also change as time passes and may be absorbed by proper supply of relief goods. The dynamics of the potential needs for relief goods can be formulated as shown in Eq. 1:

$$N(t)m = N(t - 1)m - S(t)m - A(t)m - G(t)m + \Delta N(t)m \qquad (1)$$

where $N(t)m$ is potential demand for relief goods at time t,
$S(t)m$ is supply of relief goods by local government at time t,
$A(t)m$ is supply of relief goods by agencies at time t,

G(t)m is direct supply of relief goods by volunteers at time *t*,
$\Delta N(t)$ is increase or decrease of relief demand at time *t*.

N(t)m plays an important role in the game because it is one of the indicators that are used for evaluation of the game player's performance.

The response activities of disaster-related agencies can be modeled by applying the multi-agent based simulator, which has the same structure of behavioral rule and learning process, although the type of performance may different from one agent to another.

This model deals with police services, fire services, Self-Defense agencies, medical services including the Red Cross, utility and transportation companies, volunteers, and the media. In this part, the distribution of relief goods that are prepared and stocked at the local government level is also modeled.

Disaster-Related Agency Response Model

The disaster-related agencies in the real world are each represented by an agent in the model. Each agent in the model processes the following common response activities under the given rule with the learning process:

1. To acquire information regarding damage and citizen behavior in the affected area by dispatching investigators to the scene to complement other reports from various sources. The ability to accumulate information and its degree of certainty depend on time after the quake and the number of investigators dispatched.
2. To save the information acquired in the database of the agent.
3. To determine the requirements for the affected citizens.
4. To distribute relief goods stocked at the agency level to the affected people on the basis of the estimate.
5. To choose necessary actions among the list of available actions for the respective agent, which depend on agencies.
6. To register the report of actions taken in the database of the agent.
7. To transmit the information saved in the database to headquarters.
8. To take action based on the orders of headquarters.

Relief Goods Distribution Model

As mentioned in the previous section, each disaster-related agency prepares a certain amount of relief goods that is closely related to its response activities. For example, the fire services prepares fire-extinguishing equipment for use by citizens, medical services may stock extra medicines for the emergency, and some voluntary community agencies store equipment for rescue operations. However, in Japan most responsibility for preparation of relief and rescue operations, and stocking of water, food, blankets, and so on, lies with local governments.

The distribution policy for the relief goods is, thus, determined by the emergency headquarters, which is the role-playing stage of this gaming exercise.

The function of the Relief Goods Distribution Model is to check the balance of the stock of the goods, which decreases as supply to the victims is made on the basis of headquarters' decisions, and increases as emergency assistance given by outside agencies. Needless to say, the amount of supply of any material m, $S(t)m$, should not exceed the remaining stock of m, $L(t)m$.

Operation of the Model

As explained earlier, this model is applied to support the role-playing gaming exercises in emergency headquarters. Its operation therefore needs to be intermittently controlled in time sequence. The consequences of damage caused by an earthquake, citizen behavior along with it, and the activities of disaster-related agencies are very sequential events without interruption, and are also interrelated to each other. However, it would be rather difficult to control this series of events simultaneously in the model due to its complexity. The simulation must allow intervention by the political decisions made by game players, which may be given dispersively from outside of the model. Thus, the discrete operation of the model is to be applied.

Figure 1 illustrates such discrete operation, in which the relation of three bodies, the affected people, disaster-related agencies, and the emergency headquarters (= players) are clarified. That is, at the first step, damage and its consequences up to 1 h after the quake are computed. Then, the simulation of disaster-related agencies is executed. It includes investigation of the affected area at the second step, information acquisition at the third step, and communication with the emergency

TABLE 1. Time schedule for a 1-day training program

Operation time	Stage	Game time		Notes
1000–1030	1	Day 1	1000	Establish the emergency headquarters, action begins
1030–1100	2		1200	First rescue team from neighboring local governments arrive
1100–1130	3		1500	
1130–1200	4		1800	
1200–1230	5		2100	
1230–1300	6		2400	First night in shelter
1300–1330	7	Day 2	600	International rescue team from abroad
1330–1400	8		1000	
1430–1500	9		1400	
1500–1530	10		1800	
1530–1600	11		2200	Second night in shelter
1600–1630	12	Day 3	600	
1630–1700	13		1200	
1700–1730	14		1800	Third night in shelter

The earthquake is assumed to occur at 1800.

headquarters at fourth step. The computer execution is temporally stopped at this point. It is estimated that the computation time of these four steps for 1-h events may take less than 10 min. The game players in the emergency headquarters start making an examination of the situation in the affected area based on the reports made by disaster agencies. The report may not reflect the exact situation of the affected area, of course, due to limited investigation at the time.

The players then make the necessary decisions regarding rescue and relief actions based on this uncertain information, and issue the instructions to the respective agencies at the fifth step. A set of instructions issued by players is inputted to the simulator at the sixth step, and the simulator starts execution as a second cycle. If 20 min is supposed to be allocated to players' work, one cycle of the game requires 30 min. This means that it may take 1.5 days without a break to complete the game based on a 3-day response operation. Because such an arrangement for a gaming program is not realistic, the simulation interval of one cycle may be extended from 1 h to 3–4 h so that the game can be completed within 8–9 h in 1 day.

Table 1 is an example of a 2-day time schedule of this training. This game proceeds on the assumption that an earthquake occurs at 6 p.m.

Conclusions

This project is organized as a part of the special research project on "Mitigation of Damage in Mega-Cities Caused by a Large-Scale Earthquake," funded by the Ministry of Education and Sciences. It will be completed in 5 years. The prototype of the model was supposed developed in 2003, and the experimental performance of the game will be conducted by the end of March, 2004.

Reference

Matsumura K et al (2003) Development of emergency headquarter gaming for training in earthquake responses. The report of large-scale earthquake damage mitigation for large cities. System Kagaku Kenkyujo, Report to the Ministry of Education, Culture, Sports and Technology

5. The Urban Network Game: A Simulation of the Future of Joint City Interests

Igor Mayer[1], Martijn Leijten[1], Linda Carton[1], Martin de Jong[1], Richard Scalzo[2], Ed Dammers[3], and Femke Verwest[3]

Introduction

In a thriving, densely populated and urbanized country like the Netherlands, space is at a premium. With the steady economic growth of the 1990s and the construction and expansion of homes, business parks and infrastructure, the available space and the environment are coming under increasing pressure. Major changes are also taking place on an administrative level in the Netherlands. In some cases, influential new joint ventures are formed between public, private, and social parties (Frieling 2000).

The social and administrative dynamic, and the tension that this creates in relation to spatial quality requirements, is turning into a major challenge for spatial policy. Numerous advisory bodies and policymakers are therefore advocating a spatial development policy (WRR 1998) or development planning (VROM 2001, 2002). Development planning is the opposite of admittance planning and provides increased scope for the initiatives and investments of local governments and private and social parties.

Instead of passively resisting activities and exhibiting too little flexibility, governments must aim at actively entering into partnerships with other governments, the business sector, and social organizations. Together, they must develop and realize interrelated, creative concepts, projects, and programs (WRR 1998; Healey 2000; Teisman 1997; VROM Council 2001). According to the Netherlands' Ministry of Housing, Spatial Planning, and the Environment (VROM 2002), development planning requires:

"active intervention by means of investments made by both public and private parties. The State shall then provide policy frameworks for the investments and harmonize them

[1] Faculty of Technology, Policy and Management, Delft University of Technology, PO Box 5015, 2600 GA Delft, The Netherlands; i.s.mayer@tbm.tudelft.nl
[2] ACES, Erasmus University Rotterdam, PO Box 1739, 3000 DR Rotterdam, The Netherlands; scalzo@fsw.eur.nl
[3] Netherlands Institute for Spatial Research (RPB), PO Box 30314, 2500 GH Den Haag, The Netherlands; ruimtelijkplanbureau@rpb.nl

with each other. This provides scope for the initiatives of lower governments, market parties, and social organizations and supports them."

Innovation, future orientation, integral concepts, stakeholder planning and new ways of public private financing, and cooperation are some of the relevant characteristics ascribed to development planning.

However, the above description shows that development planning may be an interesting concept but it is also very abstract and ambiguous. Moreover, the real question is how development planning works in practice and whether it actually differs from admittance planning. How can such notions as stakeholder planning, future orientation, and innovation be realized in a region? How do spatial investments, innovation, and integral concepts come about? Does development planning really result in spatial and administrative innovation, as one would expect in theory? What is clear, however, is that development planning will have to be tackled by governments and private and social parties on a regional/provincial level.

Against this background, the Netherlands Institute for Spatial Research (RPB), established on 1 January 2002, asked the Delft University of Technology to design a simulation game in which the concept of development planning can be tested in a safe environment (Mayer and Veeneman 2002; Mayer et al. 2004).

The Urban Network Game

The purpose of the simulation game was to examine the effects and conditions of development planning on the level of urban networks. It was therefore decided to focus the simulation game on the development of the Brabant City urban network. This is a recently established joint venture between the five largest cities in the province of North Brabant (a province located in the southern Netherlands close to the Belgian border) and the provincial government.

The Urban Network game was played twice, on 14 November and on 10 December 2002. The two sessions had a similar structure, but the participants had to play with two different long-term scenarios. This made it possible to evaluate the impact of lateral developments on development planning and on the administrative and spatial development of Brabant City.

Around 50 representatives from all of the relevant administrative, private, and social parties took part in each session. During the Urban Network game, participants developed a large number of innovative spatial designs and projects for Brabant up to the year 2030 and placed those projects on a large block map after consulting and negotiating with other parties. The Brabant City joint venture attempted to manage the administrative and spatial development that resulted. RPB's aim in using the simulation game was to gain a greater insight into a number of spatial concepts that are an expression of development planning, such as "urban network" and "provincial landscape."

The simulation game was intended to generate a host of ideas about the way development planning can be implemented and about the impact on development planning of lateral factors such as the economy and the environment. The project is also intended to generate ideas for a knowledge agenda, that is, a list of questions for follow-up research. The Netherlands Institute for Spatial Research intends to study the most interesting ideas from the simulation game in more detail. For the province of North Brabant, the simulation game was a good opportunity to experiment with administrative and spatial development in the context of the existing Brabant City urban network.

Outline of the Game

The simulation game was played with two contrasting long-term environmental scenarios that the Netherlands Institute for Spatial Research had developed beforehand: 1. Brabant Production Space; and 2. Brabant Aesthetical Space. The Brabant Production Space scenario functioned as the input and background for the Urban Network game held on 14 November 2002. The Brabant Aesthetical Space scenario was used in a comparable way for the gaming session held on 10 December 2002.

In concrete terms, that means that participants had to define innovative plans and projects that matched the various trends, futuristic views, and preconditions as formulated in the Production Space scenario (during the first gaming session) or for the Aesthetical Space scenario (during the second gaming session).

The environmental scenarios Brabant Production Space and Brabant Aesthetical Space outline the effects of a number of mega-trends for the province of North Brabant. Mega-trends are developments in economic, technological, socio-cultural, and other areas that fundamentally change society and physical space in the long term. The scenarios look ahead to the year 2030 and explore the effects of these mega-trends on infrastructure, housing, work, traffic, agriculture, nature, recreation, and water. The scenarios also include prognoses on development trends such as the homes and business parks required for Brabant in 2030. They therefore formulated the challenges facing Brabant City. In the scenarios, development of the urban network would have to be successful in order to compete with other urban networks in the Netherlands and with large cities in Europe.

The two scenarios Production Space and Aesthetical Space were illustrated on colored wallboards in the hall. These wallboards indicated the most important trends for each scenario with one-liners, photographs, and graphs. Other maps indicated how Brabant would look in 2020 on the basis of existing plans and an unchanged policy. Needless to say, participants could deviate from these existing plans during the simulation game. To enable the participants to really get a feel for the scenarios, two professional actors introduced the scenario before the simulation game began.

The previous history presented to the participants during the introduction to the simulation game was largely in keeping with reality. In order to highlight certain areas of tension in the simulation game, however, an imaginary leap in

time was made from 2002 to 2004. In the gaming scenario and during the introduction, the participants were told that in 2002 the five major Brabant cities and
the province of North Brabant had approved the Brabant City program, with
which they hoped to realize their joint ambitions. The participants were given
information about the actual Brabant City program and short descriptions of the
currently formulated projects in the real Brabant City program.

During the introduction to the simulation game, the participants were told that
almost nothing of this Brabant City program from 2002 had yet been realized by
the year 2004. However, the parties involved had set up the Brabant City Bureau.
The five cities and the province agreed that this bureau must mainly act as a motivating force and process manager for innovative projects that are clearly of joint
interest to Brabant City. It mainly involves large-scale and ambitious projects, so-
called key projects. These are valuable projects that would never get off the
ground without vision, harmonization, and firm management among the provincial government and the five large Brabant cities.

The participants were asked to create a "new map" of Brabant City 2030 by
consulting and negotiating with other participants and taking the scenarios into
account. The task assigned to the participants was therefore: place your own
ambitions and your joint ambitions for Brabant 2030 on the map.

A so-called block map was used for this process. This was a 3 × 5-m plasticized
map of the province of Brabant (scale 1:25,000) which was laid on a 30-cm-high
platform in the middle of the hall. During the simulation game, all projects and
plans were placed on this map, and, where necessary, were removed or replaced.
This produced an up-to-date map of all projects and plans that had been devised
and realized by participants in various parts of the hall.

The plans that were submitted were placed on the map in the form of symbols:
wooden and metal blocks for various types of urbanization, such as high-rise
buildings in city centers, suburban residential areas, greenhouses and the like;
transparent cut-out pieces of plastic for such things as nature reserves and water;
thread for line infrastructure such as roads and rail links; flags for special projects such as an airport or a theater (see Fig. 1). The map was accompanied by a
legend displaying the meaning of the symbols. Different plans were identified
immediately using different combinations of colors and flag symbols. Gradually,
therefore, projects appeared on or disappeared from this block map.

The participants negotiated and formed coalitions for projects that fitted the
scenario, and they tried to obtain financial resources and consent from other
players (in the form of tokens and signatures) for their projects. There were map
materials on each table in the hall on which participants could draw and plan the
projects. During the simulation game, the players could call in professional
designers to raise projects to a higher plane, to create more cohesion between
the projects and to illustrate the projects. The designers could themselves indicate the spatial patterns and opportunities for Brabant, draw maps, and integrate
the plans of others into area-oriented designs and concepts.

Parallel to this process, the Brabant City Contact Group, consisting of five
aldermen and a member of the Provincial Executive, and the Brabant City
Bureau attempted to give real shape and implementation to the Brabant City

FIG. 1. Projects are placed on the block map

urban network. The effects of this would become evident from the appearance of innovative, integrating (key) projects on the map and the distinctive development of the Brabant City urban network's administrative organization and procedures.

Complicated spatial and legal procedures in the simulation game were greatly simplified. Large projects required the approval of parties such as the provincial government, local government, Ministries and/or the Brabant City Bureau and could only be realized when enough tokens had been collected.

Research and Evaluation

The simulation game was played twice, on 14 November and 10 December 2002, based on two different scenarios. The gaming sessions lasted a full day and took place in the business lounge of a large football club in Brabant.

Around 50 representatives of all relevant administrative, private, and social parties participated in each session: representatives of the five large Brabant municipalities and several small municipalities, the province, project developers, Ministries, social groups such as the environmental movement and council for the disabled, and transport companies. A large number of participants took part on both days, so the two sessions also involved a learning curve. The simulation game was evaluated on the following points:

- The content-related innovation of the spatial projects: are the players capable of devising and realizing innovative and future-oriented projects in the context of Brabant City?
- The progress of the administrative processes: are the players capable, in the context of Brabant City, of bringing about administrative innovation whereby particular attention is paid to investments, process management, and strategic frameworks?

The progress of the simulation game and the results were evaluated in various ways, including observations, debriefing, evaluation forms, and interviews after the simulation game. Furthermore, the progress of the experiment with development planning in Brabant City was measured at the start of each gaming session, at lunchtime, and at the end of the day. Using eight dimensions of development planning (see Figs. 2 and 3), the participants were asked for their evaluation of the administrative and spatial process, expressed on a scale of 1 to 10. The response level for all measurements was around 90%.

Development Planning and Administrative Innovation

The first and universally shared reaction after the end of both simulation days was that the simulation game was a very realistic reflection of reality. The chairperson of the Brabant City Bureau stated, "In just one day, I experienced what I have been going through in reality for the past two years with my work for Brabant City. This has certainly opened my eyes."

Many participants cited the high speed at which the projects came about without their involvement as an important factor for the uncomfortable situation in which they found themselves. While they were trying to develop a good spatial concept, they felt the progressive processes of others were continually overtaking them. One participant aptly compared the simulation game to a pressure cooker, with the effect greatly magnified.

During both simulation days, the strategic tactics of some people were very noticeable. For example, several players cleverly used the rudimentary projects in progress to their own advantage. The project developers in particular were able to persuade many parties to place projects on the map. The small municipalities in particular were quick to turn to the project developers for advice, money, and help to realize their projects. However, while all of this was happening, the administrative representatives and process managers of Brabant City were virtually invisible. During the interim evaluation on 14 November, one project developer remarked, "I didn't even know that the simulation game was really about them."

The Brabant City administrators and process managers were very inward-looking. The competitiveness between the Brabant City cities and the occasional insularity that cropped up led to hold-ups and an element of sluggishness in the decision-making process. The main debating point was the distribution of financial costs and benefits among the municipalities. Complicated constructions were devised to regulate funding and distribute the resources, but particularly to ensure that none of the parties paid too much or received too little. In the meantime, the administrators were not available for other tasks and were therefore inaccessible to other parties. In this regard, one of the project developers remarked, "Our projects, our management is different to that in their world (the administrators). When we want to talk to them they have no time, even though our projects tie in with their network city."

One unexpected outcome was that due to the flourishing economic situation in the Production Space scenario, there were more than enough financial resources to go around. As a result, the private parties and individual municipalities were able to largely realize their own ambitions in spite of Brabant City. Some small municipalities and project developers in particular availed of the opportunity with open arms and displayed great resolve and decisiveness in realizing innovative projects. The representatives of the State were ignored increasingly often due to the bureau's lack of initiative and their failure to manage Brabant City. The Brabant City Bureau was excluded more and more from the simulation game until it was virtually ignored during the final stages of the first day and no longer played any kind of significant role.

In the time available between the two simulation days, the team, RPB, and the contact persons of the provincial government comprehensively evaluated the administrative impasse to which development planning can lead. Together, they devised a number of new strategies so that more administrative innovation could be realized on the second day. Brabant City Bureau would place less emphasis on financial resources, pay more attention to process management rather than content, contribute more to the collective development of concepts by stimulating joint designs and managing a regional development fund, be more visible, and more emphatically focus on external parties such as project developers and small municipalities. On 10 December, this new strategy worked initially, but then the same pattern as before gradually appeared. Again, one of the participants remarked, "They're still so busy talking with each other that all I can see in the simulation game is their backs. But that's the kind of inward-looking administrative attitude that you also come across in reality."

Brabant City was caught in a vicious circle: no willingness to invest without concrete projects, no projects without concepts, and no concepts without willingness to invest. The mutual trust between parties turned out to have a decisive influence on the choices they made when realizing projects and on their attitude during administrative negotiations. For example, the small municipalities chose to sell land to project developers rather than to the large municipalities, which they regarded as a threat. The large municipalities had to play a double role. They were regularly faced with the choice of going along with all kinds of local initiatives that developed at a fast pace or sticking to the sluggish procedures in the Brabant City urban network.

After the second gaming session, the participants observed that the map of Brabant Space met their expectations more than at the end of the first gaming session and that administrative management had made better progress. The participants also noted, however, that both development planning and Brabant City urban network are extremely difficult concepts in actual practice.

Interim Measurements Throughout the Process

The above observations were confirmed by the results of the interim measurements carried out on both simulation days. The results of the measurements made according to eight dimensions of development planning illustrated a predominantly negative image of the way the experiment with development planning in Brabant City progressed. Figures 2 and 3 display the progress of the scores of the participants ($n = 35$) on the basis of mean scores. The most important conclusions from these measurements can be summarized as follows.

During the first half of both simulation days, there was a significant drop in the participants' evaluation of the practical effects of the experiment with develop-

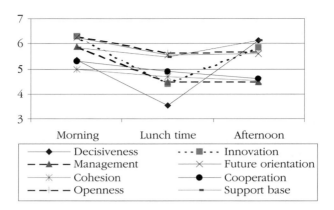

FIG. 2. Interim measurements, simulation game 1—Production Space

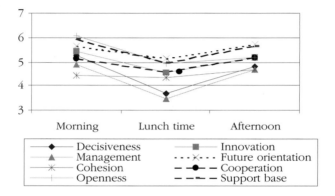

FIG. 3. Interim measurements, simulation game 2—Aesthetical Space

ment planning in Brabant. This drop is particularly significant as far as the dimensions of decisiveness, management, and innovation are concerned. The participants' evaluation of a number of dimensions rose again in the afternoon. During the afternoon of the first gaming session, there was a very significant rise in the participants' evaluation of development planning for the dimensions of decisiveness (see Fig. 2), support base, and innovation. During the afternoon of the second gaming session, these dimensions also rose again, but much less significantly. At the end of the second day, cohesion and cooperation scored as badly as ever.

On both days, however, there is an interesting dichotomy in the dimensions for development planning. This is clearly shown by the results of the measurements at the end of the first day: a reasonably positive evaluation (mean >5) for the dimensions of decisiveness, support base, innovation, future orientation, and openness. The dimensions of cooperation, management, and cohesion attained extremely poor scores (mean <5). On day two, the situation was very similar but less pronounced. Here, too, particularly management, cohesion, and cooperation attained a low score, but decisiveness was also unsatisfactory.

The conclusion to be drawn from these results is that on the first day, administrative management and innovation completely evaporated. However, because the Production Space scenario exhibited a significant economic development during the first session, giving rise to a huge demand for spatial projects, a relatively large number of projects were still realized. In other words, admittance planning largely evaporated, administrative development planning never got off the ground, but significant economic growth meant that there was still a proliferation of individual projects. Each of these projects individually was reasonably innovative and creative, but the majority of the participants were not happy with the final result, that is, the block map. To quote one of the participants, development planning, without management and at a time of major economic growth, led to a "depressing result" in terms of spatial quality.

On day two, the desired cohesion, management, and cooperation were not achieved at acceptable levels (see Fig. 3), despite the intervention of the game leaders. Partly due to the Aesthetical Space scenario, in which economic growth was somewhat less and the emphasis on spatial quality and nature was greater, the final result was less depressing, but there were also less decisiveness and spatial innovation. Because many participants were taking part for the second time and were not happy about their achievements in the previous gaming simulation, day two involved a learning element. People worked hard to bring about fundamental concepts, administrative management, and spatial quality. Nevertheless, at the end of the day people were still not very happy about the way this experiment with development planning worked out.

Discussion and Conclusions

The Dutch national government believes that regional public–private joint ventures have an increasingly important role to play in the development and innovation of spatial projects, but new administrative and spatial management instruments on a regional level are necessary in order to do this.

With the Urban Network game, the principal, the game leaders, and mainly the participants experienced and realized that the management of development planning and urban networks is a very difficult task and is full of pitfalls. Development planning will probably always function within a framework of admittance planning. However, while admittance planning is based on formal approval and can ultimately lead to coercion and sanctions, development planning mainly involves enticement and therefore positive incentives that ensure that all parties can gain and achieve something. Development planning therefore functions mainly on the basis of "soft" management instruments, such as financial distribution models, the power of persuasion, arrangements and agreements, the creation of a concept, and leadership. To achieve this, quite a profound culture change is necessary among all the parties involved. The simulation game shows that this does not evolve of itself. Particularly the element of competition between cities and the distribution of costs and benefits on a regional level are barriers that are almost insurmountable. Cities in particular tend not to go along with projects that are directly or indirectly important to them but from which others will ultimately gain even more and pay less.

Development planning in an urban network context tends to lead to an inward-looking approach on the part of municipalities and provinces. This results in slug-gishness, as a result of which private parties and small municipalities in particular lose any enthusiasm they had for the urban network and turn against it. More-over, without good management and a suitable set of administrative instruments, development planning will not lead to the cohesion and the integration of key projects.

One important peripheral condition for innovation and decisiveness in devel-opment planning is a favorable economic climate so that there is sufficient funding and demand for spatial projects. Innovation and decisiveness clearly do not live up to their promise when conditions are not ideal. The major challenge for development planning and urban networks is to ensure that support, co-operation and integration are combined with decisiveness, speed, and innovation. However, that appears to be an insurmountable dilemma, because one always seems to happen at the expense of another.

Authors' Note

A more elaborate and detailed account of the Urban Network game, the under-lying gaming scenario methodology and the results, have previously been pub-lished in *Futures 2004*, issue 3. Photographs: Zandee Fotografie.

References

Frieling DH (2000) Deltametropolis/Remaking NL. In: The density debate: seven lectures on urban settlement pattern. RIBA/University of Cambridge Conference, Manchester, pp 1–9

Healey P (2000) New partnerships in planning and implementing future-oriented devel-opment in European metropolitan regions. J Informationen zur Raumentwicklung/ Information on Spatial Development 11/12:745–750

Mayer I, Carton L, de Jong M et al (2004) Gaming the future of an urban network. Futures 36:311–333

Mayer I, Veeneman W (eds) (2002) Games in a world of Infrastructures. Simulation-games for research, learning and intervention. Eburon, Delft

Teisman GR (1997) Management through creative competition: an innovation planning perspective on spatial investment projects (in Dutch). Nijmegen University, Nijmegen, The Netherlands

VROM/RPD (2001 and 2002) Making space, sharing space. Fifth policy document on spatial planning (in Dutch). PKB part 1 and part 3, The Hague

VROM Council (2001) Quality in development (in Dutch). Advice 026, VROM Council, The Hague

WRR (1998) Spatial development policy: reports to the government (in Dutch). WRR report 53. SDU Publishers, The Hague

6. A Report of U-Mart Experiments by Human Agents

Kazuhisa Taniguchi[1], Yoshihiro Nakajima[2], and Fumihiko Hashimoto[2]

Introduction

U-Mart is a versatile simulation system, which can be used as both educational courseware and as a research program for students who learn economics or engineering. Practical knowledge of futures markets can be increased by this trading game, and to develop a machine agent will improve programming skills for students (Sato et al. 2001). The purpose of this paper is to report and analyze a series of U-Mart experiments, which were conducted in 2002 by 22 human trader agents and 20 computer-programmed software machine agents. One of the most distinguishing features of the U-Mart system is that the human agents and machine agents can participate simultaneously, but it is the conduct of the human agents that is mainly focused on in this paper. This is because the machine agents were of a random trading type, and, therefore, there were no differences between the trade strategies.

Preparatory Learning About Stock Markets and Futures Markets

The 22 human trader agents were third-year university students. They were undertaking economic majors, and were in the author's seminar class.[3] At first, they learned about futures markets and stock exchanges before the U-Mart experiments. The contents of the seminars included the history of futures markets, the stock exchange in Japan, the Tokyo, New York, and other world stock exchange systems, technical terms regarding futures markets and trading strategies according to technical analysis and fundamental analysis. The students also

[1] Faculty of Economics, Kinki University, Higashi-Osaka, Osaka 577-8502, Japan; tani@eco.kindai.ac.jp

[2] Graduate School of Economics, Osaka City University; {yoshi, hashimo}@econ.osaka-cu.ac.jp

[3] In addition to the 22 third-year students, a few fourth-year students sometimes participated in the experiments. This report focuses only on the data of the third-year students.

learned how to use the GUI-Client monitor, which is a graphical user interface of the U-Mart system for people. It took four 90-min classes to learn the entire course content. After the initial training, these 22 students participated in the experiments nine separate times.

Conditions of the U-Mart Experiments

In the U-Mart system, the futures market is not open in continuous sessions, but in a fixed-time session trading named "Itayose". This is an auction-like trading method in which all orders are contracted at the same time. The length of the trading day in the futures market of these U-Mart experiments is a virtual 24 days. It takes about 50 min for one futures market session to be completed. Itayose is held eight times on each virtual day. The interval time of Itayose is 10 s. Itayose, under which all orders are treated as simultaneous orders, refers to the method of determining the prices.

In an actual stock exchange, there are two kinds of orders available, limit orders and market orders. These stock exchanges set price limits, which limit the maximum range of fluctuation within a single trading day to prevent wild volatility. The present U-Mart system is not able to set such limits; therefore, market orders were prohibited except during the first experiment.

There are 20 random trading-type machine agents. These agents make limit orders, with a maximum of 20 yen, randomly around spot prices. They order five volumes for each order and order five times during every one Itayose.

Process of the Experiments

The series of U-Mart experiments were performed from the beginning of June to the middle of July in 2002. The experiments were conducted over five seminars and each experiment took about 50 min. The process of a series of these experiments is as follows.

Because it was easy to contract the trade by market price rather than limited price, beginners, who were indifferent to the margin, tended to trade by market price. As a result, wild volatility was observed in the market and five traders went bankrupt in the first experiment. After this experiment, market orders were prohibited in order to prevent wild volatility. In the second experiment, there was one bankruptcy that happened to input the price and the volume inversely. Occasionally, when the trade grew heated, similar accidents happened. From the third experiment onward, the market became relatively stable. Spot price data, J-30, which is a kind of stock index supplied by Mainichi Press, was adapted to the U-Mart system.

From the fourth experiment onward, artificial data was adopted; therefore, it was easy to conduct the experiments under similar conditions. This data was supplied by the Nakajima laboratory (unpublished). In the fourth and fifth experiments, roller-coaster markets were not observed. From the sixth experiment to the ninth experiment, control experiments were conducted. The aim of the control experiments was to compare the trade with or without board information per person. Participants were divided in two comparison groups.

Results and Brief Comments

Settled Profits

Regarding the trading strategy, there are no differences between the machine agents, because these machine agents use a random trading style. Therefore, they do not have different transaction results. On average, the machine agents were superior to human agents. The strategy which human agents adopted was greatly contingent on his or her character and attitude. Before the trade, each agent was given a virtual sum of one billion yen. Some of the human agents were superior to machine agents and some of them were inferior to machine agents. The average settled profits by human and machine from the second experiment to the ninth experiment are illustrated in Fig. 1.

The Frequency of the Order and the Order Volume

The average frequency of orders in one futures market session was about 32. The frequency of the order was nearly constant throughout the nine experiments. The maximum number of orders by a human agent was about 90, which was small when compared with the number of orders by machine agents, which ordered 960 times in the one futures market session. Consequently, machine agents could only respond to the transactions, which were mistakenly made by human agents.

The order volume was increased by the human agent. The order volume of the last experiment session was about three and a half times compared with the order

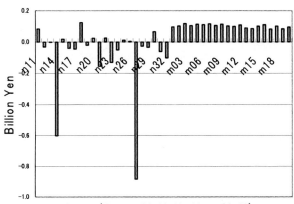

FIG. 1. Average settled profits

volume of the first experiment session. Although the frequency of orders was nearly constant throughout all experiments, the order volume increased every transaction. According to the results of a questionnaire completed by the students after the experiments, the human agents decided the order volume without referring to the market price. They seemed to have learned how to determine the order volume through the series of experiments. The volume which was ordered by machine agent was nearly constant (see Figs. 2 and 3).

Position Control

All futures contracts must be settled by offsetting. Agents are required to buy or sell to cover their transactions by the final clearing day. A short position must be bought and a long position must be sold. This is referred to as the position control. Human agents learned the importance of position control in our seminar, but it proved to be not easy to control in the trading market. In general, human agents

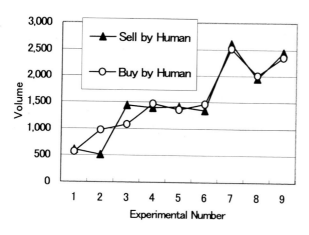

FIG. 2. Order volume by human agents

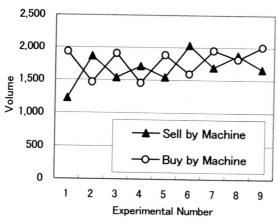

FIG. 3. Order volume by machine agents

became able to control the position after a few experimental trainings, depending on the individual. Even after the completion of all nine experiments, some human agents still could not perfectly control the position (see Fig. 4).

The Rate of Contracted Volume per Volume of Order

The contracted volume increased as the order volume increased, but the rate of contracted volume per volume of order remained almost constant by human agents. Market orders were not prohibited in the first experiment session; therefore, in this experiment alone, the rate of contracted volume is high (see Fig. 5).

A Speculator Appeared

One of the most interesting incidents in the experiments is that one participant became a speculator. Before the experiments, no one had any previous experience in investing in the stock market. However, one human agent learned the skill of investment quickly, and began to have constant high returns. He became

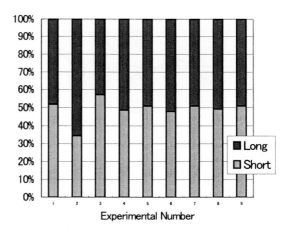

FIG. 4. Average share of short and long by human agents

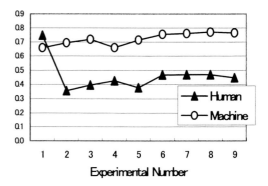

FIG. 5. Rate of contracted volume per volume of order

a successful speculator. However, according to his words, his transaction strategy was mainly based on intuition, a strategy not able to be analyzed (see Fig. 6).

Effect of Board Information (Control Experiments)

- In order to compare the effect of board information, participants were divided into two groups and the board information was displayed to one group (A group) by a monitor and was not displayed to the other group (B group) alternatively for each session. This control experiment was organized for only the last four market sessions. There was an upward trend of spot price for two market sessions, and a downward trend of spot price for the other two market sessions (see Figs. 7–10).

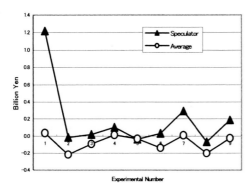

FIG. 6. Settled profits of speculator and average agents

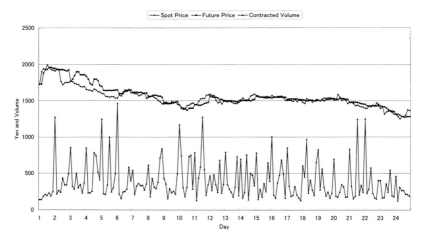

FIG. 7. Contracted price and volume (sixth experiment)

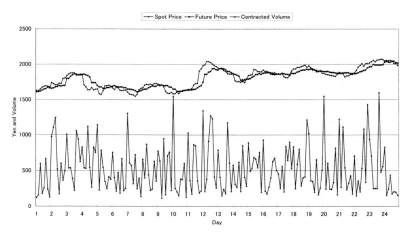

FIG. 8. Contracted price and volume (seventh experiment)

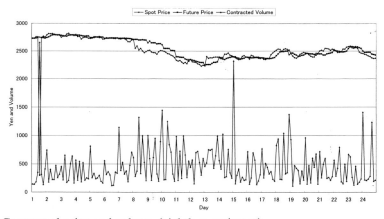

FIG. 9. Contracted price and volume (eighth experiment)

- The rate of contracted volume per volume of order was compared using analysis of variance (ANOVA) with each case depending on whether the information board was open or not. In the series of the experiments, the ANOVA table of two factors, which are the board information and the up–downward trend of the spot-price, was calculated. The significance level was 0.05 (see Table 1).
- Null Hypothesis (H_0) is as follows; the sample statistic belongs to the same population. That is to say, there is no significant difference in the rate of contracted volume per volume of order whether the board information was open or not. The test of the hypothesis produced a sample value not failing in the

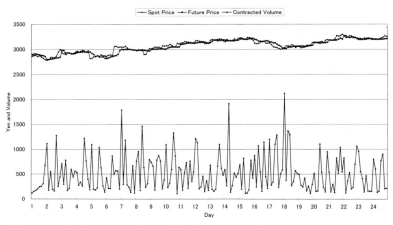

FIG. 10. Contracted price and volume (ninth experiment)

TABLE 1. ANOVA (Analysis Of VAriance)

	Source	Variation; (SS)	D. F.	Variance; (MSS)	F Ratio	F Critical P. (5%)
Group A	Up down of price	0.00176	1	0.00176	0.09345	4.02663
	Board information	0.01228	1	0.01228	0.65115	4.02663
	Interaction	0.03629	1	0.03629	1.92470	4.02663
	Residual	0.98046	52	0.01886		
	Total	1.03079	55			
Group B	Up down of price	0.00215	1	0.00215	0.06214	4.02663
	Board information	0.03883	1	0.03883	1.12330	4.02663
	Interaction	0.00040	1	0.00040	0.01167	4.02663
	Residual	1.79751	52	0.03457		
	Total	1.83889	55			

SS, Sum of squares; D.F., degree of freedom; MSS, mean of sum of squares; F Critical P., F critical point

critical region of the test, and the result was not significant. This null hypothesis (H_0) is acceptable.

The Histogram of Future Price Changes

Finally, the distribution of future price changes was considered. Transactions occur in a fixed time trading session named Itayose in the U-Mart system. The 20 yen price change class interval was selected. A histogram for the frequency distribution is shown in Fig. 10. The means and standard deviation of the future

FIG. 11. Histogram and Gaussian distribution (*line*) of future price changes

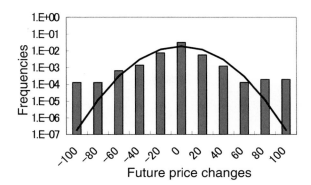

price changes of the U-Mart experiments were calculated, and a Gaussian distribution of this means and standard deviation is also illustrated in Fig. 10. Figure 10 shows that the peak of price change distribution is higher and the tails are fatter than the Gaussian distribution.

Conclusions

Regarding whether the board information was open or not, the null hypothesis was not rejected. There is no significant difference in the rate of contracted volume per volume of order. Although statistical theory provides a rationale for rejecting the null hypothesis, it provides no formal rationale for accepting it. Although the result of the experiments was not statistically significant, there may be another possibility that can be concluded from further experimentation. The Gaussian distributed price change was not ascertained by the experiments. This is the first series of U-Mart experiments that were performed systematically by more than 20 human trader agents and machine agents. However, the number of experimental data is not large, and the results obtained are restrictive. Further experiments are needed to improve our knowledge about the financial market.

Reference

Sato H, Matsui H, Ono I et al (2001) U-Mart project: learning economic principles from the bottom by both human and software agents. New frontiers in artificial intelligence. pp 121–131, Springer

7. Price Competition Between Middlemen: An Experimental Study[1]

Kazuhito Ogawa[2], Kouhei Iyori[3], and Sobei H. Oda[4]

Introduction

Recent studies of experimental price competition focus on the number of competitors. For instance, Dufwenberg and Gneezy (2000) examined whether the equilibrium price is attained when the number of competitors is two, three, and four. In these experiments, the subjects knew the supply–demand condition and the number of rounds, and offer ask prices. They are matched randomly in each round. Their result showed that the price does not converge to the competitive one when the number of competitors is two, and that as it increases, the average price approaches the competitive level. Abbink and Brandts (2002) conducted similar experiments and attained similar results.

However, Dufwenberg et al. (2002) examined the relation between the price floor (the minimum price) and the price competition. The number of competitors was two. They found that the average price without the price floor is higher than the average price with the price floor. The competition under the price floor treatment is keen because profit can still be made by bidding the minimum price at worst.

In our study, we examined how the bid–ask competition influenced the price setting. Does the bid–ask competition increase the ratio of the competitively priced pairs? The number of competitors was two and our study was in line with that of Dufwenberg et al. (2002). We designed the experiment based on the work of Spulber (1999), which dealt with the price competition between middlemen.[5]

[1] This research was supported by the Open Research Centre "Experimental Economics: A new method of teaching economics and the research on its impact on society", Graduate School of Economics, Kyoto Sangyo University and the Japan Society for the Promotion of Science, Grant-in-Aid for Scientific Research (B), 13480115, and the Ministry of Education, Science, Sports and Culture, Grant-in-Aid for JSPS Fellows, 2002–2005.
[2] JSPS Research Fellow, Kyoto University, Kyoto 606-8501, Japan; O-kazu@m3.people.or.jp
[3] JSPS PD Research Fellow, Kyoto Sangyo University; oda@cc.kyoto-su.ac.jp
[4] Faculty of Economics, Kyoto Sangyo University; iyori@cc.kyoto-su.ac.jp
[5] Plott and Uhl (1981) consider the intertemporal arbitration by middleman.

In this study, middlemen set a bid price, buy a commodity from a supplier, and then sell it to a buyer at a higher ask price.

Our results are as follows: in the final rounds, about 30% and 20% of the pairs chose the competitive alternatives under Treatment 1 and Treatment 2, respectively (see following).

Experimental Settings

The experiment consisted of Treatment 1 (T1) and Treatment 2 (T2), and they were conducted in order. The experiment was conducted at the Kyoto Sangyo University Experimental Economics Laboratory (KEEL). Subjects had no prior experience of price competition experiments. Twenty-two subjects participated under Treatments 1-1 and 2-1, 26 subjects participated under Treatments 1-2 and 2-2, 14 subjects participated under Treatments 1-3 and 2-3, and 26 subjects participated under Treatments 1-4 and 2-4. The number of rounds was more than 100. To prevent end effects, the subjects did not know when the Treatment was over.

In each session, all the subjects entered the KEEL; they received an instruction, and were told that they would receive 2000 yen for participating (about US$16 at the time of the experiment) and additional monetary reward contingent on the overall performance in the experiment.[6] The contingent part was calculated from $0.4 \times \Sigma_{i=1}^2$ Total Profit$_{\text{Treatment-1}}$.

Under Treatment 1, subjects did not know the supply or demand function. Under Treatment 2, they knew these functions. Under each treatment, before the first round began, each subject was paired with another subject according to a random matching scheme. The opponent remained unchanging during the treatment. This is different from the conditions of Dufwenberg and Gneezy (2000), Abbink and Brandts (2002), and Dufwenberg et al. (2002).

In this experiment, the subjects were asked to choose bid and ask prices as Spulber (1996) and (1999) assumed. In the first stage, subjects offer bid prices simultaneously and learn the opponent's bid price. If a subject purchases inputs, an ask price can be set in the second stage. Otherwise, the subject waits for the next round. In the second stage, only the subject who has a commodity can sell it. If both middlemen have a commodity, they chose ask prices simultaneously. The lowest-bid middleman then sells first. The other middleman faces the residual consumers and sells a commodity to them. Then, they receive the information about the opponent's ask price and their own ask price, sales, and profit. The profit of Middleman-1 is determined as follows:

$$\pi_1 = p_1 q_{D1} - w_1 q_{S1},$$

where p_1, w_1, q_{D1}, and q_{S1} represent the ask price, the bid price, the number of demand units, and the number of supply units, respectively. Especially,

$$q_{S1} = \begin{cases} 0 \text{ if } w_1 < w_2 \\ S(w_1)/2 \text{ if } w_1 = w_2 \\ S(w_1) \text{ if } w_1 > w_2 \end{cases}$$

---

[6] When the total performance was negative, only the appearance fee was paid.

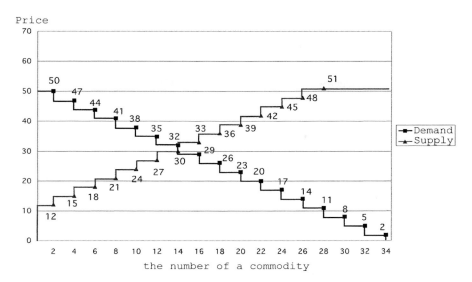

FIG. 1. The supply and demand functions used in the experiment. The shape of these functions are similar to Ogawa, et al. (2003)

$$q_{D1} = \begin{cases} 0 \text{ if } q_{S1} = 0 \\ D(p_1) \text{ if } p_1 < p_2 \text{ and } q_{S1} \geq D(p_1) \text{ or if } q_{S2} = 0, \text{ and } q_{S1} \geq D(p_1) \\ q_{S1} \text{ if } p_1 < p_2 \text{ and } q_{S1} < D(p_1) \text{ or if } q_{S2} = 0, \text{ and } q_{S1} < D(p_1) \\ q_{S1} \text{ if } p_1 > p_2 \text{ and } q_{S1} < D(p_2) - q_{S2} \\ D(p_2) - q_{S2} \text{ if } p_1 > p_2 \text{ and } q_{S1} > D(p_2) - q_{S2} \end{cases}$$

If $p^R \leq p^W$, this game has a unique subgame perfect Nash equilibrium (SPNE), where p^R and p^W indicate the sales-revenue-maximizing ask price and the Walrasian price, respectively. In SPNE, both middlemen set the competitive price as the bid and ask prices.[7]

Our supply and demand functions are step functions and are shown in Fig. 1. Competitive price is 30, 31, or 32. Maximum revenue price p^R is equal to 53/2, which is smaller than the competitive price. There is a SPNE in this setting. SPNE is (35, 29) and is different from the competitive price, because of the step functions. When both subjects choose SPNE, each profit is 36. If one of the subjects monopolistically chooses the competitive price, for example, (32, 30), the resulting profit will only be 28. Finally, we call the price set that maximizes profit the "monopolistic price set." The bid and ask prices, and the trading volume are 21, 41, and 8, respectively.

Let us examine the difference between other experiments and ours. In other experiments, subjects chose only ask prices, while our subjects chose bid and ask prices. Moreover, our experimental setting was collusion-promoting. First, our subjects did not know the number of rounds, while those in other experiments

---

[7] The detailed proof is shown in Spulber (1999) and Stahl (1988).

knew the number of rounds. Secondly, subjects played the game with the same opponent throughout the treatment, whereas pairs were randomly matched in each round in other experiments. Finally, the competitive price was not SPNE. The profit of SPNE was higher than that of the competitive price. The subjects did not have the incentive to choose the competitive price if they acted rationally. Our setting helped subjects to collude.

After Treatment 2 finished, the subjects answered the following questions.

[Q-1] "Were you aware of the bid price being higher than the opponent's?"
[Q-2] "Were you aware of setting the bid price as high as the opponent's?"
[Q-3] "Were you aware of setting the bid price to sell all the units you had in the second stage?"
[Q-4] "Were you aware of setting the ask price lower than the opponent's?"
[Q-5] "Were you aware of setting the ask price as high as the opponent's?"
[Q-6] "Were you aware of setting the ask price to sell all the units you had?"

The answers that the subjects could choose were as follows:

[A-1] I was aware of this throughout the treatment.
[A-2] I was aware of this in the early rounds but not in the later rounds.
[A-3] I was not aware of this in the early rounds but was in the later rounds.
[A-4] I was not aware of this throughout the treatment.
[A-5] Others.

Analysis

Subjects' average total profit was larger under Treatment 2 than under Treatment 1. The difference is significant at the 5% level for all cases; see Table 1. The maximum total profit and the minimum total profit were also higher under Treatment 2 than under Treatment 1.

This difference arose mainly because of the burden of dead inventory; $q_S - q_D$. Because subjects under Treatment 1 did not know the supply or demand, they searched for the profitable price sets. During searching, they often suffered from

TABLE 1. Overview of the experiments and their results

	Number of pairs	Number of rounds	Maximum total profit	Minimum total profit	Average	Variance
T1-1	11	103	3961	−10203	−126.77	10139436.85
T1-2	13	102	1982	−2761	217.54	1674217.62
T1-3	7	104	4496	−1637	1513.25	3113343.67
T1-4	13	103	4148	−11625	−928.96	16588388.76
T2-1	11	107	7636	516	3372.05	3419055.19
T2-2	13	109	10722	654	4105.46	5491465.70
T2-3	7	108	8800	907	5253.31	7635767.16
T2-4	13	107	7661	−2968	3183.73	7283718.76

dead inventory. In contrast, subjects under Treatment 2 knew the supply and demand in advance and may have selected prices to equalize supply and demand.

Let us consider where the pairs finally chose. We classify all the pairs into the following five cases.

[C-1] Convergence to the competitive price sets; (32, 30), (32, 31), or (32, 32).
[C-2] Convergence to the monopolistic price set, (41, 21).
[C-3] Convergence to the SPNE (35, 29).
[C-4] Convergence to other price sets.
[C-5] Nonconvergence.

A pair is classified into C-1 when more than 60% of the winning bid and ask prices in the 70th to the last round belong to (32, 30), (32, 31), or (32, 32). Similarly, a pair is classified into C-2 if more than 60% of the winning bid and ask prices in the 70th to the last round belong to (41, 21). A pair is classified into C-3 when more than 60 % of the winning bid and ask prices in the 70th to the last round belong to SPNE. A pair is classified into C-4 when 60% of the winning bid and ask prices in the 70th to the last round belong to a price set that does not belong to C-1 to C-3, for example, (38, 26) and (35, 27). Otherwise, a pair belongs to C-5.

Table 2 shows the distribution of convergence for Treatment 1 and Treatment 2. The distribution of Treatment 1 is different from that of Treatment 2, and the χ^2 test confirmed that this difference is significant at the 1% level.

From Table 2, about 34% of the pairs chose the competitive price set under Treatment 1. Most of them offer (32, 30), while in Dufwenberg and Gneezy (2000), no pairs chose the competitive price. Therefore, our ratio is quite high, even if the supply and demand functions are largely different from Dufwenberg and Gneezy (2000), Abbink and Brandts (2002), and Dufwenberg et al. (2002). Even if the subjects did not know the supply or demand, or were not randomly matched in each round, the ratio of the competitively priced pairs is higher than the ratio when they knew these functions and were randomly matched in each round. About 5% of pairs under Treatment 1 chose SPNE. With a lack of the supply–demand information, only a few pairs can choose SPNE exactly. However, about 16% of the pairs chose price sets near SPNE.

TABLE 2. Classification results

	Classification (%)					Total
	C-1	C-2	C-3	C-4	C-5	
T1	34.09	0.00	4.55	15.91	45.45	100
T2	20.45	13.64	20.45	13.64	31.82	100

TABLE 3. Variance of winning prices throughout treatments

	T1-1	T1-2	T1-3	T1-4	T2-1	T2-2	T2-3	T2-4
Ask	1.00	1.07	1.35	2.34	0.60	0.24	0.53	0.55
Bid	2.24	1.73	1.68	4.28	0.49	0.24	0.60	0.46

TABLE 4. Results of the questionnaire

Question	Treatment	Answer					x^2 test
		A-1	A-2	A-3	A-4	A-5	
Q-1	T1	31	38	14	4	1	0.0000
	T2	33	20	11	20	4	
Q-2	T1	10	11	30	33	4	0.0199
	T2	24	8	24	29	3	
Q-3	T1	24	3	23	38	0	0.0043
	T2	52	1	6	28	1	
Q-4	T1	27	12	7	40	2	0.1885
	T2	22	8	6	47	5	
Q-5	T1	9	4	17	56	2	0.2789
	T2	15	5	17	50	1	
Q-6	T1	50	0	18	20	0	4.74284E–10
	T2	69	2	5	12	0	

Under Treatment 2, only 20% of the pairs converged to the competitive price set. The ratio of competitive price set is smaller under Treatment 2 than under Treatment 1. However, this ratio is still higher than those of Dufwenberg and Gneezy (2000), Abbink and Brandts (2002), and Dufwenberg et al. (2002). About 20% of the pairs chose SPNE. This ratio is significantly higher than that under Treatment 1. In addition, about 14% of the pairs converged to the monopolistic price set. The supply–demand information and the experience can increase the ratio of SPNE and of the monopolistic price set. Most other pairs chose $w \in [25, 29]$ and $p \in [35, 38]$.

In summary, it appears that as more information becomes available and experience increases, C-1 decreases, while C-2 and C-3 increase. However, C-1 is higher than any other ratios in other experiments.

Treatment 1

Figure 2 shows the evolution of average winning prices under Treatment 1. Bid prices in the first five or ten rounds rose and were higher than the competitive level. The subjects competed to reveal the situation and to defeat their opponent. However, having the bid price above the competitive price incurs large losses. Therefore, the average winning bid price rapidly fell below 30. Once the average winning bid price reached [28, 30], only small fluctuations occurred up until the final round.

Let us explain the tendency of the average ask price. Except for Treatment 1-4 (Fig. 2d), the winning ask price fell in the first 10 or 15 rounds because the subjects set high ask prices and failed to make reasonable profits. Then, and until the final round, the winning ask price fluctuated upward, because the subjects intuitively understood how to make profit. The trend is confirmed by Spearman's rank correlation test. This tendency is the case in the narrow range of [32, 34].

These conclusions were confirmed by a questionnaire (see Table 4), which enabled us to understand the subjects' policy on bid price setting. First, most of

(a)

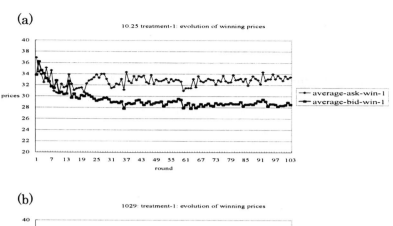

(b)

(c)

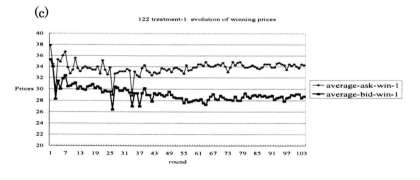

(d)

FIG. 2a–d. Evolution of average prices under Treatment 1

them tended to raise the bid price to defeat their opponent; however, as the rounds went on, this tendency gradually decreased. Finally, the subjects became aware of the advantages of setting the bid price to the same as that of the opponent. Moreover, they understood the need to set the bid price while minimizing dead inventory. Their policy on setting the ask price is summarized as follows: the subjects did not care about the opponent's ask price except when both middlemen had a commodity. Instead, they mainly paid attention to setting the ask price to that at which they could sell all of their units.

Treatment 2

Figure 3 shows the evolution of average prices under Treatment 2. The average winning bid prices belonged to [26, 29], which are lower than that of Treatment 1. Fluctuation in the early rounds was also smaller than that in Treatment 1, (see Table 3). In later rounds, fluctuation was also small except for Treatment 2-3. The average winning ask price was higher than that of Treatment 1 and belonged to [34, 37]. As shown in Table 1, the fluctuation was also smaller than that of Treatment-1. Therefore, the bid–ask spread is higher than that of Treatment 1. In most rounds, the subjects' supply equaled demand. Therefore, they did not frequently suffer from dead inventory, in contrast with Treatment 1.

The questionnaire results show that under Treatment 2, the bid price was set to the same as that of the opponent or was set in order to sell all units. This policy was satisfied throughout Treatment 2. The policy on setting the ask price was almost the same as that of Treatment 1: setting the ask price to sell all units. The subjects did not care about the opponent's ask price.

Conclusions

Although our setting is collusion-promoting and the effects of information and experience reduce the ratio of competitively priced pairs, the results are the most competitive among those experimental price competitions. Here we examine the factors that influenced the results. First, the bid price competition is winner-take-all. By this trading rule, the bid price can rise to or over the competitive level. Once the subjects offer a competitive price, they do not care about the opponent's decision. If subject A chooses 29 as the bid price and subject B chooses 30, subject A can receive zero profit.

Moreover, the result is affected by the prices that subjects choose in the initial rounds under Treatment 1. Many subjects chose bid prices higher than SPNE and the competitive level. Therefore, the competitive alternatives were the equilibrium that most of them found first. This is true under Treatment 1, especially when most of the competitively priced pairs cannot find SPNE.

Thirdly, learning affected the behaviors. Although under Treatment 2 the ratio of the competitively priced pairs decreased, some pairs learned that the competitive alternatives bring profit safely and offer competitive alternatives.

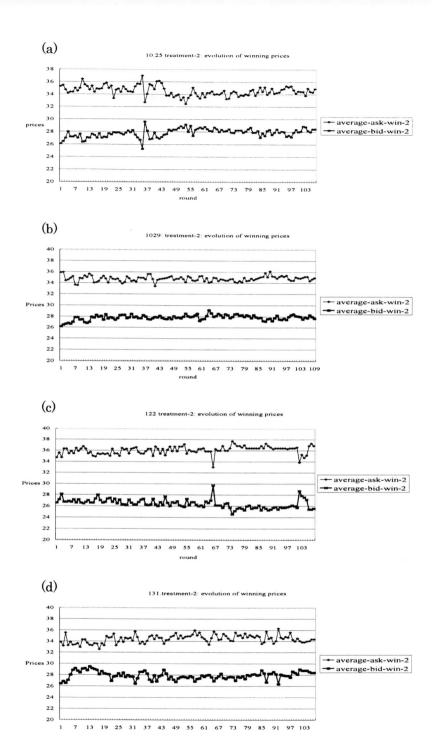

FIG. 3a–d. Evolution of average prices under Treatment 2

Fourth, the number of alternatives was too large (2500^2), even though the structure of our experiment was the same as the Prisoner's Dilemma. Because of the large number of alternatives, it may have been difficult for some subjects to cooperate with each other.

Finally, the ratio of competitively priced pairs can be reduced by the step functions, especially under Treatment 2. If we use liner functions, the ratio of the competitively priced pairs will increase. In this case, the competitive price is SPNE, and subjects do not have incentive to deviate.

The bid–ask competition is seen in real markets such as the used book industry. In Japan, the firms dealing with used books, CDs, DVDs, and TV game software have been prosperous since the 1990s. As middlemen, they have pricing power to consumers and suppliers. The price competition among these firms is keen.

Our experimental results are useful for designing a new market. Suppose that a market is planned but the participants are a few and fixed in some reason. The price collusion may happen. To prevent collusion, we can introduce price-setting middlemen and bid–ask competition. This will avoid price collusion to some degree.

Finally we consider future studies. Which is more collusion-promoting: the experience or the supply-demand information? In our study, this question remains open. Our next paper will deal with this question by introducing the treatment where inexperienced subjects have the supply–demand information.

References

Abbink K, Brandts J (2002) Price competition under cost uncertainty: a laboratory analysis. University of Nottingham, CeDEX discussion paper

Dufwenberg M, Gneezy M (2000) Price competition and market concentration: an experimental study. International Journal of Industrial Organization 18:7–22

Dufwenberg M, Uri G, Jacob K et al (2002) Price floor and competition. Working paper, Stockholm University

Ogawa K, Koyama Y, Oda SH (2002) An experimental approach to market microstructure: search and market efficiency. Proceedings of the Sixth International Conference of Complex Systems 2002. pp 124–134

Plott CR, Uhl JT (1981) Competitive equilibrium with middlemen: an empirical study. Southern Economic Journal 47:1063–1071

Spulber DF (1996) Market microstructure and intermediation. Journal of Economic Perspectives 10:135–152

Spulber DF (1999) Market microstructure: intermediaries and the theory of the firm. Cambridge University Press

Stahl DOII (1988) Bertrand competition for inputs and Walrasian outcomes. American Economic Review 78:189–201

Part II
Social Relevancies in
Simulation and Gaming

8. Facilitation in Communication: Toward a Study of an Educational Gaming Simulation

Fumitoshi Kato[1]

Introduction

In an educational gaming simulation session, a facilitator enacts multiple roles of "coach," "guide," "educator," "trainer," and "supervisor" who attempts to manage the given educational setting toward a certain educational purpose. By exploring the characteristics of one facilitator's moves, we may be able to extend knowledge about some aspects of the nature of professional practices. It then leads to our understanding of the "practice context" (Schön 1983, 1987, 1991) of a facilitation process. The idea of the practice context acknowledges that part of our knowledge, understanding, and expertise to cope with the given situation are tacit and implicit in our patterns of action.

This chapter reports on preliminary findings of a set of interview sessions with a facilitator after an educational gaming simulation session. It aims to offer further understanding of the communicative nature of professional practices as they are embedded in our action. Through the process of facilitation, the facilitator accumulates and personalizes experiences as a facilitator, and then generalizes such experiences into a private "theory" which may be applicable to subsequent opportunities to facilitate gaming simulations. Guided by the facilitator's own theory of practice, the facilitator selects and combines communication strategies in order to control the situation as the process unfolds. Based on a set of long interviews with a facilitator, some characteristics of the facilitation process are discussed in the context of a constitutive view of communication.

Conducting Interviews with a Facilitator

For the purpose of understanding the nature of the facilitation process, observational research was conducted at an educational gaming simulation session (Kato 1996, 1998). Approximately 6 months after the session, two interview sessions were conducted with the facilitator. The primary purpose of these sessions was

---

[1] Faculty of Environmental Information, Keio University, Fujisawa, Kanagawa 252-8520, Japan; fk@sfc.keio.ac.jp

to reflect upon the "practice context" (Schön 1983) of a gaming simulation in which both the facilitator and a researcher were embedded.

Videotapes recorded at the gaming simulation session were used as a stimulus for recollecting and reconstructing the situation. In these interview sessions, the facilitator was allowed to operate the VCR, to have her control the flow of the tape. The facilitator was asked to watch the videotape, and to recollect and reconstruct the situation within which she was facilitating the session. A general instruction was that in the process of reviewing the tape, whenever she found something noteworthy, she should stop (pause) and/or rewind the tape. In addition, the facilitator was asked to mention and elaborate further in cases when the recording raised particular points of interest.

Facilitator's Own "Theory" of Facilitation

The facilitator constitutes the situation through the process of communication with it, and thus the facilitator's own operational models and working hypotheses about the practice of facilitation are constituted by the situation as well. In other words, the facilitator understands the situation by trying to facilitate it. What are the facilitator's assumptions about the process of facilitation? What are the "on-the-spot" decisions made in order to maintain the flow of the gaming simulation session? What are the problems or obstacles, if any, that the facilitator faced in the process of guiding the gaming simulation session? Based on the interview sessions, some characteristics of the ways in which the facilitator coped with the situation can be identified.

Learning by Doing

One of the most important ideas that guided the facilitator's way of managing the flow of interaction is in tune with the very idea of experiential learning. That is to assume that learning is created out of experiences. In other words, the facilitator thinks that the participants will become "competent" players only through their experiences within the gaming simulation. For example, participants learn how to move around the room, to communicate with other team members, and to interpret their situation only through enacting their roles. Thus, the trial round offers an important learning opportunity for the participants.

In reviewing the videotape, the facilitator mentioned how she understood the nature of facilitation. From her past experiences as a facilitator, she came to believe that the process of gaming simulation is difficult to explain unless she makes the participants actually practice it. The participants' actual experiences of gaming simulation are important not only to help the participants understand its operation, but also to make them personally engaged in the process. Reflecting upon her past experiences as a facilitator, she talked about two "working models" of facilitation processes in the context of gaming simulation. In her talk, these two "working models" of facilitation were used to contrast two distinctive ways to help the participants understand the nature of the gaming simulation. These two models suggest possible patterns of facilitation, and can be understood as two ends of a spectrum.

At one end is an idea that the participants may learn about the operation of the gaming simulation through a detailed explanation of functional properties of the gaming simulation, such as goals and rules. In doing so, the facilitator may utilize handouts including pay-off tables and diagrams that illustrate the relationships among roles. From the standpoint of the participants, they have to go through their own thought processes in trying to understand the nature of the gaming simulation. This way of facilitation assumes that the participants need to know about the gaming simulation *before* they can actually move. Practicing presupposes theorizing.

At the other end of the spectrum is an idea that the participants may learn about the operation of the gaming simulation through actual experience of it. In this case, the facilitator may try to minimize input, and make the participants enact their roles from the earlier stages of the session itself. An assumption here is that even without much understanding about the nature of the gaming simulation, the participants should try to move from the very beginning. This way of facilitation assumes that there are many aspects of the gaming simulation that cannot be communicated via handouts and the facilitator's talk. Practicing embeds theorizing.

In one of the interview sessions, the facilitator explained that her general attitude toward facilitation processes is in tune with the latter "model" of facilitation. She thinks that understanding the operations of the gaming simulation—that is to understand the gaming simulation behaviorally—has to involve doing. As she describes:

F [1]: I guess there are various ways to facilitate the process. One would prefer to explain the procedure until all the participants understand. The other approach is to go on to actually practice, even if half of the participants don't understand, and I prefer this latter approach when I facilitate. I think it's important for them to understand how they go about exchanging cards and things like that, after going through the trial round. At that point, they would go "Aha!" and understand, and I somehow believe that many people learn in such a way.

F [2]: I go through an explanation, and then ask the participants to make sure that they understand; then they would tell me that they don't understand. In that case, I used to have an idea that I should repeat my explanation again. But instead, I'd tell them to just practice it. I think many of us prefer to understand the whole process before doing, but at least for the students I usually teach, many of them prefer to learn the process by doing. It's a better way for them to understand the process. Out of my experiences, I began to feel that learning by doing is a better approach.

The trial round creates important learning opportunities for both the participants and the facilitator. As mentioned above, participants learn behaviorally about the ways in which they can cope with the situation through their active engagement in the gaming simulation. Each of the teams can utilize this trial round to discuss about their own "strategies" in order to achieve each of their goals. Because it is a trial round, the participants are allowed to make errors. By definition, the trial round is offered for the participants to experience the process of "trial and error."

At the same time, the trial round is an opportunity for the facilitator to decide on how to make full use of the given setting. The facilitator can refer to past experiences as a facilitator, and can make adjustments if necessary. The trial round may contribute to shaping and reshaping the elements of the facilitator's repertoire of examples, images, understandings, and actions. For example, the facilitator may explore the ways in which the physical setting of the room can be used. Also, the facilitator can utilize the trial round to explore whether the participants understand the nature of the gaming simulation. The facilitator can observe how the participants cope with the situation and can also learn about the participants through their questions. It is important to note that this trial round can be understood not only as an occasion to learn about the participants, but also to learn about the facilitation process itself through communication with the situation.

Actively Inactive

Another important characteristic of the facilitation process may be described as being "actively inactive." As already introduced, the facilitator tries to be "invisible" during the gaming simulation session. In the very beginning of the observational research phase, it appeared to the author that the facilitator was *not* facilitating. Such an impression is based on the understandings and expectations about the notion of facilitation. The author's image of the facilitator's role was that to frequently intervene in the on-going process, and to give guidance to the participants. However, the facilitator rarely intervened into the process of the participants' transactions, and explicit announcements to the participants in the room were rarely made.

In accordance with the idea of behaving as a "disinterested observer," it seems that the facilitator always tries to keep a proper distance from the participants. In other words, the facilitator attempts to be "invisible," as if not present at the site. Intuitively, the very idea of invisibility does not go well with the notion of facilitation. Understanding that the facilitation process involves an active engagement, the facilitator needs to be available to the participants. In fact, in the earlier phase of transcribing the video recordings, while trying to capture some aspects of the facilitation process, the author gained the impression that the facilitator did not facilitate much. However, through the process of repeated viewing, and through an examination of transcripts, such understanding and interpretation had to be changed. The facilitator's way of coping with the situation may be characterized as "actively inactive," in that she consciously made herself invisible to maintain the participants' interaction.

In the interview session, the facilitator began to talk about her own way of coping with the situation. As she reflects, the facilitator tried not to intervene into the process of transactions between two teams. Rather, she stayed outside the circle. It seems that the idea of being "actively inactive" was proper and natural for her. Whereas it is still arguable that there may be alternative ways to facilitate the session, it became clear that the facilitator, knowingly or not, *did* what she thought the facilitator should do. She had, in her own way, reasons to be invisible on that occasion.

Pushing One's Back

In relation to the point above, the facilitator described her own image of the nature of facilitation. From her point of view, an act of facilitation requires an active engagement to the process, even though it is displayed inactively, in a humble fashion.

During one of the interview sessions, the facilitator used a metaphor to illustrate her own "theory" of facilitation. She thinks that an act of facilitation is not leading or "pulling" the participants toward a prespecified goal. Rather, the facilitation is about helping or "pushing" the participants:

F [3–1]: When you are going to move something, you first have to deal with something like friction. You have to push hard particularly in the very beginning. So, to make a smooth move, you put a sheet of paper in between . . . or, find something like a roller . . . I guess I am doing things like that. As I was watching this . . .

F [3–2]: Yes, throughout, particularly in the beginning. Once it starts to move, then they can move by themselves. But in the very beginning stage . . .

Even though there are goals embedded in the design of the gaming simulation, the ways in which the participants cope with such goals is not necessarily clear in advance. Depending on the characteristics of the participants, the facilitator may emphasize different aspects of the gaming simulation throughout the session. In other words, the facilitator is more interested in the nature of experiential learning processes to teach collaborative group processes, rather than the content of the gaming simulation itself. In that, a primary motivation that guides the facilitator's decisions is based on interest in creating an educational environment through the use of gaming simulation.

In the second interview session, she mentioned again about the idea of pushing the participants. She particularly described about the direction in which she attempts to guide the participants:

F [4]: Often, in the very beginning, I feel that they are "heavy" to move, so I guess that's the most difficult part, but once they start to move, they just proceed by themselves, so I was thinking about the direction, I mean, where they are heading. I think my role is, the facilitator's role is, like "oiling" them for a smooth move, or getting rid of obstacles in their way. So, I think the direction itself depends on them as a group.

How and in which direction the facilitator pushes the participants depend largely on the facilitator's understanding about the situation, particularly about the characteristics of the participants. From past experiences, the facilitator knows that there are various ways to push the participants depending on their previous exposures to gaming simulations. The facilitator thinks that the participants as a group will have a momentum to move themselves without much intervention from the facilitator. The facilitator thinks that her "mission" is almost completed when the participants understand the procedure, as well as the ways in which they should enact roles within the gaming simulation, and thus begin to move the process by themselves. Thus, one of the important tasks of the facilitator is to push the participants to initiate their activities, and to make them be drawn into the process of the gaming simulation.

In the early phase of the session, the facilitator tries to create a pace that seems to fit most of the participants. Depending on the characteristics of the participants, the facilitator makes a decision about the pace of the session. In turn, that pace becomes a criterion, or a reference, that guides the facilitation. Thus, once the session starts to move, the facilitator tries to pay attention to individuals in relation to the given pace of the process. By doing so, the facilitator attempts to make all the participants be involved and to keep up with the pace, while managing time for the whole session.

Discussion

A Constitutive View of Communication

Given the facilitator's theories of facilitation, it is proposed that an exploration of the nature of facilitation actions and their contexts can be theoretically based on a constitutive view of communication (Mokros 1996, 2003; Mokros et al. 1995). Within this theoretical framework, Schön's concept of the "reflective practitioner" (Schön 1983, 1987, 1991) is examined to understand practice contexts of an educational setting.

A constitutive view of communication assumes that knowledge is communicatively constructed through social interactions. Mokros (1996) noted that by viewing communication as a constitutive process, "known properties of reality are assumed to be contingent upon, or only made possible by virtue of communicative action." Thus, the constitutive view of communication directs us toward recognition that "what is regarded to be the behavior of an individual is a collaborative social sense-making activity, within which statements of identity in relationship to others are continuously realized" (Mokros 1996). This constitutive view of communication differs significantly from the informational view of communication, which sees communication as a transfer of messages (information) between a sender and a receiver who have a goal of mutually consistent information exchange. The informational view tends to pursue lawful statements utilizing a linear (cause and effect) model. Often, models proposed are based on an assumption that information can be moved from one location to another. Mokros (1993) suggests that this informational view has been "privileged" in our attempts to understand communication. From an informational view, communication is conceptualized as a transfer of message, via conduit, from sender to receiver.

A constitutive view of communication highlights the notion of meaning created within the process of communication, as well as such process itself. The view perceives that meaning is constantly at issue, as constructed, reconstructed, and maintained communicatively in social occasions. Additionally, the very process of interaction is regarded as a fundamental condition for human behavior (Watzlawick et al. 1967). The constitutive view "sees" the world in process. The image is dynamic, on-going, ever-changing, and continuous. Meanings are understood as social products, as constructions, brought about via social interactions and engagements. In other words, an individual is regarded as an active organism engaged in processes of creating meanings.

One of the most important values in applying a constitutive view of communication in a study of educational practice is that it shifts our focus from the product (outcome) of an educational setting to the process by which outcomes are derived. When seen from the informational view of communication, educational practice is understood as a transfer of information (content), for example, from a teacher to his/her students, and thus, a primary concern becomes the effectiveness of the ways in which information (content) is transferred. In contrast, from a constitutive view of communication, educational practice is viewed as a process of collaborative sense-making and not an information transfer.

Theory of Practice and Theory of Personhood

Schön's concept of the "reflective practitioner" acknowledges the importance of the interrelationships between theory and practice (Schön 1983, 1987, 1991). His ideas allow us to critically examine the "technical rationality," that separates links between theory and practice. Whereas Schön's ideas are useful for understanding the nature of "practice context," they do not explicitly explore the relationship between one's personal understandings of practice skills and one's sense of self generally acting as a practitioner. This study suggests that ideas of the theory of practice and theory of personhood (Mokros et al. 1995) may offer a framework to further examine and understand such a relationship underlying professional actions.

Mokros et al. (1995) examined the context of an on-line computer search in a library with a focus on the nature of intermediaries' interactions with users. By using a microanalytical approach, the study explored assumptions about professional practice and relational dimensions of such interactions. Through a series of analyses, the study proposes the idea of interplay between theory of (professional) practice and theory of personhood, grounded on a constitutive view of communication.

A constitutive view of communication guides us to examine the process of facilitation as relational and interactional. In a process of facilitation, the facilitator engages in the task of managing the flow of interaction, and concurrently, the facilitator is constructing and maintaining the relationships with the participants. Thus, the facilitator's moves are not only displaying to the participants what to do in the given context, but also, they are displaying about themselves, and their understandings about the relationships with the participants.

From a constitutive view of communication, the idea of the "definition of situation" becomes important in order to understand the process of facilitation. The facilitator and participants have their own images and understandings about the nature of the gaming simulation session. Through the communicative process of facilitation, they define, and redefine, the situation within which they are embedded. It is through the "definition of the situation" that roles, values, and expressive possibilities of participants at a specific place and point in time are identified (Mokros et al. 1995).

As illustrated, the facilitator has her own theories about facilitation. The facilitator may utilize a set of communication strategies to manage the flow of educational gaming simulation. At the same time, the facilitator has a claim about herself as a facilitator within that context. In their examination of the interactions between professional and client, Mokros et al. (1995) suggest:

"Thus, although a practitioner may be able to discuss a theory of practice in detail, awareness and embeddedness of this theory within a theory of personhood and especially awareness of the interactivity of these types of theories is, we assume, largely out of awareness."

As they suggest, theories of practice can be understood as embedded within theories of personhood. This study attempts to focus on such interplay of theories of practice and personhood in interaction.

Facilitation in Communication

Considering the perspective of a constitutive view of communication, a learning situation can be conceived as jointly constructed and reconstructed by both the students and facilitator through communication. Based on the discussion above, the facilitator's "definition of the situation" within the process of facilitation may be characterized. During the gaming simulation, the facilitator is, by definition, in a position as a guide who is in charge of controlling and maintaining the flow of the gaming simulation. The facilitator is engaged in a communicative, skillful practice of facilitation.

The facilitator "cannot not communicate" (Watzlawick et al. 1967), and even the facilitator's silence may function as a form of facilitation. The facilitator's communicative behavior (both verbal and nonverbal aspects) constitutes a sequence of facilitation, which may generate desirable or undesirable, intentional or unintentional, consequences within the situation. The need to quickly respond to what the participants say and do makes it impossible for the facilitator to take time to analyze the situation explicitly and deliberately choose the best course of facilitation. In fact, if the facilitator stops to do so, some interaction between the participants will be overlooked, and implicitly should choose to let it go on without interruption. In the terms of Schön (1983), the facilitator is constantly engaged in the process of "reflection in action," rather than in the process of "reflection on action." The facilitator is coping with the flow of the gaming simulation, as it unfolds, by conducting a series of "on-the-spot" experiments.

Embedded within the process of on-the-spot inquiry, it is impossible to know in advance how the facilitator's actions will affect the participants. The reality of the gaming simulation becomes accessible, for the first time, as it unfolds. Because the flow of the gaming simulation is predictable because of the set of prespecified rules to organize the gaming simulation, it is possible to systematically study these choices and consequences. Thus, for example, the facilitator can predict that his/her cue can (and will), terminate the gaming simulation. However, the ways in which the participants may react to his/her cue, and the ways in which the gaming simulation terminates, are still unknown to the facilitator unless he/she gives the participants his/her cue. In this regard, the facilitator cannot count on careful planning that will achieve the desirable outcomes in his/her facilitation. Only the act of facilitation can reveal, one by one, the direction in which the sequences of steps move the flow of interaction.

Whereas the facilitator may have had a set of careful plans and visions on facilitating the gaming simulation, its reality becomes available, probably for the first time, as it unfolds. As Schön (1983) suggests, a unique logic can be identified in the context of practice of this sort. It can be characterized as an on-the-spot experiment that operates on the logic of *affirmation*, rather than on the logic of confirmation. As he characterizes the ways in which practitioners cope with the situation:

"They seek to make the situation conform to their hypothesis but remain open to the possibility that it will not. Thus, their hypothesis-testing activity is neither self-fulfilling prophecy, which insures against the apprehension of disconfirming data, nor is it the neutral hypothesis testing of the method of controlled experiment, which calls for the experimenter to avoid influencing the object of study and to embrace disconfirming data. The practice situation is neither clay to be molded at will nor an independent, self-sufficient object of study from which the inquirer keeps his distance."

From a constitutive view of communication, every effort to facilitate the gaming simulation can be seen as *in* communication. For example, we might be able to observe that the facilitator gives cues to conclude a session within the gaming simulation by saying "I'd like to you to finish this round in about a minute"; or to change the participants' seating arrangement by saying "This team should be in the front of the room." In both of these cases, the facilitator is constructing the situation, rather than describing it. The facilitator's instructions such as "I'd like you to" or "team should be" are themselves reflections of his/her understanding and interpretation of the situation. Whereas the flow of the session can be understood as a process of joint construction by both the facilitator and participants, the facilitator, through the very act of facilitation, plays the key role in constructing and maintaining the situation.

References

Kato F (1996) An "art" of facilitation (in Japanese). Proceedings of the Eighth JASAG Annual Conference. pp 75–78

Kato F (1998) Gaming-simulation as media. In: Arai K, Deguchi H, Kaneda T, et al (eds) Gaming-simulation (in Japanese). Nikkagiren, Tokyo, pp 125–168

Mokros HB (1993) The impact of native theory of information on two privileged accounts of personhood. In: Schement JR, Ruben BD (eds) Between communication and information. Transaction, New Brunswick, pp 57–79

Mokros HB (1996) Introduction: from information and behavior to interaction and identity. In: Mokros HB (ed) Interaction and identity. Transaction, New Brunswick, pp 1–22

Mokros HB (2003) A constitutive approach to identity. In: Mokros HB (ed) Identity matters: communication-based explorations and explanations. Hampton, Mount Waverly, pp 3–28

Mokros HB, Mullins LS, Saracevic T (1995) Practice and personhood in professional interaction: social identities and information needs. Library and Information Science Research 17:237–257

Schön DA (1983) The reflective practitioner: how professionals think in action. Basic Books, New York

Schön DA (1987) Educating the reflective practitioner. Jossey-Bass, San Francisco

Schön DA (ed) (1991) The reflective turn: case studies in and on educational practice. Teachers College Press, New York

Watzlawick P, Beavin JH, Jackson DD (1967) Pragmatics of human communication: a study of interactional patterns, pathologies, and paradoxes. Norton, New York

9. The Features and Roles of Simulation Software in the Classroom

Kanji Akahori[1]

Introduction

The International Association for the Evaluation of Educational Achievement (IEA) has been conducting large-scale comparative studies of educational achievement, with the aim of gaining a more in-depth understanding of the effects of policies and practices within and across systems of education (Ministry of Education, Science, Sports and Culture 2001). The Third International Mathematics and Science Study (TIMSS) was conducted in 1999 and results indicated that Japan was only slightly trailing the leading countries in both math and science achievement. One indication of this is that the math and science ability of Japanese students surveyed ranked as fifth and fourth, respectively. However, when students were questioned whether or not they liked these subjects, Japan ranked next to last. Only 48% of Japanese students liked math or liked it very much and 55% liked science or liked it very much. These figures were both 24 percentage points lower than the international average.

Many researchers have pointed out the necessity to promote science and math education in Japan and a survey by the National Institute of Educational Research showed that student interest in science decreases as they progress through school from grades 5 to 12, as shown in Fig. 1 (National Institute of Educational Policy Research 2002).

The Ministry of Education of Japan has established several governmental policies for promoting science education in schools. These include the Super Science High School (SSH) project, the Science Partnership Program (SPP) and the development of science teaching and learning software which makes use of advanced technologies. Under the guidance of these policies the Japan Science and Technology Corporation (JST) has developed much high quality software for science education for use in both primary and high schools in Japan (Japan Science and Technology Corporation 2003). In order to make effective use of this software in education, a committee for the development and evaluation of

[1] Graduate School of Decision Science and Technology, Tokyo Institute of Technology, Meguro-ku, Tokyo 152-8552, Japan; akahori@ak.cradle.titech.ac.jp

Students' interest in science

FIG. 1. Change in student interest in science from grades 5 to 12

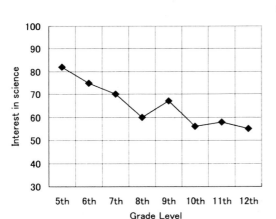

science software was established within JST (of which the author is the chair), and since that time much discussion and software development work has been undertaken. As a result, the committee has discovered several important success factors in developing software of high quality (especially within the field of science education) and integrating it into the classroom. This also sheds light onto the role of software in the teaching and learning process within the classroom.

Information technology (IT) and other educational technologies have been applied in educational institutions, ranging from primary schools to universities, not only in science education but in a wide range of fields (Sakamoto 2002). As a result of this, the effect of IT on higher order thinking, such as scientific reasoning, rational critical thinking, etc., was discussed at an international conference held in Okinawa, Japan (Akahori 2003).

Internet-based communication tools such as e-mail, chat software and bulletin boards have played a major role in learning (Akahori 2001, Rourke et al. 2001) with recent interest being shown in innovative distance education such as e-learning via the Internet and satellite technology (Bernardez 2003, CRADLE 2003). Thus the frameworks used in the teaching and learning of science using IT must be considered both within and outside the classroom environment.

This paper presents the issues involved with applying simulation software to create an interactive environment in the junior and senior high school classroom.

A Needs Analysis of Digital Software in Science Education

Before any software development took place, a needs analysis (using a survey) was undertaken to examine what kind of software was most needed by high school teachers.

The committee classified the results into the following software types:

(1) Materials based   —Science history, scientific data, video, images etc.
(2) Story based   —A series of videos presenting various scientific topics
(3) Operation based   —Simulations which respond to user manipulation
(4) Resource based   —Scientific data and related information accessed via the Internet

The purposes for the use of this software were classified as follows:

(1) Understanding scientific rules and principles
(2) Understanding the relationship between science and society
(3) Observing experiments, especially large-scale experiments or those which are difficult or impossible to carry out in a normal high school

The analysis also discovered the following views from teachers:

(1) Software would be useful in presenting topics which are impossible to conduct experiments for or for students to experience in everyday life.
(2) Video and simulation are the preferred communication medium.
(3) There is a need for a combination of computer software and laboratory-based experiments.
(4) Software should stimulate student interest and concern for science.
(5) Simulations should promote logical and deep thought in students.
(6) Simulations should enable students to try out ideas and handle their errors and mistakes gracefully.
(7) Consistency in user interface and software design is important.

Based on these results, the committee created a set of strategies to facilitate teacher acceptance in using simulation software in ordinary classes.

Features of Developed Simulation Software

The following features of the developed simulation software are most notable:

(1) Configuration of virtual environments and reaction to the interaction of students
For example, the developed wind simulation (Fig. 2) allows learners to configure the construction of a building and see how this affects wind speed and direction. Wind speed and direction can be shown at any point and this combines to stimulate the learner's motivation.
(2) Demonstration based on sophisticated calculation of equations
One of the many developed pieces of software includes a demonstration of a Rutherford scattering. This phenomenon describes the way electrons scatter when colliding with atomic nuclei. The scattering phenomenon is very important in understanding atomic structure; however, this is difficult to calculate correctly by hand because highly complex interactions between electrons and nuclei must be calculated. This simulation software allows students

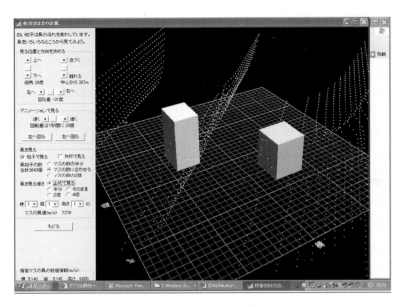

FIG. 2. Simulation of wind movement dependent on the placement of a building

to witness this interaction even though they may not be able to perform the calculations themselves, thus educating them in a fundamental concept of physics.

(3) Visually displayable results

Simulation software allows visual representation of simulation results, greatly aiding in students understanding. Hence, reaction to user changes in the simulated environment is perhaps one of the most important features of simulation software. For example, developed chemical software shows three-dimensional molecules, and students can rotate these in three dimensions (Fig. 3). This has been found to motivate learning.

(4) Real-world experiences through combining simulation and photo images

By combining computer graphics with images taken from the real world, we are able to create a more engaging environment providing a sense of real-world experience.

Science Classes Using Developed Software

The software was used in real science classes in junior high schools and high schools and produced some interesting findings:

(1) Combining the use of IT with worksheets, experiments, and the blackboard is very important

FIG. 3. Three-dimensional molecules which allow rotation

It was found that displaying the software through a projector only was too passive for most students, who soon became bored. Experienced teachers introduced other media such as printed materials and worksheets and encouraged students to take notes. These points are important because watching the simulations alone is not enough for effective retention.

(2) Teacher questioning is important

More experienced teachers often ask questions of students while using the simulation software, trying to avoid a passive learning environment. Their well-timed questions helped keep the class interactive.

(3) Student manipulation of simulations creates strong interest

While demonstrating the simulation on screen, teachers asked students to interact with it and found getting immediate feedback motivated students well (Fig. 4).

(4) Teacher's guide is essential

In addition to creating the simulation software, additional support materials of a users guide and student worksheets were also created. These proved essential in the effective integration of software in the classroom and most teachers welcomed these additions.

(5) Student interest is intensified through linking simulation software to real-world phenomena

One piece of simulation software, known as "Firework", was found to be extremely effective in motivating the learning of students. This software simulated many concepts of physics and chemistry by simulating fireworks.

FIG. 4. Operation of the simulation software by the whole class

Students could learn about sound speed, the effects of mixing primary colors, and chemical flame reactions. It shows how these factors would affect fireworks in the real world.

Results and Discussion

The project's mission was to develop quality software for science education by making use of advanced technology. The observation of its use in the classroom has led to the following findings:

(1) Most of the simulation software features, such as visualization, reaction to changes in the simulated environment from the user and integrating computer graphics with real-world images, had a very positive impact on the motivation and interest students had toward science education.
(2) Questions posed to students from teachers, while using the software, were effective in keeping the class interactive.
(3) Combining the simulation software with other media such as traditional notebooks, blackboards, and other instructional media kept students actively participating in class.

The author proposes the following instructional types based on the combination of teachers, students, media, materials, and communication modes used (T: teacher, S: student, M: material, PC: computer).

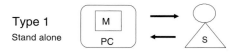

(1) Type 1: Stand-alone type

This type represents the most popular use of simulation software in the class-room, often making use of a dedicated computer room. Typically a student inter-acts with the simulation software and the effects on the simulated environment are updated on the display. Features such as visualization and the ability of the learner to adjust simulation parameters are known to be positive factors in increasing student motivation and cognition of learning, a fact which has been confirmed by this study.

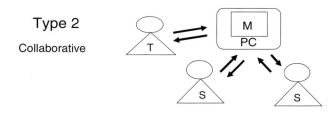

(2) Type 2: Collaborative type

This type is frequently used in elementary school computer rooms, whereby chil-dren discuss and work together to solve problems or use the Internet to research class topics.

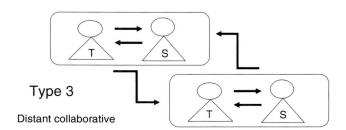

(3) Type 3: Distant-collaborative type

This type enables geographically dispersed classrooms to collaboratively, or com-petitively, solve problems posed by the simulation software using a variety of tools such as the Internet, e-mail, and bulletin boards. For example, this can be used to enable students to collaboratively, or competitively, collectively find the solution to a mathematical problem.

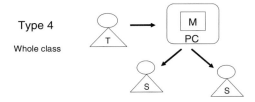

Type 4
Whole class

(4) Type 4: Whole-class type
This type makes use of a projector screen as a computer display in much the same way traditional audiovisual tools are used. Teachers conduct classes using this style easily as it mimics a traditional teaching style. However, this study has found that teachers' questions play an important role in keeping the class interactive.

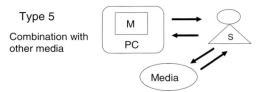

Type 5
Combination with other media

(5) Type 5: Combination type with other media
This type involves the combination of simulation software with other media, such as student exercise worksheets, experimental kits or traditional note taking.

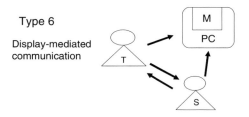

Type 6
Display-mediated communication

(6) Type 6: Display-mediated communication type
This type is often used in a computer room whereby a teacher walks around the classroom and describes the simulation or assists students. This is a form of display-mediated communication, because teachers and students communicate with each other by sharing the same display.

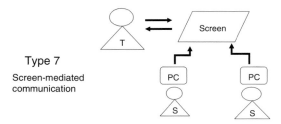

Type 7
Screen-mediated communication

(7) Type 7: Screen-mediated communication type
This type makes uses of a system known as i-mode, which was developed in the author's laboratory. Using this system, students can send questions or comments

during instruction using mobile phones or laptop computers as clients, to a central server which are then displayed on the side of the teachers projected display. Because this occurs instantly, it enables the whole class to communicate through the display, encouraging discussion and questioning without interrupting the teachers instruction.

This study has revealed how changes in the communication mode affects the classroom as a whole, and the findings relate, in particular, to the communication types 1, 4, and 5 presented above. In the future, it will be interesting to examine the effectiveness of simulation software when used with the other communication types.

Important issues gleaned from committee analysis of the gathered results were:

(1) Digital software versus hands-on experiments
(2) Multimedia versus printed materials
(3) Advanced technology versus low technology materials
(4) Advanced science versus basic scientific concepts
(5) Virtual world versus real world
(6) Media utilization versus teaching methods
(7) Science concepts versus social activities in daily life
(8) Roles of other materials such as teacher guidebooks, lesson plans and student worksheets

Acknowledgment. The author expresses his deepest gratitude to the committee members and Dr. Akira Sakamoto, who provided the opportunity to present this study.

References

Akahori K (2001) Improvement of university classes introducing topics-based discussion using the web bulletin board. Proceedings of ED-MEDIA, Finland

Akahori K (2003) Case reviews of capacity building using IT. Proceedings of International Conference of IT Based Capacity Building in Science, Okinawa

Bernardez M (2003) From e-training to e-performance: putting online learning to work. Educational Technology 43:6–12

CRADLE (2003) http://www.cradle.titech.ac.jp/index_j.html

Japan Science and Technology Corporation (2003) Science network (in Japanese) http://www.rikanet.jst.go.jp/

Ministry of Education, Science, Sports and Culture (2001) White paper database Japanese government policies in education, culture, sports, science and technology 2001: Educational Reform for the 21st Century. http://wwwwp.mext.go.jp/eky2001/

National Institute of Educational Policy Research (2002) The survey of students' awareness on importance of science learning (in Japanese). http://www.nier.go.jp/homepage/kyoutsuu/frame05.html

Rourke L, Anderson T, Garrison DR et al (2001) Assessing social presence in asynchronous text-based computer conferencing. Journal of Distance Education, 1–17

Sakamoto T (2002) E-learning and educational innovation in higher education in Japan. Education Media International, 9–16

10. Instructional Activities Game: A Tool for Teacher Training and Research into Teaching

Toshiki Matsuda[1]

Introduction

Although systems of teacher training and qualification differ between countries, it is universally essential that teachers not only study the subject matter they will teach, but also acquire professional expertise in the support and control of learners' activities. The latter implies both theoretical knowledge of pedagogy and psychology and practical instructional skills for the conduct of lessons. An additional important competency for teachers is the ability to use a variety of instructional alternatives, involving the mutual employment of knowledge and skills as the situation requires, together with good decision-making in all situations. Practice teaching in schools, as a part of pre-service teacher training, is designed to serve the purpose of providing student teachers with experience as teachers in the classroom. However, this form of practice teaching is heavily dependent on the patience of schoolchildren confronted by student teachers with underdeveloped abilities, and it is difficult to provide adequate long-term exposure to classroom situations. Therefore, the provision of training which heightens practical decision-making capabilities prior to the commencement of practice teaching should prove a useful addition to teacher-training courses. The present chapter describes the development of an Instructional Activities Game (IAG) as a first step toward filling this need for a support system in teacher training.

The usefulness of the IAG is not limited to teacher-training purposes. As already mentioned, teachers must learn pedagogy and psychology in association with the acquisition of instructional skills in a teacher-training course. Educational methodology and educational technology cover these disciplines, and "research into teaching", one of their research fields, is concerned with the design, implementation, and improvement of the delivery of lessons. In this field, it is common to analyze real lessons performed in schools. However, because there are many uncontrollable variables in an actual lesson, it is difficult to identify

[1] Tokyo Institute of Technology, Meguro-ku, Tokyo 152-8552, Japan; matsuda@hum.titech.ac.jp

causal relationships between the contents and methods of a lesson and its effectiveness. To overcome this difficulty, Allen and Ryan (1969) proposed the use of a simulation technique, "microteaching," which was devised both as a method of teacher training and as a method of research into teaching, thus giving it an experimental aspect. In addition, Yoshizaki (1983) proposed the "Stop Video Method," which employs a video recording of a real lesson, stops at an image in the scene, which is used as a key, and asks the student teacher what action he/she would take next.

A second purpose of this study is to develop the IAG as a tool for research into teaching which could replace these methods. An advantage of the IAG, compared with microteaching, is its capability, through its use of a computer, of controlling variables in a more certain fashion and recording the actions of game users more readily. Its advantage over the Stop Video Method is its flexibility in terms of changing the lesson scene. The behavior of the teacher and students in a recorded video tape is impossible to change, but in a game can be easily changed in accordance with the intentions of the game maker. On a computer it is easy to modify the behavior depicted to correspond with the game user's response.

Purpose

The aim of this research was the development of the IAG for use both as a tool of research into teaching and for teacher training. It is designed as a game executer on a computer, and therefore the development is not of specific game material, which would simulate a specific lesson, but of a game platform, on which a game maker can, using a simple method, describe various game materials. Design of the system therefore focused on the specification of a game description format that provides sufficient functions for the game maker to execute such a game.

Design of the IAG

There are various definitions of gaming (and of gaming simulations). Duke (1974) discussed the meaning of gaming as a communication method. The IAG developed in this study uses the term "game" to describe a method of teaching the features of instructional activities that are difficult to convey fully by lectures and through exercises. However, game playing will not completely substitute for lectures and exercises. It must be used as an additional method, to promote deeper understanding.

In this chapter, the design of the IAG within this context is discussed. Initially, the kinds of knowledge and skills that are assumed to be taught in lectures and through exercises, and the aspects of them that are often not fully understood are clarified.

Instructional Activities Model and Instructional Design Method

The project study assumes the use of the IAG in the Educational Technology class of a teacher-training course that teaches the fundamentals of the design, implementation, and improvement of lessons. A model of instructional activities is most important in this context as the basis for a systematic understanding of the component characteristics of lessons. There are, of course, various models of instructional activities and various methods of instructional design, for example, the various rationales and techniques derived from the theory of programmed learning proposed by the well-known behaviorist Skinner (Richmond 1965). Similarly, the architecture of intelligent-CAI (computer assisted instruction), which is based on artificial intelligence and cognitive science, has the characteristics of an instructional activities model (Barr and Feigenbaum 1982). However, both are inadequate for the usual teacher-training class because they are models for peer education. Models of teacher decision making in the classroom have been derived from research into teaching in the schoolroom, for example by Peterson and Clark (1978) and Shavelson and Stern (1981). In Japan, Yoshizaki (1988) proposed a teacher's decision-making model based on prior research; and Matsuda et al. (1992) proposed an advanced version of Yoshizaki's model, integrating several ideas from intelligent-CAI and cognitive science, and aimed at helping teachers to make better decisions by explaining how knowledge functions in the decision-making process.

In the present project, the use of the instructional activities model described by Matsuda et al. (1992) by student teachers in the teacher-training class is presumed. The reasons for this choice are as follows:

1. This model is designed to effect computer simulation of teachers' decision making, and it therefore has a high affinity with the purposes of this study, namely to create on computer a simulation game of teachers' activities.

2. The model aims to elucidate why teachers make different decisions in the same situation. This feature is important for the application of the model to both teacher education and research into teaching, especially for examining the differences between skilled decision making by veteran teachers and poor decision making by beginners.

3. The model aims to explain, systematically and comprehensively, the relationships between the various types of knowledge held by teachers. As a result, the model is sufficiently complex for use not only in lectures but also in a gaming program.

4. Matsuda et al. (1999) discuss the relationship between their model and methods of instructional design proposed in educational technology by focusing on how to acquire useful knowledge prior to actual teaching. Moreover, they have developed a training system for instructional design based on this discussion. It is possible to train students in the cycle of design, implementation, and improvement of a lesson in a consistent fashion, by integrating their system with the IAG described in the current study.

The schema of the instructional activities model of Matsuda et al. (1992), so far as it relates to the IAG, is explained below. In the model, the communication plan, which realizes the core information of a lesson plan and plays a central role in decision making, is assumed to consist of five elements, namely: prediction of a class situation, instructional aims, method of communication, lesson contents, and changes of a class situation. It is also assumed that teachers are cognizant of lesson flow patterns, including the upper hierarchy of the five elements of a lesson plan, and are used to deciding on the main flow of a lesson. In the model, these patterns are called "lesson flow scripts." Their form is affected by other knowledge, for example, knowledge about teaching methods, such as discovery learning and mastery learning, or types of explanation, which may determine the sequence in which to present information, such as inductively, deductively, and so on. Knowledge about lesson flow will in part determine the design of the sequence of a lesson, which is also chosen according to the properties of the lesson and the learners' situation.

In addition to a lesson plan, teachers also bring knowledge of teaching materials and instructional behavior. Matsuda et al. (1992) assume that the former is memorized in the form of a semantic network, such as is used to represent knowledge in many intelligent-CAI systems. The core element of knowledge of teaching materials is a learning objectives network, and it is assumed that the last "changes of a class situation" for each part of the lesson includes a condition in which certain objectives of that lesson are attained. On the other hand, knowledge of instructional behavior is assumed to be memorized as script, as proposed by Schank and Abelson (1977). Their model categorizes eight kinds of instructional behavior, including oral explanation, blackboard writing, and asking questions.

In the model of Yoshizaki (1988), a monitoring schema unifying the above knowledge serves as a mechanism to control decision making. In the simulation model of Matsuda et al. (1992), this function is realized as a production system that allows decision-making processes to be described in an "if-then" format.

Aims of and Training Situations Suited to the IAG

The two reasons for introducing the IAG into teacher training in instructional design correspond to its two functional potentials.

Firstly, in Japan, a "National Course of Study" is prescribed by the government, which also authorizes the textbooks to be used in schools. As a result, student teachers tend to think that it is possible to conduct lessons without forming an instructional plan, which, they think, will be supplied by the textbook. It is therefore necessary to make them realize the difficulty inherent in providing an effective lesson for 40 learners in a limited time period, without having prepared a specific lesson plan. Because of time restrictions, it is not always possible to allow all students to give an actual lesson, but the IAG can at least give to all the "virtual" experience of teaching. This usage of the IAG will be denoted as a "decision-making game" (DMG) from now on.

Secondly, after student teachers have been taught to make a lesson plan through lectures and exercises, the effectiveness of the teaching envisaged should be evaluated so that appropriate advice can be given for improvement. Corrective advice to students will be more effective and persuasive if given while they are in the process of a simulated lesson. The training system of instructional design developed by Matsuda et al. (1999), as described under the previous heading, can be developed for that purpose. Although the original system has an evaluative function, it is one that focuses on logical and objective errors, for example, in the combination of the five elements of the communication plan. The system needs to include additional advice if users are to improve their decisions based on the alternatives available and what would best suit the situation. In order to create a function to give such advice, it is necessary to utilize heuristic rules, but students will not necessarily be convinced by advice based on such subjective material. It is anticipated that the student teacher's motivation to consider the alternatives in a given situation will be more effectively raised if reactions and errors that are contrary to the student's anticipation are observed in the "learner" in the simulated lesson based on his plan. This type of game utilizes an individual lesson plan designed by each student, and therefore must be distinguished from the DMG above. This usage of the IAG will be denoted as a "simulated teaching game" (STG) hereafter.

The IAG is able to meet the needs of yet a third type of teacher training which arises from time to time. Curriculum change and other innovations of school procedure sometimes require teacher retraining to ensure that teachers understand the new features of lesson content or the necessity for change of various kinds, in that they have had no prior experience of the intended innovations. An example is teacher training in IT (information technology) education, which has recently become important, in many countries where the utilization of information technology in teaching, and improved computer literacy of learners, is considered desirable. This application has a different target from the former two in that it involves the in-service training of teachers, but the design of the game executer remains the same. Both types of game defined above will be relevant, requiring only a change in the contents of the games.

Function of Game Executor and Format of Game Description

(1) Principles of Game Operation and Functional Requirements of the System

Gaming is a method of communication. The basic functions of the game executor are the initiation of communication with the game user and the advancement of the game according to its rules. In designing the function to advance a game, it is important to ensure that the differences in game type, as described under the previous heading, are reflected in the operations that decide the route of the game: a DMG advances along the route of a game scenario created by the game maker, while a STG is progressed according to the lesson plan produced by the game user. A function that records, in detail, the progress of the game and the responses of the user is necessary if the game is to be used as a research tool. Figure 1 provides a diagram of the operations for the two types of game.

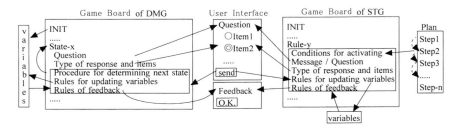

FIG. 1. Operation sequence of the decision-making game (*DMG*) and the simulated teaching game (*STG*)

In a DMG, the messages or questions for the current state of the game board are displayed, and a response is collected from the user. The response obtained is processed in accordance with a rule written for every state, which updates the value of each variable-holding attribute of the game situation and decides the next state to move to. It is possible to show feedback information geared to the user's response and the game situation. A game fundamentally repeats this operation and advances the states until the user receives feedback information when the goal state is reached. In a STG, the game executer first reads the player's lesson plan, and the plan then controls the game flow in steps using the five written elements of a plan. At each step, the system interprets the information in terms of the five elements, compares them with the rules written by the game maker, displays resultant messages or questions, collects the user's reactions, and updates the variables, based on the reactions obtained. If required, feedback to the user can be provided. If two or more rules match the information of any of the five elements in a step, the meta-rule defined in the system determines the order in which to activate them. After processing all rules matched to the current five elements, the same processing is continued repeatedly, and feedback information is displayed at the end of the lesson plan. Provided the series of the user's responses is recorded as a log of the game, the process of game execution can be reproduced later.

(2) Specification of Game Description Format

Based on the above principles of game operation, every state of a DMG can be described by the combination of (1) state-ID, (2) message for user, (3) type of response collection and items for choice, (4) procedure for determining next state, (5) rules for updating variables, and (6) rules of feedback. In a STG, the state is transposed to a rule, and can be described by a combination of (1) rule-ID, (2) conditions for activating the rule, (3) message for user, (4) type of response collection and items for choice, (5) rules for updating variables, and (6) rules of feedback. Therefore, the specification of the description format can be common for the following elements: the state/rule-ID, message for user, type of response collection and items for choice, rules for updating variables, and rules for feedback.

Correspondence with the instructional activities model must also be considered when deciding the specification of a game description format. Although it will eventually be necessary to consider the relationship between all the functions of a game and the model, this chapter focuses on the relationship between the description format of the lesson plan in a STG and the knowledge of instructional plans in the model. The model assumes that an instructional plan can be described as a series of five elements, which may be divided into sections, and which correspond to each part of the lesson flow. The instructional plan has a layered structure from the five elements level to the flow level, as shown in Fig. 2. However, if the information on flow and section is written together for all five elements repeatedly, it is convertible to a simple straight-line structure. Moreover, because Matsuda et al. (1999) have transformed a method of communication, which is included in a lesson plan as an element of each step, into "an action name + some action parameters" in their training system of instructional design, the possibility of decomposing the five elements for convenience becomes a consideration. An example of a possible description format for a lesson plan is shown in Fig. 3.

The specification of the game description format adopted at present is designed on the assumption that the form of the lesson plan is expressed as above. In addition, as is described regarding implementation of the system, it is designed as a Web application, thus making it easy to use as a research tool to collect data or in distance education as a training system, and therefore, all dialog interfaces are premised on realization by HTML. Responses from a game user are obtained as a single number in the case of radio buttons, as a list of selected numbers in the case of check boxes, and as a string in the case of a text box. In addition, the program includes a function for the construction of a multi-item questionnaire using the scale shown in Fig. 4. Answers are logged as a list of selected numbers but are transformed to a weighted sum in order to allow comparison with responses collected in radio button form.

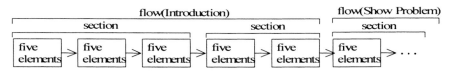

FIG. 2. Structure of an instructional plan

```
( (flow-name "1: Introduction")
  (section-name "1B02. Confirm whether students remember it or not.")
  (objects (("definition of function" "have memorized")
  ("definition of constant and variable" "can distinguish examples")))
  (predicted-states ("pay attention to class" "open the textbook"))
  (aims ("close the textbook"))
  (action-name "direct") (action-parameter "in a loud voice")
  (contents (("Close your textbook." "I'll ask you some questions.")))
  (results ("close the textbook" "pay attention to the teacher")) )
```

FIG. 3. Description of a lesson plan (example of a step)

	4: Very much like	3: Some- what like	2: Somewhat dislike	1: Very much dislike	Weight of each item
red	○	○	●	○	← 1
blue	○	●	○	○	← −1

The weighted sum of the above response is $2 \times 1 + 3 \times (-1) = -1$

FIG. 4. Example of a multi-item questionnaire

```
(ID1-a
 ((inner-var NAME "") "1:Introduction - Check attendance" ("jpg" "1A.jpg") "")
 (RADIO "1A01:Calling each student's name." "1A02:Checking vacant seats."
        "1A03:Giving a small test."         "1A04:Gathering a report.")
 (((_SW1 = 3) ID1-a2) (t ID1-b))
 (((_SW = 1) ((TIME 4)))((_SW = 2) ((TIME 2)))((_SW = 3) ((TIME 0)))
  ((_SW = 4) ((TIME 3)))(t ((ANS <- $ _SW))))
 (((_SW = 1) "Please allow sufficient time to call names.")
  ((_SW = 2) "Let's approach the seat to check it carefully.")
  ((_SW = 3) ("In cases where someone forgets to write a name on a test paper, "
             "Let's check vacant seats during the test."))
  (t "Let's check immediately whether anyone forgot to write a name on his/her
     report.")) )
```

FIG. 5. Example of a game state description (DMG)

Appendix 1 gives the specification of a game description and Fig. 5 is an example of a rule description for a DMG. As will be described, because the system is implemented by Lisp language, the description takes a list format.

Implementation of the System

Because the IAG is not only a tool for training, but also a tool for research, the system can be changed and extended in keeping with the progress of the research. A strategy can be adopted whereby some prototypes can be developed to achieve a specific game which a game maker wants to create, also making it clear how to change, integrate, and extend the game function. To enable such modifications, the system is built on the production system realized by Allegro Common Lisp with Allegro Serve, which has an extension for Web service function.

This system is not a stand-alone application but a web-based server and client application, with an executor function, and, therefore, several different games can run in parallel on it. In this situation, two or more game makers will each operate their own game separately, and the system must have a function for managing each URL of the game appropriately so that a collision cannot take place. More-over, the log of the game execution process is important as research data, so that the login management of game users is necessary.

In consideration of the above issues, the system is designed as follows. Firstly, users are classified hierarchically into two types, either game makers (= game administrators) or game users. The system identifies an administrator by the pass-word file for administrators, and manages game board data, game users' password files, log files, etc. under the subdirectory prepared for each administrator. Furthermore, although an access URL is specified when starting a game, a collision between administrators is prevented by use of the access URL http://machine-name/administrator-ID/specified-access-URL. The use of this classification means that a game maker does not need to consider collision with other game makers. In addition, because various parameters specify the initial setting of a game, the system is designed to load an initial-setting file with the entry of "administrator-ID," "password," and "initial-setting-file."

Current Game Board Development and Future Prospects

Several game boards have now been developed on the IAG system. There are boards for general instructional design classes in teacher-training courses, boards for ICT education, boards for teacher education in the new subject area of Information Technology in Japan, a board for ethics of information technology education, and a board for industrial ethics education. Although there were some requests for the expansion of game functions at the beginning of its use, more recently new demands in relation to the game execution system have not eventuated. There has been a recent request for an error-checking function for the game creation program. Research into the effectiveness of teaching by game program in comparison with existing teaching methods has been conducted, and has resulted in a request for a log analysis function. In addition to developing these new functions, the improvement or strengthening of fundamental functions, such as the dialog interface and the pattern matching function, through new game board development has also been undertaken.

References

Allen D, Ryan K (1969) Microteaching. Addison-Wesley, Reading, Massachusetts, USA
Barr A, Feigenbaum EA (eds) (1982) The handbook of artificial intelligence, vol 2. Pitman, Los Altos, California
Duke RD (1974) Gaming: the future's language. Halsted, New York
Matsuda T, Tago K, Sakamoto T (1992) A model of instructional activity toward making computer simulation systems. Japan Journal of Educational Technology 15:183–195
Matsuda T, Nomura T, Yamamuro K et al (1999) Development and evaluation of training system for instructional design. Japan Journal of Educational Technology 22:263–278
Peterson PL, Clark CM (1978) Teacher's reports of their cognitive processes during teaching. American Educational Research Journal 15:555–565
Richmond WK (1965) Teachers and machines. Collins, London
Schank RC, Abelson RP (1977) Scripts, plans, goals, and understanding. Lawrence Erlbaum Associates, Hillsdale, NJ
Shavelson RJ, Stern P (1981) Research on teacher's pedagogical thoughts, judgements, decisions, and behavior. Review of Educational Research 51:455–498
Yoshizaki S (1983) Teacher decision-making while conducting classroom instruction. Japan Journal of Educational Technology 8:61–70
Yoshizaki S (1988) Development of a model for teachers' decision making. Japan Journal of Educational Technology 10:51–60

Appendix 1. Specification of Game Description Format

- *State/Rule-ID*: Letters combined by alphanumeric characters and signs.
- *Message for user*: A list of message elements. A message element is classified to a string to show a message, a (file-extension file-name) to display a picture, a file of spreadsheet software, or an (**inner-var** variable-name string) to show a message incorporating the value of an internal variable.
- *Type to collect responses and items for choice*: One of following formats: (**RADIO/CHECK** string1 string2 . . .): A string means an item for choice. (**TEXTBOX** [columns [rows]]): A [ ] means it is possible to abbreviate. (**TABLE** (rank1 rank2 . . .)(item1 item2 . . .)(weight1 weight2 . . .)): Both rank and item are written as a string and a weight is written as a number.
- *Rules of feedback/Procedure for determining next state*: A list of (condition1 condition2 . . . message/state): A condition is described by (variable1 operator1 value1 operator2 value2 . . .). Moreover, t is usable as unconditional. Variables declared in the initial state/rule, which is named **INIT**, and the special variable _SW, which holds the value acquired as the response at that time, can be used. There are six operators for comparing numerical values, such as =, ! =, <, >, <=, >=, and four operators for judging inclusive relations of sets, such as {, }, !{, !}. The operators = and ! = are also able to apply to lists and strings. When two or more pairs of an operator and a value are specified in a condition, they are processed in the sense of logical product. A message is a string or a list of strings, which is shown as a message for the user.
- *Rules for updating variables*: A list of rules, each of which is expressed by (condition1 condition2 . . . (proc1 proc2 . . .)) A condition is in the same format as are rules of feedback. A proc is expressed by (variable operator value). The variables for use are the same as for the rules of feedback. There are six operators such as = for substitution, + = for acceleration, − > for cons to a list, <− for tail cons, => for append, and <= for tail append. In addition, a variable can be used instead of a value by attaching a **$** in front of it. If a response matches two or more conditions, variables corresponding to each condition are updated together in order from left to right.
- *Conditions for activating the rule*: A list combined with (keyword value), (keyword **//** value1 value2 . . .), or (keyword **-//** value1 value2 . . .). A keyword is either one of an identifier used to distinguish the elements of a lesson plan, or a variable name. The meaning of (keyword // value1 value2 . . .) is logical sum, such as (keyword value1) or (keyword value2) or . . . Conversely the meaning of (keyword -// value1 value2 . . .) is not (keyword // value1 value2 . . .). In addition, a special form which includes a temporary variable, such as (keyword $X), and which includes a Lisp function by attaching * in front of the Lisp function is applicable. A temporary variable $X matches any value and is useful for judging whether a different keyword has the same value, such as (keyword1 $X) (keyword2 $X), or to create a condition which includes a Lisp function, such as (keyword1 $X) (keyword2 $Y) (* > $X $Y).
  [Words printed in bold are keywords which must be used without change.]

11. Prefrontal Cortex Deactivation During Video Game Play

Goh Matsuda[1] and Kazuo Hiraki[2]

Introduction

Although video games are widely used, their influence on human cognitive function and development are not yet known. Following recent progress in brain-imaging techniques, some studies have measured brain activity, especially in the prefrontal cortex, during video game play (Kawashima 2001; Mori 2002). The prefrontal cortex plays an important role in higher cognitive functions, such as decision making and the control of complex motions. Previous studies have revealed that playing video games attenuates prefrontal cortex activity, and implied that playing video games affects cognition.

This study aimed to measure brain activity during video game play and to provide more detailed evidence of prefrontal deactivation. A 24-channel near-infrared spectroscopy (NIRS) system was used in a series of three brain measurement experiments.

Methods

Subjects

Six healthy right-handed adults, five men and one woman, between 23 and 29 years of age, participated in all three experiments. There were originally nine subjects who participated in experiment 1; six of these also participated in experiments 2 and 3. Data from these six subjects were analyzed to directly compare the results of all three experiments. All subjects provided informed consent for their participation, and the local ethics committee approved the experimental protocol.

[1] The University of Tokyo, Meguro-ku, Tokyo 153-8902, Japan; matsuda@ardbeg.c.u-tokyo.ac.jp
[2] The University of Tokyo, Japan Science and Technology Agency

Near-Infrared Spectroscopy

A NIRS system can detect relative changes in the concentrations of oxy-hemoglobin (oxyHb) and deoxy-hemoglobin (deoxyHb) non-invasively. A light source and a light detector are placed 3 cm apart on the scalp. The light detector captured near-infrared light after the light traveled 2–3 cm deep into the cortical surface. Near-infrared light tends to be absorbed by hemoglobin; a decrease of light reflects changes in hemoglobin concentration.

NIRS is not influenced by electromagnetic waves emitted from video game devices, and, because NIRS does not restrict posture, a subject can play a video game naturally.

Knowledge about the relationship between neural activity and NIRS signals is incomplete; however, variation in oxyHb is known to be highly correlated with regional cerebral blood flow (rCBF) (Hoshi et al. 2001). The increase in rCBF reflects increased neural activity at the relevant region (Jueptner and Weiller 1995); therefore, the variation of oxyHb is primarily related to corresponding neural activity as well.

A 24-channel NIRS system OMM-1080S (Shimadzu Corporation, Kyoto, Japan) was employed in this study. The channels were arranged in a 9 × 9-cm region corresponding to the bilateral dorsal prefrontal cortex (DPFC), centered over the Fz location, according to the EEG 10–20 system (see Fig. 1).

Experiment 1. Brain Activity During Video Games

Purpose

Activity in the DPFC while playing commercial video games was investigated [see Matsuda et al. (2003) for more details].

Experimental Design

Subjects sat in front of a table on which a 20-inch liquid crystal television display was placed. The task was to play a video game as if the subject was at home. Each

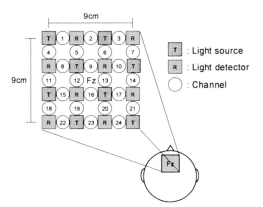

FIG. 1. Location of the light probes and the channels

subject played four kinds of video game: a shooting game, a rhythm action game, a block puzzle, and a dice puzzle.

Task duration was 5 min. There was a 30-s pretask period and a 60-s posttask period. During these periods, subjects released the game controller and gazed at the monitor calmly. All subjects started playing at the same stage. No restrictions were made for the strategy and pace of individual subject play. The order of the four video games was counterbalanced between subjects.

Before NIRS measurement, the subjects practiced each video game until the performance levels established for each game had been achieved.

Data Analysis

OxyHb, which is highly correlated with both rCBF and neural activity, was targeted as the indicator of brain activity. Each subject's data was first normalized so that pretask variation of oxyHb constituted the baseline (average = 0, SD = 1), and then that was grand-averaged at each channel . The change of oxyHb between rest and task periods was evaluated using a t-test. A channel with a significant increase or decrease in oxyHb ($P < 0.01$) was considered to indicate task-related activation or deactivation in the target area.

Results and Discussion

The channels with significant changes in oxyHb are shown in Fig. 2. More than half of the channels tested indicated deactivation during play of all of the games, with the exception of the dice puzzle game.

All channels were deactivated during the rhythm action game. Two channels, however, suggested brain activation during the block puzzle game. These results indicate that brain activity during video game play was generally static, or decreased, as compared to rest period activity.

Why did the activity in the broad area tested in the DPFC remain static, or decrease, while subjects played video games? A video game is, by definition, an attention-demanding, goal-directed task. The dorsal medial prefrontal cortex (dorsal MPFC), part of the DPFC, is related to self-referential mental activity or

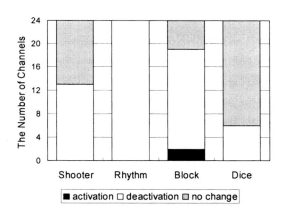

FIG. 2. The number of channels with significant oxyHb increase or decrease during video game play

self-focused attention (Gusnard and Raichle 2001). Furthermore, Shulman et al. (1997) reported that rCBF in the MPFC commonly decreases during many kinds of goal-directed task that demand positive attention to the external world. Therefore, Gusnard and Raichle (2001) suggested that the MPFC is activated for spontaneous self-monitoring in a resting state, and that it becomes attenuated once externally focused attention is required.

Experiment 2. The Effect of Positive Attention to Visual Stimuli on Deactivation of the Prefrontal Cortex

Purpose

To investigate the effect of positive attention to visual stimuli on deactivation of the prefrontal cortex, we measured DPFC activity during passive viewing of either a silent image of a video game, or a nonvideo game event. If prefrontal cortex deactivation during video game play is derived from positive attention to external visual stimuli, deactivation during video game viewing should be lower than that during video game play.

Experimental Design

The experimental apparatus was similar to that of experiment 1, and a block design was employed. A trial consisted of a 30-s pretask period, a 60-s task period and a 30-s posttask period. In the pretask and the posttask periods, the subject gazed at a gray cross, centered on the display. Six video images were used as stimuli. Four of the images were recorded from the same opening scenes of the four video games used in experiment 1 (video game condition). In addition, natural scenery (mountains, grass, and flowers) and a 5×5 square mosaic image were presented (control condition). The mosaic image was created from the video image of the rhythm action game using a pixilated filter from Adobe Premiere software, and each square was filled with the mean color of pixels in the square. During the task period, one of the six images was presented to the subjects, and the order of the images was counterbalanced among the subjects. Subjects were asked to silently view the images. Subjects were verbally debriefed after NIRS measurement.

Data Analysis

Channels that indicated significant activity in the task period were estimated using the same procedures used in experiment 1. In addition, data from experiment 1 were reanalyzed for comparison with the results of this experiment.

Results and Discussion

Prefrontal Activity During Video Observation

Figure 3 illustrates the number of channels activated or deactivated during video image viewing. More than half of the channels were deactivated, and there is no

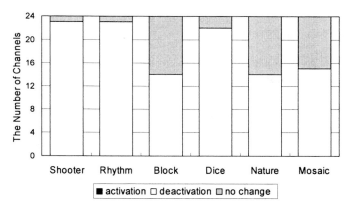

FIG. 3. The number of channels with significant oxyHb change in each observation

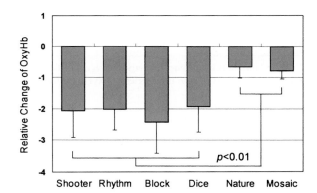

FIG. 4. The mean of oxyHb decrease at deactivated channels

activated channel. This indicates that DPFC activity during watching video images was reduced as compared with the activity at rest. On the other hand, the mean intensity of deactivated channels, namely the decrease in oxyHb, during video game viewing, was significantly greater than during viewing in the control condition (F(5,110) = 16.43, $P < 0.0001$). There was no significant difference between control conditions or among video games (see Fig. 4).

What can account for the difference between the video game and control conditions? Five of the six subjects commented that during the postexperiment debriefing they had simulated the video game in their minds during the video game observation. We did not instruct the subjects not to think, but rather told them to view the image silently. Therefore, subjects might have engaged cognitive attentional processes during simulation similar to those involved during actual video game play. In contrast, subjects reported that they passively observed non-video game images, so it is likely that the intensity of deactivation depends on the degree of attention to images rather than on their visual properties.

We must also consider subject familiarization with the images. All subjects had played the four video games in experiment 1 and were more familiar with video games than with the control images. Familiarity might be involved in the extent of observed prefrontal deactivation.

Comparison of Play and Observation

Table 1 presents similarities in prefrontal activity between the play condition in experiment 1 and the observation condition in experiment 2, for each game. Figure 5 displays the time series of oxyHb at channel 1 as representative of the channels deactivated commonly in all eight conditions. More than half of the channels were commonly deactivated in each game, and the correlation coefficients were generally large. Paired *t*-tests for the mean decrease of oxyHb at commonly deactivated channels revealed that oxyHb declined more in the play condition than in the observation condition in all games, with the exception of

TABLE 1. Similarities between the play and the observation condition

Game category	Shooter	Rythm action	Block puzzle	Dice puzzle
NCC (/24)	17	23	12	21
MC	0.767	0.763	0.638	0.531

NCC, the numbers of common deactivated channels between the two conditions; MC, the mean correlation coefficients for the time series of oxyHb between the two conditions in those channels

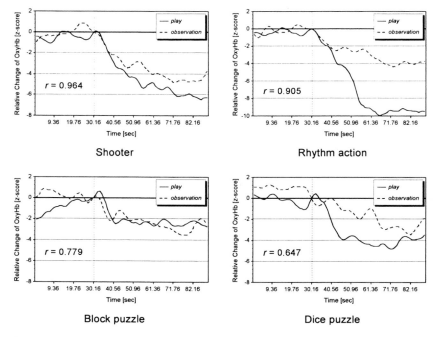

FIG. 5. The time series of oxyHb at channel no. 1. A *dotted vertical line* denotes the beginning of the task period, where a z-score is plotted as zero. The *r* on the lower left represents the correlation coefficient between the play and the observation conditions

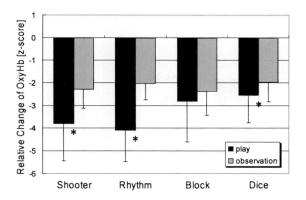

FIG. 6. The mean decrease of oxyHb in common deactivated channels between the play (experiment 1) and the observation (experiment 2) conditions. An *asterisk* represents a significant difference between the two conditions in a relevant game

the block puzzle game (see Fig. 6). These results suggest that there is less deactivation while watching a video game than while playing one, although the pattern of prefrontal activity between the two conditions is very similar. Imaginary play elicited similar brain activity but less positive attention, as compared with actual play.

Experiment 3. The Effect of Finger Movement on Prefrontal Deactivation

Purpose

The difference between playing and viewing games is reflected not only in the degree of attention paid to visual stimuli but also in whether finger movement is involved. In order to examine the effect of simple finger movement, DPFC activity was measured while a subject tapped his or her thumb on a game controller.

Experimental Design

The experimental apparatus was the same as in experiments 1 and 2, except that headphones were worn by the subjects. A block design was adopted, and one trial consisted of a 15-s rest period and a 15-s task period. Throughout the session, a cross appeared in the center of the display as a fixation point and a slow (2 Hz) or a fast (5 Hz) hi-hat beat sounded from the headphones. The color of the cross was gray for the rest period and green for the task period. In the task period, the subject tapped his or her left or right thumb on the button of the game controller in response to the hi-hat beat. The subject gazed silently at the cross during the rest period. Each tapping condition, right–slow, right–fast, left–slow, and left–fast, was repeated for five trials. The order of these conditions was counterbalanced among the subjects.

Data Analysis

The channel that indicated a significant task-related increase or decrease in oxyHb was estimated a using t-test ($P < 0.01$).

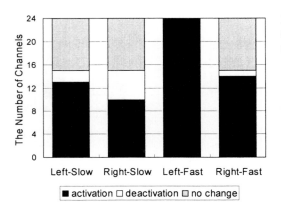

FIG. 7. The number of channels with significant oxyHb change during thumb tapping

Results and Discussion

As shown in Fig. 7, more channels were activated in the task period in the fast-tapping conditions than in the slow-tapping conditions, and more with the left thumb than with the right thumb, at either beat. Stronger activation during left tapping arose, presumably, because all subjects were right-handed and left tapping was more difficult for them.

These results did not show the widespread deactivation observed during video games, and we conclude that the prefrontal deactivation elicited by video games is unrelated to simple finger movement.

Conclusions

Wide deactivation in the DPFC during video game play was observed in experiment 1. In addition, the results of experiment 2 indicated that similar regions were also deactivated during video game observation. Because simple finger action activated these same regions, we conclude that DPFC deactivation during video games is mainly due to the visual aspects of video games and, further, that it depends more on a player's positive attention to the game than its visual attributes.

Acknowledgment. This study was partially supported by the Foundation for the Fusion of Science and Technology.

References

Kawashima R (2001) Self-development of the brain (in Japanese). Kumon Publishing, Tokyo
Mori A (2002) Fear of a brain game (in Japanese). NHK-Book, Tokyo
Gusnard DA, Raichle ME (2001) Searching for a baseline: functional imaging and the resting human brain. Nature Reviews Neuroscience 2: 685–694

Hoshi Y, Kobayashi N, Tamura M (2001) Interpretation of near-infrared spectroscopy signals: a study with a newly developed perfused rat brain model. Journal of Applied Physiology 90:1657–1662

Jueptner M, Weiller C (1995) Does measurement of regional cerebral blood flow reflect synaptic activity?—Implications for PET and fMRI. Neuroimage 2:148–156

Matsuda G, Hiraki K, Shimada S et al (2003) Hemodynamic measurement of video game players using near-infrared spectroscopy (in Japanese). Studies in Simulation and Gaming 13:21–31

Shulman GL, Fiez JA, Corbetta M et al (1997) Common blood flow changes across visual tasks: II. Decreases in cerebral cortex. Journal of Cognitive Neuroscience 9:648–663

12. The Quantity and Context of Video Game Violence in Japan: Toward Creating an Ethical Standard

Akiko Shibuya[1] and Akira Sakamoto[2]

Introduction

Video game entertainment, as well as animation, may be a symbol of Japanese culture for children and adolescents around the world. While children eagerly devote their time to playing video games, parents and teachers express their concerns, particularly about their violent contents, which may adversely affect children. After the schoolyard massacre at Columbine High School in Colorado, these concerns have been increasingly growing in the United States.

On the effect of violent video games, more than 40 empirical studies have been reported (for reviews, see Dill and Dill 1998; Griffiths 1999; Shibuya 2001). Although recent studies indicate playing violent video games is likely to increase aggressive behavior (Anderson and Dill 2000; Sherry 2001; Sakamoto et al. 2001a; Ihori et al. 2003; Katori 2001), some results were inconsistent (Yukawa and Yoshida 2000). This inconsistency in experiments suggests that the effect of violent video games on aggression depends on the quantity and context of violent scenes, as well as the personality, sex, and age of the individuals.

On the basis of television violence studies, Table 1 shows the predictions for which variables are likely to increase and decrease learning aggressive behavior. Among 17 variables, the effects of 12 variables (X1–12) were based on Wilson et al. (1997), and those of the other five variables (X13–17) were suggested by video game studies (e.g., Ballard and Wiest 1996; Brooks 1999; Calvert and Tan 1994; Yukawa and Yoshida 2000; for a review, see Shibuya and Sakamoto 2002). Table 1 also reports the effects of graphicness, reality, rewards, and competition which were empirically assessed in video games experiments (Ballard and Lineberger 1999; Sakamoto et al. 2001b; Anderson and Morrow 1995).

Content analysis has been conducted on the quantity and context of popular video games in the United States (Lachlan et al. 2000), but no content analysis

[1] Institute for Media and Communications Research, Keio University, Minato-ku, Tokyo 108-8345, Japan; akikoguma@nifty.com
[2] Department of Psychology, Ochanomizu University, Bunkyo-ku, Tokyo 112-8610, Japan; sakamoto@li.ocha.ac.jp

TABLE 1. Predicted and tested impact of contextual factors of video game violence on learning aggressive behavior

Contextual factors	Variables	Predicted impact	Tested impact
Extensive/graphic violence	X1 Extent	△	
	X2 Graphicness	△	△
Nature of perpetrator	X3 Attractive perpetrator	△	
Reasons for violence	X4 Justified	△	
	X5 Unjustified	▼	
Presence/ availability of weapons	X6 Presence of weapons	△	
	X7 Availability of weapons	△	
Realism of violence	X8 Reality	△	△
Rewards and punishments	X9 Rewards	△	△
	X10 Punishments	▼	
Depictions of pain/harm	X11 Depictions of pain/harm	▼	
Humor	X12 Humor	△	
Role playing/interactivity	X13 Role playing	△	
	X14 Interactivity	△	
Competition/activity/difficulty	X15 Competition	△	△
	X16 Activity	△	
	X17 Difficulty	△	

Predicted impacts were based on Wilson et al. (1997) and on reviews of video game studies. △ = likely to *increase* aggression. ▼ = likely to *decrease* aggression

with category definitions has been reported in Japan. The previous content analysis analyzed best-selling games, which may not be popular among children or adolescents, and its categorization did not consider interactive video game features. This study analyzes the quantity and context of violence of popular video games selected by children, and the contexts of analysis include interactive video game features.

This study posed the following research questions:

1. What is the prevalence of violence in childrens' favorite video games in Japan?
2. Among those games that contain violence, (1) How frequently is each variable found? (2) Is violence justified rather than unjustified? (3) Is violence rewarded rather than punished? (4) Are violent acts performed competitively rather than cooperatively?

Methods

This study analyzed the 30 most popular video games based on two surveys, which were conducted on 900 fifth graders (ages 10 to 11) in December 2001 and February 2002 (Sakamoto et al. 2002). Both surveys used a questionnaire to ask children to list their three favorite video games. The 900 children attended eight large elementary schools, which were randomly selected from urban and rural areas in Japan. Because the favorite games selected by children may have been biased toward new games, the surveys were conducted twice to reduce the risk of bias.

Some games appeared in both surveys, and a total of 41 video games were selected for this study. The unit of analysis was the individual video game.

Eleven undergraduate and graduate students (ages 19–24 years) acted as coders and analyzed the quantity and context of violent scenes in video games. First, they predicted if there would be violent acts after looking at the guide that came with the video game. If coders expected violent acts, they were asked to play until the first violent act, and then to continue playing for another 30 min. If coders did not expect violent acts, they were asked to check the content for 2 h or until they had verified that there was no violence. At least two coders were assigned to each game to play and code the contents, and all of the games played on the screen were videotaped for coding.

Next, the video games were divided into long games, which were narrative stories continuing for more than 30 min, and short games. For a long game, two sessions of 30 min were played by at least one coder. Games were also separated into either single-player games or multi-player games, which were games where more than two players could join the game in a major mode. For multi-player games, another session was played by two other players and also coded by both of them. Finally, two to five sessions were coded by two to four players for each game.

The definition of violence was that defined by Wilson et al. (1997),

"any overt depiction of a credible threat of physical force or the actual use of such force *intended* to *physically harm an animated being or group of beings*. Violence also includes certain depictions of physically harmful consequences against an animate being or group that occur as a result of unseen violent means."

Prevalence of violence was coded by whether violent acts were found.

On the basis of literature review (e.g., Wilson et al. 1997; Potter 1999; Shibuya and Sakamoto 2002), categories were operationally defined (Tables 2–10). Whereas the categories were within a framework of television violence in Lachlan et al. (2000), video game specific features, such as role playing, interactivity, competition, activity, and difficulty, were analyzed in this study. Media-specific categories were also created for other variables, such as justification, reality, rewards, and punishments (e.g., X4-4, X5-4, X8, X9-3 to 9-6, X10-3 to 10-6).

For all 41 games, and among all 11 coders, reliability coefficients were calculated for all 82 categories (Wilson et al. 1997). Half of the median reliability coefficients were above 0.95. On only three of the 82 variables was the median lower than 0.70, and they were "pleasant sounds or music" (0.67), "visible pain or harm" (0.67), and "clearly audible stereo effects" (0.67). All categories were considered acceptable.

Results

Prevalence of Violence

Among 41 video games, 35 games (85%) contained at least one violent act. The other categories were coded for only the 35 games with violent acts.

TABLE 2. Extent and graphicness of violence

	Categories	Predicted impact	Mean (range)	SD
Extent		△		
X1-1	Violent acts caused by player (# of pushing/ handling the controller)	△	173 (1–961)	239
X1-2	Violent acts caused by others (#)	△	149 (3–885)	226
X1-3	Perpetrator (#)	△	17 (1–63)	18
X1-4	Targets (#)	△	36 (1–240)	54
X1-5	Length of violent scenes (min)	△	12 (1–30)	8
				Presence (%)
Graphicness (any X2)		△		**29**
X2-1	Close-up focus (bigger than 2/3 of screen)	△		23
X2-2	Blood or gore	△		9

n = 35, numbers were per 30 min

TABLE 3. Nature of perpetrator

	Categories	Predicted impact	Presence (%)
Attractive perpetrators (any X3-1 to 3-4, visible human only)		△	**54**
X3-1	Under 20 years old	△	26
X3-2	Attractive appearance (e.g., strong, pretty)	△	29
X3-3	Attractive personality (e.g., kind, intelligent)	△	20
X3-4	Hero (e.g., hero in TV animation)	△	20
X3-5	Visible	△	91
X3-6	Human	△	74

n = 35, only player-controlled characters

Extent and Graphicness of Violence

Table 2 reports that only 23% of the games had close-ups, and only 9% had blood or gore. More violent acts were committed by player-controlled characters (mean = 173 per 30 min) than by other characters (mean = 149). Games had more targets of violence (mean = 36) than perpetrators (mean = 17).

Nature of Perpetrators

Player-controlled characters were perpetrators and targets of violence in all 35 games. Table 3 reveals that 54% of the games involved at least one category of attractive perpetrators. Perpetrators were under 20 years old in 26% of the games, and had attractive appearances and personalities in 29% and 20% of the games, respectively. Heroes were perpetrators in 20% of the games.

Reasons for Violence

Table 4 shows violent acts were justified in 77% of the games, and also unjustified in 71% of the games. The most frequent justification was "players *cannot*

TABLE 4. Reasons for violence

Categories		Predicted impact	Presence (%)
Justified violence		△	**77**
X4-1	Retaliation	△	11
X4-2	Protection of others/society	△	46
X4-3	Protection of own life	△	34
X4-4	Player *cannot* continue the game without violence	△	74
Unjustified violence		▼	**71**
X5-1	Against innocent target (e.g. nonfighter, citizen)	▼	9
X5-2	Personal gain (e.g., money, status)	▼	20
X5-3	Emotional instability (e.g., anger, fear)	▼	9
X5-4	Player *can* continue the game without violence	▼	60

n = 35

TABLE 5. Presence and availability of weapons

Categories		Predicted impact	Presence (%)
Conventional weapons (any X6-1)		△	**66**
X6-1a	Sword or knife	△	51
X6-1b	Firearm (e.g., gun, pistol)	△	40
X6-2	Bomb	△	46
X6-3	Heavy weaponry (e.g., missiles, tank)	△	29
X6-4	Natural means (e.g., punch, kick)		80
X6-5	Ordinary material (e.g., stone, vase)		49
X6-6	Supernatural means (e.g., monster summons)		54
Availability of weapons		△	**34**
X7	Major weapons used were easy to get/use	△	34

n = 35

continue the game without violence," which was present in 74% of the games, and the most frequent category of unjustified violence was "players *can* continue the game without violence," which occurred in 60% of cases.

Presence and Availability of Weapons

Table 5 reports that conventional weapons were used in 66% of the games. Swords or knives were used in 51%, and firearms were used in 40%. The most frequent form was natural means, which were present in 80% of the games. Regarding availability, major weapons were easy to get or use in only 34% of the games.

Realism of Violence

Table 6 reveals that violence "possible to be imitated" was found in 43% of the games, while "existing/ordinary places" were found in only 23% of the games.

TABLE 6. Realism of violence

Categories	Predicted impact	Presence (%)
Increasing reality (any X8-1 or 8-6)	△	**91**
X8-1 Possible to be imitated	△	43
X8-2 Existing/ordinary places	△	23
X8-3 3D background and photographic CG	△	60
X8-4 Characters move smoothly/rich facial expression	△	37
X8-5 Audible conversation (vs. readable in texts)	△	20
X8-6 Major characters are humans	△	37
Decreasing reality (any X8-7 or 8-8)	▼	**23**
X8-7 Large command/information area (bigger than 1/6 of screen)	▼	20
X8-8 Permitted as sports	▼	3

$n = 35$

TABLE 7. Rewards and punishments

Categories	Predicted impact	Presence (%)
Rewards (any X9: after a violent act)	△	**94**
X9-1a Self-praise	△	46
X9-1b Praise from others	△	43
X9-2 Receive materials/money	△	57
X9-3 Score increased or moved up a level	△	43
X9-4 Pleasant sounds/music	△	40
X9-5 Pleasant graphics/movie	△	17
X9-6 Players *can* continue the game	△	83
Punishments (any X10: after a violent act)	▼	**57**
X10-1a Self-condemnation	▼	0
X10-1b Condemnation from others	▼	11
X10-2 Lose materials/money	▼	14
X10-3 Score reduced or moved down a level	▼	9
X10-4 Unpleasant sounds/music	▼	14
X10-5 Unpleasant graphics/movie	▼	14
X10-6 Players *cannot* continue the game	▼	17

$n = 35$

The most frequent category was "3D background and photographic CG," which was present in 60% of the games.

Rewards and Punishments

Table 7 shows violence was rewarded in 94% of the games, but only punished in 57% of the games. The most frequent form of reward was "players *can* continue the game," which occurred in 83% of the games. The most frequent punishments were "players *cannot* continue the game," which was present in 17% of the games.

Consequences of Violence

Table 8 reports pain and harm were depicted as consequences of violence in 94% of the games. The most frequent category was "visible," which was present in 80% of the games, and the second was "audible," which was in 66% of the games.

Humor

Table 8 also shows that humor was present in 60% of the games. Mild humor was present in 43% of the games, and hostile humor in 34%.

Role Playing and Interactivity

Table 9 reveals that players can name or move a main character up a level as role playing in 37% of the games. The most frequent category was "free to move around the field," which was present in 86% of the games.

TABLE 8. Consequences of violence and humor

Categories		Predicted impact	Presence (%)
Depictions of pain/harm (any X11)		▼	**94**
X11-1	Audible (e.g., screams, groans)	▼	66
X11-2	Visible (e.g., fall down, distorted face)	▼	80
X11-3	Visible body damage (e.g., injury)	▼	9
X11-4	Written with words	▼	23
Humor (any X12)		△	**60**
X12-1	Hostile humor (e.g., irony, sarcasm)	△	34
X12-2	Mild humor (e.g., joke, parody)	△	43

$n = 35$

TABLE 9. Role playing and interactivity

Categories		Predicted impact	Presence (%)
Role playing (any X13)		△	**100**
Able to name/move a main character up a level (X13-1 or 13-2)		△	37
X13-1	Able to name a main character	△	31
X13-2	Able to move a main character up a level	△	26
X13-3	Able to choose a main character	△	51
X13-4	Able to choose either male or female main character	△	37
X13-5	Narrative	△	74
X13-6	Able to select conversation/action	△	49
X13-7	Free to move around the field	△	86
Interactivity (any X14)		△	**77**
X14-1	More action than pushing the controller	△	0
X14-2	Vibration	△	69
X14-3	Head mount display (HMD) (e.g., virtual reality)	△	0
X14-4	Clearly audible stereo effects	△	49

$n = 35$

TABLE 10. Competition, activity, and difficulty

Categories		Predicted impact	Presence (%)
Increasing competition (any X15-1 to 15-5)		△	**94**
X15-1	Showing winner or loser	△	49
X15-2	Showing rank (among more than two)	△	31
X15-3	Showing score	△	34
X15-4	Presence of antagonist	△	66
X15-5	Able to compete with other players	△	49
Decreasing competition		▼	**29**
X15-6	Able to cooperate with other players	▼	29
Activity (any X16)		△	**71**
X16-1	Quick reaction	△	71
X16-2	Fast pace	△	46
Difficulty (any X17-1 to 17-3)		△	**89**
X17-1	Difficult to find the point to push controller	△	63
X17-2	Difficult to handle the controller	△	69
X17-3	Limited access to save	△	20
			Mean (range) SD
X17-4	Number of failures (e.g., forced game over, lowest rank, losing, in 30 min)	△	2.86 (0–13.75) 3.19

$n = 35$

Competition, Activity, and Difficulty

Table 10 reports that players were able to play competitively in 49% of the games, but cooperatively in only 29%. In addition, at least one form of competition was found in 94% of the games. The most frequent form of the competition was "presence of antagonist," which was present in 66% of the games. Table 10 also shows that at least one form of activity was present in 71% of games, and at least one form of difficulty was found in 89% of the games.

Discussion

On the basis of the research questions and results, the following conclusions were reached:

1. There was at least one violent act in 85% ($n = 35$) of the children's favorite video games in Japan.
2. Among the 35 games, features that are likely to *increase* learning aggressive behavior are as follows:
   A. Attractive perpetrators were found in 54% of the games.
   B. Conventional weapons were used in 66%.
   C. Violence was rewarded in 94% and punished in only 57%.
   D. Humor was found in 60%.
   E. Violent acts were played competitively in 49% and only cooperatively in 29%.

Features that are likely to *inhibit* learning aggressive behavior are as follows:
F. Only 23% of the games contained a close-up focus in their graphics.
G. Violence was possible to be imitated in 43%.
H. Players were able to name or move a main player-controlled character up a level in only 37%.
I. Pain and harm were depicted in 94%.
J. Violence was justified in 77% and unjustified 71%.

The games analyzed here had less close-up focus (23% vs. 78%), less blood or gore (9% vs. 27%), but had more firearms (40% vs. 8%) and more humor (60% vs. 41%) than those in Lachlan et al. (2000). These discrepancies, however, may be due to the differences in methods (e.g., games selected by children vs. best selling games; 60–120 min vs. all violent interactions in 10 min).

Although this study analyzed two to five different sessions of two to four players, its high reliability suggests each video game has a specific pattern of violent acts created by a game designer. If the video game industry does *not* want children or adolescents to increase their aggression, some changes can be made. There should be less violence, which should be less justified; less rewarded; and punished more. Violence should not be used competitively, and it should be used by less attractive perpetrators. There should also be less use of conventional weapons. For example, creating another *more rewarded* nonviolent option in addition to violent acts makes violence *less* justified and *less* rewarded, and might make the game more interesting instead of simply forcing "routine" violence. If the players have their games ended after committing violent acts on some characters, it might also inhibit aggression as *punishment*. This may also make the games more challenging.

On the basis of the empirical studies about effects of the quantity and context of video game violence, it may be possible to make a violence index or score that can predict the degree to which each game contributes to learning aggressive behavior (Shibuya and Sakamoto 2002). Once the violence index is created, it would provide useful information for parents, teachers, and game designers to prevent children and adolescents from learning aggressive behavior from video games.

This study focused on only the violent features of video games in the process of learning aggressive behavior; however, children are also learning other things including new words and challenges, communication, and problem solving. Further studies are needed to empirically assess various types of effects of video games on children and adolescents.

Acknowledgments. This research was supported by the Konami Corporation; the Broadcasting Policy Division in the Information and Communications Policy Bureau at the Ministry of Public Management, Home Affairs, Post, and Telecommunications; and Keio University. The authors thank Shigeru Hagiwara, Shintaro Yukawa, Nobuko Ihori, and Kei Mitsumori for their support and suggestions. The authors also express their appreciation to the 11 coders who participated for their patience and comments.

References

Anderson CA, Dill KE (2000) Video games and aggressive thoughts, feelings, and behavior in the laboratory and in life. Journal of Personality and Social Psychology 78:772–790

Anderson CA, Morrow M (1995) Competitive aggression without interaction: effects of competitive versus cooperative instructions on aggressive behavior in video games. Personality and Social Psychology Bulletin 21:1020–1030

Ballard ME, Lineberger R (1999) Video game violence and confederate gender: effects of reward and punishment given by college males. Sex Roles 41:541–558

Ballard ME, Wiest JR (1996) The effects of violent videogame play on males' hostility and cardiovascular responding. Journal of Applied Social Psychology 26:717–730

Brooks MC (1999) Press start: exploring the effects of violent video games on boys. Ph.D. dissertation, University of Texas at Austin. Dissertation Abstracts International, 60 (12B):6419

Calvert S, Tan S (1994) Impact of virtual reality on young adults' physiological arousal and aggressive thoughts: interaction versus observation. Journal of Applied Developmental Psychology 15:125–139

Dill KE, Dill JC (1998) Video game violence: a review of the empirical literature. Aggression and Violent Behavior 3:407–428

Griffiths M (1999) Violent video games and aggression: a review of the literature. Aggression and Violent Behavior 4:203–212

Ihori N, Sakamoto A, Kobayashi K, et al (2003) A panel study on causal relationships between video game use and aggressiveness in elementary school children: effects on physical violence (in Japanese). Studies in Simulation and Gaming, pp 139–148

Katori T (2001) Effects of violent video games on aggression and interactivity (in Japanese). Paper presented at the 42nd Annual Meeting of the Japanese Society of Social Psychology, Aichi, pp 602–603

Lachlan K, Smith SL, Tamborini R (2000) Popular video games: assessing the amount and context of violence. Paper presented at the Annual Meeting of the National Communication Association in Seattle, Washington

Potter WJ (1999) On media violence. Sage, Thousand Oaks, CA

Sakamoto A, Ozaki K, Narushima R, et al (2001a) The influence of video game play on human violence and its process: two social psychological experiments of female university students (in Japanese). Studies in Simulation and Gaming 11:28–39

Sakamoto A, Kobayashi S, Mouri M (2001b) Effects of violent video games on aggression among female undergraduates: impacts of reality and rewards (in Japanese). Paper presented at the 65th Meeting of the Japanese Psychological Association, Tsukuba, p 804

Sakamoto A, Yukawa S, Shibuya A, et al (2002) A report on a panel survey about effects of broadcasting and electronic media on children and adolescents: effects of media violence on aggression (in Japanese). (A report for the Ministry of Public Management, Home Affairs, Posts and Telecommunications)

Sherry JL (2001) The effects of violent video games on aggression: a meta-analysis. Human Communication Research 27:409–431

Shibuya A (2001) Effects of violent video games on aggression: a comprehensive review (in Japanese). Bulletin of Keio University Graduate School Human Relations 53:55–67

Shibuya A, Sakamoto A (2002) Effects of violent video games on aggression: a review and proposal of a content analysis (in Japanese). Paper presented at the Spring Meeting of the Japan Association of Simulation and Gaming, Chiba, pp 18–23

Wilson BJ, Kunkel D, Linz D, et al (1997) In: National television violence study, vol 1. pp 3–268 Sage, Thousand Oaks, CA

Yukawa S, Yoshida F (2000) Violent video games and aggression: impact of game format, presentation style, and participation (in Japanese). Paper presented at the 41st Meeting of the Japanese Society of Social Psychology, Osaka, pp 74–75

13. Background and Current Status of Learning Games in the Field of Japanese School Education

Haruo Kamijo[1]

"Learning Games Study Group"

I am the leader of Jugyou Zukuri Nettowaaku (the Quality Class Network), which is a private research organization for Japanese teachers/professors of elementary schools, junior and senior high schools, and universities who study various teaching methods. This organization has approximately 400 members and also holds a study group specialized in "learning games." This group, whose name is Gakusyuu Geimu Kenkyuukai (the Learning Games Study Group), was founded on May 9, 1999, and now has 200 school/university teachers/professors as members. They conduct research on learning games to be used mainly in Japanese classes as well as in other classes, special activities, and ethics classes.

As the result of the research, a collection of "learning games for training thinking power" have been published to be used in coursework for subjects such as Japanese, math, science, and social studies. These publications were designed to have immediate effects in classroom situations, and eight such publications have been published so far. I also chair this study group.

Game-Like Teaching Methods That Were Long Ignored in Japanese Schools

In the field of Japanese school education, game-like teaching methods were ignored for a long time. For example, the special section "Tips for Developing Game- and Quiz-like Teaching Materials" in the October 1985 issue of the educational magazine *Classroom Teaching Studies* (Meijitosho Publishing) says:

1. A famous editor who dealt with educational publication commented as follows in the editorial: "I heard that crossword puzzles were quite popular among young teachers . . . So, I went to a bookstore to see how popular this activ-

[1] Leader, Jugyou Zukuri Nettowaaku (the Quality Class Network), Japan; haruo.kamijo@nifty.ne.jp

ity was, and I found that there were more than 10 kinds of magazines. I was amazed by this fact, but I hesitated to create a feature topic on this because children loving this activity did not seem like a good enough reason." This example tells us that dealing with "games" as an article theme in educational magazines was believed to be taboo before 1985.

2. In the special article "Answer within 500 Characters: Yes or No for Introduction of Games and Quizzes to Classes," ten researchers and practitioners basically agreed to the idea and introduced their comments. One of them said that "it is a 'cool' idea to introduce games and quizzes to classes. It seems that people now tend to like something nice and easy and that they avoid heavy and serious issues. I have a feeling that games and quizzes can be introduced to classes as long as classes become more active. What is important here is to know the consequences of using the quizzes." As seen in this comment, the general belief was that the quizzes and games in classes only played minor roles. Therefore, "games and quizzes" were never considered as an important element that would really support classes.

3. Next, one of the researchers who wrote papers for the special section wrote as follows: "In the United States (and other English-speaking countries), 'games' are an established educational research field. In Japan, on the other hand, 'games' are only regarded as play. It is thought that games are a form of hobby and have nothing to do with education. Especially in Japan, no one has come up with the idea to introduce simulation games to school education. This is because, in Japan, the duality theory claiming that play and study are two different things dominates." The idea that "play and study are two different things" was still strongly believed in the world of Japanese education, and it even prevented the concept of "classes using games" from spreading.

The three comments introduced above represent what was thought of game-like teaching methods in the Japanese educational scene until the middle of the 1980s. To summarize, these comments argue that schools are places where students learn and study in a serious manner, and games and quizzes must be ignored.

Drill Games First Appearance in the 1980s

Drill games became popular in the middle of the 1980s. Note that, at that time, these games were basically drills, but used some puzzles and games. One that became hugely popular used math puzzles. Students were to play the games by themselves.

There was an elementary school teacher who was given the nickname "the king of learning games." The following is the game this teacher created:

1. This is a Chinese character puzzle for third-year elementary school students.
2. Students are to collect Chinese characters that contain a radical that is specified by the teacher.

3. For example, when students are to collect Chinese characters containing the "tree" radical, they collect appropriate Chinese characters and draw each of them in boxes already provided with the "tree" radical.

4. Students who cannot read all the Chinese characters can use a dictionary.

5. Each of the Chinese characters completed in the boxes will be translated into scores. Students obtain 10 points for each of the Chinese characters that they complete. Some Chinese characters (e.g., 5) are given out that will give the students bonus points. If any of the Chinese characters drawn by students match the Chinese characters given by the teacher, the students who drew that Chinese character get 20 points instead of 10 points.

6. The student who gets the highest score wins the game.

There had previously been some simple games like collecting "Chinese characters containing the tree radical," but the attempt to emphasize the coincidence factor using bonus points started around that time. Since then, small tools such as dice, a deck of cards, and various other cards have been actively introduced to classes. Introduction of such tools was considered revolutionary because, until then, "being serious" had been the standard in Japanese school education.

As pointed out above, such learning games at that time mainly focused on "learning through practice" and "learning through memorizing." Through such quizzes and games, most games attempted to allow students to enjoy learning Chinese characters or mathematical calculations, or to enjoy memorizing names of places, or plants and animals.

Two Significant Changes Observed in Schools in the 1990s

The learning games mentioned above underwent two sets of significant changes in the 1990s, one of which was "classroom debate." This became popular in the middle of the 1990s, mainly in Japanese classes and social studies classes, resulting in wide awareness of the existence of fully-fledged learning games. The other change was a recent trend called the "malfunctioning classroom" or "malfunctioning school" which drew much attention in the late 1990s. This led to attention to games that would motivate school children to enjoy studying.

First, the "classroom debate" that became popular in the middle of the 1990s is discussed. When the educational magazine *Quality Class Network* (Gakuji Publishing), that I am currently the chief editor for, and the National Association of Debate in Education, born from this magazine, were first introduced to the public, classroom debate was very popular. At the beginning of the January 1996 issue of "History and the Future of Classroom Debate," I wrote as follows:

As of October 1995, classroom debate is rapidly spreading. I am now witnessing how a certain study area can spread at an explosive pace. For example, the following events were observed in the last 30 days.

On September 9, NHK's program called "Ohayo Nippon" broadcast a classroom debate by second-year elementary school students instructed by Ms. Junko Sakuma, and the title of the debate was "Are cockroaches necessary?" The program showed a general process flow of how the topic was determined, how research was conducted, and how the students carried out the debate.

On September 21, the *Yomiuri Shimbun* said: "Elementary schools and junior high schools are now starting to incorporate debates into classes and introduced a debate about 'notifying a patient of cancer diagnosis' conducted by the class of Mr. Osamu Ikeda from Zuiun Junior High School." The newspaper also introduced the comment by Mr. Hiroshi Adachi of Mutsukawa Elementary School saying: "Debates . . . make me humble and allow me to see things from various perspectives."

Going back to September 4, the *AERA* magazine reported The first Elementary School Student Debate Contest, where 56 schoolchildren participated from 11 elementary schools in Saga prefecture. Also, the magazine introduced the Debate Koushien planned by the Classroom Debate Study Group (Leader: Mr. Nobumasa Fujioka). A large number of television programs and newspapers were attempting to make this event into a story. This event will be described later.

Media in general often report that "debate has eliminated bullying." The Japanese language division of the Agency of Cultural Affairs is now planning to create an instructional video to be distributed to the school boards across Japan in the next spring. As an additional piece of information, more than 70 people participated in regular meetings (every other month) of the Classroom Debate Study Group in September (I am one of the attendants of the meeting). We expect to welcome more than 100 practitioners and researchers participating in the meeting in November.

While the mass media were paying close attention to this whole debate issue, some issues of classroom debate instruction books were published each month, publication of a specialized magazine *The Wind of Classroom Debate* began, and research and information–instruction exchanges were actively conducted, mainly in electronic meeting rooms. Roughly speaking, large-scale changes in Japanese society such as "post-cold war restructuring" were considered to be the background for this increase in popularity. Debate has become hugely popular twice so far in recent Japanese history: once after the Meiji Restoration, and once after World War II. Therefore, the big debate boom this time is the third one. Debate tends to become popular when the concept of "political issues must be determined by public opinions" is considered desirable.

To summarize, learning games in the 1980s gave us the impression that they hid agonizing practice and memorizing under forms of play that involved winning and losing. However, due to the new trend called classroom debate, the fact that there existed intellectual games and simulation games became widely understood.

This debate trend was also an innovating event in the field of Japanese education.

Next, the trend called the "malfunctioning classroom" or "malfunctioning school" that emerged in the late 1990s is illustrated.

The terms "malfunctioning classroom" and "malfunctioning school" made their appearances to represent the "troubled school," which became the major issue in Japanese educational circles in the late 1990s. I wrote a series of articles about the malfunctioning classroom for the educational magazine *Quality Class Network* over a 2.5-year period, starting from October 1997.

The very first article started as follows:

The "malfunctioning classroom" phenomenon has caught a lot of attention. One of the pioneering news reports on this subject was "Document 97" by NTV, broadcast on Sunday, April 6, 1997. Its theme was straightforward: "the malfunctioning classroom." This program did not get too much attention from the general public since it was broadcast from 0:15 at night; however, the fact that "the malfunctioning classroom" was openly introduced on television shocked educators.

In the *Soka Report* (April 2, 1997), there was an article introducing an interview with Mr. Hiroshi Niiya, producer and director of the news department at NTV. The title of the article was "Elementary school students who do not sit, and use verbal and physical violence . . . / Classes cannot be conducted in the metropolitan area." Below is the beginning of the interview:

The term "malfunctioning classroom" does not sound familiar. What does it mean?

The Higashi-Osaka Teachers Association started to use this term. Higashi-Osaka is on the east side and adjacent to Osaka City. This term has not been given any specific definition, but in general, it indicates conditions as described below:

1) Children do not stop talking and continue to be noisy even after their homeroom teacher enters the room. Students will not listen to the teacher.
2) Some students do not even sit at their desks. Sometimes half a class leaves the room, or when the situation gets worse, some use verbal or physical violence against their teacher. Such a situation where classes cannot be conducted at all is referred to the "malfunctioning classroom."

I did not know that. Is this phenomena correlated with the entire quality or level of the school?

Not all cases. There are some differences in problem levels among elementary schools in the metropolitan area, but more or less, they are experiencing the same type of problem.

Each teacher takes charge of his/her class and teaches all subjects; therefore, each classroom is quite often called the "class kingdom" and exactly what goes on within the class is rarely known by others outside it. It is usually the case that teachers do not even know the status of the classroom next door. When injuries or other accidents occur, however, gradually the reality of the malfunctioning classroom is reported in newspapers or other media. In this program, I thought I would like everyone to know that this type of problem is now occurring in elementary schools.

During the course of discussion regarding this malfunctioning classroom issue, Mr. Shotaro Takahashi, whose article about education was published in the *Asahi Shimbun* on November 15, 1998, made the following comment:

Japanese schools have employed the "uniform class method" since the school system was established in the beginning of the Meiji period. In this method, all students in the same class used the same textbook and they studied the same thing. What supported this traditional style was the series of rules that students were to sit at their desks and listen to their teacher quietly while maintaining a good posture, and students were to volunteer their opinions only after they were allowed to do so by their teacher. Each class was able to hold 40 students and to keep it that way, which was quite rare for a developed country, because the abovementioned class rules were properly observed. Now, the malfunctioning classroom phenomenon is affecting the "classroom culture" that has lasted for over 100 years."

To summarize, this comment implies that the classroom culture based on the duality theory, comprising play and study, must be reviewed.

In response to this comment, school teachers who approached education with traditional seriousness gradually started to show their interest in learning games. The result of a survey on the malfunctioning classroom conducted and published in 2002 by the National Institute for Educational Policy Research indicated that approximately 80% of elementary school teachers reported that they are actively creating "classes in which students can participate and experience," and learning games are the core of such classes. These games are not of course the practice or memorizing types that were used in the 1980s; they are learning games that are more of the on-site study type that "foster thinking power" and "heighten reliability," and classroom debate is taken into consideration in these games.

The "Animación a la Lectura," introduced from Spain, and the "Structured Group Encounter," known as a type of psychological education, are major examples. Games are the core of both teaching methods and have successfully captured the minds of teachers, who after encountering the malfunctioning classroom phenomenon now think that having only serious classes does not let children grow.

Five Major Trends Related to New Learning Games

I would like to briefly introduce five kinds of learning games that appeared after the classroom debate boom and the malfunctioning classroom phenomenon occurred:

– Animación a la Lectura: This is a Spanish reading game. For example, readers are to help each other to fix the order of story parts that were originally in random order. Children will enhance their ability to read while enjoying the game. The first translated book about this game was published in April 1997, and its title was "Animación a la Lectura." Since then six more books on the same topic, including translated versions, have been published. Educational videos have also been created.
– Structured Group Encounter: This is a Japanese game in which players will experience structured meetings, and its purpose is "self-discovery and understanding of others." There will be exercises such as "one person in a pair closes his/her eyes and physically relies on the other with open eyes." Over 30 books about this game have been published between 2000 and 2002, and these books

are know-how books based on clinical psychology theories that can be used at schools.

- Public Communication Game: This is a game that aims to develop logical thinking ability. For example, a word that would not be used in daily living is selected, and its correct meaning is presented along with other incorrect meanings made up by the question presenter. Players are to guess the correct one. This game is published as "Learning Games for Enhancing Logical Expression." It was first introduced to the public in May 1998 in the 11th volume of *Challenging Classroom Debate*, a specialized magazine by the National Association of Debate in Education. This game has been practiced widely in combination with debate education.

- Project Adventure: This is a teaching methodology using adventure games and was introduced from the United States. For example, participants hold hands and make a circle. Then, they try to move a hula-hoop along the circle and time how long it takes for the hula-hoop to come back to the starting point.

- Japanese language learning game: This is used in teaching Japanese as a second language. Games are similar to the ones used in teaching English. For example, participants are divided into two groups and one of the groups will have a garage sale. The other group will try to get as large a discount as possible. An increasing number of original games have been created.

Current Research Points

Since 2000, there has been an increasing number of experience-type learning games. In addition to the games introduced above, some drama-type games such as "improvising games" are now used in school education. Also, game-like teaching methods are used in cross-cultural or environmental education.

Here, there are two research points. The first one is "review." When using simulation games in an educational way, the most important step is that learners talk about impressions of the games and exchange opinions afterward. However, according to traditional Japanese methodology, teachers "sum up" at the end of the class for the students.

Quite frequently, although students gained good experience through the games, teachers summarize the whole experience for the students saying, for example, "There are three elements that you can learn from these games." Therefore, review after games has not been established as a methodology.

The second one is how to conduct "facilitation." In the traditional uniform teaching method in Japan, teachers divide teaching materials into great detail and give these parts to the students. Then, the teachers use them one by one to teach. Such "small-step methodology" is the mainstream in Japan.

Differing from conventional class principles, in participation/experience-type games, some degree of freedom will be necessary. Here, once a teacher presents what the learning theme is, he/she will see how learners learn by trial and error. Such a class principle for teachers has not been established yet.

Although the research on the abovementioned learning games have just started, Japanese teachers who are usually good at making small customizations seem to be gradually producing good results. I believe that research on learning games in Japan will greatly advance when the study concepts of review and facilitation spread to sites of education.

14. *Yutori* Is Considered Harmful: Agent-Based Analysis for Education Policy in Japan

Atsuko Arai[1] and Takao Terano[2]

Background and Motivation

Recently, there has been heated debate about education policy in Japan. It has been suggested that the new education policy known as "flexible education, free from pressure" or "Yutori Kyouiku" in Japanese, reduces a student's academic achievement. Some have also said that "flexible education" can lead to further stratification of Japanese society, as lower income groups tend to attach less value to education (Kariya 2002).

This chapter describes how the influence of education policy upon student motivation for learning changes seriously with disparities in the social stratum. By social stratum, we mean the educational investment based on wealth gap, and the strength of motivation, because home environment and the socioeconomic class to which students belong influence academic ability and academic advancement. We examine these mechanisms in a virtual artificial society (Epstein and Axtell 1996) on a computer. This research proposes a novel application in social science and pedagogy through an agent-based approach (Terano et al. 1998). The main conclusion is simple: "Yutori Kyouiku" is considered harmful for both higher and lower level students.

Related Work

Research on Education and Social Stratum

There is much literature worldwide on the relationship between achievement and social stratum. For more than half a century there has been research on the existence of a hierarchical difference in connate ability (Davis 1955). In addition,

[1] Publishing Division, Editorial Department, Jiji Press Ltd., Chiyoda-ku, Tokyo 100-0011, Japan; araia@jiji.co.jp
[2] Graduate School of Systems Management, University of Tsukuba, Bunkyo-ku, Tokyo 112-0012, Japan; terano@gssm.otsuka.tsukuba.ac.jp

other studies have investigated ability and attitude toward education. Willis (1977) stated that the culture of the industrial classes in Britain includes a negative attitude toward education. Educational expectation and a child's enthusiasm for education differ according to the academic background and occupation of the parents. Parents with a high level of education have a greater interest in their child's schooling. These parents work directly with their children and their schoolwork or they provide a positive environment to facilitate their children's studies. From a psychological viewpoint, McClelland (1961) stated that the difference in student motivation for learning stems from the social stratum.

In addition, Bourdieu and Passeron (1970) investigated a hierarchical difference of "cultural capital" at home, and they pointed out the relationship between academic achievement and the hierarchy. Cultural capital means cultural experience accumulated in the home. This includes, for example, experiences of family outings to concerts or museums, linguistic competence, and the number of books in the house.

Our work will focus on the above-mentioned education and social stratum research, and we have summarized the following two points on students' academic abilities and motivation for learning influenced by parents.

1. The economic factor: the amount of money spent on education by parents affects a child's academic advancement. Education expenses include direct costs, that is, what parents pay for schooling, and indirect costs, for example, what parents pay when they take on a tutor for their child.
2. The cultural factor: the learning environment in the home and parental encouragement. Various experiences in the home stimulate the child's intellectual curiosity, and this influences the child's motivation for learning.

Research on Education Policy in Japan

Advanced, industrial countries are preoccupied with academic credentials. Japan is no exception. Recently, education reform in Japan has aimed at getting rid of excessive competition in entrance examinations. A culture of excessive emphasis on academic credentials had produced heated competition in entrance examinations, which had led to a variety of educational problems, including bullying at elementary and lower secondary schools, refusal to attend school, and school violence.

In education sociology, it is said that "social birth" will occur after "biological birth" in a society preoccupied with academic credentials. In Japanese society, it is determined by the entrance exam (Amano 1989). With the acquisition of academic credentials, people can be reborn into a different class from their class of origin. Therefore, many people have been keen to acquire academic credentials; so entrance examinations have become more and more competitive.

After the 1990s in Japan, education reform was introduced aimed at improving entrance examinations and easing competitivness. Curriculum reform produced the "flexible education, free from pressure" or "Yutori" policy. This policy meant a decrease in curriculum contents, students spending less time in class, and it has reduced pressure on children to study and has lightened their workload. It has also produced concern about the decrease in students' motivation for learning.

In our research, we focus on the above-mentioned policy. We have summarized the following two points which are mainstays of Japanese education policy.

1. Competitive entrance examinations: The government has planned improvements to scholastic attainment; educational content has been upgraded, quality and quantity of curriculum contents have been increased. The advancement rate for students wishing to attend university has risen sharply. The students' scholastic attainments have improved overall. However, some students could not keep up with this regime and dropped out of the competition.

2. Flexible education, free from pressure: Curriculum contents and class time have been decreased, and the level of study has been eased. Reduction in the number of subjects for university entrance exams has eased competition for university entrance. External pressures on the student having been reduced, the incentive for the challenge of the examination is weaker. This has exacerbated gaps in students' academic abilities and has resulted in a polarization of education, that is, there are students studying hard at every situation, and students influenced by the situation.

Artificial Society Model

The scenario for a model of an artificial society where agents act is described below (see Fig. 1). We employ three kinds of agent (see Table 1). Each has different motivation for learning in an artificial society. Agents will sometimes receive challenging tasks, and obtain rewards in proportion to their levels of motivation, and finally, they will advance their levels of academic achievement. However, as educational expenses are necessary to achieve the task, income varies with the level of academic achievement.

TABLE 1. Personality of agents

Personality	Student A	Student B	Student C
Color	Red	Blue	Sky blue
Next stage	Green	Red	Blue
Academic ability	30	20	10
Faculty	0.9–0.1	0.9–0.1	0.9–0.1
Property	1000	600	300
View	3	3	3
Motivation for learning	Strong	Average	Weak

We also implement different education policies in this society, such as increasing or decreasing competitive entrance examinations between agents, depending on their motivation for learning.

The education policy, in this case, mainly involves increasing or decreasing the amount of work to be done, or changing the level of difficulty of work by changing course curriculum. Another factor is that agents, as students, receive income from their parents and are influenced by parents' motivation to educate their children. Thus, agents already have specific motivations for learning under the given conditions.

Motivation for learning is, as a rule, based on achievement-oriented activity according to theories of motivation. Motivation for learning can also be influenced by extrinsic motivation (Weiner 1992). Extrinsic motivation refers to education policy and influence of parents' motivation: see the model in Fig. 1.

1. Competitive entrance examinations: the difficulty of the task has been increased, and the number of examinations has been reduced. As the possibility of the students' advancement to university decreases, the examination becomes more competitive.
2. Flexible education, free from pressure: the difficulty of the task has been decreased, and the number of examinations has been increased. As the possibility of the students' advancement to university increases, competition is eased.
3. Influence of parents: agents are subjected to the same influences as students. Agents' motivation for learning is changed when a certain threshold is exceeded, and it makes agents want to accept the challenge of a difficult task.

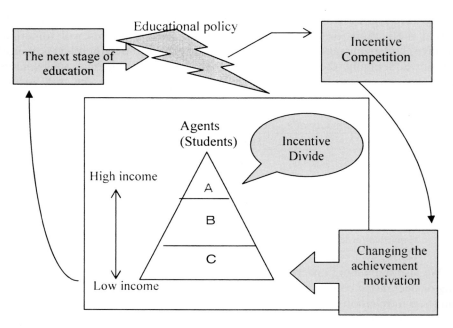

FIG. 1. Artificial society model

Experiments

In this section, we describe the results of the following two experiments:

1. Change of academic abilities under external pressure "Competitive entrance examination," "Flexible education, free from pressure," and "Influence of parents."
2. Shift of social stratum under the above conditions.

Change of Academic Ability Model

The objective of the series of experiments was to understand the relationship between student academic ability and education policy in the social stratum. We carried out the experiments by changing the level of difficulty of tasks, observing differences of motivation for learning, and observing changes in education costs.

Results showed that the competitive entrance examination is the most effective for student A in raising academic abilities. Influence of parents plus entrance examination competition is the most effective for students B and C in raising academic abilities. Improving the difficulty of the task, and changing the agents' action rule into the "high motivation for learning model" was also effective in increasing academic abilities. On the other hand, all agents' academic abilities dropped under the Yutori policy.

In addition, we measured results to check for hierarchical differences using the Gini coefficient. The Gini coefficient is a distribution-free statistic to measure the inequality of wealth in a society. A large Gini coefficient indicates an unequal society (Epstein and Axtell 1996). The Gini coefficient became 0.35 with Yutori in the unequal academic ability model, and the academic ability gap expansion was the greatest here. The Gini coefficient fell to 0.22 when the influence of parents plus competitive entrance examination was introduced under the same condition, and the academic ability gap eased. Figures 2 and 3 show the results of these two cases.

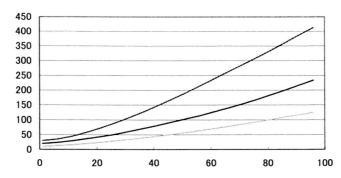

Fig. 2. Model of the smallest academic ability gap under "Influence of parents + competitive entrance examination." *X-axis* is the simulation step, *Y-axis* is the degree of student academic ability. *Upper curve* indicates student A, *middle curve* indicates student B, *lower curve* indicates student C

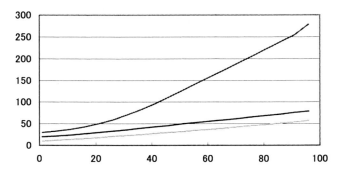

FIG. 3. Model of the largest academic ability gap under "free from pressure." *X-axis* is the simulation step, *Y-axis* is the degree of student academic ability. *Upper curve* indicates student A, *middle curve* indicates student B, *lower curve* indicates student C

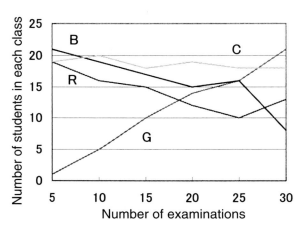

FIG. 4. Transition of student personality brought about shifting the stratum. Student G, R, B, C is a result of a hierarchical movement after this simulation. It moves to a high-ranking hierarchy in order of C→B→R→G. For example, student A changes to G (super A), and student B changes to R

Shift in the Social Stratum Model

The objective of the series of experiments was to understand the shift in the social stratum caused by education policy and "Influence of parents". We carried out the experiments by changing the entrance examination opportunities, and observing changes of education costs. The student agents accept the examination challenge, and, as a result, they are promoted to a higher degree, and this means moving to the next stratum. In this case, opportunities for students to go to the next stage of education have been produced by increasing the number of examinations, according to "free from pressure." Initial number of students in each class was equally set at 20 and the number of examinations was set at 5–30 in this experiment. It was simulated by each of 100 steps.

Results show the student A group moved from A to G instantly, produced by increasing the number of examinations. Student groups B and C found it diffi-cult move to the higher position, despite an increase in the number of examinations. However, when the number of examinations exceeded 20, a hierarchical movement occurred rapidly (see Fig. 4). In addition, when "Influence of parents" was introduced in this case, and the motivation for learning of student B · C was changed, a hierarchical movement was produced.

Initially, we forecast that many students could pass the examination irrespective of their stratum if Yutori was introduced in this society, moreover the occurrences of the shift in the social stratum would be increased. However, the phenomenon was actually seen in the limited hierarchy as follows:

- Student A change to G: happens easily
- Student B change to R: happens according to circumstances
- Student C change to B: happens according to circumstances
- Student C change to R or G: difficult to occur.

Discussion

From the experiments described in the previous sections, we have observed the following:

1. The academic abilities of all students decreased with the Yutori policy. Especially remarkable is the decrease of students' academic achievement in the medium or lower layer of the social stratum. In addition, the gap in academic abilities between the upper-ranking layer and the medium or lower layer expanded. Students in the upper-ranking layer have always been favored under every situation.

2. Even if the quantity of curriculum content is reduced and the level of study becomes easier, students do not always benefit.

Conclusions

This chapter describes an agent-based simulation of the influence of education policy upon stratified students' academic abilities. We have proposed that the academic achievement gap in the social stratum is not caused by academic ability or investment in education, but by the action rules for task achievement, that is, by the motivation to learn. It suggests that education policy should aim at cultivating students' motivation to learn.

Future work includes exploring the various factors for the causal relationship between levels of academic achievement and education policy, because, in general, levels of academic achievement depend on national education policy and education systems (Green 1997).

References

Amano I (1989) The dilemma of Japanese education today. In: Shields JJ (ed) Japanese schooling: patterns of socialization, equality, and political control. Pennsylvania State University Press, University Park

Bourdieu P, Passeron JC (1970) Reproduction: in education, society, and culture. Sage, Beverly Hills

Davis A (1995) Social-class influences upon learning. Harvard University Press

Epstein J, Axtell R (1996) Growing artificial societies. MIT Press

Green A (1997) Education, globalization and the nation state. MacMillan

Kariya T (2002) The polarization of education. JapanEcho, Vol. 29 No. 4 http://www.japanecho.co.jp/sum/2002/290403.html

McClelland DC (1961) Achieving society. Van Nostrand

Terano T, Kurahashi S, Minami U (1998) TRURL: Artificial world for social interaction studies. In: Proceedings sixth International Conference on Artificial Life (ALIFE VI), pp 326–335

Weiner B (1992) Human motivation: metaphors, theories and research. Sage

Willis P (1977) Learning to labor: how working class kids get working class jobs. Saxon House, Westmead

Part III
Strategies and Policy Exercise

15. Simulations and Social Responsibility: Why Should We Bother?

Ivo Wenzler[1]

What Is Corporate Social Responsibility?

Corporations operate in complex business and social environments where the shareholders are not the only stakeholders that influence, and are influenced by, what the corporation does. There is a growing number of overlapping social and political entities that show a keen interest in a corporation's business and are increasingly putting pressure on each corporation to demonstrate a socially responsible behavior. This behavior is manifested in how a corporation is dealing with issues such as business ethics, community investment, environment protection, governance, human rights, transparency of the marketplace, and the quality of the workplace.

There are many definitions of what corporate social responsibility means, mostly dependant on which side of the issue the author sits. The one definition I find most helpful is by Business for Social Responsibility,[2] saying that corporate social responsibility (CSR) means achieving commercial success in ways that honor ethical values and respect people, communities, and the natural environment.

Becoming socially responsible requires corporations to address the legal, ethical, commercial, and other expectations that society has of them. The decisions made have to fairly balance the claims of all key stakeholders and the corporation should take responsibility for current as well as future impacts of those decisions. The mechanism for this is a comprehensive set of policies, practices, and programs that need to be fully integrated into business operations, supply chains, and decision-making processes throughout the corporation.

[1] Accenture, Apollolaan 150, 1070AT Amsterdam, The Netherlands; ivo.wenzler@accenture.com; Technical University Delft, Jaffalaan 5, 2628 BX Delft, The Netherlands; i.wenzler@tbm.tudelft.nl
[2] Business for Social Responsibility (BSR) is a global organization that helps member companies achieve success in ways that respect ethical values, people, communities and the environment. Web site: www.bsr.org.

Becoming and staying a socially responsible business, and being able to effectively sustain or improve commercial success, is not easy. There are a number of challenges ahead, having to do with:

- The inherent complexity of the CSR issues;
- The difficulty in developing the right CSR vision and strategic choices;
- Building and sustaining CSR-related business capabilities; and
- Being able to translate these capabilities into an improved performance.

In the following pages, some of these challenges are outlined in more detail, and then the role that different types of simulations and games can play in helping corporations are presented, as well as the groups interacting with them, to address these challenges in an innovative and effective way.

What Are the CSR-Related Challenges?

Parallel with the growing pressures on corporations to think and act in a socially responsible way, there is a growing proliferation of CSR codes, standards, indicators, and guidelines. These standards or guidelines, regardless of whether they are initiated by governments, pressure groups, or corporations themselves, are continuously adding to the complexity of the CSR landscape. Some of this complexity can be reduced by externally and/or internally driven consolidation and streamlining efforts, but if the corporations want to effectively deal with this growing complexity, this will not be enough.

This leads to the *CSR challenge #1*: How can an organization ensure that it is not only aware of all the relevant CSR codes, standards, or guidelines, but it has an appropriate understanding of the effects they might have on the organization's way of doing business and the business results it is seeking to achieve?

To be even given a chance of being successful, CSR not only needs a prominent place in the corporate core mission, vision, and value statements, but it must be continuously and proactively promoted and acted upon within and outside the corporation itself. This means making the strategic choices that fully reflect this vision, and then making sure that these choices are translated into operational business decisions.

This leads to the *CSR challenge #2*: How can an organization effectively incorporate and integrate social responsibility concerns into their vision, culture, strategic choices, and business decisions at all levels of the organization?

While the advocates of CSR want to see demonstrable social and environmental improvements, it is safe to assume that the vast majority of shareholders want to see a demonstrable improvement in financial performance. This is also likely to be the case for investors. Although they increasingly view CSR as a strategic business issue, they also have a basic expectation that once implemented, CSR activities should provide a healthy return on investments. Corporations themselves are also keen to understand what their CSR initiatives have accomplished, so that they can focus scarce resources most effectively. Some of the things they are interested in are:

- Understanding how CSR initiatives influence their growth potential,
- What are the most effective leverage points; and
- What are the trade-offs of various strategic (investment) options?

These benefits can be externally and internally driven. Customers are increasingly drawn to brands and companies with good reputations in CSR-related areas. In addition to price, quality, and convenience, they are increasingly using value-based criteria for buying products (such as sweatshop-free or child labor-free, low environmental impact, nongenetically modified materials). CSR-related brand image and reputation with the public, as well as within the overall business community, is definitely having a positive effect on business performance. Employee-related CSR initiatives also have significant potential. Improved working conditions, lower environmental impacts, and employee involvement in decision making often lead to increased productivity and reduced error rates.

This leads to the *CSR challenge #3*: How can an organization effectively demonstrate to its shareholders that its CSR-related policies and activities do not only honor ethical values and respect people, communities, and the natural environment, but at the same time have a positive impact on commercial success and business performance?

In addition to revenue, the level of operational costs affects the financial performance of every corporation. A most common perception within a business community is that implementing CSR initiatives will undoubtedly increase operational cost and in that way negatively affect business performance. This perception does not necessarily provide a full and valid picture. Some CSR initiatives can actually reduce operational costs quite significantly. For instance, many CSR-driven recycling initiatives can cut waste-disposal costs and, in addition, can generate income by selling recycled materials. By improving working conditions, the corporate ability to retain employees will increase, which will result in reduction in turnover and associated recruitment and training costs.

This leads to the *CSR challenge #4*: How can an organization effectively demonstrate to its shareholders that its CSR-related policies and activities can effectively reduce the operating costs of doing business, and in that way also contribute to the overall business performance?

One of the significant developments within the CSR landscape is the sharp increase in stakeholder activism. The general public, as well as various stakeholders, are looking to the private sector to help with a myriad of complex and pressing social and economic issues, and they have come to expect ever more of businesses when these issues are in question. There is also a growing demand for transparency and growing expectation that corporations measure, report, and continuously improve their social and environmental performance.

Different stakeholders (shareholders, analysts, regulators, activists, labor unions, employees, community organizations, news media, consumers) are also increasingly asking companies to be accountable not only for their own CSR-related performance, but for performance throughout their whole value chain (suppliers, business partners, clients). This is expanding the boundaries of corporate accountability and contributing to the already high complexity of CSR-related issues.

These developments are requiring corporations to pursue a more sophisticated stakeholder engagement. The question is no longer "whether to engage" but "how to engage." To be able to influence the perceptions and behavior of the public, their stakeholders, business partners, or industry colleagues they need to be more proactive in providing information, listening to, understanding the concerns, and pursuing partnerships around CSR issues.

This leads to the *CSR challenge #5*: How can an organization effectively and efficiently engage all of the stakeholders in a meaningful dialogue about issues of concern?

Any corporation that subscribes to the CSR agenda will often have to develop and implement a whole set of new business capabilities, either related to the relationship with their clients, shareholders, and business partners on the one side, or their employees on the other. These capabilities have to ensure that the corporation can reach its CSR-related objectives in the most efficient way possible, and in this way close the gap between what the corporation says it stands for and the reality of its actual performance. An example of such a capability that is increasingly becoming more important is innovation—ability to innovate and ability to quickly translate the ideas into improved performance.

This leads to the *CSR challenge #6*: How can an organization effectively develop, test and implement CSR-related business capabilities, both in terms of processes and systems needed for sustained performance?

The most important element of transforming a particular business capability into actual business results is workforce performance. The lack of critical workforce skills, the lack of workforce understanding of CSR-related business strategy, and the lack of workforce understanding of the connection between their jobs and overall corporate strategic priorities has a detrimental effect on that performance. Employees cannot be held accountable for socially responsible behavior if they are not aware of its importance and are not provided with the skills, information, and tools they need to act appropriately in carrying out their job requirements. That is why each corporation that is serious about their CSR agenda should accelerate their CSR capabilities by improving the skills, motivation, and commitment of their employees. In addition to that they should build employee confidence in future success by helping them experience the benefits of change and their ability to be successful.

This leads to the *CSR challenge #7*: How can an organization reduce the gap between existing and required CSR-related understanding, knowledge, skills, culture, and attitudes?

The seven challenges outlined above do not pretend to capture the whole landscape of issues a corporation faces in its attempt to become and stay a socially responsible business, but they do capture the core of it (see Fig. 1). These challenges are also not necessarily mutually exclusive or collectively exhaustive, but

	Outward oriented	Inward oriented
Policy level	Challenge #1 – Understanding of the effects CSR standards can have on the business!	Challenge #2 – Effective integration of CSR issues into a corporate vision! Challenge #3 – Demonstrate that CSR has a positive impact on commercial success! Challenge #4 – Demonstrate that CSR related policies can reduce the operating costs!
Operations level	Challenge #7 – Reducing the gap between existing and required skills and attitudes!	Challenge #5 – Effective engagement of all stakeholders in a meaningful dialogue! Challenge #6 – Effective development of CSR related business capabilities!

FIG. 1. Overview of seven key corporate social responsibility (CSR) challenges

they do provide a reasonably good framework for linking the needs corporations have and different types of simulations and games that can be used in addressing these challenges.

Why Should We Bother with Simulations and Games?

When talking about simulations and gaming there are probably as many definitions and categorizations as there are professionals developing and implementing these tools. As with modeling there are no good or bad models, only the useful ones and not so useful ones. The same is true for categorizations and definitions in the simulation and gaming field. There are no good or bad definitions, only the more useful ones and less useful ones. The categorization and definitions used here are not intended to be correct or universally applicable, but they have been very useful in my work. This is especially the case when I need to explain to my colleagues and my clients what simulations are and what can they do (see Fig. 2). The seven categories I use are:

- Market simulations;
- Policy simulations;
- Dynamic business modeling;
- Capability simulations;
- Day-in-a-life simulations;

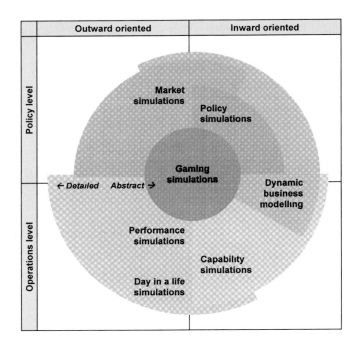

FIG. 2. Simulation and gaming categories (types)

- Performance simulations; and
- Gaming simulations.

Market Simulations

Market simulation is a representation of dynamic relationships between different actors within a certain market structure, where the behavior in the market is a direct result of the causal relationships between these actors and the decisions they make. The effect of causal relationships is based on actual decisions, assumptions, and decision rules, which are formalized by using mathematical equations, allowing for the simulation of the market behavior over time.

CSR-related use: Market simulations can help corporations and their stakeholders build insights and understanding of the effects that CSR policies and practices can have on how a particular market works. In addition they can help corporations explore what effects that changes in CSR codes, standards, or guidelines might have on their way of doing business, both externally in their relationship with the market and internally in their relationship with employees.

Policy Simulations

Policy simulation is a representation of a particular policy environment or issue, where the behavior of actors and the effects of their decisions are a direct result of the interaction between these actors and the relationship structure between them. This structure as well as the level and character of interaction are determined in most cases by actors themselves during the simulation run.

CSR-related use: Policy simulations can help corporations and their stakeholders build insights and understanding of a number of CSR-related policy issues, and then help them explore and validate a set of related policy assumptions. In addition they can help corporations increase their awareness about the possible effects these policies might have on performance, once implemented. Policy simulations can also be used to discuss, define, and then promote a CSR-driven corporate vision and culture, both within and outside the corporation itself.

Dynamic Business Modeling

Dynamic business modeling is a representation of a dynamic behavior of a business system, where the behavior of the system is a direct result of the casual relationships between different elements of the system. The effect of causal relationships is based on assumptions and decision rules, which are then formalized by using mathematical equations, allowing for the simulation of the systems behavior over time.

CSR-related use: Dynamic business modeling can help corporations prototype and validate business assumptions specific to CSR-related business and market structures, as well as determine the impact of strategic decisions on their commercial success and business performance. In other words, dynamic business modeling can help corporations create a better understanding of what the CSR initiative could accomplish once implemented, so they can focus their resources more effectively. Dynamic business modeling based simulations can serve as a living business case, helping corporations explore and validate the impact of CSR initiatives on operating costs, investments needed, and revenues. They can also help define what the most effective leverage points are, and what the trade-offs of various strategic investment options (in both the size and timing of benefits) are. The results of these simulations can then help demonstrate to the shareholders the level of business benefits coming from CSR policies and activities.

Capability Simulations

Capability simulation is a representation of a dynamic behavior of an existing (or future) business process, where the behavior of the process is a result of a number of discrete events following one after another. The characteristics of these discrete events are based on assumptions and decision rules, which are then formalized by using mathematical equations, allowing for the simulation of the process behavior over time.

CSR-related use: Capability simulations can help corporations prototype and validate business assumptions specific to CSR-related business processes. They can help determine how the processes will perform under different circumstances and whether the corporation can reach its business process-related objectives.

Exploring the effects of different CSR issues on process performance can help determine process bottlenecks, find out how significant they are, and develop possible solutions to eliminate them. Capability simulations can also help in determining which process alternatives will deliver a more sustainable performance and what capacity in people and IT systems a corporation needs to deliver a desired CSR-related business process performance.

Day-in-a-Life Simulations

Day-in-a-life simulation is a one-to-one representation of a particular real-life business environment, with participants working in an integrated way with their new IT systems and processes, acting on their new roles and responsibilities, and using actual data and business cases. Everything is real, except the consequences.

CSR-related use: Day-in-a-life simulations can first provide insight into the relationship between the CSR-driven changes in the organization, processes, and IT to a large number of employee and stakeholder groups or individuals. Secondly, these simulations can help to reduce the gap between existing and required CSR-related knowledge, skills, and attitudes by providing a safe environment for learning. By building the confidence in corporate ability to be successful in dealing effectively with CSR issues, day-in-a-life simulations can increase the employee and stakeholder motivation, confidence, and commitment to success. Thirdly, these simulations can significantly reduce the time needed to reach the target CSR-related business performance.

Performance Simulations

Performance simulation is a representation of a particular business issue or environment, where all the elements of the business environment and the relationships between these elements are predesigned and integrated into a computer program. Results of player's decisions are path dependant.

CSR-related use: Performance simulations can help corporations quickly and effectively enable CSR-related knowledge, skills, and attitudes within a large numbers of individuals, by providing them with a safe, interactive, and self-directed environment for learning. By building the confidence in each individual's capability to be successful in dealing effectively with the CSR issues, capability simulations can also significantly increase the employee and stakeholder motivation, confidence, and commitment to success. As with the day-in-a-life simulations, capability simulations can also significantly reduce the time needed to reach the target CSR-related business performance.

Gaming Simulations

Gaming simulation is a representation of a set of key relationships and structure elements of a particular issue or a problem environment, where the behavior of actors and the effects of their decisions are a direct result of the rules guiding the interaction between these actors. Most of the time, the representation of the problem environment is a metaphoric or symbolic one, and at the higher level of abstraction.

CSR-related use: Gaming simulations, being the most generic category of simulations, can help corporations in a whole range of CSR-related issues. Due to their mostly higher level of abstraction, these simulations can be very effective in providing the insight and understanding of what CSR is, why it is important, and how it can be effectively implemented. Gaming simulations can be also very effective in helping corporations negotiate, build consensus, and promote a shared CSR vision and related value statements. Besides building the understanding, these simulations can enable a whole range of general management skills and attitudes, and help corporations build the confidence, motivation, and commitment to act on these newly required skills and attitudes.

Figure 3 outlines which simulations can be used to address particular CSR challenges, and to what extent. The idea behind the framework is to help simulation and gaming professionals and their clients match the needs of a corporation with the appropriate simulation approach.

The applicability of different simulation types on CSR challenges To some extent ● To a large extent ⬤	Market simulations	Policy simulations	Dynamic business modeling	Capability simulations	Day-in-a-life simulations	Performance simulations	Gaming simulations
#1 – Understanding of the effects CSR standards can have on the business!	⬤	⬤	●				●
#2 – Effective integration of CSR issues into a corporate vision!	●	⬤	⬤				●
#3 – Demonstrate that CSR has a positive impact on commercial success!	●	●	⬤	●			
#4 – Demonstrate that CSR related policies can reduce the operating costs!			⬤	●			
#5 – Effective engagement of all stakeholders in a meaningful dialogue!	●	⬤	●	⬤	●	●	⬤
#6 – Effective development of CSR related business capabilities!			●	⬤	●		
#7 – Reducing the gap between existing and required skills and attitudes!				●	⬤	⬤	⬤

Fig. 3. CSR challenges/simulation types matrix

Conclusions

All these different types of simulations have been very effectively applied to a whole variety of issues outside the corporate social responsibility arena. They have proved to be an effective approach in helping corporations build sufficient understanding of market dynamics, develop and assess different strategies, design and test business capabilities, and, last but not least, improve their human performance.

The challenge facing simulation and gaming professionals is to replicate this success within the arena of corporate social responsibility and help corporations, as well as the groups interacting with them, to address the CSR-related challenges in an innovative and effective way.

An example of a successful application of simulation and gaming for CSR is a game developed by the Rabo Bank branch office in Bernheze, Netherlands.

The bank was facing two issues: (1) How to increase the awareness of what socially responsible entrepreneurship is, both within the bank as well as within the communities the bank is serving, and (2) how to create a vision of how to effectively develop and implement socially responsible entrepreneurship in the local communities; a vision that is not only shared with but acted upon by all relevant actors in that community.

With these questions in mind the bank developed a board game called "The Game of Profit and Values" (Spel van Winst en Waarden)[3] and played it with the employees of the bank, the bank clients (members), members of the local government, representatives of political parties, and representatives of business associations. Based on the experiences and insights created by playing the game, the bank (together with their clients) shaped a vision on socially responsible entrepreneurship in the local communities.

---

[3] Rabo Bank; Nieuwe Verbindingen: Duizend-en-een communities in praktijk; Juni 2003 (ISBN 90-807510-1-6).

16. Motivation Styles to Speak Out, Decision Rules, and Group Size as Determinants of Group Decision Making: Simulation of Meetings

Nireka Adachi[1], Masayori Ishikawa[2], and Koichi E. Okamoto[3]

Introduction

Recent years have witnessed a number of corporate scandals, such as systematic violation, in Japanese society. The scandals have made profound impact on our society, and, most of all, the fact that acts clearly regarded as illegal were accepted in these corporations increased public distrust of them. Today, we can find active movement in which companies change their corporate governance to one that emphasizes the importance of management responsibility and transparency of management. The more transparency required of the decision process in a company, the more attention is paid to whether appropriate decision procedures are followed. The purpose of this study is to show that a conventional decision procedure that helps the majority has substantial and considerable impact on adoption of a proposal, and suggest preventive procedures against unethical and antisocial decision making.

Majority Makes Minority Silent

Those who attend a meeting may or may not have some information that other members of the meeting do not. Therefore, they may attend meetings to find and share information like as those who attend brainstorming meetings to generate and share novel ideas. Contrary to their speculation, Stasser and his colleagues found that members of meeting could not share unshared information through discussion and consequently failed to find out an alternative (a superior decision alternative in their experiments) (Stasser 1992, Stasser and Titus 1985, Stasser et al. 1989).

Stasser and others also found the probability that participants at meetings put shared information into discussion was high, and those members spent

---

[1] Research Institute of Science and Technology for Society (RISTEX), Minato-ku, Tokyo 105-6218, Japan; nadachi@ristex.jst.go.jp
[2] Research Center for Nuclear Science and Technology, The University of Tokyo/RISTEX
[3] Faculty of Human Sciences, Toyo Eiwa University/RISTEX

more time repeating information that was already shared (Stasser et al. 1989). In such a situation, "validity" of shared information increased, because shared information was referred to and was supported by many members. On the contrary, the probability that members throw unshared information into discussion was low. Because unshared information was supported by few members, the probability of being repeatedly thrown into discussion was also low.

The recognition that an opinion is supported by the "majority", in some cases a false recognition, discourages people from giving an opinion that is different from the *majority*. This silence also encourages the *majority*. We can see a vicious cycle, the "spiral of silence," in this process. The process deprives the *minority* of motivation to express their opinion, and induces them to conform their opinion to one of the majority at the same time (Ikeda 1993, Kameda 1997, Kameda and Sugimori 1995, Noelle-Neumann 1993).

Procedure Dependency of Decision Outcomes

Controllability of group decision making at the macro social level has been one of a number of important issues (Saeki 1980). On the other hand, Kameda pointed out that the same is true of group decision making at the face-to-face level (Kameda 1996, Kameda and Sugimori 1995), and warned of unreflective use of conventional procedures in group decision making.

As Kameda pointed out, there is a conventional procedure which, potentially, also has influence on group decisions at face-to-face level. For example, to say "Is there any objection? . . . Then, there being no objection, the proposal has been adopted," is the one used in meeting. This is a common practice employed for the smooth running of meetings (Robert et al. 2000), and therefore it can give rise to an atmosphere that discourages members from daring to voice their dissent, because this procedure seems to implicitly demand approval or disapproval (in this case, approval is implicitly demanded). Considering the general situation of the meeting already moving toward approval, or the situation in which the chair is the supervisor of the members and intimidates them, it is easy to understand the influence of this procedure. Adachi and Ishikawa (2003) demonstrated its negligible influence on the adoption rate of proposals. Although such procedure has been used without much attention, their research suggests that it can become a means by which hard-line supporters push through their impossible demand.

Research

Among the influential procedures that affect group decisions, there is one that elicits impediments and barriers inherent in group decision making. The purpose of this research is to examine a procedure that helps the *majority* and increases the adoption rate of proposals by taking advantage of such impediments and barriers.

When a proposal is submitted and members discuss adopting it, it is necessary for those who do not support it to make others aware of the existence of opponents. The possibility of rejecting the proposal must be higher if it can be shown that not only one person but many disapprove of it. Nevertheless, there may be a case that the chair takes a decision on it without full discussion with the phrase mentioned above. This procedure has potential danger to make members mistakenly recognize dominant opinion as consensus of members and come around to this opinion without knowing their own opinion status (Kameda 1997). In fact, it is found that an opinion or an alternative which is more actively discussed by group members is likely to be recognized as dominant, and will finally get more votes cast in support (Kameda and Sugimori 1995). In other words, this procedure includes the expectation that members who did not express their opinion come to support seemingly dominant opinion based on their false recognition, and enables us to utilize actively the mechanism by which the social reality that seems as if an opinion is supported by the *majority* is generated.

Based on the above discussion, we explore the effect of this conventional procedure in terms of the ease of forming a *majority* view in a decision-making group, that is, we study whether the easiness affects the adoption rate of the proposal, considering following three aspects.

(1) Motivation styles of members to speak out: In order to form a *majority* to pass their proposal, it is necessary for many supporters to express their opinion, and it is also important for each supporter to do so as soon as possible. Whether supporters can pass their proposal depends on the number of supporters who express their opinion spontaneously. However there are opportunists who try to decide whether to express their opinion, waiting and seeing how the meeting goes. Although it is possible to have a *majority* if those opportunists speak out, their keeping silent results in a *minority* position, and may lower the possibility that the proposal is passed. The same is true of opponents against proposals.

(2) Decision rules: Decision rules, such as unanimous rule and majority rule, have more direct influence on adoption rate. For example, in Robert's rule, not a simple majority (1/2 majority rule) but a two thirds majority (2/3 majority rule) is required to set a stricter standard (Robert et al. 2000). In this study, we also set a 2/3 majority rule, and compare the effect of it with the 1/2 majority rule.

(3) Group size: Many studies demonstrated that group size has various influence on group decision making (Adachi and Ishikawa 2003, Kameda 1997, Kameda and Sugimori 1995). Additionally, as the size of a group becomes large, the competition for a chance of speaking also becomes severe. Therefore, in this study, we take group size into account, and also examine whether this factor affects the adoption rate.

Method

Computer Simulation

- **Group composition.** In computer simulation, each member supports or is opposed to the adoption of a proposal submitted by one of the supporters, and the opponents always have one more member than the supporters irrespective of group size. Therefore, in this situation, if all members vote by secret ballot before discussion, opponents are sure to gain a majority.

- **Motivation style of members to speak out.** People seem to have a certain type of motivation to express their own opinion in group discussion settings. In this simulation, it is also assumed that there are three types of members in the group, namely, "proponent", "follower", and "opportunist."
  - **Proponent type:** The proponent is motivated to speak out in any situation without hesitation, and in our study both opponents and supporters have one proponent member. It is also assumed that a proponent who belongs to supporters submits a proposal and, therefore, is the member who opens the debate on it.
  - **Follower type:** The followers are the members who do not bring themselves to speak up unless at least another member expresses the same opinion as them. In the simulation program, the follower becomes "active" (stands as one of candidates for next speaker) if any one of the members belonging to the same faction (i.e., opponents/supporters) express his/her opinion before the follower. If more than one member is active, the next speaker is selected among them in a random order. The maximum number of followers in the supporters is four and in the opponents is five: in the supporter faction the number of followers varies from one to four, and in the opponents faction varies from zero to five.
  - **Opportunist type:** The rest of the members are opportunists. The opportunists are members who take a wait-and-see approach in such a meeting. Whether an opportunist gives his/her opinion depends on the number of members who have the same opinion with them and have already expressed it. More concretely, the opportunists do not become active until the members who take the same view with them occupy more than half of the members who have already presented their own view. If more than one member is active at the same time, the next speaker is selected among them in a random order.

    Whenever the number of members who belong to the same faction and have already made remarks is less than half the speakers, they quit as candidates of the next speaker. Additionally, opportunists keep taking a wait-and-see attitude and do not become active unless more than five members, irrespective of faction, state their own opinion.

- **Conformity at the time of taking a division.** As noted above, emergence of a *majority* makes members who keep silent (especially opportunists) be more likely to conform their opinions to ones of the *majority*. In this study, we assumed that a vote taken after discussion is not by a secret ballot which is relatively easy to reveal honest feeling, but by showing of hands which is difficult to do so. Then, in the simulation, at the time of taking a decision, opportunists in opponent/supporter factions who will not speak throughout the discussion, although all supporters/opponents have already stated their opinion, are expected to conform their opinion to the *majority* and are counted as supporters/opponents.

- **Length of meetings/number of speeches.** In the process of forming a *majority*, the impact of first speech of a member on the others seems to be the strongest. Then in this simulation, it is assumed that each member makes remarks only once in a meeting. The length of a meeting in this simulation is represented by the number of member speeches and is limited to the total number of members. If all members speak once, or there is no candidate for the next speaker, then the discussion is over and members go to a vote.

Factorial Design

Factorial design is 2 (decision rules: 1/2 majority rule, 2/3 majority rule) × 3 (group size: 11-member group, 17-member group, 29-member group) × 6 (number of followers in opponents: from 0 to 5). Based on this design, the frequency of the case in which a proposal was adopted was analyzed by the number of followers in supporters. The simulation was run for 500 (corresponding to 500 cases of meeting) per cell.

Results

To examine relationships among factors, we selected a model from 2 (decision rules) × 3 (group size) × 6 (number of followers in opponents) × 2 (frequency of adoption) models within number of followers in supporters by a backward method. Except the case in which there is only one follower in supporters, saturated models were significant.

In the case of one follower in supporters, a 3 (group size) × 6 (number of followers in opponents) × 2 (frequency of adoption) model was significant ($G^2 = 28.91, df = 36, p = 0.703$). This selected model showed conditional significant relationships between group size and adoption rate (frequency of adoption of a proposal). This result shows the extent of influence of group size on frequency of adoption changes according to the number of followers in opponents. However, a model including decision rules was nonsignificant ($G^2 = 18.29, df = 10, p > 0.05$). There are no two-way interactions between decision rules and group size, and decision rules and the number of followers. On the other hand, interaction group size and adoption rate ($\chi^2 = 700.2, df = 2$), the number of followers in opponents and adoption rate ($\chi^2 = 17423.8, df = 5$) are significant ($p < 0.0001$).

In the case of two followers in supporters, a saturated model including factor of decision rules is significant ($G^2 = 58.94, df = 10, p < 0.0001$). The three-way interactions among decision rules, group size, and adoption rate are significant ($\chi^2 = 9.87, df = 2, p < 0.01$). The adoption rate was significantly associated with decision rules and number of followers in opponents ($\chi^2 = 11.92, df = 5, p < 0.05$), with group size, and the number of followers in opponents ($\chi^2 = 657.1, df = 10, p < 0.0001$). Also, adoption rate significantly interacted with decision rules ($\chi^2 = 5.78, df = 1, p < 0.05$) and group size ($\chi^2 = 1966.6, df = 2, p < 0.0001$), and the number of followers in opponents ($\chi^2 = 8398.4, df = 5, p < 0.0001$) (see Fig. 1).

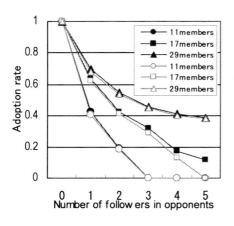

FIG. 1. Adoption rate of a proposal in case of two followers in supporters. *Outlined marks* indicate cases with the 2/3 majority rule and the other marks indicate cases with the 1/2 majority rule. From Adachi et al. (2003). Copyright 2003 by Shakai-gijutsu. Reprinted by permission

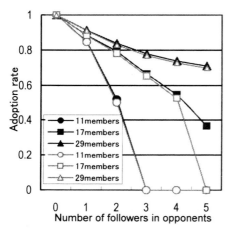

FIG. 2. Adoption rate of a proposal in case of four followers in supporters. *Outlined marks* indicate cases with the 2/3 majority rule and the other marks indicate cases with the 1/2 majority rule. From Adachi et al. (2003). Copyright 2003 by Shakai-gijutsu. Reprinted by permission

In each case of three and four followers in supporters, saturated models were significant as the case of two followers ($G^2 = 113.9$, $df = 10$, $p < 0.0001$; $G^2 = 158.2$, $df = 10$, $p < 0.0001$, respectively). These models include significant three-way interactions of adoption rate with decision rules and group size ($\chi^2 = 21.52$, $df = 2$; $\chi^2 = 31.48$, $df = 2$), with decision rules and the number of followers in opponents ($\chi^2 = 38.64$, $df = 5$; $\chi^2 = 83.5$, $df = 5$), and with group size and the followers number ($\chi^2 = 1164.8$, $df = 10$; $\chi^2 = 1353.2$, $df = 10$). Decision rules ($\chi^2 = 12.07$, $df = 1$; $\chi^2 = 19.14$, $df = 1$), group rules ($\chi^2 = 2714.9$, $df = 2$; $\chi^2 = 3827.8$, $df = 2$), and the number of followers in opponents ($\chi^2 = 7464.4$, $df = 5$; $\chi^2 = 7193.6$, $df = 5$) are all associated with adoption rate (all p values < 0.0001).

The effects of decision rules were found except in cases with one follower in supporters. The different effects of decision rules seemed to be due to the number zero of adoption rate which appeared in the case of the 17-member group (see Figs. 1 and 2). From the supporters' perspective, in the case of groups with 11 members, they are required to win more than 2.33 opponents (3 opponents, virtually) for adoption of a proposal. However, when 2/3 majority rule is applied, they cannot win the required members. The reason why they cannot is because there are only from 0 to 2 "floating voters" (i.e., opportunists in opponents) if the 6 opponents in a group with 11 members have from 3 to 5 followers in them. The same is true of 17-member groups. The number of opportunistic opponents that supporters in 17-member groups need to win is 4 when 2/3 majority rule is applied, but if there are more than 5 followers (6 members altogether including a proponent) in opponents, the number required cannot be won.

Based on this discussion we limited the number of followers in opponents to 0–4, and examined whether factor of decision rules is still significantly associated with adoption rate and other factors using a 2 (decision rules) × 3 (group size) × 5 (number of followers in opponents) × 2 (frequency of adoption) log-linear analysis within each case of 2–4 followers in supporters. The analysis indicated that a model included 3 (group size) × 5 (number of followers in opponents) × 2 (frequency of adoption) three-way interactions is significant ($G^2 = 4.91$, $df = 30$, $p = 1.00$; $G^2 = 2.88$, $df = 30$, $p = 1.00$; $G^2 = 0.94$, $df = 30$, $p = 1.00$, respectively). Adoption rate significantly interacts with group size and with the number of followers in opponents (all p values < 0.0001).

Discussion

The purpose of this study is to examine a conventional procedure which encourages the formation of a *majority*, and the influence of the formation of the *majority* on the adoption of proposals. In particular, we focus on speech motivation, decision rules, and group size because they seem to be major factors in forming *majorities*. In summary, the following are the results from our simulation.

In the case that many supporters of a proposal made remarks in succession while only one follower in opponents made a remark, the proposal was adopted with more than 40% probability at least. When there were four followers in supporters, the probability increased to about 90%. It shows the difficulty to kill the proposal in the situation that he/she is almost out on a limb. Under the circumstances that there are many opportunists in opponents, it is hard for an opponent to be supported by those who do not express their attitude by remarks. In the case that there are many followers in supporters, most remarks in the meeting will be occupied by the opinions of the supporters, and almost no opportunistic opponents will have a chance to make any remarks (i.e., they are not motivated to make a remark).

To reduce the adoption of a proposal, it is important to increase followers of opponents. However, provided that there are at least two followers of supporters, our study shows that the contribution to the reduction of proposal adoption by increased followers of opponents lessens as the group size grows. Especially when the group has 29 members, this phenomenon becomes most apparent. When there is a group with 29 members including more than two followers in supporters, the proposal is adopted with more than 40% probability even if there are the same or more followers in opponents. The simulation suggests that proposals have higher possibility of adoption as the group size grows, because opinions of opponents are likely to fall into obscurity while supporters' opinions appear stronger.

Change Decision Rules

In this simulation, we found that each member's motivation to speak out and group size are influential factors in the adoption of proposals, but we did not find an effect of decision rules. As explained previously, for adoption of proposals in the group with 11 members, supporters are required to win more than 1 opponent over to their side under 1/2 majority rule and they need to win more than 3 opponents under 2/3 majority rule. In the case of a group with 17 members, supporters are required to win more than 1 opponent to their side under 1/2 majority rule and they need to win more than 4 opponents under 2/3 majority rule. In the case of a group with 29 members, supporters are required to win more than 1 opponent over to their side under 1/2 majority rule and more than 6 opponents under 2/3 majority rule.

On the other hand, we checked with a number of nonspeakers in opponents of each simulation who did not make any remarks at all. In most cases in which only nonspeakers of opponents were left, the number of these opponents, as mentioned above, supporters want to win, exceeded the number required for the majority rule of 2/3 (e.g., in the case of group with 29 members including 4 followers in supporters and 4 followers in opponents, more than 6 nonspeakers in opponents are left with a 73.6% probability and the probability is the adoption rate of proposals in this case). Therefore, it can be said that almost all cases in this simulation clear the standards of the 2/3majority rule, and standards of the 1/2 majority rule did not function. It is necessary to elucidate whether the 1/2 majority rule is appropriate for the adoption of proposals in the situation where many members will not make remarks.

To avoid the emergence of a *majority* or to minimize the influence of it as much as possible, the following parliamentary procedure may be effective; (a) ask all members to make remarks. If it is difficult for all of the members to do so, (b) balance remarks between supporters and opponents based on the number in each side. (c) Avoid repetition of similar remarks. (d) Limit the number and time of speech of each member. Points (b) to (d) are incorporated into Robert's rules (Robert et al. 2000). Regarding (a) and (b), in the case of a business meeting, it should be arranged for subordinates to make remarks ahead of time to their supervisor, because we cannot eliminate the possibility that conformity, a factor in group dynamics, will function.

Even if the above rules are respected in meetings, the procedure of supporting a *majority* in votes could happen. What would the opponents do if they were asked to raise their hands to show their disapproval in the situation in which they know they are expected to support the proposal? Such a procedure might be used as if to encourage opponents to express their disapproval (at least it can show there are opponents) of the proposal, however, the result would usually be the very reverse. For the opponents, especially opportunists who are unwilling to speak out voluntarily, the "show-of-hands" voting is hard to reflect their opinions.

Thus there are important implications in changing the vote methods according to the importance of matters. Although the effects of decision rules are not clear in this study, we can take Robert's rules as an example which ask members to change decision rule from 1/2 to 2/3 majority rule based on the understanding that adoption standards should be more severe.

Right to Speak and Level of Conformity

The purposes of this study are to show systematically how decision procedures in meetings affect adoption rates of a proposal and to propose some procedures that are effective to counter pressure to accept (in some cases anti-social) proposals. However, all of our results cannot be generalized. What remains to be studied is as follows:

In this study, it was assumed that the speaker could make remarks only once in a meeting and discussion time (i.e., the length of a meeting) is limited to the accumulation of speech time of all members. However, the same member is likely to make remarks repeatedly in an actual meeting; the opportunity to speak is not always once per member and temporal conditions change according to the situation. Moreover, the repeated speech of the same speakers could play a role in pressuring others to conform to them, and at the same time, it could result in a monopoly of time and decrease other members' motivation and chances to make remarks within the allotted time. These must affect the voting on the adoption of proposals. It goes without saying that the extent of time restriction is deeply related to the matter of time monopoly.

Speech opportunity is also related to the right to speak. In this study, it is presumed implicitly that members make speeches in a sequence and alternately without being disturbed by the other members (smooth adjustment among members). However, in natural conversation, it is often that others disturb speech and speakers consciously or unconsciously decide who will be the next speaker and what should be talked about subsequently (Psathas 1995, Yamada and Yoshii 1991). We can easily imagine that blocking the speech of opponents and transferring the voice to supporters repeatedly facilitates forming a *majority*. It indicates strongly that the position and power relationships of the members should be taken into consideration when addressing the matter of rights of speech.

In addition, it was assumed in our study that the members had the same level of pressure while voting. According to social impact theory (Kameda and Nidaira 1993, Latane and Wolf 1981), however, social influence is a function of the strength, the immediacy (spacious and temporal distance), and number of people (or, more precisely, sources) present. In future study, dealing with the issue of group conformity and opinion change, those three factors, such as additional influence by accumulation of opinions, should be considered.

Acknowledgments. The authors are grateful to Dr. Jinmin Wang of the Research Institute of Science and Technology for Society for providing some useful ideas. This research is a part of work at the Research Institute of Science and Technology for Society.

References

Adachi N, Ishikawa M (2003) Pitfalls of decision making [in Japanese]. In: Okamoto KE, Konno H (eds) Social psychology of the risk management of accidents. Shin-yo-sya, Tokyo, pp 157–186

Adachi N, Ishikawa M, Okamoto KE (2003) Motivation styles to speak out, decision rules, and group size as determinants of decision making [in Japanese]. Syakai-gijutsu Kenkyu 1:278–287

Ikeda K (1993) Psychology of image of society [in Japanese]. Saiensu-sya, Tokyo

Kameda T (1996) Procedural influence in consensus formation: evaluating group decision making from a social choice perspective. In: Witte EH, Davis JH (eds) Understanding group behavior, vol 1: consensual action by small groups. Understanding group behavior. Lawrence Erlbaum, Hillsdale, NJ, pp 137–161

Kameda T (1997) Quest for wisdom of group decision making [in Japanese]. Kyoritsu, Tokyo

Kameda T, Nidaira I (1993) An analysis of sequential consensus formation processes: a computer simulation of Nemawashi procedure [in Japanese]. Paper presented at the 41st annual meeting of the Japanese Group Dynamics Association, Kumamoto, Japan

Kameda T, Sugimori S (1995) Procedural influence in two-step group decision making: power of local majorities in consensus formation. Journal of Personality and Social Psychology 69:865–876

Latané B, Wolf S (1981) The social impact of majorities and minorities. Psychological Review 88:438–453

Noelle-Neumann E (1993) The spiral silence (2nd ed). University of Chicago Press

Psathas G (1995) Conversation analysis: the study of talk-in-interaction. Sage

Robert III HM, Evans WJ, Honemann DH et al (2000) Robert's rules of order newly revised, 10th ed. Perseus, Cambridge, MA

Saeki Y (1980) Logic of decision making [in Japanese]. University of Tokyo Press, Tokyo

Stasser G (1992) Information salience and the discovery of hidden profiles by decision-making groups: a "thought experiment." Organizational Behavior and Human Decision Processes 52:156–181

Stasser G, Titus W (1985) Pooling of unshared information in group decision making: Biased information sampling during discussion. Journal of Personality and Social Psychology 48:1467–1478

Stasser G, Taylor LA, Hanna C (1989) Information sampling in structured and unstructured discussions of three- and six-person groups. Journal of Personality and Social Psychology 57:67–78

Yamada T, Yoshii H (1991) Ethnomethodology of exclusion and discrimination [in Japanese]. Shin-yo-sya, Tokyo

17. Openness: A Key to Good Team Performance

Minako Fujiie[1], Sigehisa Tsuchiya[2], Akira Tanabe, and
Koichi Sekimizu[3]

Introduction

We have carried out research and activities aimed at improvement of team
performance of nuclear power plant (NPP) operators in Tokyo Electric Power
Company (TEPCO). Every operator belongs to a team, and operation jobs are
performed by teams. It is very important to improve team performance not only
by enhancing each member's technical skill but also by promoting good communication among team members.

Training Program for Improvement of Team Performance (TIPS)

In preceding research on the team performance of NPP operators, it became
apparent that some teams communicate well, and others do not (Fujiie 1996). We
also know from research that a team whose communication among its members
is good in normal situations can demonstrate high performance in an emergency.
We then developed a training program called TIPS to improve communication
in normal situations. TIPS is designed to make operators reaffirm and realize the
importance of communication and teamwork. It consists of a video case study
and game work, and allows all trainees to participate.

Effects of TIPS

Almost all NPP operators in TEPCO participated in TIPS training as part of their
scheduled training program.

---

[1] Tokyo Electric Power Company, Yokohama 230-8510, Japan; fujiie-m@rd.tepco.co.jp
[2] Chiba Institute of Technology, Narashino, Chiba 275-0016, Japan
[3] Aitel Corporation, Kawasaki 210-0862, Japan

It is difficult to evaluate the effects of TIPS objectively. The decrease in the number of problem cases is not effective because the number of cases is quite few, and it is quite difficult to catch the infinitesimal improvement of team states. Therefore, a questionnaire was used to determine participant sentiment as a subjective evaluation of TIPS.

The answers showed that TIPS acquired, in general, favorable comment and was effective in respect of making participants reaffirm the importance of communication and teamwork. Three questions and their responses are shown in Fig. 1.

Q1. Did you reaffirm or realize the importance of communication and team-work by TIPS?

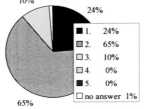

1. realize well
2. realize
3. don't know
4. cannot realize
5. cannot realize at all

Q2. Do you think TIPS is useful to improve communication and teamwork?

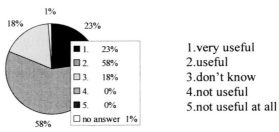

1.very useful
2.useful
3.don't know
4.not useful
5.not useful at all

Q3. Do you want to take more training program like TIPS?

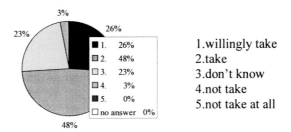

1.willingly take
2.take
3.don't know
4.not take
5.not take at all

FIG. 1. Questions asked of participants and their responses

Investigation of the Ideal Team

Background and Purpose

TIPS improves team performance by indirectly making participants aware of the importance of communication. In the next step, we decided to develop a training program in which we proposed "what team state is good".

Clarification of Concept

We clarified our concept of an "ideal team" by the following measures:

1. Brainstorming among BWR Training Center (BTC) instructors and people with experience of operators, etc.
2. Questionnaire to all NPP operators in TEPCO.

As a result, 11 items were extracted as requirements for an ideal team:

1. Directions and chain of command are clear.
2. Role assignment is clear.
3. Team members are active (much opinion comes out).
4. Advice, indication, and suggestion can be performed freely.
5. A key man who encourages the team is present.
6. There is no strong authority gradient.
7. Team leader acts as the members' spokesperson and is their representative to outside entities.
8. Every team member has an opportunity to understand each other's character.
9. Good advice from outside is accepted.
10. Learns other teams' good points.
11. There is an innovative education system in the team.

We added a further 3 items from free descriptive replies to the questionnaire:

12. Information is shared within the team.
13. Target and purpose of job are clear.
14. There is a team atmosphere that backs up and supports individual team members.

The above items comprise the concrete expression of the requirements. In order to develop the exercise model we must arrange these items in several dimensions, and determine which dimension is the most important. Therefore, we examined the work of Roth (1999) and Montgomery et al. (1992).

Roth (1999) advocated six dimensions to measure the teamwork for NPP operator teams. They were information exchange, communication, supporting behavior, team initiative/leadership, task coordination, and adaptability.

Montgomery et al. (1996) developed six dimensions to measure the teamwork of NPP operator teams. They were communications, openness, task coordination, team spirit, maintenance of task focus in transitions, and adaptability.

We selected five dimensions from their research as follows:

1. Communication
2. Openness
3. Cooperation
4. Leadership
5. Adaptability

We arranged the above 14 requirements for the ideal team into five dimensions as shown in Fig. 2.

An arrow drawn from adaptability to communication, for example, means that if adaptability is improved, it is expected that communication will also be improved. The numbers in each node (dimension) represent the number of arrows from and to the node, respectively. It suggests that improving a dimension that emits many arrows effectively enhances team performance.

In Fig. 2, leadership, adaptability, and openness have the most emitted arrows. Therefore, by improving these three dimensions, it is expected that we can improve team performance effectively.

Among the three dimensions we focus on openness, because of the following reasons:

1. From the results of the questionnaire, operators selected three items as being important. These are (1) that directions and chain of command are clear, (2) that team members are active (much opinion comes out), and (3) that advice, indication, and suggestion can be performed freely. Two of these three belong to the dimension of openness.

2. It is pointed out that a lack of openness is one major cause of many organizational accidents.

Therefore, we paid particular attention to openness in making the ideal team, and developed a means to improve openness.

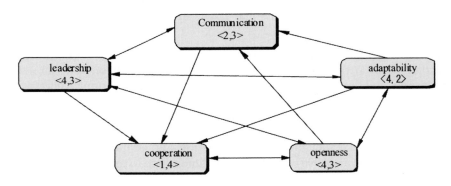

FIG. 2. The five dimensions of the ideal team and the links between them

"King of Fisherman"—A Policy Exercise That Aims to Improve Openness

Openness

Openness is essential to create shared mental models that allow team members to predict the needs of the task and anticipate the actions of other team members in order to adjust their behavior accordingly. Creating and maintaining open communication among team members is a most difficult challenge, although almost everybody is aware of its importance. This is because, in most cases, openness is merely an espoused theory of action and not a theory in use.

The most commonly recognized aspect of openness is the freedom to speak one's mind. Senge (1990) stated that there are two different aspects of openness: participative and reflective. While participative openness leads to people speaking out, reflective openness leads to people looking inward. Reflective openness is typified by the attitude, "I may be wrong and the other person may be right." It involves not just examining our own ideas, but mutually examining the thinking of others. Unless the two forms of openness are integrated, the behavior of being open will not produce real openness.

In response, we developed the policy exercise named "King of Fisherman" (KOF) and introduced it to the training program for the NPP operators in TEPCO.

The objective of this policy exercise is to open the mind of operators toward participative and reflective openness. The exercise provides them with insights into their theory-in-use and into any discrepancies from their espoused theory, as well as into the causes of any unawareness of discrepancies. In addition, it provides operators with an appreciation of how they may be personally responsible for creating the defensive pattern that they decry in their organization.

Outline of KOF

The outline for the KOF exercise is as follows: a fishing fleet works in a stormy sea, and the fleet consists of a mother ship and five fishing boats. The radar screen of the mother ship is shown in Fig. 3. The boats are located in a line in the lower left of the figure. Each boat is operated using the operation board on the right side of the figure. The fishing fleet aims to catch as many fish as possible while overcoming obstacles and minimizing miss operations.

Composition of KOF

The operators participated in KOF training in their own teams. Two persons, a leader (Shift Supervisor) and a subleader (Assistant Shift Supervisor), operate the mother ship and command the fishing boats. A member (operator) controls each fishing boat. The mother ship can see extensive ocean space on the radar screen. This simulates the daily Shift Supervisor situation in which they can grasp

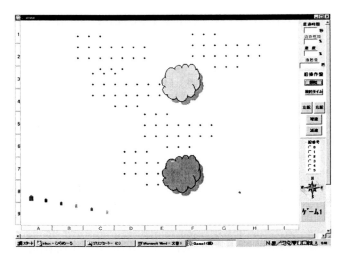

FIG. 3. The radar screen of the mother ship in the King of Fisherman exercise

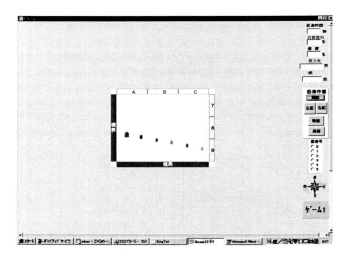

FIG. 4. The radar screen of a fishing boat in the King of Fisherman exercise

wider information than operators. As shown in Fig. 4, the fishing boats can see only a narrow ocean space on the radar screen, although all things close to them are visible. This simulates the situation of the daily operators in which they can grasp narrow but precise information. On the radar screen, a fine blue point represents a Pacific saury (1 point each). The red circle at the lower right is a sea bream (10 points each). Pacific saury and sea bream can only be caught by the fishing boats. In addition, tuna (20 points each) are expressed with a green circle, and can only be caught by the mother ship. However, tuna are not visible by radar unless the mother ship comes close to them.

The form of the gray cloud in Fig. 3 represents a typhoon. If a boat enters into this typhoon and cannot escape from it within a limited time, the number of fish caught falls to zero. This is because the catch must be disposed of in order to avoid sinking. If boats collide with each other, the catch is also reduced to zero for the same reason.

Fish and typhoons are moved automatically. In order to increase the amount of fish caught, it is necessary to frequently exchange active information or opinions between the mother ship and the fishing boats. This corresponds to participative openness. Furthermore, the mother ship must listen to opinions and ideas from fishing boats. If the ideas of the mother ship are different from those of the fishing boats, is it possible for mother ship to doubt its own ideas. If this is so, the mother ship shows reflective openness. The exercise is carried out three times. The first two exercises are performed to check participative openness. In the third exercise, the radar of a mother ship is intentionally damaged in the middle of the exercise. This is to examine whether the mother ship has reflective openness.

The time taken for one exercise is about 10 min. A discussion is held between each exercise, and at the last stage a debriefing is performed. During discussions and debriefing, a facilitator makes participating members aware of the importance of openness, and urge to mastery, by intervening naturally.

System Configuration of KOF

The system configuration of KOF consists of seven personal computers (PCs) connected with a local area network (LAN). Among these, one PC is assigned as a server. One more PC is assigned as the mother ship and the remaining five PCs are for fishing boats. The positions of fish and typhoons are calculated on the server. This information is sent to each PC through the LAN. The information of the position of boats and the fish caught is brought together to the server.

Application of KOF

The KOF was applied to the Human Factor Training curriculum of the operators in the TEPCO nuclear power plants in 2002 fiscal year. Almost all NPP operators played the KOF, giving a total number of participants of about 600.

Response of the Participants (selected from sentiments written just after the exercise)

- The participants were enthusiastic about the exercise.
- The nature of the daily tasks of the teams was apparent in the exercise.
- The participants were able to grasp the characteristics of the other team members.

- Participants were given good opportunity to consider the team performance.
- The lecture was able to be understood and then the exercise was able to mastered in practice.
- The above feedback shows that good results were obtained using KOF.

An Example of Team Performance

It is possible to evaluate the openness of the team by analyzing communications during the exercise from the following points:

1. The members informed the leader with data such as the position of tuna and requested the information necessary for fishing from the leader.
2. The leader directed the members properly, and collected sufficient information from the members.

The participative openness in the team can be evaluated by the above two points.

Table 1 shows a checklist that is used to evaluate team performance during the confusing situation in which the radar of the mother ship is faulty and the information from the mother ship is incorrect. In the checklist, the items from numbers 1 to 5 are related to catching sea bream. Because the sea bream is valuable (10 points), the leader almost always informs the members of the location

TABLE 1. An example of evaluation results after the radar of a mother ship fails

No	Items	Evaluation	Person in charge
1	Having expressed that sea bream were not seen	○	Operator
2	Having recognized the possibility that sea bream cannot be taken	○	Leader
3	Abandon taking of sea bream	△	Leader
4	Having reported to the leader when sea bream were taken	△	Operator
5	Interest was shown in the position of where sea bream were taken	×	
6	Having expressed to the leader that Pacific sauries were not where the operator was directed to	○	Operator
7	Having been ordered to move from the place where fishing for Pacific sauries was successful	○	Operator
8	In the situation in 7, the operator gave his opinion without following the leader's direction	×	Operator
9	Operator stayed at the place where he was able to find Pacific sauries, although the instructions of the leader indicated that there were no fish at that location	×	Operator
10	Situation in which the operator pointed out the leader's error		Operator
11	Having recognized the possibility that Pacific sauries cannot be taken if operators follow the leader's directions	○	Leader
12	Having stopped directions regarded the position of Pacific sauries	×	Leader
13	Having taken the discussion time	○	Leader
14	Identification of the cause of problems	×	

of where to find it. However, in this confusing situation, the members cannot find it by following the directions from the leader.

The items from numbers 6 to 12 are related to catching Pacific sauries. As many Pacific sauries move together, the members move around to catch them without information from the leader. These items evaluate the members' capability to point out the incorrectness of the leader.

Item 13 evaluates the leader's capability to pause the game and to confirm the status in the confusing situation. Item 14 evaluates the team capability to identify the reason for the confusion.

Based on this checklist, examples of the observations and evaluation results are shown below.

- Some teams reached the conclusion that the radars of the fishing boats were incorrect, without thorough inspection, when the radar of the mother ship broke down and information discrepancies appeared between the mother ship and the fishing boats. This was frequently observed on the teams that had a strong authority gradient.
- After the radar of the mother ship became faulty, fishing boats followed the directions of the leader. However, they could not find sea bream. They expressed that there were no sea bream at the point to which they were directed, and they went looking for sea bream in other locations. Three fishing boats caught sea bream at locations they found themselves. Only one fishing boat informed the leader of finding sea bream, without any location information. The leader misunderstood that one fishing boat's radar was correct and others were in error. Later directions from the leader were based on this mistake, and as a result, caused many problems.
- The mother ship did not ask for any information from the fishing boats and the fishing boats did not give any information to the mother ship. Even in such a situation, the leader seemed to think that he was receiving precise information from the fishing boats. This situation caused poor team performance. As shown in this example, team members were often unaware of the actual situation of their own openness.

Discussion and Conclusion

From the information of the KOF exercise and the daily work of participants, it became clear that teams that had a strong authority gradient in daily work also showed a strong authority gradient during the exercise. This means that the attitude of the participants during the KOF exercise reflects their team state in a normal situation. In conclusion, it is expected that a policy training exercise such as KOF is useful for improving team performance, and transferring feedback from the exercise to real-world jobs.

For further research, we are planning to analyze data from the KOF exercise in detail to classify the behavior of the participants. It should be useful to link the data pattern to participant openness in order to make each participant realize his/her own openness.

References

Fujiie M (1996) Development of training program 'TIPS' for improvement of team performance. Proceedings of IERE Workshop Human Factors in Nuclear Power Plants, pp 27–30

Montgomery et al (1992) Team skills evaluation criteria for nuclear power plant control room crews (working draft available in the NRC Public Document Room)

Roth EM (1999) Approaches to measuring team performance: recent research results

Senge PM (1990) The fifth discipline. The art and practice of the learning organization

18. A Business Game with Social Consequences

Joseph Wolfe[1]

The ISAGA 2003 conference has as its main theme the "Social Contributions and Responsibilities of Simulation and Gaming." This theme indicates the field can and should make an effort to improve society through its work. It is accepted that games are effective teaching devices (Wolfe 1997, Keys and Wolfe 1990) so it is reasonable to believe they can be used to bring about desirable social outcomes if the game's structure incorporates ethical and social lessons.

Business games have obtained wide acceptance in North America's business schools (Faria 1998) and are slowly gaining acceptance in other countries (Wolfe 1993). Given the pervasiveness of business gaming, it can be used, if properly designed and administered, to expose players to many of the ethical and social dilemmas they will face in their business careers. Unfortunately many games, especially those dealing with the top management levels of firms where such decisions once made have the greatest long-term impact on the company's constituencies, are sadly deficient (Wolfe and Fritzsche 1998). This chapter presents how a recently developed top management business game challenges its players to face the realities of decisions that manifest social consequences.

Background

Those in business leadership positions must deal with a wide range of conflicting constituencies or stakeholders. Using this approach, those who have an interest in the firm's success are often at odds with each other (Friedlander and Pickle 1968). The company's owners or shareholders want strong financial returns; the employees want good pay, kind supervision, and job satisfaction; customers want quality goods and creditors want liquidity, while the community and the government want social responsibility and lawful behavior. Not all these needs can be met and in the haste of everyday business not all groups have an equal ability to demand that their needs be satisfied. Thus, the company's leaders can, and often

[1] Experiential Adventures LLC, Tulsa, OK 74133-4206, USA; Jwolfe8125@aol.com

do, serve the needs of some more than others. Given a degree of discretionary latitude, managers without strong moral or ethical compasses can easily make decisions that intentionally or unintentionally harm various groups less able to make their needs felt.

Global Business Game (Wolfe 2003) is a computer-based top management game that focuses on the strategic decisions made by managers in a worldwide company making television sets. The game's design was based on a content analysis of the major textbooks associated with the fields of strategic management and international business (Wolfe and Rogé 1997, Klein et al. 1993). Thus the game's model and its details were driven by the field's definition of what must be learned about the academic discipline rather than upon the author's own world view. Players, based on the game complexity level chosen by the game's administrator, have a number of options placed before them by the game's opening scenario. Business can be conducted in up to six different countries and there are a number of ways that the firm can try to obtain long-term success. In the course of their activities, a number of optimizing decisions must be made even though incomplete information accompanies each decision-making situation. When this occurs, players must let their conscience or ethics be their guides, thus providing them and their instructors, through in-class discussions and game debriefings, to probe the issues involved.

Critical Incidents

The Global Business Game features ten critical incidents or vignettes requiring executive action. Some involve strategies for changing the firm's structure; others deal with market entry tactics, while five feature issues that raise ethical issues and the social consequences of decisions made by a firm's top management group. During the game, the Game Administrator can invoke up to three critical incidents per quarter. When a response is called for, firms must choose one of four options that are presented to them. The options themselves all "solve" the problem but one response is the "best" one as it guarantees the firm either the greatest amount of long-term damage control or the greatest amount of conformity to the spirit of the law under which the firm must operate. The remaining alternatives are less satisfactory and can actually harm the firm's performance while the ideal response improves its performance. This is because, depending on the alternative chosen, the algorithms relating to the critical incident may change in positive or negative degrees depending on their propriety. Any algorithmic effects are the strongest in the most recent quarters with all effects dissipated within 1 year.

Table 1 summarizes the dilemmas presented in one of the game's societally related critical incidents and Table 2 provides an example of how the critical incidents are presented in the Player's Manual (Fig. 1). An analysis of each alternative is presented in the Game Administrator's Manual while explaining the propriety of each response.

TABLE 1. Critical incidents with ethical and societal implications

Incident	Title	Issue(s)
1	Bill Fisher's new Salary bonus system	How to motivate a sales force but using a bonus system that may discriminate against older sales representatives.
2	You have to get their attention	Gaining access to market channel participants but with a method they may violate anti-trust and fair competition practices.
3	The new automaton technician	Dealing with a sexually charged factory environment while attempting to implement an equal opportunity employment policy.
4	Ferdie Milano fights back	Company damage control and the proper response to an age discrimination lawsuit.
5	"Hell No to This Baksheesh Stuff!"	Dealing with what constitutes a bribe or improper payment to a foreign agent as well as how to conduct business in cultures where this is an acceptable business practice.

Critical Incident 6 "Hell no to this Baksheesh Stuff!"

You have recently sent Robert Frazier, one of your country liaison executives, around the world with your operations manager, Joseph Graham, to scout possible new plant locations. They are now summarizing their estimation of the prospects for building new plants overseas.

FIG. 1. Player's manual critical incident presentation

"As far as I can see, we have a large number of choices, especially in Asia, which is also closest to our Hong Kong supplier." Bob Frazier continued, "Our labor costs would be very low and the infrastructure available to us would be adequate for an assembly operation like ours."

"I have to agree with you on that," Joe Graham responded. "But I have a real problem with some other things, especially with the ethics that some of those foreign businessmen showed me. And I thought it was even worse in the case of some of the government people we met."

"Well, you'll just have to get used to that . . . they've operated this way for years and that's how it's done over there." Bob then leaned across the table to emphasize his point. "Even more, it's good to get on their good side, and a little bit of *baksheesh* can save you a whole lot of time and money in the long run."

This comment seemed to trigger an anger that had been boiling inside Joe all during the trip. "I don't care if you call it *blat*, *baksheesh*, or *grease*! It's all illegal, and I don't think we should have any part of it. It just galls me that we have to line the pocket of some puny little bureaucrat just to process some papers that he's supposed to do in the first place! I know there has to be a law somewhere against this."

On that note a rambling discussion ensued. It was pointed out that the U.S. Foreign Corrupt Practices Act of 1977 allows for personal payments to foreign government and company officials as gratuities for performing "nondiscretionary" services or engaging in activities that are appropriately within the scope of their job descriptions. In this case, a small payment is not illegal. It was pointed out, however, that problems arise over what are considered "small" versus "large" payments, and what are "nondiscretionary" versus "discretionary" actions or are actions outside the scope of the official's strict job duties.

Given that your company may eventually build a plant in a country where you will face this problem what position do you think your company should take?

Responses

1. Avoid building any new plants in Asia, where the practice of *baksheesh* is widespread.
2. Avoid breaking any American laws by conducting all negotiations on plant sites in a "neutral" nation such as Liechtenstein, Vanuatu, the Netherlands Antilles, or the Cayman Islands, where such activities are not illegal or are not monitored closely. This option would add the equivalent of US$250 000 to the cost of construction your next plant in either Japan or Thailand and would be amortized along with the original investment expense.
3. Be practical and follow the "rules of the road" and deal with the problem on a plant-by-plant and country-by-country basis. This response would cause your Miscellaneous Account to be debited the equivalent of US$75 000 for each plant subsequently built in Thailand or Japan.
4. Hire local middlemen to represent your company in all negotiations with government officials and relevant businesspersons. This option would add US$80 000 to the cost of building any APEC factory.

Results

A comparative examination of the economic versus socially correct repercussions of the various alternatives available to the game's top managers for all critical incidents reveals that in three of the five cases the most socially enlightened response is the least economically attractive alternative. In the two remaining cases the socially correct response is the second-most economically attractive option. The long-term results of each decision, while indeterminate for critical incident 5, always weigh against the choice that is the most socially responsible. Thus, the firm choosing what is best for society, or society's implementation through governmental laws and regulations of the social goods of equal employment opportunity, freedom from sexual harassment, and the protection of the elderly in the workplace, is punished economically. Given the short-term and long-term gains players can realize by not pursuing the socially correct alternative, it can easily be seen why they, and their real-world counterparts, make decisions that injure various social classes and individuals.

Capacity Options

A number of strategic options are available to firms in The Global Business Game. Each option has societal consequences with some being more pervasive than others. One strategic decision that must be immediately faced by the firms in this industry is one of obtaining low manufacturing costs. Two of the ways that real-world companies deal with this problem is to seek lower-costing raw materials or to automate away each finished product's labor component. The most common method, and the one with the greatest societal impact, however, is to seek lower hourly labor costs by either forcing concessions from the plant's workers or by simply moving all or a great proportion of the firm's production facilities to countries with weak unions and/or low hourly wages. The flight of factories from the United States to Mexico, and then onto various Pacific Rim countries, exemplifies this strategy in action where none of America's television sets are now made in the United States and almost all are made in the Pacific Rim.

   While this strategy results in lower-priced goods to the consumer and potentially higher rewards to the firm's stockholders, severe losses are suffered by the home country's wage earners through lost employment. Additionally, society at large suffers through the loss of revenues on personal and corporate income and property taxes. Managers making capacity location decisions have to wrestle with the company-related short-term disadvantages and long-term gains associated with the array of options they have. They also have to deal with how their particular capacity decisions affect those societies that are near and far away. The following example illustrates how players in The Global Business Game experience the results of eight different capacity acquisition options.

The Situation

This scenario entails a Japanese firm wishing to enter the relatively wealthy and homogeneous American market for mid-sized television sets. The company presently has enough capacity to serve its own near-term Japanese market, but any increase in its overall sales, and the retention of its ability to compete in this global industry, requires an increase in its plant and equipment. There are several ways this expansion can be accomplished. All entail relatively high initial monetary and managerial investments, however, with varying company-related direct and indirect costs and long-term consequences to the countries within which the investment would reside. The dilemma facing the firm is one of placing this capacity "correctly" given the social consequences it may suffer as well as the costs associated with those consequences given the impact they have on the company's ability to remain profitable and competitive.

Eight capacity-expansion options, from a variety of options available, are presented in Table 2. Most of the options more or less decrease its commitment to its home country of Japan while increasing its commitment to foreign production operations. Regardless of which option is chosen, each one has its own set of economic advantages and disadvantages. Using objective, quantitative decision-making criteria, all have costs and benefits, although the problem is confounded by the fact these costs and benefits are not completely calculable and therefore their consequences are not completely predictable. For this example, the results are presented after running the simulation for seven quarters or decision rounds while keeping all other decisions such as product prices, sales staff incentives, and research and development budgets constant across all firms.

The Results

The cumulative profits reported in Table 3 indicate the comparative virtues of a firm having a low-cost advantage in this type of industry which is a mature

TABLE 2. Japanese capacity expansion options

Option	Action
1	Supply the American market's needs through an expanded Japanese plant.
2	Supplement the current Japanese plant through capacity obtained from a new plant built in Thailand.
3	Supplement the current Japanese plant through capacity obtained from a new plant built in Mexico.
4	Supplement the current Japanese plant through capacity obtained from a new plant built in the United States.
5	Eliminate the Japanese plant and transfer its capacity to a new, larger plant built in Thailand.
6	Eliminate the Japanese plant, build a new plant in Mexico and transfer Japan's capacity to the Mexican plant.
7	Maintain the Japanese plant and build new plants in the United States and Mexico
8	Liquidate Japan's factory and build new plants in Mexico and Thailand.

TABLE 3. Expansion option earnings performances

Option	Total profit (millions)
1	¥1005.0
2	¥200.0
3	¥315.0
4	¥605.0
5	¥875.0
6	¥155.0
7	¥210.0
8	¥1005.0

oligopoly. Firms that avoided Japan's high labor cost environment by building plants in the low-cost countries of Mexico and Thailand, in combination with low shipping costs into the American and Japanese market caused by their proximity to those markets, brought about higher long-term profits. All firms absorbed early high switch-over and/or startup costs, but once these capacity adjustments had been made those moving all or most of their capacity out of Japan reaped long-term benefits.

Although the bottom-line results indicate the benefits that primarily accrue to the firm's owners, society itself obtains rewards and damages from each company's action. These rewards and damages can be quantified through wages and tax revenues gained or lost given the society or country closest to the firm's sphere of activity.

Conclusions

Business instructors who want to expose their students to the dilemmas facing the socially responsible firm can use appropriately designed simulations to accomplish this purpose. The Global Business Game possesses a number of avenues by which this can be accomplished. Players, in the name of company profits, are often tempted, as is the case for real-world managers, to put the firm's economic needs before the needs of society's other members. The root problems for the predicaments posed in The Global Business Game revolve around which public is more important to the firm, the perceived gain to be obtained by placing the firm first over others, the likelihood that the transgression will be caught and punished, and an inability to completely quantify and qualify the results associated with each alternative. A proper discussion and debriefing by the instructor for the cases given here can do much to highlight the breadth and depth of the issues involved which will hopefully result in ethically and morally correct behavioral guidelines for all players to follow in their business careers.

References

Faria AJ (1998) Business simulation games: current usage levels—an update. Simulation and Gaming 29:295–308

Friedlander F, Pickle H (1968) Components of effectiveness in small organizations. Administrative Science Quarterly 13:289–304

Keys JB, Wolfe J (1990) The role of management games and simulations in education and research. Yearly Review of Management 16:307–336

Klein RD, Fleck RA Jr, Wolfe J (1993) A role for management games in internationalizing the business school curriculum. Journal of Management Education 17:159–173

Wolfe J (1993) A history of business games in English-speaking and post-socialist countries: the origination and diffusion of a management education and development technology. Simulation and Gaming 24:446–463

Wolfe J (1997) The effectiveness of business games in strategic management course work. Simulation and Gaming 28:360–376

Wolfe J (2003) The global business game: a strategic management and international business simulation. South-Western, Mason, OH

Wolfe J, Fritzsche DJ (1998) Teaching business ethics with management and marketing games. Simulation and Gaming 29:44–59

Wolfe J, Rogé JN (1997) Computer-based general management games as strategic management learning environments. Simulation and Gaming 28:360–376

Part IV
Designs and Tools of Simulation and Gaming

19. An Evaluation of Role-Playing Gaming on Reformation Toward Sustainable Rural Society: How to Awaken a Regional Context in Citizens

Shinobu Kitani[1], Kiyoshi Arai[2], Tadashi Hasebe[1],
Noriaki Nomura[3], and Fumihiro Nakano[1]

Background

In the process of regional environmental planning, it is clear that the regional plan should be decided along regional views of the town. The views have been brought about in a relationship between local citizens and regional environments.[4] In such a case, how can we awaken citizens' view of a region in the global wave? We have made a new role-playing gaming simulation of a regional environmental planning process for a small town in Japan, and have already obtained some meaningful results. Our role-playing game is intended to function as an instrument that makes citizens aware of regional views of the town, the base of which we call a regional context. Although a regional context is supposed to be common knowledge to citizens of the town, we consider that the context cannot be described as a set of instrumental knowledge.[5]

The principal feature of our role-playing game is that strangers to the town perform role play as proxies of real citizens, and there is one-to-one correspondence between strangers and citizens. In this study, we make a second run of the game based on the theme, "reflect upon five public enterprises to reform the town", where we provided two indices to measure citizens' awareness in addition to protocol analyses of citizens' feeling toward strangers and their opinions of the planning.

[1] Graduate School of Agricultural Science, Tohoku University, Sendai 981-8555, Japan; skitani@mail.tains.tohoku.ac.jp
[2] Faculty of Social Systems Science, Chiba Institute of Technology, Japan
[3] Graduate School of Engineering, Tohoku University, Japan
[4] We consider these views to come from a mediance, which Bergue (1990) defines as a meaning of relationship between local environment and society concerned.
[5] Polanyi (1966) says some knowledge cannot be informed systematically and calls this tacit knowledge. We regard a regional context as a kind of tacit knowledge.

Outline of the Role-Playing Game

Definition of the Game

Our concept of role-playing gaming is given briefly [see Kitani et al. (2003) for a detailed explanation]. Players who participate in the game are placed in one of two kinds of group. One is a set of real citizens who are living in the same town and the other is a set of virtual players who have never lived in the town and stand in for their corresponding citizens. Real citizens make decisions according to their views of the town. On the other hand, virtual players make decisions based on their individual views, which are expected to be (hopefully largely) different from those of real citizens.

Basic Design of the Game for Regional Planning

Real players are real citizens of the town, where they know each other very well. On the other hand, virtual players are strangers to the town. They are under-graduate students who are living in a big city. These virtual players are informed of the corresponding citizen's visions for the future of the town as well as their socio-economic status through questionnaires in advance, and make an on-the-spot investigation of the town just before the main stage of the game.

The key points regarding the information available to the players are as follows:

- Citizens can only observe the discussion of virtual players, and are prohibited from joining it. After the first discussion, each of the citizens has a chance to give additional information to their virtual player, and then the second discussion is observed.
- Throughout the game, the citizens are not informed of whose roles virtual players fill, except their own.
- Each virtual player is instructed to express their opinions during the discussion by taking in the corresponding real player's socio-economic status, social roles, and their vision of the town. Moreover, they are also clearly instructed to express their own opinions that are not based on the corresponding real player's preference, but rather on their own preference.

The first and third conditions guarantee the independence of the first and second games. The second condition guarantees anonymity of virtual players' opinions for real players. This condition would be necessary for real players not to bring about a feeling of antagonism related to their practical life in the town.

Trial Run and Reconsideration for Improvements

A Pilot Experiment of Our Game

We made a trial run of our regional planning game (RPG) at the town of Kaneyama, which is located in the north-east of Japan's main island of Honshu, in September 2001. There are many historical and traditional buildings in Kaneyama, and the local government has expended much effort in conserving them. Citizens in Kanayama are also cooperative with the government, but they are now confronted with a garbage collection problem, which would have something to do with conserving the historical structures. Under the background of the town, we selected five issues for discussion: (A) global environment, (B) historical features of the town, (C) protecting sanitation, (D) acceptable practices for dumping garbage, and (E) maintenance and management of the collection spot. The first three points are objectives of town planning (what and why) and the latter two are related to the means of planning (how); however, we intentionally did not inform all players of the structure of the issues.

The results are shown in Kitani et al. (2003), in which we analyzed the results from three points of view: citizen's awareness of a regional context, regional environmental learning for citizens, and environmental education for students. After observing student discussions, we found that some citizens who felt a sense of incongruity with students' discussions could not convey their thoughts regarding their lifestyle in the town, and proposed an unconventional idea such as "take care rules" on garbage collection instead of penal regulations for offenders. Citizens also learned the breadth of environmental problems.

Improvements in the Game for Positive Proof of Citizens' Awareness of Regional Views

There are some points to be reconsidered in the Kaneyama RPG. In view of instilling a regional context, they are summed up as follows:

- The issues for discussion were not set up to be connected with a regional context.
- Methods to verify that the RPG facilitates a regional context were subjective.
- Players (both citizens and proxies) had no strongly opposite opinions on each issue.
- Facilitator did not function as a controller of discussion.

We could not determine what issues to which citizens realized a regional context.

The location of Kaneyama gave rise to the first point. That is, this town is among the mountains and citizens there have comparatively few chances to mix with people from large cities and they often view the town from the inside. Therefore, we set up the issues for discussion to make citizens learn the regional environment of the town in connection with the global one. The second point requires us to investigate the change of citizens' image of the town by more objective methods. The third point suggests that a set of citizens was biased, namely, the attributes of participants (real citizens) were similar to each other. According to the fourth point, we should delegate power to the facilitator to handle the discussion. To solve the last point, we must choose relevant citizens allowing for their attributes, especially their occupations and living areas.

Role-Playing Gaming for Awakening a Regional Context Toward Sustainable Rural Society

Discussion Theme and Issues for Discussion

We made a second run of our role-playing gaming. The gaming was planned to clarify how the RPG could contribute to awaken a regional context in citizens. Therefore, we selected a suburb of a rural core city as the subject of our study, where a regional context in citizens would be forgotten because of the wave of urbanization. Miharu town is about 10 km away to the east of Koriyama city with a population of 330 000. The population of Miharu is 19 000 and a considerable number of people conduct farming activities. They are active in renovating and keeping the farm life of the town, which has many traditional facilities and degrees of natural beauty.

The discussion theme in the RPG is "reformation of farm village" allowing for such figures of the town, and pick up five issues for discussion: (A) international cultural exchange, (B) interchange between cities and Miharu town, (C) daily farm life and culture, (D) environmental protection in nature, and (E) farm management to maintain the village. These issues all correspond to public enterprises embarked on by the Miharu town office, namely (A) management of House of Rice Lake (a small town in Wisconsin in the USA which forms a twin town with Miharu), (B) selling land and house for city dwellers (a village "Kamisuki"), (C) management of the center of country life ("Denen-Seikatsu-Kan" for traditional agriculture park), (D) maintenance of rural landscape around Lake Sakura), and (E) support for agricultural corporate bodies (management of herb garden). It should be noted that the former two issues relate to interchanges with outside of the town and the latter three relate to activities within the town. This classification was made in consideration of the first point of reflection.

Sampling of Citizens for Gaming

On the five issues stated above, we must carefully choose citizens as real players. Real players are expected to have various opinions on each issue, considering the last point of reflection. Real players in the game were the following seven citizens:

[1] a 53-year-old housewife who lived in a farmhouse far from the center of the town
[2] a 59-year-old man, manager of the center of country life "Denen-Seikatsu-Kan"
[3] a 60-year-old man, public officer of Miharu town
[4] a 56-year-old man, new citizen who came from a big city to live in Miharu
[5] a 48-year-old woman, mushroom farmer
[6] a 56-year-old man, land owner who lives near the herb garden
[7] a 55-year-old woman, employee of the store at the center of town selling fresh products of Miharu

Works of citizens [4] and [7] have no direct relation to agricultural product activities, citizen [5] has been to Rice Lake, while citizen [1] has not. Citizens [2] and [3] have a duty to be in politically impartial positions. Citizens [5] and [6] live in farm village around Lake Sakura, while citizen [1] is living more than 5 km away from Lake Sakura. These differences in attributes would make them express different opinions on local issues.

Investigation of Citizens' Images on Farm Village

We investigate citizens' images on a farm village at the end of the first and second discussions in the main stage of the RPG. Here we consider that the image can be figured by analytic hierarchy process (AHP) investigation. Our AHP model has two levels. The upper level consists of three criteria: nature and ecology, life and society, and history and culture. At the lower level, four pictures are relevantly picked up from pictures related to five public enterprises stated previously. This investigation system is designed in personal computers.

Procedure of the Game

Table 1 shows the procedure of the game. The procedure is similar to the one used in the trial run at Kaneyama. There are three differences in the procedure from the Kaneyama RPG. First, the facilitator does not ask all players to express their opinion on all issues, but chooses a few players who would have definite opinions on each issue and gives a free discussion at the end. Second, after each RPG involving student discussion at the preparation stage (which may be called PG), the images of players on the farm village are surveyed using a PC. Third, we make virtual players play in the board game after the end of the last RPG (the fourth RPG). The aim for this is to activate their discussions and to give more strong incongruity to real citizens, which would avoid the third point to reflect upon.

An Evaluation Framework of the Gaming in View of Awakening a Regional Context

An Assumption Model on the Type of Citizens in Whom a Regional Context Can Be Awakened

In order to meet the fifth point of reflection, we make an assumption that citizens would be classified into three types as follows:

Type A: citizens who are always aware of regional views throughout the game.
Type B: citizens who are not aware of regional views because they look to other views before the game.
Type C: citizens who cannot be aware of regional views throughout the game due to a lack of experience in a farm village.

TABLE 1. Procedure of the game

	Real players	Virtual players (proxies)
	Seven citizens living in Miharu town with a population of 19 000	Seven students living in Sendai city with a population of 1 million
RPG in rehearsal		
Preparation for gaming	• Answer paper questionnaire	• Discuss five points between students, no assigned roles[-AHP] (meeting room)
	• Not be informed of the point at issue, only be informed of the whole theme. (Reformation of farm village)	• Assign roles to students (one-to-one correspondence to seven citizens). After studying Miharu town by materials, and checking corresponding citizen's attributes on questionnaire, discuss five points by taking their corresponding citizens (1st RPG).[-AHP]
		• Research Miharu town by on-the-spot survey, and 2nd RPG.[-AHP]
Main stage		
Phase 1	Discuss five points between citizens. (meeting room) [-AHP]	Wait in a partitioned room. Cannot observe citizens' opinions.
Phase 2	Answer to proxy's inquiries. (go to each partitioned room)	Ask some questions to corresponding citizen to play as a proxy.
Phase 3	Only observe proxies' RPG, prohibited to join in. (meeting room)	3rd RPG [-AHP] (meeting room)
Phase 4	Make requests to proxies, give answers to proxy's inquiries. (in partitioned room)	Refer to citizen's requests, ask necessary questions. (in partitioned room)
Phase 5	Only observe proxies' RPG and the board game,[a] prohibited to join in. (meeting room)	4th RPG. After the discussion, play the board game.[a-AHP] (meeting room)
Phase 6	Discuss five points between citizens.[-AHP] (meeting room)	Only observe citizens' discussion, but prohibited to join in.
After the RPG	Answer proxies' inquiries about the game. (in partitioned room)	Inquire of corresponding citizens, how well they played. (in partitioned room)

[-AHP]: AHP investigation
[a]The board game is designed to decide the budgets of five enterprises cooperatively. The structure of the game is omitted here

As Fig. 1 shows, we pay attention to citizens of Type B and expect our RPG to facilitate awakening a regional context in them. In fact, our elaboration to contrive to awaken the context would be useless when the RPG is applied in the town where people are almost all Type A.

Methods to Verify Awakening a Regional Context

We have three methods to investigate which citizens are classified into Type B. First, we make a protocol analysis on the minutes on citizens' feelings on student discussions, advice to their students, and their opinions at the second discussions between citizens. The second method is to compare citizens' interest in five issues

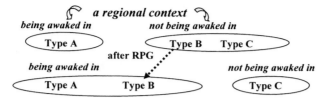

FIG. 1. An assumption model on the effects of the gaming

TABLE 2. Alternation of citizens' interests on issues

Citizens	Issues for reformation of farm village				
	(A)	(B)	(C)	(D)	(E)
[1]	3 3	**3 4**	**3 4**	**3 4**	**3 4**
[2]	3 3	3 3	**4 4**	**4 4**	**4 4**
[3]	**3 4**	3 3	3 4	**4 4**	3 4
[4]	3 3	**4 4**	*4 3*	**4 4**	3 3
[5]	3	2	3	3	3
[6]	2 2	3 3	3 3	3 3	**4 4**
[7]	*3 2*	**2 3**	3 3	2 2	3 3

Each pair of numbers means the levels of interest which were chosen according to four ranks at the end of the first and second discussion. **Bold type** shows that the level of interest heightened or there was no room to heighten because of the largest level. *Italic type* shows that the level of interest lowered. The second interests of citizen [5] could not be surveyed because she left as soon as the second discussion ended.

at the end of the second discussion with those of the first one. The third method is to examine alternations of citizens' images of the farm village.

Before analyzing the result of RPG by these three methods, we impose three necessary conditions for awakening a regional context in citizens;

• They state opinions emotionally, feeling incongruity with student discussions.
• Interest on issues reflecting the inside of town is enhanced after RPG.
• Image of life and culture are conjured up more so than that of nature.

Analysis of the Results of Experiment—Necessary Conditions for Awakening

First, we can see five citizens who felt a kind of incongruity. They are citizens [1], [2], [3], [4], and [7] and only citizen [2] expressed his opinion eagerly at the last stage. To be concrete, he said, "It seems to be difficult for outsiders to understand our discussions, so we citizens must send strong messages on our visions for Miharu town to outsiders actively." We can tentatively classify citizens into three groups {[1][3][4][7]}, {[2]}, {[5][6]}.

Table 2 shows the alternation of citizens' interests between the first and second discussions. As a whole, interest on issue (A) (international cultural exchange) showed little change, and we can see upward tendencies in interest of the other four issues. Going into details of citizens, interest of [7] on issue (B) (interchange between cities and Miharu town), of [1], and [3] on issue (C) (daily farm life and culture), of [1] on issue (D) (environmental protection in nature), and of [1], and [3] on issue (E) (farm management to maintain the village) all heightened. On the other hand, interest of [4] on issue (C) lowered. That is, we can infer that interest on matters (C), (D), and (E) within the town became higher than those outside the town, excluding citizens [4] and [7]. Therefore, it is possible for us to consider that a regional context was not awakened in citizens [4] and [7], although they felt a sense of incongruity on student discussions.

Figure 2 shows citizens' images of the farm village before and after observing the third and fourth RPG by their students. The images are shown in terms of weights on the three upper criteria: nature and ecology, life and society, and culture and history. In the figure, we can see that there are two citizens whose images changed markedly. The image of nature and ecology of citizen [2] shifted to that of life and society, and that of culture and history of citizen [4] shifted to that of nature and ecology.

Classification of Citizens According to the Assumption Model

Although citizens in the group {[1],[3],[4],[7]} would not have expressed opinions related to regional planning in Miharu, we might consider that RPG awakened a regional context in citizens [1] and [3] because of their alternation of interest in issues. For citizen [2], we could not find his alternation of interest in issues related to inside of town, but this can be considered a result of the ceiling effect. Moreover, we found that citizen [2] had heightened his image of life and society.

Getting our results in shape, we would conclude that the final classification of citizens is groups {[1],[2],[3]}, {[4],[7]}, and {[5],[6]} in consideration with the first classification. The difference between {[4],[7]} and {[5],[6]} would be that citizens in the former group felt incongruity in students' discussion but a regional context was not awakened in them, and citizens in the latter group seem to have had a

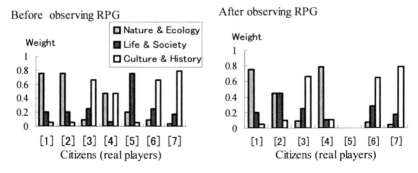

FIG. 2. Image of a farm village before and after observation of students' RPG. The second weights of citizen [5] could not be surveyed because she left as soon as the second discussion ended

robust conviction on the town building and discussed regional views from the beginning of the game. In conclusion, {[5],[6]}, {[1],[2],[3]}, and {[4],[7]} are classified into Type A, Type B, and Type C, respectively.

Discussion

The citizens that discussed regional views of Miharu throughout the game were citizens [5] and [6], who live near the spot where the three public enterprises (C), (D), and (E) are being carried out or planned. Citizens in whom a regional context of Miharu farm village was not awakened were citizens [4] and [7], who had little experience in farm life. The most significant fact is that a regional context might have been awakened in three citizens, and two of them work at public or related offices. Under the present circumstances, public officers might have a tendency to ignore a regional context because they feel they should manage to make the town compare with others or the standard of living all over the country. To defend this currency, it would be extremely important for people who work on public projects to have a perspective on the town that takes root among citizens living there.

We could verify the positive effect of our RPG on awakening a regional context in some key citizens. Although citizens who would discuss regional environmental issues along a regional context might be in the minority (here [5] and [6]), it is possible to consider that our RPG might enable us to increase the number of such citizens by incorporating some citizens who are temporally unaware of the peculiarity of regional environments of the town.

Conclusions

By the second run of our new role-playing game in Miharu, we could grasp details of its effect. Our RPG has already been confirmed in its effect of giving a new viewpoint to town planning by a trial run. Adding some devices and improvements to the trial run, we could find out what type of citizens would have been aware of regional views of the town. That is, the RPG of context-discordance[6] gives us a methodological validity to support a regional planning in awakening a regional context in critical citizens.

Moreover, our RPG seems to be instructive in environmental education for students[6]. They can learn regional environmental problems comprehensively from a certain regional society.

---

[6] We named our concept of RPG "context-discordance RPG"(Kitani et al. 2003).

[7] Greenblatt (1988) gave five learning objectives for using gaming simulations: (1) increasing motivation and interest, (2) teaching: conveying information, (3) skill development, (4) attitude change, and (5) self-evaluation or evaluation by others. The aim of our gaming simulation can be referred to (4) and (5).

References

Berque A (1990) Mediance: de mileux en paysages. Gip Reclus, Montpellier, Français (Translated into Japanese by Miyake K (1994) Fudo to shite no Chikyu, Chikuma-shobo, Tokyo)

Greenblatt CS (1988) Designing games and simulations: an illustrated handbook. Sage, Newbury Park, CA, USA

Kitani S, Arai K, Hasebe T (2003) A new role-playing gaming on regional environmental planning: a framework and trial run. Studies in Simulation and Gaming 13:149–156

Polanyi M (1966) The tacit dimension. Routledge and Kegan Paul, London

20. Congruent Facilitation of Simulations and Games

Elyssebeth Leigh[1] and Laraine Spindler[2]

Introduction

In a review of material published in the journal *Simulations and Gaming* over several years, we found only about 10% of the articles addressed the issue of facilitation skills. While most authors provided information concerning specific briefing and debriefing processes, only a few provided details about the capabilities required of a person directing a simulation or game as a learning activity. Because simulations and games are complex and somewhat unconventional learning modes, it seems likely that those writing in the field are, at least partly, unaware or unconcerned about the capabilities and knowledge they themselves develop as they acquire the capacity to create the kind of learning experiences about which they write.

Until events necessitated critical reanalysis of our practice, we were similarly unconcerned about our own facilitation skills. Once we began examining facilitation processes, new insights into the facilitation role emerged. These insights especially concern the way in which personal preferences appear to have a major influence on choices and behaviors when facilitating experiential learning activities. Two sets of choices emerge as particularly relevant. The first concerns choices about the type of simulation or game; the second concerns the preferred facilitation style and observable behaviors. These preferences seem to be more significant in shaping individual choices than do the goals and purposes of the learning that is the focus of the experiential activity. We first wrote about these in 1998 (Leigh and Spindler 1998) and have continued to report our explorations in subsequent papers (Leigh 2003a, 2003b; Leigh and Spindler 2004).

In this chapter we briefly describe our earlier work, and extend the proposition that personal attributes and teaching and learning philosophies often have greater influence on choices and actions than requirements of specific educational outcomes. For example, given similar learning outcomes, someone who sees learning as a highly structured process requiring tight control is likely to choose a quite different approach and facilitation style to someone who regards learning as an emergent process dependent on interactions among learner, processes, and content.

[1] Faculty of Education, University of Technology, Sydney, Australia;
elyssebeth.leigh@uts.edu.au
[2] Institute for International Studies, University of Technology, Sydney, Australia

At ISAGA 2003 we used a collaborative research strategy to pilot an exploration of these propositions. We developed instruments to assist in identifying philosophical stances, preferences for simulations and games formats, and facilitation practices. During the workshop, participants were able to use these instruments to identify personal patterns among these frameworks. Within the collaborative workshop there was sufficient support for our propositions to encourage further research.

Defining Simulations and Games

When discussing definitions and types of simulations in use around the world it is easy to see that the choices are immensely varied. What "are" and "are not" simulations, and how to manage, design, learn from, and behave in simulations are all subjects of debate. While preparing this chapter one of us was invited to complete two electronic surveys about the field. One was for a technology-based Australian simulation association and the other for an international teaching and research center. Neither provided a definition of "simulation" apparently assuming that anyone completing the survey shared their (unstated) assumptions about what the term means. This assumption, that there is no problem about the "meaning" of the term, emphasizes the need to provide our own definition which is:

Simulations and games include all interactive representations of perceived reality past, present, future—used for learning purposes (Leigh 2003b)

Such a broad definition allows consideration of the widest possible spectrum of activities and we encourage readers to think about their own definitions, and to regularly review their personal schemas for the field. To pursue our exploration of the facilitator's role and choices we use three arrangements from a broad range of possible models for categorizing simulations. We are aware that other equally useful arrangements exist and intend to include consideration of them in future work.

A Spectrum Approach

Taylor (1977) used a "spectrum" approach to explain to educators of town planners the potential of simulations and games as teaching media. He arranged them from "most" to "least" *real* as models of human activity. He considered case studies to be "most real" and electronic simulators to be "least real" based on how materials mediate learning. Case studies are almost "real" with little distance between player and "reality" while mechanical simulators interpose extensive technology-based mediating elements between players and reality. Taylor's spectrum is nearly 30 years old and computer-based simulators now provide near-perfect representations, e.g., flying a plane. His spectrum still emphasizes the importance of taking into account the mediating role and impact of technology and materials.

A Relational Approach

Ellington (1999) used a Venn diagram (Fig. 1) to define seven formats including:

FIG. 1. A relational approach based on the
work of Ellington (1999)

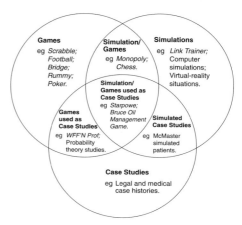

1. *Pure games*
2. Games used as simulations
3. *Pure simulations*
4. *Pure case studies*
5. Simulations used as case studies
6. Case studies used as games
7. Simulation games used as case studies

The arrangement of the formats is especially useful for choosing activities for particular learning contexts. For example, a game has rules and time constraints but need not be *like reality*, while a simulation must *specifically represent* an aspect of reality (or potential reality), and a case study must enable *in-depth analysis* of content.

Although useful in understanding *materials and rules* etc., neither of these approaches explains how to manage the learning process.

A Drama Perspective

To do this requires something different, so we have chosen Christopher and Smith's (1987) categorizing of activities as "open" or "closed," drawing on concepts from theatrical drama to distinguish between two quite different types of games (see Table 1).

Closed games rely on the facilitator for control and authority to arrive at predetermined learning points. While the route to solutions may vary, the overall action and debriefing processes do not. In contrast, open games inhibit the facilitator from being someone who "knows the desired answer." They structure the role to minimize a facilitator's capacity to help participants arrive at "the right place," because there is no one right place. Rather, the experience is that of a journey during which participants encounter moments of insight, while initiating events and experiencing emotions that may direct their attention in any number of likely, or unanticipated, directions. Facilitators support and guide, reassure and encourage; they do not direct, and certainly do not teach the meaning of events.

Assumptions About Facilitation

Both closed and open forms of simulations or games can contribute to rich learning experiences. However, each makes quite different assumptions about how

TABLE 1. Features of closed and open simulations, based on Christopher and Smith (1987)

Focus	Closed games	Open games
Framing question	Here is a **problem**. Your task is . . . "How to solve it?"	Here is a **situation**. Your task is . . . "What to do?"
Focus of the briefing phase	Togetherness	Diversity of players and views
Role of facilitator	Benevolent authority figure	Not the leader (this may be resented)
Rules for the action	Players all have same rules	Few rules, little detail. Chance events occur on players' whims.
Scenario/setting/ participant roles	Play begins at a moment of crisis. Each step proceeds logically from the one before. Action is goal oriented/forward looking. Stimulus is toward cooperative problem solving: emphasis on outcome.	A journey: multiple plots diffuse action. Stages not clearly marked. Changes occur because of players' actions. No clear order and balance. Minor actions spin off in apparently illogical manner. Emphasis on reactions. Diverse happenings. Emphasis on behavior, not outcomes.
Outcomes: focus of debriefing	Players derive pleasure from shared experience. There are problems and answers. Conflict can be reconciled.	Players find themselves more thoughtful than pleased. There is a lack of certainty and an awareness of new possibilities.

learning occurs and how participants and facilitators are to behave. A closed game assumes that participants need guidance and the facilitator is there to provide it. An open game assumes that participants create the experience *they* need to have, in order to learn. It further assumes that disorder and confusion are likely to emerge as part of this process, and that this provides a "container" within which "deep learning" is likely to occur. The facilitator must not disturb the emergence of such disorderly chaos, but can offer support as participants travel forward to the destination being created by their actions. The intended outcomes of such activities are of course often quite different. Where open simulations will usually concern themselves with themes such as managing in times of uncertainty and learning about emotionally charged contexts, closed simulations tend to be designed for acquisition of facts and information.[3]

We propose that facilitators who regard knowledge as an "object" to be possessed, acquired as "facts," and "contained" in words will prefer the more structured form of closed games, whatever the purpose. Conversely, facilitators who regard knowledge as *emerging from the process*, acquired through both emotional responses and examination of facts and "things," will prefer the sense of "journey" allowed in open simulations and the way that the unexpected and unanticipated become vital forces for understanding, and go beyond acquisition of data and facts.[4] As we explored these perspectives, we developed the concept of the "vigilant observer" (see Fig. 2) and identified two factors linked to developing the capability for using open games.

---

[3] Please note we consider these to be a description of tendencies and not assertions about the precise nature of either form of activity.
[4] As noted above, such different approaches will almost always produce quite different learning outcomes.

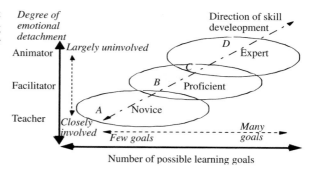

FIG. 2. Emotional detachment and learning goals, linking *novice*, *proficient*, and *expert* presenters of simulations

We used this concept to develop a spectrum with endpoints of "moderator" and "improviser" signaling the respective attitudes to the task of managing the learning. The improviser is more comfortable with open simulations and has similar characteristics to the animator described by Boud and Miller (1996) with an emphasis on emotional detachment and acceptance of ambiguity. A moderator prefers closed simulations and regards their task as being to ensure achievement of concrete intentions. The improviser works with what emerges from the action, being able to improvise from moment to moment, seeing the goal as assisting individuals to attend to their own experiences rather than directing attention to designated topics. Figure 3 illustrates differences between moderators and improvisers emerging as the outcome of personal decisions made (often tacitly) about such things as: the relative importance of content knowledge; the need to control the action; the power relationships between learner and teacher roles; and beliefs about what constitutes appropriate methodologies.

Our concern is that novice facilitators, unable to differentiate between closed and open forms may make errors in their management of the learning including:

- *Stretching closed simulations beyond their design parameters, by treating them as open and therefore*
  - encourage participants to "unpack" ideas that are not fully within the scope or goals of the game but appear interesting
  - claim an activity provides more variety than it can sustain
  - expect a game to operate as open and telling players how to make it so
- *Limiting the potential of open simulations by treating them as closed and therefore*
  - require specific outcomes to be achieved
  - ignore emergent learning, in favor of preset expectations
  - contain action in narrower constraints than the designer's intentions
  - rescue learners that are temporarily lost in a "morass" of potentials
  - fail to encourage exploration of new potentials being created

We are more interested in errors related to treating open games as if they are closed for two main reasons. The first is that such errors can generate a lot of emotional turmoil for both participants and facilitator if anyone begins to develop unrealistic or unattainable expectations about the others' roles and

When performing as a Moderator of learning contexts	When operating as an Improviser in learning contexts
The goal is to *control behavior* by managing group dynamics and individual activity	The goals is to understand the *flow* and patterns of the action so as to support and challenge the learning
This is achieved by making learning structures stable and self-evident	Patterns of learning are expected to emerge, be explored and supported
Operational (implicit) assumptions are that learning requires	Operational (implicit) assumptions are that learning creates
• Orderliness and attention to detail	• turbulence (emotional, and physical)
• Stability, with the teacher in control	• discovery
• Emotional constraints	• challenges to beliefs and practices

FIG. 3.
A continuum of approaches to managing learning, adapted from Leigh and Spindler (1998)

behaviors. The second is that any potential for learning may be lost if participants and facilitator become seduced by the emotional turmoil and are unable to identify what learning is actually available (and indeed occurring).

To better understand problems in managing open simulations, and to develop a means of improving the learning from our own experiences, we began to consider how teaching and learning preferences are shaped by educational philosophies and influence facilitation choices. Consideration of "learning styles" and "personality types" provides a brief introduction to thinking about how novice and experienced facilitators may better appreciate the implications of their choices in regard to games formats through better understanding their own profiles.

Learning Preferences

David Kolb developed the concept of learning as occurring in a cycle, suggesting that adults prefer one or two of four steps in the cycle, but must use all four for new learning to be fully integrated (Kolb et al. 1979). He suggested it is possible to map individual preferences in a way that enables anyone to understand more about their own "beginning point" and become alert to the way this may shape their approach to learning activities. Honey and Mumford (1986) modified this approach by mapping the learning preferences in the form of a kite. Their model, as shown in Fig. 4, suggests the following key characteristics of each of the four points of the kite:

Activist—fully engages without bias in new experiences
Reflector—stands back to observe experiences from different perspectives
Theorist—adapts and integrates observations into complex logical theories
Pragmatist—tries out ideas, theories, and techniques to see how they work in practice

The assessments developed by Honey and Mumford indicate the degree to which individuals hold particular preferences. Plotting these along the axes provides a visual image of individual learning style. Figure 4 shows this approach, with the kite of one of the authors superimposed on the grid as an example of what it can produce. This kite suggests that its owner prefers action to "kick start" new learning and has a pragmatic need for learning to be relevant to current

FIG. 4. Learning styles as a set of preferences, adapted from Honey and Mumford (1986)

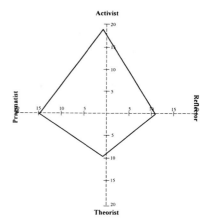

practice. Observation and analysis remain subservient to action. The kite's owner prefers to teach and learn via simulations and games, with a strong affinity for open simulations as a challenging and rewarding way to help adult learners integrate present knowledge and new information.

A person with a preference for extensive reflection and careful analysis prior to action will be less likely to enjoy the "free form" nature of open simulations that require quick responses and allow little time for in-depth analysis of options. The comparative strength of each one's preferences is likely to dictate responses to specific activities. Thus, knowledge of one's own learning preferences and its impact on the design and delivery of learning processes can assist facilitators to both extend their own repertoire of teaching strategies and be better prepared for the widest possible array of learners' responses.

Personality Types

It is logical to assume that understanding and beliefs around teaching and learning practice are likely to have an impact on choices of learning activity. The same could be said of individual personality characteristics. In general terms, personality theories aim to explain psychological aspects of human beings, particularly commonalities and differences. A well-known model influencing development of personality theory is that of Jung (1974). He described four mental "functions" and noted that:

1. Everyone can perform all of them
2. Each function has an opposite function; each pair of functions has an opposite pair
3. Each individual prefers using some functions, and pairs, more than others
4. These habits can be generalized to describe types of people

Figure 5 illustrates the format known as the Myers Briggs Type Indicator (MBTI) (Briggs Myers 1999). This is based on the work of Jung, and is an instru-

S and N
We take information in via our senses. When this **Sensation Function (S)** dominates perception, we prefer sensate things: certainty, precision, simplicity, practicality, concreteness. The **Intuition (N)** function perceives patterns and possibilities. An **N** sees objects as parts of patterns,
implications, possibilities or theories. The **N** dreams, nothing is the same way twice; there must
be change.
Until they understand these differences the two functions will not value each other. **S** calls **N** a
lazy dreamer, and **N** considers **S** a plodder.

T and F
As we take in information we use it via thinking and feeling. **Thinking (T)** analyses elements to
reach an objective *truth*. Information is dealt with objectively, impersonally, logically. Thinkers
make good planners because they lay events out in order. **Feeling (F)** types do not just *have*
feelings; they use them to make **value judgments** to build relationships, compare things, act
compassionately. **T** is irritated by **F**'s personalizing, who sees **T** as a cold fish.

P and J
A Perceiving **(P)** person takes in a lot of information before deciding and taking action. A Judging **(J)** person takes in less information and decides more quickly. **P** may be slow; **J** may "shoot
from the hip". (Putzel 2001)

FIG. 5. Brief summary of Myers Briggs type indicator typology (Briggs Myers 1999)

ment used regularly as part of our adult education programs to provide students
with an understanding of the variety of individual preferences. Just as learning
style preferences may influence preferences for teaching methods, so it is likely
that different personality types will respond differently to particular methods and
strategies.

We suggest that people with S, T, and J preferences (as per the information
in Fig. 5) are likely to prefer closed simulations because of the opportunities
they provide for clear, detailed analysis and the development of logical, well-
structured arguments about specific learning outcomes. Conversely, we propose
that those with N, F, and P preferences are more likely to choose open simulations because of the prospects for exploring patterns, creating original action,
building relationships, and working with lots of information. We are cautious in
our predictions, as we have as yet only worked with limited data; however, we
received encouraging support at ISAGA 2003 and briefly report on that aspect
of the research, in what follows.

Collaborative Exploration—ISAGA 2003

In developing our approach for the workshop at ISAGA 2003, we opted to work
with a number of theoretical frameworks that can be arranged in orthogonal
(right-angled) relationships, thus identifying four distinct stances in regard to
each concept being examined. The three models we chose to work with concern
(1) adult learning principles, (2) project management types, and (3) a personality profile called "Tetramap" (Brett and Brett 2004) which draws on a combination of western and eastern philosophies to identify four distinct types of
approach to learning and being. Each of the models can be arranged such that
the factors can be seen as aligned in terms of "more than" and "less than," bal-
ancing aspects of each measure rather than possessing or not possessing each of

Fig. 6. A representation of Turner's project types

the factors being considered in each model. For example, Turner identified four types of project based on two related factors of knowledge of methods to be applied and tools to be used. Figure 6 shows how these factors help to define four project types. Different individuals will feel more comfortable with some project types (e.g., projects with well-defined goals and methods) than with others (e.g., projects with methods that are not well known or tools not well defined).

These models are all ones we use elsewhere in our adult education programs and each provides an insight into a different aspect of the teaching and learning processes in which we are engaged.

During the ISAGA 2003 workshop, participants reviewed the models choosing stances that seemed most like their own, and then self-selected into groups reflecting their choice patterns. The groups then examined its members' preferences for open or closed simulations based on a discussion of the work of Christopher and Smith (1987). We had posited that the more structure participants chose, the more they would be likely to chose closed simulations and vice versa. In addition we proposed that there would be fewer differences within groups than across groups. These propositions were well supported by the choices made by individuals within the workshop groups.

We want to emphasize that our concern is not to label what is good or what is not good facilitation practice, but we are hoping to establish what attitudes and practices might underlie good facilitation practice for different forms of simulation and games. We are concerned that it is possible to "strangle" learning by using a facilitation approach that does not suit the form of the activity.

Concluding Comments

Open simulations do not, at the beginning, provide time for careful analysis. Participants are thrust into action in a nondefined state by the momentum of the action and only slowly come to a realization that their learning is being formed by the activity, as well as their observation and analysis of it. Closed simulations, in contrast, generally provide more time for analysis giving a facilitator scope to guide learning in a defined and logical manner.

Moving between forms appears to become easier as facilitators acquire understanding of their own and others' learning preferences. It remains difficult for those who judge learning designs from within parameters of formal logic and consider uncertainty as a needlessly difficult approach to imparting knowledge.

Of course, when knowledge itself is uncertain in its content and overall relevance, then adherence to logic is difficult, and facilitators may be more able to perceive how open simulations offer a way forward beyond the logic of the ancient Greeks. In developing his thesis of "Gaming: the Futures Language" Duke (1974) captured the essence of the dilemma quite well. Although he did not allocate a place for emotions in simulations, he was acutely aware of the nature of the "gestalt" they offer for humans needing to explore multiple meanings simultaneously. Duke's concern was with the design and use of the process, more than with the skill of the user.

We believe the paucity of information about managing simulations of all types creates an urgent need to develop ways to help facilitators learn about matching their skills and preferences to the use of particular simulations and games, and then developing skills for using all forms of simulations and games. Self-knowledge may be a key factor. From this preliminary exploration, indications are that individual differences and preferences may influence much about choices and actions in facilitation. As difficulties in facilitation may occur as a result of incongruent facilitation strategies (Leigh and Spindler 1998) it may be important for facilitators to develop an awareness of their preferences for particular modes of learning and personal styles. This will assist in making effective choices about the styles of simulations and games initially and ways they will need to challenge their beliefs in order to develop more flexible facilitation styles.

References

Brett Y, Brett J (2004) Tetramap, see http://www.tetramap.com/
Briggs Myers I (1999) Introduction to type. Australian Council for Educational Research, Melbourne
Boud D, Miller N (1996) Working with experience. Routledge, London, UK
Christopher EM, Smith LE (1987) Leadership training through gaming. Kogan Page, London
Duke RD (1974) Gaming: the futures language. Halsted, New York, USA
Ellington H (1999) Games and simulations—media for the new millenium. 1999 SAGSET
Honey P, Mumford A (1986) The manual of learning styles. Maidenhead, UK
Jung C (1974) Psychological types. Princeton University Press, Princeton, NJ
Kolb DA, Rubin IM, McIntyre JM (1979) Organizational psychology an experiential approach. Prentice-Hall, Englewood Cliffs, USA
Leigh E (2003a) A touchy subject—people factors in simulations. SimTECT 2003, Adelaide
Leigh E (2003b) What is expected of the facilitator of interactive learning? In: Percival HGF et al (eds) Interactive learning through gaming and simulation. ISAGA/SAGSET, Edinburgh
Leigh E, Spindler L (2004) Simulations and games as chaordic learning contexts. Simulations and Gaming 35. pp 53–69
Leigh E, Spindler L (1998) Vigilant observer: A role for facilitators of games/simulations. In: Geurts J, Joldersma C, Roelofs E (eds) Gaming/simulation for policy development and organizational change. Tilburg University Press
Putzel R (2001) XB manual for a learning organization. St. Michael's College, Colchester, VT
Taylor J (1977) Instructional gaming procedures in planning education. In: Megarry J (ed) Aspects of simulation and gaming. Kogan Page, London, pp 103–115

21. The Loss of Concentration by the Effects of the Timing of Commercial Breaks

Noriko Nagata[1], Sanae H. Wake[2], Mieko Ohsuga[3], and Seiji Inokuchi[4]

Introduction

Concentration is a key word in various fields, such as media, entertainment, and training. Concentration is the key to success in business and sport, thus we often talk about how to develop our powers of concentration and what its mechanism is.

Commercial breaks are often placed at the climax of stories in television programs in Japan. By placing television commercials just after a climactic scene, the producer intends the audience to watch both the commercial and the story after the climax without fail. However, commercials placed in the middle of the climax will discourage the audience attention and concentration (Anon. 2002). Furthermore, the audience might feel uncomfortable watching the scene just after the commercial is played.

We can see, therefore, that planning a program can seriously affect the audience, especially children. The authors are anxious that children that are now in their developing years might grow into adults with poor concentration after they have watched such television programs repeatedly. In this chapter, we present the influence of the timing of commercial breaks on the loss of attention in children.

Various research studies on attention have been published in the field of psychology. The level of concentration has been evaluated mainly by brain waves (α waves, fmθ waves) (Sakamoto 2000, Miyata 1997), and the rate of the occurrence of fmθ waves is related to the number of times a person blinks (Miyata 1997). It

[1] School of Science and Technology, Kwansei Gakuin University, Sanda, Hyogo 669-1323, Japan; nagata@ksc.kwansei.ac.jp
[2] Department of Information and Media, Doshisha Women's College of Liberal Arts, Kyotanabe, Kyoto 610-0395, Japan; swake@dwc.doshisha.ac.jp
[3] Faculty of Information Science and Technology, Osaka Institute of Technology, Hirakata, Osaka 573-0171, Japan; ohsuga@is.oit.ac.jp
[4] Faculty of Human and Social Environment, Hiroshima International University, Kurose, Hiroshima 724-0695, Japan; inokuchi@ieee.org

is known that concentration is related to breathing as expressed with such common expressions as "to hold one's breath" or "take one's breath away" (Miyata 1997). In addition, there have been some evaluations of concentration in the media, such as television games (Sakamoto 2000) and interactive art (Tsutada et al. 1997). However, to date there has been no research concerning the effects of television commercials on concentration.

Therefore, a preliminary psycho-physiological experiment concerning breathing, heartbeat, and blinking was arranged. The experiment was based on the hypothesis that when the peak of concentration is disturbed, the next peak of concentration will be delayed, or in other words, the recovery of concentration will be delayed (Nagata et al. 2004).

Method of Psycho-Physiological Experiment

There were four subjects in this experiment: a 2-year-old girl, a 3-year-old girl, an 11-year-old girl, and a 13-year-old girl. They were shown a television program for young children for about 30 min as the stimulation. The contents of the program are shown in Table 1. There were two commercial breaks (CM1, CM2). CM1 was a 1-min commercial placed after the first half of the story (Story A) came to a suitable stopping point, and CM2 was a 1-min commercial placed during the climax of the second half of the story (Story B). In addition, after CM2, 18s of the scene just preceding the commercial was replayed, and then the story was continued. The breathing, heart rate, and blinking of the subjects during the program were measured.

TABLE 1. Contents of the television program and scenes before and after commercials (from Tottoko Hamutaro "Tottoko Panic! Hinamatsuri")

Story	Synopsis	Scene no.	Start time	Contents
Story A	At the Hinamatsuri party, a member of	ScA1	12:05	Dolls displayed on tiers fall slowly (with a background music of "the Destiny").
	Hamuchans (T-kun) carelessly upsets dolls displayed on tiers.	ScA2	12:14	Dolls lay scattered on the floor.
		CM1	12:20	CM1
Story B	Hamuchans try to put dolls back on the	ScB1	19:09	T-kun is approached by the dog, and cries "NO!" while running.
	tiered stand, but a	CM2	19:27	CM2
	dog disturbs them.	Replay	20:24	(= ScB1)
	T-kun runs about trying to attract the	ScB2	20:42	The dog begins to jump at cornered T-kun.
	dog's attention.	ScB3	20:53	The master appears and catches the dog. T-kun is saved.

General Results of Experiment 1

Figure 1 shows the rates of blinking and breathing, and the amplitude and curve of breathing for the 3-year-old girl.

When the blinking rate increased, the rate of breathing decreased and its amplitude tended to increase. From observations during the experiment, we found that the subject usually lost her attention to the screen while yawning, and she often blinked. This could show that she had lost her attention at that time, or in other words, it could be said that she was relaxed or bored.

Also, when the subject seldom blinked, we found that both the rate of breathing and the amplitude of breathing were very small. It could be said that she had, "her breath taken away", that is, she was tense or her attention was concentrated. By comparing the rate of breathing, various amplitudes of breath, and the progress of the stimulation, we found that concentration could be classified into four categories as shown in Table 2.

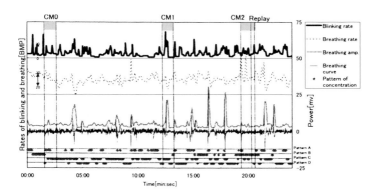

FIG. 1. The psycho-physiological state before and after the commercials for a 3-year-old girl

TABLE 2. Four categories of the pattern of concentration

Pattern of concentration	Breathing rate	Breathing amplitude	Contents of stimulation	State of subject
A	High	High	High tempo and cheerful song. Noisy chase scene	Concentration with excitement
B	High	Low	Chase scene. Looking the other way (shaking head)	Unstable
C	Low	High	Ordinary scene	Relaxed/bored
D	Low	Low	Melancholy and passionate song. At the turn of the scene	Concentration with tenseness

202 N. Nagata et al.

Detailed Results of Experiment 2

In Fig. 2 we show an enlargement of Fig. 1 so that the details of the experiment before and after the commercials were placed are visible. The state of the subject during the experiment is also shown in Fig. 3.

Figure 2a indicates before and after CM1 was played. From a tense condition (pattern D) at the climax of the television program (ScA1), where the amplitude of the subject's breathing was increased, her condition gradually relaxed after the first part of the story (ScA2) ended. By placing CM1 here, the subject's breathing was initially delayed (at point *a1*, Fig. 2, with what is called "holding her breath"). Then, with deep breathing (point *a3*), after sudden blinking (point *a2*), her tension was released and she became relaxed at once (Fig. 3a). Five seconds later (point *a4*), even though it was during the commercial break, her status changed to tense concentration (pattern D). (Pattern B, seen in the second half of the commercial break, was caused by the subject's turned back, so it was unrelated to this experiment.)

In Fig. 2b, which was before and after CM2 was played, the subject was extremely excited (pattern A) while she watched the chase scene of the program (ScB1). The increase of her breathing rate at point *b1* was caused by her stamping as she could not restrain her excitement. As a consequence of CM2 being placed in this situation, there was no sudden blinking, which was seen in Fig. 2a, but weak blinking (point *b2*) continued for nearly 10 s. During this period, the subject absently opened her eyes wide and turned her eyes away from the television screen (Fig. 3b). Next, a breathing disorder with a short amplitude (point *b3*) was observed and this unstable condition continued until the commercial break ended (pattern B). The subject began to pay attention to the television when the story was resumed; however, after 5 s, the subject noticed it was a replay (Fig. 3c). Both the rates of blinking and breathing went up and changed to pattern B again. After that, she didn't pay strong attention to the climax scene (ScB2). Finally, she concentrated on the final scene (ScB3). As can be seen, patterns C and D were the main patterns during CM1; however, pattern B was often seen during CM2, and therefore, they show very different aspects.

Discussion

Results for the 3-Year-Old Subject

From the observed results, it appears that when the concentration is disturbed by a commercial break, it takes longer to reach the next concentration peak. These observations are in accordance with our hypothesis. In other words, commercials at the climax of a story delay the recovery of concentration. Also, we verified that replaying a scene after a commercial break is one factor that disturbs attention.

It was also found that relaxation is required before concentration and that the timing of relaxation was important. We obtained results that support

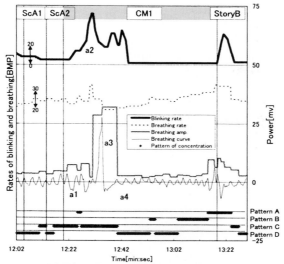

(a) Played at a natural pause in the story.

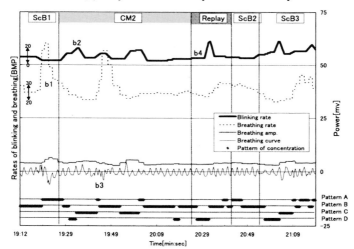

(b) Played at the climax of the story.

FIG. 2. Detailed results of the experiment before and after the commercials were played (an enlargement of Fig. 1). **a** Played at a natural pause in the story; **b** played at the climax of the story

FIG. 3a–c. Appearances of the subject after playing the commercials. **a** Five seconds after CM1 starts (*middle*); **b** 5s after CM2 starts; **c** 5s after the replay starts

existing knowledge, which says that tension and relaxation are important for concentration.

Furthermore, it is not true that there is no attention during commercial breaks. If timed properly, it is clear that more attention is paid to them. This is because relaxation is enhanced at the start of a commercial break when a scene is able to relax the viewer just before the commercial break starts. Thus, it is confirmed that it is more effective to place a commercial break after the climax of a story rather than halfway through the climax, because the audience will pay more attention to it.

Other Results

Lastly, we will briefly mention the other results. First, the heart rate data obtained was so noisy that it could not be evaluated this time. It is considered that there was a problem in the way the heart rate sensor was worn, and some improvements are necessary to obtain the data correctly.

Second, in the results for the 2-year-old subject, it was observed that the blinking rate increased slowly during the commercial breaks, as shown in Fig. 4. However, there was no difference in response to the commercials between after the climax and at the climax, and there was also no particular response to the replay scene. This can be explained by the difference in the stage of cognition development due to the subject age.

Third, the 11-year-old and 13-year-old subjects seemed to pay weak attention to the stimulation on the whole. We counted the total time and the frequency of when the subjects took their eyes off the screen during the program, as shown in

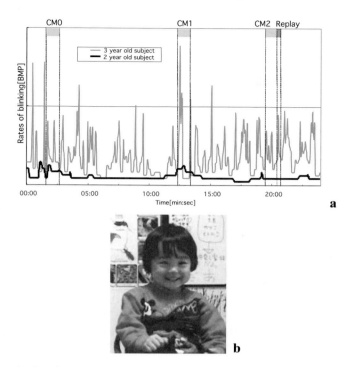

Fig. 4a,b. Results for the 2-year-old subject. **a** Comparison of the blinking rates between the 2-year-old and 3-year-old subjects; **b** appearance of the subject

TABLE 3. Total time and frequency of when the subjects took their eyes off the screen during the program

Subject	Story A (579 s)		Story B (460 s)	
	Total time	Frequency	Total time	Frequency
2 years old	5 s (1%)	2	5 s (1%)	2
3 years old	22 s (4%)	6	8 s (2%)	4
11 years old	96 s (17%)	35	38 s (8%)	18
13 years old	72 s (12%)	25	74 s (16%)	31

Table 3. For the 3-year-old subject, the frequencies during both the first and the second half of the story were low, and a loss of attention was not observed. The 2-year-old subject took her eyes off the screen only four times (10 s in total) over 17 min and her concentration was strong. On the other hand, the 11-year-old and 13-year-old subjects took their eyes off the screen more than 50 times (2 min in total). Such results are considered to be caused by various factors such as the stimulation, the experimental environment, and the difference between individuals.

Fourth, we confirmed the effects of the timing of commercials in this experiment, however, we could not confirm from observations whether a commercial break had occurred.

Such considerations will be addressed in future research.

Conclusions

We conducted a psycho-physiological experiment with an index of concentration to evaluate the influence of the timing of television commercial breaks on children's attention. As the result of the experiment, it was shown that concentration, blinking, and breathing are mutually related. Furthermore, disturbing the concentration has the tendency of delaying the recovery of concentration. Therefore, by watching television programs over and over, we are afraid that the number of children who cannot maintain their attention may increase. Moreover, from the point of view of presenting commercials effectively, it is advisable that commercial breaks occur after the end of a story rather than during the climax.

In the future, we will seek to improve the experimental method of evaluating concentration. Also, we will continue to study methods that will have a good influence on the audience for not only commercials, but also for various kinds of media. We believe that media companies that carry out program creation with top audience ratings as their main goal should be made aware of the findings discussed here.

References

Anon. (2002) CM and shopping "not concerned with each other" is 60%. In: "Be" Asahi-Shimbun, 2002.10.26 (in Japanese)

Miyata Y (ed) (1997) Applied psychophysiology. New Psychophysiology vol 2. Kitaoji Shobo, Kyoto

Nagata N, Wake SH, Ohsuga M, Inokuchi S (2004) The effects of the timing of commercial breaks on the loss of attention. IEICE Trans. INF & SYST. vol E87-D, No 6, pp 1484–1487

Sakamoto A (2000) Video games and violence: controversy and research in Japan. In: Children in the new media landscape: games, pornography, and perceptions. Goeteborg, Sweden: The UNESCO International Clearinghouse on Children and Violence on the Screen. pp 61–77

Tsutada H, Kato H, Kimura A, et al (1997) A physiological analysis of tensity of performer and audience in interactive art (in Japanese). TVRSJ 2:9–16

22. Utilization of Neural Networks and Genetic Algorithms to Make Game Playing More Exciting

Norio Baba[1] and Wang Shuqin[2]

Introduction

During the past several decades, soft computing techniques such as neural networks (NNs), fuzzy logic, and genetic algorithms (GAs) have contributed much to the construction of various intelligent systems. Recently, the authors tried to utilize those techniques to the field of gaming (Baba 1999a, 1999b; Baba et al. 1995, 1996, 1997). In particular, neural network technology has been applied to mimic each player's way of playing in the Commons Game (Powers et al. 1980). Furthermore, GAs have been utilized for finding an appropriate rule to make the Commons Game much more exciting (Baba 1999b; Baba et al. 1997).

In this chapter, NNs and GAs are applied to the Environment Game (Baba et al. 1986). It is shown that NNs are quite helpful for making a copy of each player's strategy. Furthermore, it is also shown that GAs can be utilized for making this game exciting.

Environment Game

Historically speaking, gaming has its origin in war games (Hausrath 1971). However, after World War II, it has been applied to various peaceful applications (Duke 1974; Baba 1984). A large number of business games have been developed for the purpose of training students in business school (Shubik 1975; Cohen et al. 1964). Furthermore, some environmental games (Ausubel 1981; Baba et al. 1984) have also been developed in order to help people think seriously about the environmental state of the world. In the following, we briefly touch upon the Environment Game (Baba et al. 1986; Baba 1986).

---
[1] Information Science, Osaka-Kyoiku University, Kashiwabara, Osaka 582-8582, Japan; baba@is.osaka-kyoiku.ac.jp
[2] Northeast Normal University, China; wangsq562@nenu.edu.cn

Personal Computer Gaming System

In the Environment Game, players represent the directors of four chemical companies whose factories face the sea. Because the sea is surrounded by land on all sides, all company management decisions can strongly affect the environmental state of the sea. If they invest large sums of money to improve their financial state without giving due consideration to the possible deterioration of the sea, a serious environmental situation could emerge. Therefore, they must manage their company in such a way as to avoid the environmental deterioration of the sea.

Objectives of the Game

The game is designed to:

(1) help people to learn about the red tide issue of an inland sea.
(2) give people a chance to manage a company whose factories face an inland sea.

Detailed Explanation of the Rules of the Game

The game can be played for more than 20 years with one game director and four players representing the four companies facing the inland sea. At the beginning of the first year, an equal amount of money, for example $1000, is given to each of the four players. Each player must then decide how much should be invested for producing chemical goods and how much to avoid environmental deterioration (Fig. 1).

In each round, players should decide the following three values:

I The amount of money to be invested for producing chemical goods.
Z The amount of money to be saved for constructing new equipment for decontamination.
U The amount of money to be utilized for operating the current equipment for decontamination.

Because there are three kinds of chemical goods, each player should specify, in deciding the value of I, which chemical good will be invested in. The first chemical good G_1 may create large profits with some risks. The third chemical good G_3 would only produce small profits (but with rather high probability). The second chemical good G_2 can be considered as the one taking the position in between G_1 and G_3. In other words, investment for producing G_1 is somewhat speculative, while the other alternatives represent sound management. Let us explain this more clearly. In each round, the game director receives a piece of paper from each player on which the values of I, Z, and U are written. The director then inputs all of these values into a personal computer. If the director pushes the RETURN key, two dice rotate and stop. The amount of money invested in each chemical good increases or decreases depending on the sum of the numbers of the two dice, as shown in Table 1.

TABLE 1. The rule of change of the rate of profit with dice

Chemical good	Dice	Then	Else
G_1	3, 4, 5	2.2	0.90
G_2	6, 7	1.7	1.00
G_3	8, 9, 10, 11	1.4	1.10
G_1, G_2, G_3	2, 12	1.5	1.5

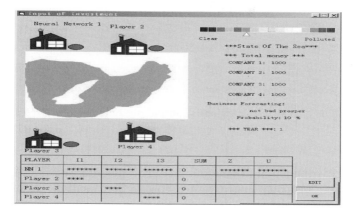

FIG. 1. A graphic display which appears on the personal computer screen in the initial round

Assume that the ith player invests at the jth round $I_1^i(j)$, $I_2^i(j)$, $I_3^i(j)$ on G_1, G_2, and G_3, respectively (Table 1). If the sum of the two dice is 3, 4, or 5, the player receives

$$I_1^i(j) \times (2.2 + \xi_1^i(j)) + I_2^i(j) \times (1.00 + \xi_2^i(j)) + I_3^i(j) \times (1.10 + \xi_3^i(j))$$

where $\xi_k^i(j)$ ($k = 1, 2, 3$) are normally distributed random variables with zero mean. If the sum of two dice happens is from 6 to 11, on the average $I_1^i(j)$ decreases and $I_2^i(j)$ (or $I_3^i(j)$) increases (Table 1). If the sum of two dice is 2 or 12, the player receives

$$(I_1^i(j) + I_2^i(j) + I_3^i(j)) \times (1.5 + \xi_4^i(j))$$

where $\xi_4^i(j)$ are normally distributed random variables with zero mean.

The probability that the sum of two dice is 3, 4, or 5 is small. Therefore, investment in the first chemical good G_1 is rather risky. However, it may produce a large profit. On the contrary, the investment on the third (or second) chemical good means sound management. (Even if the sum of the two dice is 3, 4, or 5, the total amount of money invested in G_2 or G_3 does not decrease much.)

The graphic display as described in Fig. 2, gives players in each round a range of information: the state of the sea (environment), the financial state, and business forecasting. If the players invest their money only to gain profits, and do not

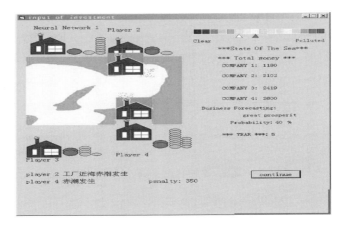

FIG. 2. A graphic display which appeared on the personal computer screen in the fifth round

care about environmental protection, the environmental state declines and the color of the sea becomes tinged with yellow. If they continue with such selfish decisions over several years, a red tide may appear on the sea near their factories. If they change their policy and care about environmental protection, the red tide may disappear in several years. However, if they still continue to invest a lot of money to produce chemical goods and none for environmental protection, they would be ordered to cease all operations at their factories.

The game can end in two ways:

1. If serious environmental deterioration of the sea occurs, the game terminates and each player loses money. The top right hand corner of Fig. 2 shows that there are 16 environmental states of the sea. (1 is the best state, and 16 is the worst). The initial environmental state of the sea is 6. Depending upon the policies chosen by the players, the environmental state of the sea becomes better or worse. If the environmental state of the sea advances to the 16th state, the game comes to an end because environmental catastrophe has occurred. All players lose their capital.

2. The game comes to an end between the 21st and 30th rounds. (Each round has an equal probability of 0.1 with which the game terminates.) The player who gets the largest amount of money wins the game.

As the game proceeds, the players receive various instructions from the personal computer. For example, in several rounds the player that has contributed most to environmental protection is honored and given an amount of money by the government (see Fig. 3). When the environmental deterioration of the sea becomes a serious problem, players are asked to pay consolation money to the fisheries industry. The players should decide the amount of consolation money taking into account the damages that may have been inflicted on the fishery. If the

Fig. 3. A game screen that shows the personal computer has chosen the fourth player as the one that has contributed most to decontamination of the sea

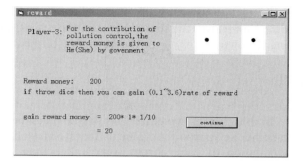

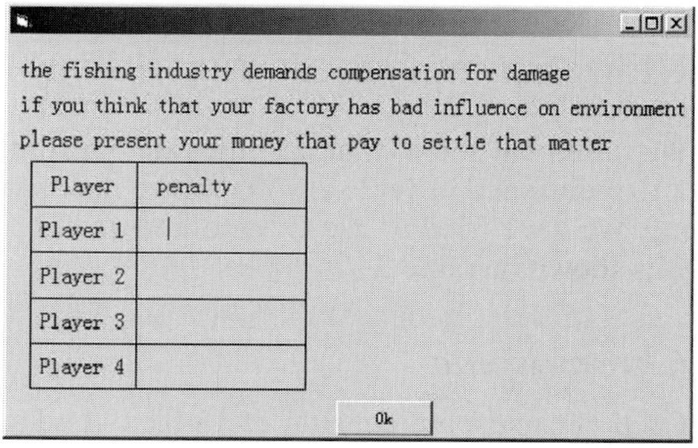

Fig. 4. Compensation for the fishing industry. Each player must decide how much money should be paid for serious damage in the sea

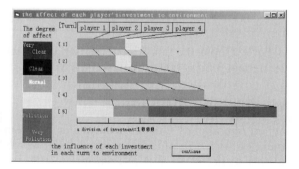

Fig. 5. Information concerning how players have influenced environmental contamination over the past 5 years

amount decided by is the players is not enough, they will be asked to pay an additional amount (see Fig. 4).

After every five turns the players have a conference time. As shown in Fig. 5, they are given information concerning how they have influenced the environmental deterioration. The game director, and all of the players, should evaluate the decisions made by each player during the last five rounds. They should choose an integer from −2 to 2 and write it on a sheet of paper provided by the game director. (2 indicates the best contribution to environmental protection and −2 indicates the worst). Each player should write 0 for their own score. The game director receives the sheets from the players and inputs all of these scores (including his own scores) from the keyboard of the microcomputer. If the total score of a player is less than −4, the player has to pay a penalty. If the total score of the player is larger than 4, the player receives a financial reward.

About 15 years ago, one of the authors and his students succeeded in constructing a personal computer gaming system of the original Environment Game.

In this chapter, we utilize this personal computer gaming system to investigate whether an appropriate value of the rate of profit can be found by GAs. However, evaluation of each chromosome takes time, so we decided that the neural network can be utilized for making a copy of each player.

Utilization of Genetic Algorithms

We think that some change in the rate of profit such as 2.2, 0.90, 1.7, 1.00, 1.4, and 1.10 mentioned in Table 1 would make the Environment Game much more exciting. We have tried to use GAs to find an appropriate value in each of the intervals shown in Table 2.

Chromosome

Each chromosome consists of 18-bit 0–1 sequences in which each 3 bit corresponds to a real number in each closed interval shown as the following graphic.

000~111	000~111	000~111	000~111	000~111	000~111

For example, the first 3 bit corresponds to a value in a closed interval $[1.9, 2.3]$. If the first 3 bit is 000, it corresponds to 1.9.

Evaluation Function

When one applies GAs to a particular problem, the way to return a measurement of the worth of a chromosome must be carefully decided. The main theme in this section is to find an appropriate rule which makes playing of the Environment Game much more exciting. Therefore, the evaluation function should be constructed from a such point of view. That is to say, we have to set up the evaluation function by carefully considering: "What kind of play is exciting for players?"

TABLE 2. The range of each profit rate

Rate		Rate range	Rate		Rate range
2.2		1.9~2.3	0.90		0.75~0.93
1.7	→	1.4~1.75	1.00	→	0.88~1.02
1.4		1.15~1.3	1.10		0.98~1.10

Here, our object is to find an appropriate value for each rate of profit. We have tried to evaluate each chromosome by taking the following data into account:

a) Number of times that the top player has been replaced by other players.
b) Variance of the total points.
c) State of the environment at the 20th round.
d) Final state of the environment.
e) Total number of times that participating players have been rewarded.

Utilization of Neural Networks for Evaluating Each Chromosome

Figure 6 shows the outline of how the appropriate value has been found by GAs. In the following, let us give a comment concerning the evaluation of each chromosome in step 3 of Fig. 6.

As already explained, the evaluation of each chromosome is executed by the result of play. However, one may not be able to expect to find an appropriate value for the rate of profit by using only the gaming results by human players. Let us explain this more clearly.

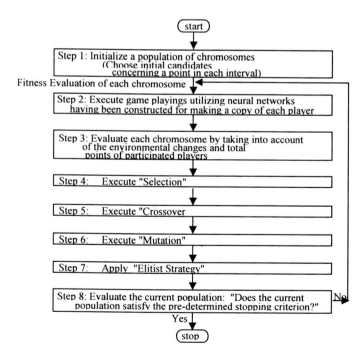

FIG. 6. Flow chart of genetic algorithms

Assume that 100 chromosomes are chosen at random in Step 1. Usually, at least 1.5 h is needed for each game run. Therefore, in order to evaluate 100 chromosomes at the first generation, we need at least 150 h. This means that a huge number of hours are needed to execute GAs for scores of generations, and are likely to exceed the scope of human efforts. So we decide that the neural network can be utilized for making a copy of each player by using the computer gaming system of the Environment Game.

The neural network model (shown in Fig. 7) utilized for making a copy of each player has eight input units, one hidden layer, and five output units. We have chosen the following input variables, which may significantly affect the amount of money to be invested by players:

A) State of the surrounding sea.
B) Total amount of money.
C) Does the surrounding sea show signs of the red tide?
D) Average amount invested in each of the chemical products.
E) Average amount used for environmental protection.

As outputs from the neural network model, we have chosen the following variables:

a) Amount of money being invested for I_j ($j = 1, 2, 3$).
b) Amount of money Z and U being used for environmental protection.

New Rule Concerning the Rate of Profit

As an initial population, 100 chromosomes were generated randomly. Simple GAs were utilized. As shown in Fig. 8, the highest value of the evaluation of the chromosomes is 0.85. This value was not been updated until the 100th generation. The chromosome whose evaluation was the highest corresponds to the values shown as Fig. 9.

To investigate whether this new rule is appropriate, some students played the game using this new rule. We felt that almost all of the students concentrated

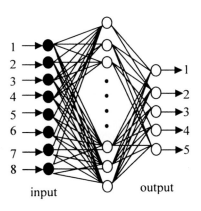

input   output   FIG. 7. Neural network model

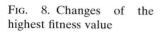

FIG. 8. Changes of the highest fitness value

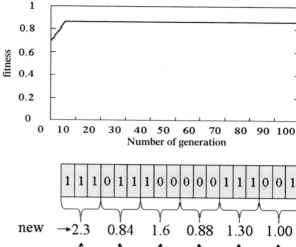

FIG. 9. The new rule concerning the rate of profit

more on the game than before. They also expressed that the new game[3] was far more interesting than the original game.

Conclusions

We investigated whether it is possible to find an appropriate rule in the Environment Game by utilizing GAs and NNs.

To show the effectiveness of the utilization of intelligent techniques such as GAs, NNs, and others in the field of gaming, more simulation studies are needed. These investigations will be addressed in our future studies.

References

Ausubel JH (1981) The greenhouse effect: an educational board game. Instruction booklet, IIASA

Baba N (1984) The commons game by microcomputer. Simulation and Games 15: 487–492

Baba N (1986) Personal computer gaming method. Nikkan Kogyo Shinbun, Tokyo

Baba N (1999a) Application of neural networks to computer gaming. In: Tzafestas SG (ed) Soft computing in systems and control technology. World Scientific, Singapore, pp 379–396

---

[3] Here, the "new game" means "the game which utilizes the values of the rate of profit obtained by GAs."

Baba N (1999b) Utilization of GAs in order to make game playing much more exciting. Proceedings of KES'99. Adelaide, Australia, pp 473–476

Baba N, Uchida H, Sawaragi Y (1984) A gaming approach to the acid rain problem. Simulation and Games 15:305–314

Baba N, Sawaragi Y, Takahashi H, et al (1986) Two microcomputer-based games. IIASA working paper

Baba N, Kita T, Oda K (1995) An application of artificial neural network to gaming. Proceedings of SPIE 2492:465–476

Baba N, Kita T, Takagawara Y, et al (1996) Computer simulation gaming system utilizing neural networks and genetic algorithm. Proceedings of SPIE 2760:495–505

Baba N, Kita T, Takagawara Y, et al (1997) Computer gaming systems utilizing NNs and GAs (in Japanese). Trans. SICE, Sougou Ronbun, 36:434–448

Cohen KJ et al (1964) The Carnegie tech management game.

Duke R (1974) Gaming: the future's language. Sage

Hausrath A (1971) Venture simulation in war. Business and Politics, McGraw-Hill

Powers RB, Duss RE, Norton RS (1980) The commons game. Instruction booklet

Shubik M (1975) Games for society. Business and War, Elsevier

23. Effective Learning Through Gaming Simulation Design

Willy C. Kriz[1], Matthias Puschert[2], Angelika Dufter-Weis[2], and Juliane Karl[2]

Introduction

In order to survive, people, groups, organizations, and societies need to adapt continuously to the change of inner and outer conditions. Therefore, human beings and social systems must be able to learn. Learning on the individual level implies acquiring knowledge, skills, and competencies in order to cope successfully with different circumstances. Learners need to change their inner conditions. Through cognitive (re)construction of mental models, learners change their perception and interpretation patterns of reality. Simultaneously, individuals must deal with the environment in which they live. Learning at the level of social systems signifies the change of systems cultures and structures. Organizational learning affects the (re)construction of social representations and norms of groups and the development of social systems' processes in order to create sustainable and humane societies.

With the use of gaming simulation, a general competence in dealing with change processes can be developed. Simulation games can also be used for supporting the acquisition of knowledge and competencies in a domain-specific context for the training of specific skills. Gaming simulation and the design of simulations with debriefing can be used as methods of training to foster individual learning processes. Simultaneously, the use and design of simulation games effects learning at the organizational level. New sensibilities and awareness, new team skills, competencies and cognitive capacities, new action rules, attitudes, and values that are formed in the run and design process of simulation games give direction, and are implemented to produce new organizational approaches, structures, and corporate cultures (Kriz 1998, 2001). Gaming simulation enhances a shift of existing organizational cultures and structures and in this way contributes to the change process of social systems. This leads to a preferred (re)construc-

[1] Assistant Professor, Department of Psychology, Ludwig-Maximilians-University Munich, Leopoldstr. 13, D-80802 München, Germany; wkriz@edupsy.uni-muenchen.de
[2] Ludwig-Maximilians-University, Munich, Germany

tion of real situations through the constitution of new action patterns, norms and roles, and the change of the physical and social environment itself. In this way, organizational learning, individual learning in organizations (e.g., in school, university, company, etc.), and the cultural change of organizations form the basis and offer fundamental social contributions to maintain healthy and peaceful societies.

A Training Course with Gaming Simulation Design

In the process of experiential learning, the playing of simulations games, their design, and debriefing are all important aspects of the learning cycle. We developed a 560-h gaming simulation-based training course on systems competence (the program takes 1.5 years). During the course, participants not only play simulation games and experience different forms of debriefing, they also learn how to facilitate and debrief simulation games ("train the trainer"). In addition, they design simulation games as well as debriefing sessions ("train the designer"). See Table 1.

The main contents and objectives of the program are: fostering of systems thinking (especially skills for analysis and sustainable development of complex system dynamics), fostering of teamwork skills (especially training of competencies for better problem solving, decision making, communication, and exchange of mental models in groups), and learning about methods of gaming simulation. Within the program, simulation games are designed that should contribute to the sustainable development and cultural change of selected social systems.

During Seminar 1, students participate in different simulation games in order to gain basic skills in systems competence and to learn about methods of gaming simulation (e.g., policy exercises, role play, pure games and experiential learning activities, simulation games and played simulations, computer simulations). In this seminar, trainers lecture on theory (lecture and discussion), present various techniques (e.g., tools for building models and systems analysis, brainstorming techniques, decision-making techniques, debriefing methods, etc.), and run illustrative simulation games.

During Seminar 2, the participants gather information and knowledge, and prepare methods, techniques, and simulation games in small project teams (with coaching by the trainers). The participants are the ones that lead the activities of the second seminar: facilitate and debrief simulation games, train methods and techniques (similar to Seminar 1). In addition, optional workshops are offered: a special course in outdoor training methods (e.g., with low and high ropes course elements and special combinations of outdoor exercises and gaming simulation), a seminar about computer simulation, and use of system modeling software and a workshop on large-group simulation games. Special problems and effects of large group games are not only discussed in theory, participants of the workshop also prepare and facilitate a large group game with more than 100 participants.

TABLE 1. Structure and contents of the training program for systems-competence with gaming simulation

Activities in the whole group of participants	Individual tasks (I) and teamwork in project teams (T)	Training hours
Seminar 1: Introduction		2h
Seminar 1: Basic course		50h
	I: Writing learning diary	7h
	I: Design a modification/variation of a simulation game presented in Seminar 1	6h
	I: Paper about theoretical contents	15h
Sum step 1		80h
Seminar 2: Introduction		2h
	T: Prepare the facilitation of exercises, presentations, and simulation games	40h
Seminar 2: Train the trainer, conduct games and debriefing		60h
	I: Writing learning diary	7h
	I: Design a modification/variation of a simulation game presented in Seminar 2	6h
	I: Paper about theoretical contents	15h
Sum step 2		130h
Seminar 2a (option)—outdoor training		20h
Seminar 2b (option)—large group game	T: Prepare and conduct a simulation game for 100 participants or more	40h
Seminar 2c (option)—computer simulation and modeling software		40h
Sum step options		100h
Seminar 3: Introduction		8h
	T: Design of simulation game, prepare the facilitation of self-designed prototype game	80h
Seminar 3: Train the designer, conduct of designed games with debriefing		60h
	I: Writing learning diary	7h
	T: Writing game-manuals (facilitator and participants manual)	15h
Sum step 3		170h
Seminar 3a (option)—projects	T: Work as co-trainer and/or co-designer in real gaming and simulation projects (in small teams) for customers (possible to write thesis)	40h
Seminar 3b (option) attending guest lectures of gaming and simulation experts		10h
Sum step 3 options		50h
Seminar 4: Excellence in gaming simulation	Seminar at Venice International University	30h
Total sum with all options		560h

During Seminar 3, the participants again have the opportunity to form teams, in which they are to design simulation games. There again the trainers play a supervisory role. Self-created prototype games are presented, conducted, and tested. The trainers facilitate a continued meta-debriefing within the whole design process. Again, additional optional activities are offered at this stage of the training program: guest lectures with experts and participation in real projects. Students can also choose to write their thesis on a topic related to gaming simulation (e.g., evaluation of self-designed games, empirical studies about the effects of training programs, etc.).

Seminar 4 focuses on gaming simulation for intercultural communication (with participants and lecturers from different countries) and on "excellence in gaming simulation." There again simulation games are designed in teams, although in a very short period of time. Topics of the designed games are intercultural communication and additional specific themes linked with current design projects of the lecturers.

Empirical evaluation studies of this training course, based on measurements both before and after, show significant improvements in knowledge and competencies, and a clear effect of knowledge transfer via training, as compared with control groups without such training. Studies highlight especially the combination of education team skills and in systems thinking through gaming simulation, which leads to a more sustainable systems management. As a result, the students' systems competence especially increases during the phase of designing their own games (Kriz and Brandstaetter 2003).

The design of games and simulations is used as a training method in order to improve students' acquisition of knowledge and skills, and to aid in the formation of shared mental models within groups. Among the group of participating students, the design of simulation games creates a virtual reality that leads to a change in their social representations of reality. The construction of models and the design of corresponding simulation games tends to be more effective than simply participating in rigid-rule simulation games (even if they are properly designed by simulation and gaming experts; Kriz 2003). The translation of experiences gained from the design of a simulation game and from the playing of the self-designed games to the real life system lead to a deeper understanding of that system's structure. This understanding may lead to intervention in the system in order to improve its functioning. The design of simulations and games by stakeholders can be defined as a type of "free form game." Participants have the opportunity to settle their own learning goals, construct models of reality, and define game rules. The design process as a self-organizing learning environment helps reveal the communication modes of the group as well as the individual mental models and systems representations of the participating designers. Common values, goals and rules, social representations of reality, and common strategies for complex systems management can be mutually shaped. In this way people are more committed to their own ideas and visions of change. Therefore, the probability of an effective change process within the reference system of the designed game increases.

The participating students are educated in the training course to become designers themselves. In this way, participants, as designers of gaming simulation, should also become change agents to develop and implement appropriate learning environments in educational organizations. The process of game design as a part of the curriculum at the University of Munich enhanced the preferred change of the institution itself. The learning process and the learning culture at the university is effecting change in the direction of a new and preferred culture that provides students with more opportunities for self-organized learning, team learning, and experiential learning.

Participants of the training courses are students of the educational sciences (future educators) and they design games that they intend to use later on in their own classrooms. Some of these education students and recent graduates have gone on to design games with their own pupils. More than 25 teams designed games in the last 5 years with a large spectrum of different gaming simulation methods, different contents, and varied learning objectives (Kriz and Reichert 2001). The learning aims of these games range from the development of personal and social skills to domain-specific and methodical competencies.

Five short examples that have already been successfully evaluated within the context of diploma thesis and which were also implemented in the school curriculum are:

- A simulation game about environmental education and teamwork in the classroom; target group are pupils of 3–4th grade primary school (age: 8–9 years); dealing especially with eco-farming and cooperative farming;
- A simulation game for mathematics education, team building and team development in the classroom; target are pupils of 8th grade high school (age: 13–14 years); fostering mathematical abilities (linear relations, proportionality, fraction terms) and social communication skills;
- A role-play game about creating a positive climate and good relationships in the classroom and about integration of outsiders and handicapped in the class; target group are pupils of 3–4th grade primary school (age: 8–9 years);
- A simulation game for intercultural communication, conflict resolution, and consensus building within value conflicts, building awareness for implicit social norms; target group are pupils of 10–12th high school, university and vocational training (age: 16 years and older);
- A frame game for learning how to learn and to develop better learning strategies; target are pupils of 5–10th grade high school (age: 10–15 years).

The next section shows a large group game, which was designed within the course.

Cruz del Sur—A Large Group Game

The game was designed as a highlight for a 1-week Boy Scout camp with nearly 1000 participants with ages ranging from 7 to 25 years. The learning goals for the whole week were: cross-cultural learning, improvement in communication, and strengthening of the solidarity between the participants. The organizers divided the scouts into five age groups and each was settled on its own "planet" (camp group).

The configuration of the game was five planets, five different cultures, and five completely different ways of thinking and living. However, only together can they save the galaxy from apocalypse. Only if all of them act together can they avert the danger. This is the task of the 1-day large group game Cruz del Sur (Fig. 1).

Every planet has its own culture, its own history, and its own rules. The five planets together with several uninhabited planets are part of a galaxy named Cruz del Sur. (The star constellation Cruz del Sur, the Cross of the South, actually exists. It can be seen in the sky of the southern hemisphere.)

The first planet is Acrux. The Acruxianer are travelers and merchants. They trade with everything available and buy all goods, objects, food, new games, information, etc. Most important is that they are the only species that can transport goods through the galaxy, because they have the necessary freighters. This is their asset for the realization of the common goal.

The second planet is Becrux. The Becruxianer are a high-tech society focusing on technical solutions and statistics. The contribution of the Becruxianer to the common goal is the design of a symbol. Toward the end of the game, they have to arrange all players in the pattern displayed by the symbol.

Fig. 1. The participants form a "human" Cruz del Sur

Third is Gacrux. It is a cold, barren, and inhospitable planet without resources. Therefore, the Gacruxianer have to trade to get everything they need to survive. The task of the Gacruxianer is to learn as much information as possible about the other planets and to document everything with photos. Because of their studies, the Gacruxianer will gather information about the apocalypse.

The inhabitants of Decrux, the fourth planet of the galaxy, spend most of their time designing and making jewelry and other beautiful items. They also like to play and have religious ceremonies. Through the ritual the Decruxianer get their food and will also find out about the apocalypse. So their assignment is to send groups to the other cultures and inform them about the dangerous threat which can destroy the whole galaxy. Later on they are also told how and where the apocalypse can be prevented.

The fifth and last planet is called Ecrux. The population of Ecrux is a very conservative, reactionary macho-culture. Men like to drink tea and to play games, while women have to make tea and design games. Because Ecrux is the only planet where yellow exists, this makes the planet very important for building the symbol at the end of the game, because many people from other cultures need something yellow in the end.

At the beginning of the game the participants have to adapt to their own culture and to master the challenges inherent to living on their planet. Then they have to contact the other cultures, trade with the other planets, and learn more about them. Furthermore they have to follow a number of rules:

General Rules:
- Communication between the cultures is only allowed on the planets and not while traveling from one planet to another.
- The population of a planet is divided into groups of 10–20 people by lot. The groups have to stay together for the rest of the game. Every activity has to be done by the whole group.

Rules for Traveling:
- About half of the population should always stay on the planet to welcome visitors. This is necessary so that visitors can be received at any time and get a comprehensive impression of the planetary life and culture. The game leaders can decree laws of exception for any planet upon request of that planet's regional government.
- Only predetermined groups are allowed to travel. Two group members at most are allowed to be absent while traveling.
- While traveling, only personal property can be taken, e.g., one's own lunchbox. For transporting goods, special freighters (labeled backpacks) are required.
- Galactic turbulences aggravate traveling in the star system. Every inhabited planet is surrounded by a critical zone, which travelers have to get through in order to reach the planet.
- A small number of high-tech, one-man spaceships can pass through those critical zones without being affected.

Regional Governments:
- At the beginning of the game, each group elects one representative for the regional government of its planet. Each regional government has one president which is elected by the representatives.

At first glance, one could be under the impression that the planets are not necessarily dependent on each other. As the game proceeds the situation changes. In the course of their research, the Acruxianer find out that a black hole closes in on the galaxy at a very high speed and threatens to destroy the entire galaxy. If they fail to swiftly inform the other cultures and develop a solution together with all of the other races, then all of the planets are doomed.

What can be done to save them? To prevent the apocalypse the inhabitants of all five planets have to work together. Many things are needed and important parts of the solution only exist on each one of the planets. Every culture plays an important role, but they need one another to survive. During the game, the cultures have to find out what they can do to prevent the catastrophe and what the role of each culture is. In the end they have to create a symbol, which shows the star constellation Cruz del Sur, made of blue and yellow plates. This symbol has to be built on one of the uninhabited planets of the galaxy.

If all the cultures work together and manage to construct a "human" Cruz del Sur they will save the galaxy from the catastrophe and win the game (Fig. 2).

FIG. 2. The catastrophe has been prevented

After the game, a debriefing took place in the same small groups that already existed during the game. Its major goal was to find out whether the following learning objectives had been achieved:

- Cross-cultural communication
- Tolerance toward other cultures
- Solving of problems and challenges
- Interaction and group dynamics

Because of the large number of participants, the debriefing was done in written form. Also, problems and questions were addressed in order to promote reflection of what had been learned and to transfer new insights won during the game to everyday life as a scout. It was important to show what the simulation had to do with reality. The participants played in the same age groups which normally exist for pioneers. These groups have many problems in everyday life and so the organizers tried to solve these problems by playing a game.

Closing Remarks

Recent education graduates and participants of the training course have also started to use gaming simulation in processes of organizational development of school administrations. Increasingly, more appropriate learning environments are constructed in the educational system, with a great potential to create effective learning processes and to advance educational social systems. In addition, the designed games of the training programs phase III deal with different social issues and in this way contribute to the development and preferred change of social systems and society itself.

To push this forward Cruz del Sur, for example, is now adapted for use in schools. In summer 2004, it will be played in two high schools with 850–900 pupils per school to develop the pupils' skills in teamwork and social competence and to contribute to a better climate of confidence and mutual assistance in the school system as a whole.

References

Kriz WC (1998) Training of systems—competence with gaming/simulation. In: Geurts J, Joldersma C, Roelofs E (eds) Gaming/simulation for policy development and organizational change. Tilburg University Press, Tilburg, pp 287–294

Kriz WC (2001) Human-resource development with gaming and simulation: structure, contents, and evaluation of a training program. In: Villems A (ed) Bridging the information and knowledge societies. Tartu University Press, Tartu, pp 143–153

Kriz WC (2003) Creating effective interactive learning environments through gaming simulation design. Journal of Simulation and Gaming 34:495–511

Kriz WC, Brandstaetter E (2003) Evaluation of a training program for systems-thinking and teamwork-skills with gaming and simulation. In: Percival F, Godfrey H, Laybourn

P, et al (eds) The international simulation and gaming research yearbook, vol 11. Interactive learning through gaming and simulation. Edinburgh University Press, pp 243–247

Kriz WC, Noebauer B (2002) Teamkompetenz. Konzepte—Trainingsmethoden—Praxis. Vandenhoeck and Ruprecht, Goettingen

Kriz WC, Reichert S (2001) Maths galaxy—a game for mathematics education. In: Villems A (ed) Bridging the information and knowledge societies. Tartu University Press, Tartu, pp 213–223

24. For the Knowledge Society: How to Involve Human Resources in Gaming

Arata Ichikawa[1] and Mieko Nakamura[2]

Introduction

The most important resource in the knowledge society will definitely be orga-nized human beings. The assumptions, opinions, and objectives of people and their organizations will be primary facts for future gaming research.

Peter F. Drucker (1985) pointed out that "scientific" is not synonymous with quantification. He teaches that "scientific" presupposes a rational definition of the universe of science as well as the formulation of basic assumptions that are appropriate, consistent, and comprehensive. He insisted that the first task for management science is to define the specific nature of its subject matter. To gaming researchers, what he wanted to emphasize seems to be that this should include, as a basic definition, the insight that the business enterprise is made up of human beings.

Drucker's thoughts on management science, as mentioned above, have had an influence on not only our business game research, but also our gaming research in general. As gaming simulation should be understood to be human or human–computer simulation of social processes, our approach to gaming research focuses on communication, information sharing, knowledge creation, and decision making for teamwork in a small group.

Although our gaming research is still in its embryonic stage, this chapter pre-sents a series of dialogues and actions in a game without using built-in computer simulations in observing the conversational learning process of a gaming team. This empirical presentation shows the current state of teamwork activity of players in a Japanese management style.

In the following sections, we address management and business gaming in order to define what gaming is universally in line with Drucker's thoughts on management.

[1] Department of Business Administration, Ryutsu Keizai University, Ryugasaki, Ibaraki 301-8555, Japan; ichikawa@rku.ac.jp
[2] Department of Sociology, Ryutsu Keizai University, Ryugasaki, Ibaraki 301-8555, Japan; mnakamura@rku.ac.jp

Finally, "structured facilitators" will be briefed as a new agenda for gaming research.

The Gaming Society

Play for Gaming

Gaming societies are groups involved with games of strategy in our social systems. A gaming society could be a gaming camp or a gaming family in terms of the relatively limited number of members.

The gaming society is a supersymbol society, or rather, we can call it a "super-society." The gaming society is not an artificial society or a virtual society, but is an artificial world in the natural world.

Roberts et al. (1959) suggested, from a perspective of anthropology, that games of strategy which are models of social interaction should be related to the complexity of the social system; games of chance should be linked with other expressive views of the supernatural, and there is a possibility that games of physical skill may be related to aspects of the natural environment. They discussed further that games of strategy may be linked with the learning of social roles, games of chance with responsibility and achievement, and games of physical skill with self-reliance.

What we learned from the three categories of Roberts et al. (1959) is that a serious game of strategy presents a comprehensive vision of the social system. Historically, games of strategy were simulations of chase, hunting, or war activities. Therefore, the process of a game is always a reflection of our society.

When we consider the knowledge society in context of our daily life, games of strategy would be a reflection of the society of knowledge workers. Gaming should become more popular in the future because gaming is a knowledge activity of human beings.

Drucker (1985) assumed that organizations are organs of society. In this context, an organ is a group that performs a special function. Each organization fulfills a specific social purpose and satisfies a specific need of society, community, or individual. Serious games of strategy could deal with the some specific concerns of society. Those games teach us to think of what they are supposed to be doing and what their tasks are. Play, in his words "Management," is the organ of the game. The specific purpose and mission of the game is to play the tasks. However, in every playing problem, every decision, every action, there is the additional dimension of time. Play in every round of the game has to consider both the present and the future; both the short term and the long term because games of strategy may be related to mastery of the social system.

Duke (1974) stated that gaming is a future's language. He argues that the primary purpose of any game is to convey gestalt. In this context, gestalt implies the logical integration of all that we have learned in sectional disciplines, which is explored to experience possible problems that must be faced in the future. In Duke's terminology, all future languages are problem-specific and they have an ability to present a future orientation. Thus, most games have a setting other than a current time frame. Putting all the above-mentioned perspectives into practice, Duke (1974) defined gaming as a gestalt communication mode. In addition, he proposed a concept of supersymbols: new symbols that are created with a specific meaning each time a player enters a new round.

An evolving society tends to own its symbol interpretation. The gaming society will create supersymbols in each round as time advances in the future. We can say that the gaming society appeared as a knowledge society before we moved from the postindustrial society to the knowledge society.

Gaming Players

According to Drucker (1985), a manager has two specific tasks. The first is creation of a true whole that is larger than the sum of its parts. The second is to harmonize in every decision and action the requirements of immediate and long-range future. This notion is applicable to the tasks of gaming players.

Gaming players have almost the same tasks as managers. Because games of strategy may be related to mastery of the social system, the essential task of gaming players is to create an image of gestalt.

Gaming Communications

Duke (1974) defined gaming as a gestalt communication mode. Designing a game requires generating the conceptual map as the organ of the game. The conceptual map is a designer-perceived model of the complex society. The purpose of the game may be to assist some research team in the articulation of the system. In the game run, they should experience communication at least whenever realizing that they communicate differently with the same model.

The most perfect communications may be purely "shared experiences," without any logic whatsoever (Drucker 1985). Communication is best known to be perception. This means that one can communicate only in the language of the recipient. As the terms have to be based on experience, they will not be able to receive terms without their own experience.

Drucker's conclusions on managerial communications are: communication requires shared experiences; communication works only from one member to another; communication is the mode of organization.

The Gaming Organization

The organizational structure of a game has to be that of a team. Because the sharing of experiences during communication among players about a topic that is complex and future-oriented, players must be organized into a team of limited number.

The thoughts of Drucker (1985) on team principles are useful for us in the analysis of the management by gaming players. For example, he pointed out that there is usually a team leader as a permanent appointment. Even so, leadership at any one time changes according to the specific stage of its progress. An important limitation of the team structure is size, which is from 7 to 15 at most. If the size of a team gets bigger, its strengths, such as flexibility and the sense of responsibility of the members, are reduced.

According to the theory of communications, at least 2 people can team up and they can play many roles with another in a wide diversity of communication types, thus forming a very complex team. According to the theory of group dynamics, 3 people produce multiple communication pathways and the possibility of subgroups in the team. The biggest team may be from 15 to 25 members. Teams of 25 are teams of teams with 2 to 9 members. The biggest team of teams could range to up to 81 members who belong to nine smaller teams.

A Serious Game of Strategy

Decisions by Consensus

An effective decision is essential in any game of strategy. To achieve efficiency, a game of strategy can be made to consist of subparts, making it possible to concentrate on each subpart sequentially without being distracted by the relations among subparts.

Strategy depends on values of the society of local people. According to Drucker (1985), in Western society, all the emphasis is on the answer to the questions whenever making a decision. Many books on decision making that try to develop systematic approaches to giving an answer are available in Western society. In Japan, the important element in decision making is defining the question. It is in this step that we, the Japanese, aim at attaining consensus. Consensus is the essence of the decision to our society. The answer to the question, which is considered the decision for the Westerner, follows its definition.

In the remainder of this section, the Japanese style in management and business gaming is explored to see if the consensus orientation plays a major role in decision making. For this purpose, we employ the Paper Plane Game as a management and business game tool. The original name of the game is "Planes or bust," designed by Legg (1994).

This is an operational game that teaches students or workers optimized production technology principles by playing the eight steps of the process flow of a manufacturing system. The input material is A4-size paper and the output is simply two pieces that are folded with particular marks on them and stapled together in an Origami-like structure of an airplane. The rule of the game is easily understood. The time of the run varies between 45 and 120 min according to the level of knowledge of the players. We have found that it takes more time for higher management people to play the game than it does for operations people. We analyze the difference as follows.

Even though the Paper Plane Game was designed as an optimized production-oriented operational game, it has four characteristics that suit the purpose of this chapter: (1) highly abstract level, (2) planning capability, (3) different roles, and (4) real manufacturing involving the players as human resources. The players of the game are expected to play alternately in both levels of management and operation. In another words, they will play as members of a functional organization as well as those of a team.

When one of the authors, Nakamura (1999), participated in the game for the first time, the result was very disappointing. The disappointment was caused by one of the participants, who was from the West, who gave the solution to the game to other participants before it was run. He seemed to have enough scientific knowledge to run the game efficiently by finding the bottleneck of the process of the production model. He instructed the participants on how to play the game, and, as a result, all the participants except him were forced to work like machines in an operational mode.

Management and Business Gaming

Preparation for Research

We organized a gaming team consisting of eight participants who had several years experience in Japanese management (Ichikawa and Nakamura 2000, 2002). Nakamura also participated in the game as a facilitator. The other author, Ichikawa, also participated in the game as an observer in charge of videotape recording.

The steps of the game are shown in Table 1.

Initial Inertia

In Inertia 1 in Fig. 1, players organized themselves and chose the leader Pa (Player A) and the subleader Pb. They then shared their own knowledge relating to the game. The person standing to the rear is the facilitator F.

In Inertia 2, the group reached the conclusion that the bottleneck was in the operation with the longest processing time. This was given 30s per unit in the conceptual map. All the players worked in this operation once in order to

TABLE 1. Steps of play

Phases	Initial inertia	Playing	Debriefing
Period	60 min	15 min	45 min
Organization	Team	Functional structure	Team
Tasks	Organizing a team, understanding the conceptual map, sharing players' knowledge relating to the problem, pre-play practicing, and making decisions	Working their own jobs as role players, noticing wrong decisions, and adjusting for better decisions	Discussing with an endogenous review and then with an exogenous review

FIG. 1. The progress of play

measure the actual time of the operation and to find which player was the best worker in terms of time efficiency. As a result, Pc was appointed to this task with a working time of 34 s per unit, which was longer than that of the conceptual map.

Although Nakamura had run the game several times for college students, it was the first time that the actual work time for a particular job of each player was measured.

In Inertia 3, with the assistance of subleader Pb, the leader Pa, standing alone, took the initiative in making all the players exchange understanding of the game from their own perspective in the game. As a result, an overall vision of the game was established and shared.

In Inertia 4, Pc alone started practicing his operation, which was the bottleneck of the production process, in order to make his work more efficient. The other players tried to examine each role with the assistance of others and the facilitator.

Inertia 5, which was a preplay practice phase, shows that all the players moved to a simulated manufacturing site. Pc practiced by himself in the actual game site. The other players try to examine the whole site.

In Inertia 6, the leader Pa measured the running time of the whole production process while the other players worked as assigned.

In Inertia 7, just after the preplay practice phase, another player Pd appeared to help with the leadership. The second subleader Pd could afford to see all the production because he was not busy. The leader Pa (standing with folded arms), realized that he could not take the leadership role during production because he was busier than he expected. This was also true for subleader Pb. As a result, the shared understandings were partly reviewed.

Playing

Playing 1 in Fig. 1 shows a scene at the beginning of the 15-min production, where the leader Pa bought materials in bulk according to the production plan for efficiency.

In Playing 2, Pc tried to send a hand signal but no one responded, including the leader. It seemed that there was no communication between members of the group in the initial part of the production time.

In Playing 3, the players started to use voice communication instead of hand signals as they realized that the hand signals Pc employed were of no use.

In Playing 4, the leader Pa counted the volume of production to confirm when the planned volume was achieved.

In Playing 5, because the players estimated that only a few minutes remained, the leader Pa bought another sheet of material to continue the production.

Debriefing

In Debriefing 1 in Fig. 1, a situation required the involvement of the facilitator F, while all the players involved themselves deeply in operational activities to escape from deep mental concentration on detail. In Debriefing 2, the subleader

Pb took the leadership role in commencing debriefing with sign language. Debriefing 3 shows that nonverbal communication was used effectively. However, it seems that the leader Pa would not share experiences with others, electing to sit and observe rather than actively participate. In Debriefing 4, the second subleader Pd continued to exchange experiences with others by using sign language. In Debriefing 5, the experience-based communications lasted for five min before the end of the game.

Play: Responsibilities, Principles, and Practices

We have observed the game involving players who are experienced in management roles in Japan. It was assumed that there is some analogy between management and "play." We have also tried to find differentials between them with a perspective of the artificial world to the natural world.

Play has not been paid serious attention for gaming research because it is a very abstract concept to understand. In addition, play is a type of design rather than analysis, such that this kind of research on design has tended to have little to do with academic respectability. In reflecting on the play of the game mentioned above, we have to conclude that play is a multidimensional discipline and is an intellectual, analytical, and empirical subject.

This game teaches us that the success of play depends on the exact responsibilities of the players. Armstrong (1979) suggested some principles of natural learning, learner responsibility, setting objectives, finding and engaging in active learning tasks, obtaining feedback on performance, and applying what was learned. With self-direction of the players, no human facilitators would be required to run a game except for the moment at which debriefing starts (refer to the explanation of Debriefing 1) unless we disregard Gresham's Law.

According to Simon (1977), an important principle in organization design is Gresham's Law of Planning. This law postulates that operational work tends to drive out management and communication. To overcome this spontaneous event in an organization, every member of the organization must manage their human information processing.

We have also found that shared leadership made the game successful. If shared leadership had not led the play of the Paper Plane Game, the game would have been an optimized production-oriented operational game. In this chapter, structured facilitators are factors that facilitate shared leadership. Seers et al. (2003) summarized structured facilitation of shared leadership: the task requires role differentiation and multiple exchange relationships, larger group size up to the point where coordination requires formalization, higher ratings of each other's abilities to contribute toward goals, and so on. For games that have structured facilitators, the group size may range between 6 and 13 members. The group size of the case presented was within this range.

Play could be defined as the sum total of responsibilities, principles, and practices of the players.

Conclusions

We are evolving from the information society to a knowledge society. In this chapter, we initially focused on gaming in general, and discussed the thoughts of Peter F. Drucker in the context of building a gaming theory. This study subsequently focused on play or actions in a game. We tried to interpret the principles and practices of play by applying Drucker's thoughts as much as possible to theory building. Play should be a design process of the players and an organized body of experience. Play fosters the experience, the understanding, the knowledge, and the skills for the future with responsibilities, principles, and practices. Play will become an integral part of gaming research. We think that the concepts in management can apply whenever gamers try to build a theory of gaming.

According to Faria (1998), business simulation game users are mostly business policy instructors (58.9%) and are less likely to be accounting or finance instructors (10.3% or 13.0%). Only 28.7% of management instructors used games in higher education, which suggests that there will be a great opportunity for gaming research in this field. Drucker (2001) stated:

"The essence of management is to make knowledge productive. Management, in other words, is a social function. And in its practice, management is truly a liberal art."

Notes

This chapter is based on the authors' presentation at a special session called "Peter F. Drucker's Thoughts and Gaming" at ISAGA 2003. In this session, any game aspects on any of Drucker's thoughts on management were presented for exploration not only on business games, but also on management in general for the 21st century.

Peter F. Drucker is a writer, teacher, and consultant specializing in strategy and policy for business and social organizations. He is best known to Japanese middle management as well as to Japanese executives. He himself shows an interest in Japanese culture and wrote a book on Japanese painting. W. Edwards Deming is another teacher and consultant specializing in quality planning, who, like Drucker, contributed to the recovery of Japanese industries with economic growth.

All the photos are adjusted to lower resolution to protect the players' identity.

References

Armstrong JS (1979) The natural learning project. Journal of Experiential Learning and Simulation 1:5–12

Drucker PF (1985) Management: tasks, responsibilities, practices (revised version). Harper Business, New York

Drucker PF (2001) The essential Drucker. Harper Business, New York

Duke RD (1974) Gaming: the future's language. Sage, New York

Faria AJ (1998) Business simulation games: current usage levels—an update. Simulation and Gaming 29:295–308

Ichikawa A, Nakamura M (2000) A self-evaluation based on the discussion and decision in experts' business gaming. Developments in Business Simulation and Experiential Learning 27:48–49

Ichikawa A, Nakamura M (2002) Exploring the decision-making process by a learning team of middle managers: a dialogue and action protocol analysis using a simulated environment. Journal of Ryutsu Keizai University 37:1–14

Legg L (1994) Planes or bust: an OPT scheduling game. In: Armstrong F, Saunders D (eds) The simulation and gaming yearbook vol 2: interactive learning. Kogan Page, London, pp 209–219

Nakamura M (1999) Dilemma and depression in the ninth year. Simulation and Gaming 30:356–360

Roberts JM, Arth MJ, Bush RR (1959) Games in culture. American Anthropologist 61:597–605

Seers A, Keller T, Wilkerson JM (2003) Can team members share leadership? In: Pearce CL, Conger JA (eds) Shared leadership, Sage, Thousand Oaks, pp 77–102

Simon HA (1977) The new science of management decision (revised edition). Prentice-Hall, New Jersey

Part V
Paradigms in
Simulation and Gaming

25. Social Contributions and Responsibilities of Simulation and Gaming: Thoughts on the Retirement of Gaming Simulations

Cathy S. Greenblat[1]

Introduction

Changing Lives

In 1956, Brigitte Bardot, a 22-year-old French actress, caused a sensation in her home country and around the world in the film *And God Created Woman*. French censors condemned the film as immoral, demanding that it be edited before it could be shown; it lost money in France where it received terrible reviews. Internationally, however, it was a box office success and Bardot, known as BB, became an international sex symbol. She was best known for the many nude or semi-nude scenes in which she appeared in various films, for her appearances in *Playboy* in 1964 and 1969, and for her flamboyant lifestyle. She starred in an average of two films per year and made several record albums before she retired from acting at a very young age of 39 in 1973. In 1995, more than 20 years after her retirement, she was chosen by *Empire* magazine (UK) as one of the "100 Sexiest Stars in Film History" (#9); in 1997 the same magazine ranked her #49 in their list of "The Top 100 Movie Stars of All Time." The June 14, 1999 issue of *Time* magazine named her one of the 20th century's twenty most beautiful stars.

On the Internet, there are many web sites devoted to BB, and many offer old posters and photographs of her for sale. Brigitte Bardot retired to her home in St. Tropez, on the French Riviera, where she has devoted much of her time over the last 30 years to work on behalf of animal rights.

Just 100 km down the road from St. Tropez is Nice, where I currently live. I moved there at the beginning of 2002, having decided that the gratifications of my career in the academic world were no longer as great as they had been. Last January, I officially retired from my Professorship at Rutgers University, and I am loving my new life in this beautiful area. My major current endeavors include swimming, kayaking, exploring the wonderful area where I now live, seeing old friends, and making new ones. Reading on my terrace is a favorite pastime, too. Of course, nobody is selling photographs on the Internet of me in my past life as a gamer and sociologist.

---

[1] Professor Emerita of Sociology, Rutgers University, USA; cathyg@bigplanet.com

FIG. 1. Greenblat photographs from past and present. **a** From my terrace, 2004; **b** with Dick Duke (center), London, 1973; **c** ISAGA, Caracas, Venezuela, 1976; **d** ISAGA, Kyoto, 1991

Retirement has permitted me to devote more time to what used to be a long-term hobby, and to couple it with my background in sociology to produce photo essays. One project, undertaken in a residential facility in California for people with Alzheimer's disease, will appear in book form from the University of Chicago Press in spring 2004, under the title *Alive with Alzheimer's*. Thanks to Kiyoshi Arai, there is a small exhibition of some of my photographs in the conference center for the next few days, including the one shown in Fig. 2, which appears not only in my book, but on the cover of a book for caregivers of people with Alzheimer's that will be published in June 2004.

I recently shipped most of my collection of gaming materials to the Universidad Politecnica de Valencia, where Amparo Garcia Carbonell will put them into an accessible archive in the main library of the School of Telecommunications. Dennis Meadows has also added a sizeable amount of material, and we are enthusiastic that in their new home, our materials will fuel the thinking of new scholars. In short, I am a retired gamer.

This brings me to the topic of my talk today. I hoped that the Brigitte Bardot images would awaken those of you who arrived here in Chiba after long journeys, but they are also central to the issues that I want to discuss. I am honored by the invitation to address you in this first Plenary Session at the ISAGA 2003 meetings in Japan, and I have elected to share some thoughts with you about the "retirement" of gaming simulations and gamers. My questions are: What happens to gaming simulations when they get old? Or what should happen to them? What differentiates those gaming simulations that have longer lives from those that lose their useful roles early? What does that tell us about what we need to do to keep our materials viable and effective?

Fig. 2. Heather and Goldie #6, 2001.
From Greenblat 2004 with permission

"Wannabees" and "Has Beens"

In the film world, it is common to talk about people with high aspirations that they have not attained, or have not yet attained, as "wannabees," a slang form of "want to be." Thus someone might be referred to as a "wannabee star." If untalented or unlucky, she or he may always be a wannabee; or some of them will succeed. Having succeeded, however, offers no certainty of continuing fame or demand. Actors, and more often actresses, may lose their appeal, often due to age, and then are referred to as "has beens."

Perhaps it is useful to think of gaming simulations in similar terms. Some games, like many wannabee actors and actresses, never achieve recognition in the first place, never come to have a national or international reputation. Some of these are simply ineffective and poorly designed. All of us who have taught courses or workshops in game design have seen heartfelt efforts that were just not good enough to send them out into the field, and we have seen some of these weak products at professional meetings, too. Some of these wannabee games do not "make it" because they are not good models of the social world. The designer has failed to understand or to represent the relevant dimensions of the social system of concern to him or her, and when the gaming simulation is operated, it lacks critical elements or the linkages between elements prove ineffective. In other words, the simulation elements are not well constructed. Others fail because the game elements are weak. The designer may have had a good grasp of the model, but failed to create a teaching/training tool that engaged the interest of the participants, was manageable for the operator, could be used within the time and space parameters available, etc. (see Greenblat and Duke 1981).

As in the film world, there are other reasons for failure. One is bad luck. Some fine gaming simulations have been designed by people who simply did not find the right connection for putting the game into the field where it could be seen and utilized by others. In short, the designer was not at the right place at the right time. One of the valuable contributions ISAGA, NASAGA, JASAG, and other gaming organizations have made has been offering designers the chance to showcase new games, allowing them to obtain feedback on weaknesses as well as encouragement for continuing to develop their models.

Yet other gaming simulations have only been played in private venues. In this address, I am referring to the games designed by colleagues whose work is done in their role as consultants, rather than in the academy. Because the gaming simulations designed for corporations under these conditions are frequently not presented to colleagues and the work is not published in peer-reviewed journals or at conferences, we are neither able to learn from them nor to critique them. The private stages of these gaming simulations are behind closed doors. However excellent they may be, they do not become known in the larger community of gamers.

Other gaming simulations enjoyed considerable success in their prime, but they were retired after their "youth" faded. Here I think that there are two reasons. Some of these items did not last because for years we have been plagued with the problems of lack of effective mechanisms for medium-scale production and distribution of gaming simulations. For example, some of you will remember *Me, the Slow Learner* by Don Thatcher and June Robinson, or Fred Goodman's *End of the Line*. I found both superb, and I had personal copies of them, but their distribution was extremely limited. Among my own creations, I particularly cherished *CAPJEFOS*, a game that I designed with a team of colleagues from Africa with UNESCO funding. It was widely commended as a tool for instructing and sensitizing participants to the problems of development at the village level in Africa. *CAPJEFOS* never made if off the local stage, and some key demonstrations around the world, however, because I never found a publisher for the large kit needed to run it.

Other gaming simulations had more success, and were reproduced in large quantities and were used in many settings. Nonetheless, they have been retired (and rightly so), although they are still remembered and praised. I think of three examples right away. *Metro-Apex* was extremely sophisticated, having emerged from years of work by Dick Duke and reflecting his great talent for modeling and creating a dynamic game. *Metro-Apex* was used widely and frequently to train engineers, politicians, and others on the dynamics of city life and of the creation of effective air pollution controls. But it was built for an old model mainframe computer. The technological revolution in computing in the past 30 years simply swept it off the "playing field" because the task of rewriting the elaborate program to a personal computer would have been enormous. Furthermore, the issues of air pollution control, while certainly not solved, became less central to subsequent administrations of the American national government.

A similar fate befell two of my own gaming simulations, although for somewhat different reasons. *The Marriage Game*, which I designed with Peter Stein and Norman Washburne in 1970, was disseminated widely because we created it in a form that allowed production of players' materials in a book form published by Random House, a major US publisher. We sold over 25 000 copies of the first edition, and we revised it about 3 years later, selling about the same number of copies. *The Marriage Game* continued to be used for several years, but the social world of dating and marital relationships was changing rapidly, and our model was each year less accurate. Delicate balances needed to be adjusted; new data for salaries, rents, vacation costs, etc. needed to be inserted; new patterns of gender-based negotiations had to be taken into account in the model. Several years later, therefore, the simulation needed another "face-lift." We chose not to do another revision, because all of us had other projects that had captured our time and imaginations.

A third example is *Blood Money*, which I designed with John Gagnon in the mid-1970s. It modeled the difficulties faced by people who suffered from hemophilia: the disease in which one's blood lacks factors 8 and 9, the clotting factors. Our model built in the complex interconnections between unpredictable attacks of bleeding, the need for immediate blood transfusions, and the interdependencies of patients, physicians, insurers, and blood suppliers. Playing *Blood Money* generated high emotion, and many participants, including top physicians working with hemophiliacs, indicated that through playing it they developed a much greater appreciation of the social psychological stresses of living with this chronic illness. The National Hemophilia Foundation awarded us a Special Achievement Award at its 1977 annual meeting, and numerous regional and local chapters of the foundation assembled kits and ran the game with diverse groups of players.

A few years later, major scientific advances allowed hemophiliacs to obtain and take home to their freezers concentrated factor 8 and 9. This freed them from the complex system we had modeled, and from the recurrent crises they had experienced with each bleeding episode. I would be happy if the story ended there, with the game going into retirement because of these changes in medical science. Sadly, as we know from global health reports, however, this blood factor, extracted from hundreds of pints of whole blood, became HIV infected, leading to the death of thousands of hemophiliacs in the early years of the HIV/AIDS epidemic. Obviously, *Blood Money* no longer reflected the situation of hemophiliacs. It was still an excellent **game** in terms of how it ran and the impact it created in participants, but it no longer **simulated** the real life situation, which had become even worse (see Greenblat 1994 for elaboration).

Moving to a New Stage

Let me offer a more complicated example of why some gaming simulations need to be retired, or to move to other stages. This saga is about a game that is known to many of you in the audience, thanks to the work of two Japanese colleagues, A. Sakamoto and M. Kashibuchi, who translated *Pomp and Circumstance* from English and have done very interesting teaching and research activities using it.

In 1978 Linda Rosen, John Gagnon, and I had a subcontract from a Ford Foundation grant in reproductive health, held by Dr. Susan Philliber. She asked us to design an evaluation tool to assess the impact of teaching about sexual and contraceptive decision making to young people in school and other settings. We were concerned that often both the students and the teacher are made equally uncomfortable by the discussion of sexuality within the traditional classroom format. Both student and teacher are understandably hesitant to reveal personal information, and so discussions of a deeply personal topic often become impersonal and detached from real-life problems. Thus, we decided to simulate, on a very abstract level, the social and personal pressures and the costs and rewards of adolescent decision making about sexual activity and contraceptive use. The main function of the game was to serve as a vehicle for the creation of a relaxed context for discussion of sensitive questions: the forces which operate and the costs and rewards of choices made by adolescents during the junior high and high school years regarding sexual activity and contraceptive use.

Pomp and Circumstance proved to be an effective evaluation tool, and Dr. Philliber and the Ford Foundation reviewers were pleased with our effort. However, Dr. Philliber soon discovered that a sizable number of the teachers in her study argued that the gaming simulation should have been the teaching approach, not the vehicle for evaluating what they felt were less effective modes of teaching. The teachers considered *Pomp and Circumstance* an innovative, imaginative, and effective tool for conveying the lessons about risk taking and failing to use contraception as did others who subsequently used it. Students echoed the enthusiasm of the teachers.

The last thing I wrote about *Pomp and Circumstance* was in 1988, 10 years after the design process ended. In *Designing Games and Simulations*, I noted our failure to find a publisher to effectively disseminate the game. I was optimistic, however, and stated (Greenblat 1988):

"We answered most letters of inquiry with a promise of information in the future; we provided a few kits to people who were adamant about their immediate need and enthusiastic about the use of the game. On the whole, the game sat on our shelves. As of this writing, there appears to be a major impetus in the United States to increase and improve sex education, and we plan to return more effectively to the tasks of publication and dissemination in the coming months."

How wrong I was! In fact, the information about *Pomp and Circumstance* provided in the Japanese translation of *Designing Games and Simulations* by Professors Arai and Kaneda led to enthusiasm about it in Japan, and a new life for the game thanks to the efforts of Dr. Sakamoto and Ms. Kashibuchi. Their interesting research has been shared with JASAG colleagues and reported in several publications, including *Simulation and Gaming* and the *International Journal of Psychology*.

But in the United States, there was no basis for a continuing use of *Pomp and Circumstance*, again for two important reasons, which offer game designers an interesting lesson about threats to the "careers" of the materials they create. First, the model itself has become somewhat less accurate because there have been changes in adolescent sexuality and in the social context of adolescent sexual life in this 25-year period (see Alan Guttmacher Institute 2002). It is not clear that this information explosion has created great changes in behavior, but adolescents do know more about sexuality than they did in the late 1970s and the school-based programs are thus not the only source of information for them. Nonetheless, we would argue that the model in *Pomp and Circumstance* is still useful, but for younger players. Another major source of threat to the current validity of the underlying model is that the HIV/AIDS threat did not exist when we designed *Pomp and Circumstance*. The risks of adolescent sexuality represented were risks of pregnancy, not of HIV infection. Given the low risk of AIDS transmission for most adolescents, probably we would not put that element into the game itself, but would let it be brought in through the post-play discussion.

A second set of factors presents a much more potent challenge to *Pomp and Circumstance* as a tool for sex education in the United States at the present time. Here I refer to the vastly changed conditions of sex education in the two decades since we designed it. *Pomp and Circumstance*, the "young star of 1978," if used today in the US schools, would be considered not simply out of date but a dangerous and immoral influence!

Consider the conditions under which we began. In a paper given at the Third International Congress of Medical Sexology in Rome in 1978, Dr. Rosen and I wrote:

Many factors in American society promote the use of effective birth control techniques. Contraceptives and contraceptive information are legally available, relatively inexpensive, and socially approved. Our culture generally supports the notion of limiting family size and spacing childbearing over time, while strongly disapproving of births that take place out of wedlock. Nevertheless, the illegitimacy rate—that is, the number of children born to unmarried females—has increased dramatically in the past decades ... Efforts to reverse this trend have focused on making contraceptives more accessible to the adolescent, and on educating the potential contraceptive user. Some form of sex education is available in many secondary school systems. At present, however, these programs teach the adolescent about the biological facts of reproduction and the hazards of premarital pregnancy, but neglect the student's personal concerns about sexual activity and contraception.

In the last decade, however, at the socio-cultural level in the United States there has been a pronounced shift to the right in terms of sexuality education, a shift that began long before, but became fully obvious in the mid-1990s. The conservative anti-sex forces are now a social movement composed of activists and supporters and lobbyists for their point of view who are affiliated with the Republican Party. People with their point of view are now powerful in Washington and other locations. They keep an eye on all aspects of sexuality (nationally and locally) and they use all of the techniques of a skilled lobbying group to influence government officials and the media about specific sexual issues (gay marriage, funds for research, the content of sex education, etc.).

In terms of sex education, they posit that sexual activity for adolescents is shameful and psychologically damaging. They argue that condoms are in fact ineffective at preventing HIV infection and pregnancy, hoping thereby to increase the fear elements around such sexual activity. For both these reasons, they are opposed to teaching about contraceptives in the schools; rather, they believe that the only effective, moral, and health-corrective programs of sex education are abstinence-only programs. Currently, "Federal law establishes a stringent eight-point definition of 'abstinence-only education' that requires programs to teach that sexual activity outside of marriage is wrong and harmful—for people of any age—and prohibits them from advocating contraceptive use or discussing contraceptive methods except to emphasize their failure rates," (Darroch 2000).

This trend toward abstinence-only sex education has sharply increased since Congress attached a provision to welfare legislation in 1996 that created a federal entitlement program for abstinence-only-until-marriage education. Section 510(b) of Title V of the Social Security Act channeled 50 million dollars to states for 5 years to support abstinence-only sex education. Educational programs using federal funds must teach that a "mutually faithful monogamous relationship in the context of marriage is the expected standard of human sexual activity" and that "sexual activity outside of marriage is likely to have harmful psychological and physical effects" [Section 510(b)]. In addition, any program receiving federal funds must not provide any information inconsistent with these definitions. The effect of this federal funding on sex education in the classroom has been dramatic. Since 1996, funding for unevaluated abstinence-only-until marriage education has increased by nearly 3000%. A recent study shows that 23% of secondary school sexuality education teachers in 1999 taught abstinence as the only way of preventing pregnancy and STDs as compared with 2% in 1988 (Landry et al. 1999). Another study reported a sharp decrease in the percentage of teachers supporting teaching about birth control, abortion, and sexual orientation and concludes that many students are not receiving accurate sexuality information.

As of October 2002, only 22 states required schools to provide a broad sexuality education, while 38 states mandate education on HIV/AIDS and other STDs. However, despite these mandates, many states give local school boards and policy makers broad oversight in determining what is taught in local school districts. Studies show that of public school districts that teach sexuality education, 35% require abstinence-only-until marriage programs and either prohibit discussion of contraception (including forbidding teachers to respond to student questions) or require contraception teaching to focus only on its shortcomings (Boonstra 2002). Similar arguments and supporting data are offered in analyses by Irvine (2002) and by Levine and Jocelyn (2002).

In such a context, *Pomp and Circumstance* would be viewed as dangerous because it fosters open discussion of contraception and it includes the message that such contraception is effective. It would be viewed as immoral because it does not condemn premarital sexual activity, implicitly or explicitly. Had it been in active use as this campaign began, it would have been forcibly retired immediately.

Implications: Abstraction and Evaluation Considerations

We have little regret about the retirement of technological tools that have become outdated, although we may regret the retirement of the Concorde before we could afford to take a flight in it or think nostalgically about the original Macintosh that we loved. Gaming simulations, too, I have argued, should be seen as candidates for retirement when they no longer serve their old purposes and when new purposes are not best served by them. As we have seen in the examples above, sometimes the models are outdated, and sometimes the teaching-training conditions no longer favor (or permit) the approach. Some of the best and most important games, while no longer viable, have made important contributions, and spawned new generations of materials. They, like Brigitte Bardot, may continue to garner awards, and to be remembered in the Top 100 lists.

Some gaming simulations have a longer shelf life because of their higher levels of abstraction, but I believe that it is possible to push that level of abstraction too far. I come from a particular school of gaming. I believe that the best teaching and training tools are gaming simulations based on social science methodology, on research data; they embed systemic models of organization and society. They have different outcomes as they are played by different groups of participants, but the range of outcomes is limited by the built-in systemic constraints and reward. Debriefing of these games includes references to concrete knowledge of specific social conditions, not just to generalized discussion of conflict or communications difficulties or power relations.

I admit that while I have had fun playing some simple games, I find them fundamentally uninteresting. I consider that the weight falls far too heavily on the debriefing and the debriefer to connect the lessons of play of the game to the real world conditions. Because the lessons then come from talk, more than from the play itself, they are easily forgotten. Because they are so vague, however, these simple games may last longer. However, I prefer the "early retired" to the "ongoing but unmemorable."

In addition, thinking about the potential for gaming simulations to become less efficacious over time, as real-world conditions change, means that we need to think about evaluation differently. Many games are designed and used without an evaluation component. We continue to use them because of anecdotal responses, not because we know that the desired changes in knowledge, attitudes, and behavior have been brought about through participation. We do not seriously inquire about what they know or do differently. Even where such evaluation is done, it is likely that it is done only in the early stages of use. My discussion of the changing effectiveness suggests that we should build in ongoing measurements of the outcomes of participation. This would put our work on a more scientific basis, and would increase our credibility with sponsors and users.

While reminiscing about *Pomp and Circumstance* to write this paper, I looked on the web to see what Dr. Philliber, the person who hired us to design the game, was now doing. I discovered that she is a major figure in the evaluation world, and recently gave the keynote address at a conference on evaluation in the United Kingdom. One of her arguments in that presentation offers good advice to us, I believe (Philliber 2002):

Another characteristic of good evaluation is timeliness. Our evaluations are only useful when they function more like smoke detectors than autopsies. We must set up our work so that it produces a continual flow of data to program staff, helping them make midcourse corrections and continuously improve their work. When our reports are late, when data only appear 2 years after the program is over, something is learned but my, how much more learning would have been possible if this work had been an organic part of the program, data flowing along with the work. Benchmarks, interim outcomes, milestones—these are the in-between things that make us more useful.

Moving Forward

Kiyoshi Arai has been telling me for 2 years that the situation is changing, and he is a trusted friend, whose judgment and talent I greatly respect. He assures me that we are on the threshold of a revolution and a regeneration of gaming. How could I resist his urging to come and witness it here, at these meetings? In the next few days of this conference, I look forward to learning what many of you have been doing in gaming during my short retirement and to casting an eye on the bright future Kiyoshi foresees.

We have much to discuss with one another and I am sure we will do so in the spirit of an old Chinese proverb:

"Acquiring knowledge is a joy, and sharing knowledge is an ultimate joy."

References

Books, Articles, Presentations:

Alan Guttmacher Institute (2002) Facts in brief: sexuality education. http://www.agi-usa.org/pubs/fb_sex_ed02.html, cited on

Boonstra H (2002) Teen pregnancy: trends and lessons learned. In: The Guttmacher report on public policy. February pp 7–10

Darroch J, Landry D, Susheela S (2000) Changing emphases in sexuality education in US public secondary schools, 1988–1999. Family Planning Perspectives 32:204–211, 265

Greenblat C (1988) Designing games and simulations. Sage, Newbury Park, CA

Greenblat C (1994) Designing games and simulations (in Japanese). Translated by Arai K, Kaneda T. Kyoritsu Shuppan, Tokyo

Greenblat C (2004) Alive with Alzheimer's. University of Chicago Press

Greenblat C, Rosen LR (1978) Sex education and pre-marital pregnancy: an innovative approach. Presented at the Third International Congress on Medical Sexology, Rome, Italy, October

Greenblat C, Duke RD (1981) Principles and practices of gaming simulation. Sage, Beverly Hills, CA

Irvine J (2002) Talk about sex: the battles over sex education in the United States. University of California Press, Berkeley

Kashibuchi M, Sakamoto A (2000) Pomp and circumstance: the instructional effectiveness of a simulation game in sex education. International Journal of Psychology 35:156

Landry D, Kaeser L, Cory R (1999) Abstinence promotion and the provision of information about contraception in public school district sexuality education policies. Family Planning Perspectives 31:280–286

Levine J, Jocelyn E (2002) Harmful to minors: the perils of protecting children from sex. University of Minnesota Press, Minneapolis

Philliber S (2002) Reflections on the practice of evaluation: the bottom line cometh. Keynote address delivered at the United Kingdom Evaluation Society meeting in London

Gaming Simulations:

Metro-Apex. Designed by Richard D. Duke. Published by Mark James, Director of Computing Services, COMEX. Davidson Conference Center, University of Southern California, Los Angeles, CA 90007

The Marriage Game. Designed by Cathy Stein Greenblat, Peter J. Stein, Norman F. Washburne. Published by Random House, New York, NY

Blood Money. Designed by Cathy Stein Greenblat, John H. Gagnon. Published by National Heart Lung and Blood Institute, POCE, Bethesda, MD

CAPJEFOS: a simulation of village development, revised version. Mimeographed. With Philip Langley, Jacob Ngwa, Saul Luyumba, Ernest Mangesho, Foday MacBailey. (Original: 1984, published by UNESCO, Division of Man and the Biosphere, Paris, France)

Me, the Slow Learner. Designed by Don Thatcher, June Robinson. Published by Solent Simulations, Fareham, Hants, England

End of the Line. Designed by Frederick L. Goodman. Published by Institute of Higher Education Research and Services, University, Alabama

26. Enhancing Policy Development Through Actor-Based Simulation

Jan Klabbers[1]

In institutional networks, policy is made by interaction among a plurality of partisans (Lindblom and Cohen 1979). Each participating actor needs information specialized to their partisan role. Knowledge in such a context is an outcome of negotiated meaning. Therefore, it is a social construction. This type of knowledge is context dependent and not accumulative per se as historical and political conditions change, and with it the negotiated meaning. This implies that facts and their significance change.

Individual actors produce knowledge within the limits and possibilities of their discourse. Discourse, according to Foucault (1972), is a system consisting of rules of formation and volitions that control what can be said within a particular field. It defines the styles of reasoning prevalent in scientific disciplines and political discourses. As a consequence, each scientific discipline, following its discourse, speaks with a different voice.

Policies, framed by interaction among a plurality of partisans, put science at the policy/science interface in a double role:

- the role of provider of information and truths within a specific discourse from the perspective of an outside observer;
- the role of a fellow partisan in the policy-development process, via (institutional) interactions with other policy actors. Here the sciences play the role of insider/stakeholder.

Especially the second role requires a model of problem solving, which is different from the traditional problem approaches of science (see the discussion on four models for problem solving).

Devising Courses of Action: The Macro-Cycle

Devising courses of action aimed at changing existing situations into preferred ones presupposes:

[1] KMPC, The Netherlands; Department of Information Science and Media Studies, University of Bergen, Norway; jklabbers@kmpc.nl; http://www.kmpc.nl

- a vision of the future, which is integrative and strategic,
- methods to achieve such preferred situations,
- a participatory setting to take on board a variety of perceptions of the stake-holders involved.

The vision of the future gives shape to the goals of such a project. The methods should enhance expanding the range of useful options, to assess future consequences of such options, and to shape programs of intervention or action. The participatory setting is needed:

- to support the process of assimilation of the results of inquiry by the intended policy actors. The objective is to influence positions, perceptions, and attitudes.
- to implement the outcomes of the assimilation process via interventions and actions in the ongoing policy-making process to realize the objectives of the project undertaken.

The implementation process provides information feedback that may lead to adjustment of the original goals. The resulting cycle of policy- or action-oriented research is illustrated in Fig. 1.

Methodology of Simulation Game Design: The Micro-Cycle

Developing and applying methods to produce results in the form of useful options, and assessments of future consequences of such options is part of the so-called empirical or model cycle.

Because the focus of this chapter is on simulation and gaming, the model or artifact represented is a particular simulation game, designed to deal with certain issues of the reference system involved. If pending problem identification, the focus of study is on conflict resolution, consensus building, environmental policies, education, intercultural communications, or city planning, then more precise information is needed to guide the abstraction process during simulation game design. This information is partly dependent on the prevailing gaming methods, and partly on the styles of reasoning of the disciplines involved.

In the various disciplines, different styles of reasoning play a significant role. They define the substantive corpus of assertions and ideas about aspects of the

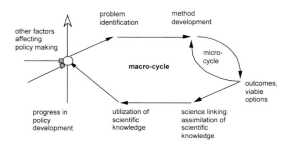

FIG. 1. Macro-cycle of policy- or action-oriented research (adapted from Klabbers 1982)

world, which are mediated through a variety of representations such as nonverbal codes, ritual acts, words, mathematical formulas, etc. Classifications, embedded in such styles, enable the definition of objects that correspond to aspects of the world. Classifications in the behavioral and social sciences are more difficult to handle than in the natural sciences. "The classification 'quark' is indifferent in the sense that calling a quark a quark makes no difference to the quark" (Hacking 1999). Taking an example from war, poverty, or ethnic conflict, the terms "refugee" or "terrorist" (as a kind of classification) are interactive kinds because they interact with objects of that kind, namely people, including individual refugees and terrorists. They become aware of how they are classified and modify their behavior accordingly. They form an interactive, self-referential kind. Quarks in contrast do not form an interactive kind; the idea of a quark does not interact with quarks. The classification "quark" is invariant, while the classifications "refugee" and "terrorist" fluctuate with social conditions. In game sessions, such "looping effects" between the classifications and players (actors) of that kind need to be addressed explicitly. Understanding the meaning of the distinction between indifferent and interactive kinds is a prerequisite for the design of adequate simulation games.

Currently available examples are role-playing games, board games, behavioral simulations, computer-assisted and computer-supported simulation games, and web-based games. The position and perceptions of the stakeholders involved frame the goals of the project. The resulting problem setting defines the information needs that the designers have to take on board. The various disciplines involved not only pursue certain styles of reasoning, they also offer diverse classification systems to enhance the abstraction process.

Problem Framing in the Social Domain

Problem identification in the social domain is not straightforward. Actors represent different positions and try to secure certain interests. Consequently, their perceptions vary. Nevertheless, the process of problem identification is the key input to action- or policy-oriented research. It sets the preconditions for a feasible project. It is a process of problem framing during which, interactively, the actors name the elements and attributes to which they will pay attention, and frame the contexts in which they will handle them (Schön 1983).

In problem framing, two heterogeneous elements are linked to each other: normative elements (norms, values, principles, ideals, goals) and empirical elements, that is, situations or conditions (Hoppe and Peterse 1993; Douglas and Wildavsky 1983). Values, norms and ideas are appreciations of products, processes, systems, and relationships attributed by people. Therefore, problems are social constructs. Problems and situations are shaped by a variety of concepts and frameworks. Moreover, scientists from different disciplines represent different knowledge claims that are based on their distinct styles of reasoning. In pluralist societies it is worthwhile to distinguish between consensus and dissension about values (and norms). In addition, the perception of existing and the anticipation of future situations are based on more or less certainty about available knowledge. Both viewpoints result in the types of policy problems shown in Table 1.

The scheme of Table 1 refers to the epistemological implications of data laden with theory, and the ethical meanings of facts laden with values.

Connected to tricky ethical and policy problems is the question how science deals with uncertainty about knowledge acquisition and assimilation. Wynne (1992) noticed that the discussions about uncertainty on many policy issues seem to rely implicitly on the naive notion that inadequate control of societal risks is due only to inadequate scientific knowledge. He criticized this idea, and added the concept of "indeterminacy" as a category of uncertainty. Indeterminacy acknowledges the fact that many of the intellectual commitments, which constitute our knowledge, are not fully determined by empirical observations. The latter implies that scientific knowledge depends not only on its degree of fit with nature, but also on its correspondence with various social constructions of reality.

Funtowicz and Ravetz (1993) use the term "post-normal science" for issue-driven research in a context of hard political pressure, values in dispute, high decision stakes, and high epistemological and ethical systems uncertainties. They use the term "post-normal" to indicate that the puzzle-solving exercises of normal science [i.e., science in the rationalist (Kuhnian) sense, see next section, models 1 and 2] are no longer appropriate when society is confronted with the need to resolve policy questions regarding tricky transnational and transgenerational social issues. Post-normal science should allow us to understand the background of conflicting interpretations. Such coexisting different interpretations are often perceived as conflicting certainties. Gaming offers a suitable approach to handle them adequately.

Within the scope of this chapter it is worthwhile to reflect further on characteristics of the science/policy interface. Vickers (1965) distinguished two levels of judgment: policy making in a strict sense, and executive decision making. Policy making is a process of appreciation that links two types of judgment: a judgment of facts and a judgment on the significance of these facts for the appreciator (policy actor). Executive decision making is based on instrumental judgment. It refers to technical issues of carrying out policies, of finding the right instruments. Although policy actors, while framing governing relationships, may be confronted with a tricky policy problem, this does not imply that they will define the related executive problem. For a variety of reasons, policy actors may refrain from formulating the executive problem. Vickers (1965) pointed out that once a policy actor realizes that there is a policy problem, it is up to him to decide what the

TABLE 1. A typology of policy problems (adapted from Hoppe and Peterse 1993)

Views on values	Certainty about knowledge acquisition	
	Certain about knowledge	Uncertain about knowledge
Consensus	Manageable knowledge problems	(in-)tractable knowledge problems
Dissension	Tricky ethical problems	Tricky policy problems

executive problem will be. Subsequently, it is the executive's responsibility to solve it.

Taking into account the many intangibles of social problems, how can science enhance social problem solving?

Four Models for Problem Solving

Science so far has offered various forms of support in addressing social issues. Paraphrasing Weiss (1977), three models for problem solving are widely used:

1. The "knowledge-driven model," in which "research has thrown up an opportunity that can be capitalized on."
2. The "decision-driven model," in which scientists respond to a problem largely posed by decision makers.
3. The "survey model," in which scientists engage in a complex search for opinions and behavior from a variety of sources.

All three models are, according to Lindblom and Cohen (1979), examples of analytical problem solving, because they refer to alternative ways of bringing knowledge to bear. They reflect a notion of knowledge that has its origins in the intellectual traditions in science and in the philosophy of science. The more information a person acquires the more knowledgeable the person becomes. In this tradition, knowledge is viewed as a collection of abstract, context-independent concepts, and discrete instances of truths or information. The underlying notion of knowledge puts science in the position of observer, providing information or truth. This position is built on the belief that science should serve nonpartisan purposes.

As mentioned earlier, in organizational networks policies are actually made by interaction among a plurality of partisans (Lindblom and Cohen 1979). At the policy/science interface, scientific institutes in many cases become a fellow actor in framing and dissemination knowledge. This puts science in the double role, mentioned above. As policy making is a way of problem solving, it continuously aims at enhancing the learning capacities of the actors involved. This approach to problem framing requires a fourth model of social problem solving.

4. The "participative model" of problem solving via which scientists develop the right conditions for sharing of knowledge and practice among the fellow actors by designing adequate learning environments to enhance joint capacities. Gaming—actor-based modeling—fits very well into this methodology.

Actors, Agents, and Algorithms

Taking into account the framework of participative social problem solving, it is worthwhile to reflect on the generic structure of simulation games, especially from the viewpoint of actor-based modeling and simulation. Special attention needs to be paid to the term "agent."

Hacking (2002) argues that people are self-conscious. They are very aware of their social environment. They are agents that act under descriptions. Such actors or agents are concerned with how we know what is, about the nature of the relationship between the ones who know and what is known.

The generic form of simulation games distinguishes between three interrelated building blocks (Klabbers 1999):

- Actors, assuming roles,
- Rules, and
- Resources.

Actors can be individuals, groups, organizational units, and institutes. Key characteristics of actors are: self-referential capacities, self-awareness, and the potential of self-reproduction. Actors produce, reproduce and transform rules, procedures, and practices to establish and sustain mutual engagement, and to make use of resources such as natural resources, people, information, etc. They are agents in Hacking's sense, not in the sense of agent-based modeling. For reasons of convenience, the terms "actor" and "agent" are distinguished in the context of this chapter by using the term "agent" for nonhuman agents, called "actants" by Mutch (2002), or "cyborgs" by Hacking (2002). The reasons are as follows. *While actors act under descriptions, agents act under prescriptions, embedded in the rules.* Actors act under descriptions, and they are aware of this because they are reflexive. Agents, as in agent-based modeling, are not reflexive and are controlled by algorithms, that is, a set of interrelated rules.

Through computers, simulation modeling has emerged as a viable and independent scientific discipline in its own right with a wide variety of areas of application such as engineering, environmental modeling, and economics. It is used as a viable method within the realm of complexity science. Three different approaches to complexity are distinguished (Klabbers 2002a): algorithmic, organizational, and organized complexity.

Algorithmic complexity refers to calculability and reproducibility of systems (Stewart 2001). It relates to the quantity of information to describe a system (Cohen and Stewart 1995) to the minimal precursor pattern, the minimal template, to (re-)construct the pattern (Katz 1986). Moreover, algorithmic complexity is based on a systematic theory of models, relating the observer to the observed (Casti 1994).

Organizational complexity relates to organizations in transition (Stewart 2001). This branch of complexity theory has its roots in evolutionary biology and the study of ecosystems, which increase or decrease in complexity as their component systems co-evolve (Kaufmann 1993). These processes select a unique and specific course through unimaginable large sequence spaces. Specific organization, structure, and process produce order within huge sequence spaces (Stewart 2001). This could be possible by grasping the context, or boundary conditions that lead to a unique history, and requires knowledge of local circumstances (local knowledge).

Both distinctions do not take into consideration basic features of organizations that are self-observing, as they primarily pay attention to the perspective of the observer.

FIG . 2. Illustration of a multi-actor-based model, embedding an multi-agent-based model (Klabbers 2002b)

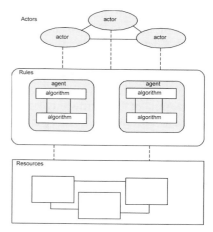

Organized or social complexity emerges through the self-awareness of the internal actors who have to deal with high levels of complexity of the internal organization vis-à-vis the environment. To a certain extent this complexity emerges through the coproduction of the actors.

Agent-based modeling is related to algorithmic complexity. It represents the rule-base of social systems. In agent-based simulations, the algorithms are functionally integrated with the simulation of resources. They potentially complement the capacities and abilities of the actors to steer the social system involved.

This understanding brings forward the scheme shown in Fig. 2 for connecting actors, agents, and algorithms in the framework of actor-based modeling.

In computer-supported, actor-base, model part of the rules, including the agents and their algorithms, are embedded in the computer configuration.

The framework of Fig. 2 conveys an important message. Agent-based models are embedded in actor-based models. They enhance the competencies of the actors. For that reason, they are complementary to the competencies of the actors and not in competition with them. This understanding should influence the way agent-based models are designed. Agent-based models are allopoietic or artificial systems. The behavior of such a system is controlled by the function it fulfills in the larger social system and by the input it receives from its environment. It is viewed as an instrument, produced and used by another external system to reach its goals (Maturana and Varela 1980). The other external system in this case is the actor-based system with its self-referential and self-organizing capacities.

The Macro-Cycle of Policy- or Action-Oriented Research Revisited

The schematic of the macro-cycle (see Fig. 1) presupposes a chain of activities that is reasonably well defined. However, the discussion on the typology of policy problems, on problem framing, and indeterminacy throws a spanner in the works. It turns out that with respect to social issues, because they are tricky, the steps of the macro-cycle are iterative in nature, and the macro-cycle runs the risk of not reaching closure due to shifting political interests. The actors involved may get bogged down in naming the elements and attributes to which they will pay attention, and framing the contexts in which they will handle them. This observation implies that the micro-cycle of simulation game design is intertwined with problem framing, as input to the design process, and with assimilation and utilization of the knowledge and understanding, as input to the policy-making process. Untangling such a string is not straightforward.

Simon (1969) broadened the notion of design by pointing out that everyone who devises courses of action aimed at changing existing situations into preferred ones is involved in design. This endeavor is what I call "design-in-the-large" (Klabbers 2003a). Simon argued that the intellectual activity that produces material artifacts is not fundamentally different from the one that prescribes remedies for the sick patient or the one that devises a new sales plan for a company or a social welfare policy for a state.

Based on Simon's views, I have distinguished between two levels of design: "design-in-the-small" (DIS), referring to simulation game design as such, and "design-in-the-large" (DIL), referring to changing existing situations into preferred ones. Both levels of design are closely interconnected. The macro-cycle of Fig. 1 depicts DIL, while the micro-cycle represents DIS. The interplay between both levels of design shapes the science/policy interface. To provide a scientific underpinning of the macro-cycle, elsewhere, I have elaborated on the principles of a science of design (Klabbers 2003b).

Even if the interplay between both levels of design is successful, there is no guarantee that the policy makers will take on board the recommendations and lessons learned. Other inputs into the policy-making process, such as shifting interests of constituencies, conflicting interest of public management, and upcoming elections, may gain such influence that valuable outcomes of such a project will disappear in a drawer.

Limited Liability and Responsibility

Those professionals involved in simulation gaming, actor-based modeling included, have theoretical models, and speculative conjectures couched in terms of those models. They also have views about how gaming works and what you can do with it; how simulation games can be designed, modified, and adapted. Typically, the simulation game does not behave as expected. The world resists (see the macro-cycle of Fig. 1), and scientists have to accommodate themselves to that resistance. They can do it by correcting the major theory under investigation, revise beliefs about how the game works, and they can modify the game itself. The end result is a robust fit between all these elements (Klabbers 2001).

The scientization of the industrialized world and the related proliferation of professional knowledge have become essential for the functioning of society. They stress a rationalist conception of knowledge with scientists in the driver's seat. Traditional professional knowledge is not well suited to coping with complex and unique situations. Problem solving such as encountered in agent-based modeling brings forward a narrowly technical rationality, emphasizing a rationalist framework for interpreting knowledge. The related problem-solving strategies are too limited in scope when dealing with social issues. They disregard competing frameworks based on multiple perceptions (Klabbers 1996).

Because the rationalist notion of knowledge is predominant, local knowledge embedded in the social relationships between the owners has received much less attention in professional practice. Moreover, it is difficult to tap. Therefore, unique circumstances leave much room for additional knowledge claims. This process of scientization spreads knowledge and uncertainty to agencies outside the science community, turning the target groups, the appliers of scientific results and other stakeholders in the political realm in business and the public domain into active coproducers in the social process of knowledge creation, linking, and utilization. They interpret scientific knowledge in heterogeneous ways and mould it to local needs. According to Beck (1992), such reflexive scientization opens "new possibilities of influence and development in the processes of production and application of scientific results." Beck is ambivalent about the consequences.

Summarizing, traditional knowledge claims by professionals are not well suited to deal with tricky ethical and policy problems.

Summary

Through the line of reasoning presented in this chapter, I have pointed out that gaming—actor-based modeling—offers a powerful and fruitful methodology to deal with tricky social issues. However, it is not in the position to take responsibility for its contributions to solving social issues. It is not in the driver's seat to take control of the future. Game designers and facilitators can enhance social problem-solving processes by offering suitable interactive learning environments for negotiating meaning and improve joint capacities. Even if the potential of simulation gaming to enhance social problem-solving is high, as professionals we can take only limited responsibility.

In the Enlightenment tradition, we may believe that more information and knowledge will automatically lead to better judgment and improved circumstances. In the policy arena we tend to forget that building and maintaining governing relationships once in a while will lead policy makers to repress, or ignore information. We need to ensure that policy makers will take the risk of getting involved in the participative modeling approach, depicted through the macrocycle. That, as such, should be considered quite an accomplishment.

References

Beck U (1992) The risk society. Sage, London
Casti J (1994) Complexification. Explaining a paradoxical world through the science of surprise. Abacus, London

Cohen J, Stewart I (1995) The collapse of chaos. Discovering simplicity in a complex world. Penguin, New York

Douglas M, Wildavski A (1983) Risk and culture. University of California Press, Berkeley

Foucault M (1972) The archeology of knowledge and the discourse on language (Sheridan Smith AM Trans.). Pantheon, New York (original work published in 1969)

Funtowicz SO, Ravetz JR (1993) Science for the post-normal age. Futures Sept:739–755

Hacking I (2002) Inaugural lecture: Chair of Philosophy and History of Scientific Concepts at the Collège de France 16 January 2001. Economy and Society 31:1–14

Hacking I (1999) The social construction of what? Harvard University Press, London

Hoppe R, Peterse A (1993) Handling frozen fire: political culture and risk management. Westview, Oxford

Katz MJ (1986) Templets and the explanation of complex patterns. Cambridge University Press, Cambridge

Kaufmann SA (1993) The origins of order. Self-organization and selection in evolution. Oxford University Press, Oxford

Klabbers JHG (1982) Futures research and public policy making: a context of use for systems theory and gaming. In: Kallen D, Kosse G, Wagenaar H et al (eds) Social science research and public policy making: a re-appraisal. NFER-Nelson. Cy. Windsor, England

Klabbers J (1996) Problem framing through gaming: Learning to manage complexity, uncertainty and value adjustment. Journal Simulation & Gaming 27(1):74–92

Klabbers JHG (1999) Three easy pieces. In: Saunders D, Severn J (eds) The international simulation and gaming research yearbook, vol 7. Simulation and games for strategy and policy planning. Kogan Page, London

Klabbers JHG (2001) The emerging field of simulation and gaming: meanings of a retrospect. Journal Simulation and Gaming 32:471–480

Klabbers JHG (2002a) Enhancing corporate change: the case of strategic human resource management. In: Frizelle G, Richards H (eds) Tackling industrial complexity: the ideas that make a difference. Proceedings of the 2002 conference of the Manufacturing Complexity Network. University of Cambridge, UK, 9–10 April 2002

Klabbers JHG (2002b) Information science: What kind of science is it? Working paper for Information Science Research Seminar. KMPC, Bemmel-NL

Klabbers JHG (2003a) Simulation and gaming: introduction to the art and science of design. Journal of Simulation and Gaming 34:488–494

Klabbers JHG (2003b) Gaming and simulation: principles of a science of design. Journal of Simulation and Gaming 34:569–591

Lindblom CE, Cohen DK (1979) Usable knowledge. Yale University Press, New Haven

Maturana H, Varela F (1980) Autopoiesis and cognition: the realization of the living. Reidel, Dordrecht

Mutch A (2002) Actors and networks or agents and structures: towards a realist view of information systems. Organization 9:477–496

Schön DA (1983) The reflective practitioner. Basic Books, New York

Simon HA (1969) The sciences of the artificial. MIT Press, London

Stewart P (2001) Complexity theories, social theory, and the question of social complexity. Philosophy of the Social Sciences 31:323–360

Vickers G (1965) The art of judgement: a study of policy making. Chapman and Hall, London

Weiss CH (1977) Using social research in public policy making. Heath, Lexington: D.C.

Wynne B (1992) Uncertainty and environmental learning. Global Environmental Change 2:111–127

27. Complex Project Management and Gaming Simulation Methodology: Enriching Interfaces Between the Mission and Performance

Shigenobu Ohara[1] and Kiyoshi Arai[2]

The Evolving Project Management World

What Is Project Management?

The International Project Management Association (IPMA) publishes a project management guidebook for the management professions and defines terminology and competency guidelines. The guidebook describes a project as "an undertaking, which is in principle characterized by a set of unique conditions such as objectives, clear time, cost, quality, and other conditions." Another definition shared among the professions states that "project management is the planning, organization, monitoring, and control of all aspects of a project and the motivation of all involved to achieve the objectives safely within agreed time, cost, and performance criteria" (Motzel et al. 1999). Project management is primarily supported by a systems approach. It harmonizes a cross-disciplinary pool of intellectual assets so as to comply with the highly sophisticated needs and technical requirements of an analysis of any engineering or management system. In fact, over the last few decades, the engineering industry has prospered in aeronautical-space constructions, building architecture, the construction of factories, and the installation of public infrastructures and networks. In these types of projects, the focus is on how to assemble modules or components into an integrated system of quality, on time and within budget. This type of project management is referred to as "delivery oriented."

A Big Shift from Hardware to Software

Changes in this hardware approach are more or less limited to the interdisciplines between technical systems. So as to improve this approach and enhance the capability of the overall organization, project contexts and knowledge areas of discrete management were defined in 1985 by the Project Management Insti-

---

[1] PMCC Research Center, Japan; University of Technology, Sydney, Australia
[2] Chiba Institute of Technology, Chiba, Japan; k-arai@pf.it-chiba.ac.jp

tute (PMI), an American professional association. A guide and handbook of project management was published and for a decade has become the bible of the American software industry. This type of project management is known as "modern project management" (Duncan 1996). This emerging industry needed to change the mindset of system engineers from computer hardware to a focus on the software side of business. Organizational training was implemented in the United States to disseminate knowledge and to foster project managers. In fact, PMI increased membership from 5000 to 100000 members with various jobs in software engineering (PMI 1999).

Value Activities in Organizations

Enterprise activities are basically undertaken for the pursuit of value generation. Public enterprise provides services for benefit while private enterprises produces products or services for profit. In a free economy, enterprise activities are competitive except for those of central government. Nevertheless, there is the need to cope with changes in a globally linked society. Undoubtedly, innovation is a key to enterprise management, but unfortunately despite the trend, innovation takes place rarely and slowly. Numerous reasons have been offered to explain such issues of awareness, difficulty, and system. In the project management context real project-oriented organization is rare but line-oriented organization is still dominant today. Operational activity is continuous, repetitive, and ongoing, while project activity is unique, temporary, and ephemeral. Therefore, innovation is found only in project work with a specific agenda of novelty and uniqueness such as research and development. What is vital for the expansion of innovation is to give equal importance to both the system's organization and the mindset within the project.

A Business World of Complexity

The Interface Between Industry and Service

Information communication technology (ICT) has drastically changed business styles and innovation has been accelerated by software and network technology. Software creates multiple interrelations between business and services across industry (Quinn et al. 1997). Needs are deeply rooted in the improvement of services for the customer, in terms of speed and reliability of response systems. New opportunities have arisen in such areas as e-government, e-commerce, and e-learning with new forms of versatile business models in portal services, supply chains, and customers relations. According to a government report in 2001, the ICT-related services market grew to a turnover of 10 billion dollars. (Ministry of Public Management, Home Affairs, Post, and Telecommunications 2002). ICT has penetrated every industry from manufacturing, finance, logistics, and energy, to construction. Despite this wide variety of multiple interfaces, it is surprising that project management is still confined within a paradigm of delivery-oriented thinking. A body of knowledge is built on several hypotheses:

1. A system requirement is determined (well defined) and resources are allocated.
2. A system context is clearly understood.
3. Quality, cost, delivery, scope, and resources are all principal goals to be managed.
4. Best process and best practices are applied throughout.

Mission-Oriented Project Paradigm

Major customers today expect a solution by applying software to business. This is not merely a delivery of a software application package at site level, but includes consultation to clarify a customer's mission at the front-end level. The mission is a holistic view or desired context as outlined by the project initiator. The starting point of a project is a mission profiling of its complexity, from out of which projections may indicate areas of future value. Trust or responsibility for performance is a significant criterion at the back-end level. System building is a bridge between the front and the back ends. It is now clear that project management must deal with a "project value chain" from scheme consultation, system building, and operational performance (Ohara 2001). Performance provides proof of value generation through applying intellectual activities and assets so as to create quality in depth and breadth. Whether it is specific or small, software has interfaces with many disciplines and business practices. In a business environment, the basic hypotheses are different and are summarized in the following:

1. The system requirements are not determined and created from a fuzzy mission (ill defined).
2. The mission includes multiple issues to be demystified.
3. A value chain is designed to integrate compound projects.
4. Competency, capability, and broader knowledge of the best process and practices are applied.

What Is Complex Project Management?

Building a Knowledge Framework

P2M is the first standard guidebook of mission-based complex projects or program management developed in Japan (Ohara 2001). The guidebook is edited for practical use with complex project issues. To satisfy the hypothesis, a survey was designed to select "high-performing companies" from the "only-one-type" category in business models and not from "number-one" type in size of market share or sales. The intent of this survey is to understand the big picture of the process of how ideas are generated and how complex missions are conceived, born, and bear fruit. In fact, the building framework of program management is a reflection of patterns perceived in CEOs case hearings. Profiles of these attitudes are summarized as zero-based thinking, competence focus, flexibility to change, and time-to-time valuation. Although similar attitudes are observed in big firms, commitment to action is either weak or less motivated. New leadership is another aspect to pay attention and observe within the innovation process of project thinking. It is more visible and implicative in small to medium enterprises, as the CEO plays a variety of roles: leader, idea generator, facilitator, and manager. The CEO launches the mission by asking for proposals from the middle and builds several projects by integrating the process with the project. These critical patterns are reflected in program integration management.

Program Integration Management

What is integration? In its current definition, it means controlling or coordinating different activities, attempts, interests, and results. However, here integration means unification of projects deduced from missions. It comprises six areas of management.

1. Profiling management
2. Program strategy management
3. Architecture management
4. Platform management
5. Program lifecycle management
6. Program valuation management

Lynn Crawford plays a leading international role in the standardization and global forum of project management, helping to clarify differences and similarities of project management guides. Her encouraging comments are "**P2M** is potentially the most significant advance towards genuine integration," and "it heralds a revival of intellectual depth to the field that has been in the process of codification of knowledge and practices" (Crawford 2002).

Process of Integration

Any project or program starts from a "mission" and not from "goals or objectives". A mission is full of multiplicity, and interfaces to cross-disciplinary areas. To clarify the context, a mission should be written in clear plural scenarios from which issues, objectives, and goals are illustrated in a semantic network relationship. Strategy is developed to select the best out of scenario options and project portfolio. Needless to reiterate, the selected scenario must be essentially readable, highly feasible, and potentially innovative. In case the scenario is evolved to realization, major components of projects are explored and identified. A group of these interlinked projects would be depicted in a program lifecycle. When putting a scenario into practice, the program architecture is indispensable in designing structural, functional, and operative connectivity configurations. The word architecture originated from out of building design, and this framework is applied to information engineering (Scheer 1998). In complex hybrid projects, project modeling is essential to identify and put them in order, before phased planning is implemented. In the turbulent environment of today, which needs flexibility to changes, a support system for quick decisions is mandatory. At the least, people have to recognize the distinction between delivery-oriented and mission-oriented types and to classify scheme, system, and service project models. The rationality of this idea lies in looking into the vital views of "human talents and team space." For many years, it has been debated that the leadership of project managers and the teamwork of their members are keys to success or failure. Applying the concept of "Ba" or team space, is a more persuasive explanation as to how teamwork is activated to produce extraordinary outcomes. Ba is liberated from the climate and rules regulated by mother organizations, and members are permitted to do what they desire if the leader is good enough to guide and coach them (Itami et al. 2000). Here, "project platform" is a concept of team community supported by a digital network. It includes a space for doing tasks, enforcing digital communications, and respecting disciplines and the culture of different professions. The project platform is also useful for decision making for drastic changes. Project management limits itself to deal with the internal changes of technical systems or of its related environment. However, it was proven that external changes like a financial crisis or disruptive technology might cause the total collapse of the value of a project. Lessons are reflected in a decision system for introducing "project real option" (Taketomi and Ohara 2002) methodology in **P2M**. Likewise in complex projects, more value indicators are needed for efficiency for goals, process, stakeholders, and ill-defined issues across the industries. **P2M** adopted a "balanced scorecard" (Olve et al. 1999) for project valuation. Once again, it is worth noting that the core idea of project and program management is value creation, and its integration is the heaviest part of the management framework.

Framework Building and Methodology

Conventional Methodology of Project Management

In a stable environment with hardware systems as the core of management, a major methodology was targeted to clarify system structure, time horizon, and progress. Work breakdown structure (WBS) is a typical tool to clarify a system structure by defining top-down hierarchy. Phased project planning (PPP) assists in effective visualization by a phased approach at milestones. Earned value management system (EVMS) is a dominant measuring tool to see time and cost package estimations of progress. Taking into account the hypotheses of complex project management, tools usually applied by the conventional methodology of project management are hardly adaptable.

BOK-Type Methodology and Cognitive Science

"A body of knowledge," (BOK), as defined by the previously mentioned American PMI, defines a range of essential knowledge for project management. Competency is a different concept involving many skills and talents found in managing projects by the European International Project Management Association (IPMA). Competency is thought to be a hybrid of knowledge, attitude, and experience, and it is shown in competency-based guidelines. Approaches are different between America and Europe. A project manager plays the role of trouble shooter when facing a crisis. He/she has a broad knowledge and competency in engineering and management, from out of which appropriate ideas of trouble shooting are generated. Why and how are they generated? According to cognitive psychology, memories of experience and knowledge are stored in a versatile frame package and his/her ideas are formulated by a combination of frames to create a shooting framework (Minsky 1986). Although BOK is written in IDEF system definition (Integrated Computer-Aided Manufacturing (ICAM) DEFinition), **P2M** is edited as a framework so that a project manager may select knowledge subframes to build competency at his or her discretion. This is because one right way does not exist. A project manager is required to do many right things rather than choosing one right way, as in a multiple choice situation.

SSM and Abduction Methodology

In dealing with the framework building of business solutions, seven steps are commonly traced starting from stating the vision, defining the mission, generating or reading ideas, conceptualizing issues, designing the architecture, operating systems, and finally obtaining business values. Although this business process is well known in many forms, the practical framework is not yet fully in place. Conventional project management uses only the fifth and sixth steps, but acts as though all seven steps have been implemented and it is because of this that business failures are caused. Soft systems methodology (SSM) (Checkland and Scholes 1990) is a brilliant system of unusual elegance and in a novel style quite different from the conventional systems approach.

SSM aims at the clarification of the semantic aspect of the issue before action or symbolic modeling by a cyclic process of exploring and learning, because the issue is interpreted from multiple angles without any single answer. The mission is composed of objectives, measures, and actions in a root definition, and after clarification is made, the conceptualized system is tested by CATWOE analysis. In the experiments of SSM, it was found that an innovative idea is not necessarily generated, but rather unfortunately confined in the old paradigm. Abduction methodology (AM) by Charles Sanders Pierce and its development (Yoshikawa and Yagiu 1997) is an effective approach in terms of idea generation. An inventor or a creative entrepreneur proposes "a package idea of a solution" as a mission or idea by zero-based thinking but fitted into the future. The idea is innovative and valuable, has potential and is often practical. His/her competency and insight has been trained in the real business world. The mission is deemed as a requested solution package to be read in depth and deployed in the system. Abduction competency is fostered in any successive thinking of reduction and deduction methodology.

Adaptation of Gaming Simulation Methodology to P2M

Ohara and Arai have both proposed the methodology adaptation to program management, and started reframing gaming simulation within the scope of program management (Arai et al. 2003). The more the study has advanced, the more interfaces are found for future collaborative work. Klabbers states, in his congress paper (Klabbers 2003), that "gaming simulation is a transdisciplinary field of inquiry and practice, which requires an appropriate epistemological and methodological basis." Gaming simulation and **P2M** have a lot in common even on an ontological, epistemological, and methodological basis, and their collaboration can only be fruitful, which is easily recognized in a paper given to the international audience (Ohara 2003).

Program management is derived from condensed knowledge in the business field, while gaming simulation is born out of science, technology, and practice. Business looks for profit or benefit, and science has been pursuing facts by induction and deduction. This striking difference of attitude has led to little collaboration in the field of social systems (Arai 2003). However, it is interesting to learn that gaming simulation is opening the door by linking hypothetical worlds to the realistic world in an SSM way where the combination of theoretical models and their real world grounding is extremely important (Deguchi 2003). Fresh interpretations and practical gaming technology are producing new initiatives in such arenas as context building, policy exercise, learning, education, communication, and training. All of them are closely related to and helpful to program management. Commonality of approach is found at least in the following agenda:

1. Demystifying the holistic view or semantic context of program missions or issue findings.
2. Focusing the human community and interactions among players and facilitators.
3. Forecasting system dynamics and systemic behaviors.
4. Designing architecture for effective hardware and software systems or their compounds.
5. Assessing program value or performance in multiple dimensions.

Conclusion

Challenging projects are triggering innovation. P2M has opened a way to the heart of the labyrinth of complex business systems designed to manage missions and implement business. The methodology used is a set of interlocking principles

266   S. Ohara and K. Arai

and disciplines within particular project fields. However, it is important to apply, nurture and develop the new methodology. It is fortunate to discover that gaming simulation provides a methodology in the link between conceptualized systems and the real world.

References

Arai K (2003) A new horizon of simulation and gaming: difficulties and expectations of facilitating science, technology and practice. Proceedings of 34th International Conference of ISAGA 2003

Arai K, Kitani S, Hasebe T (2003) Discordance of project context: a program management approach to community environmental planning. Proceedings of 17th World Congress on Project Management, Moscow, 2003

Checkland P, Scholes J (1990) Soft systems methodology in action. John Wiley & Sons

Crawford L (2002) World PM trends and the position of P2M in the global community at the project management workshop held in Osaka and Tokyo by ENAA and PMCC, 2002

Deguchi H (2003) Agent-based modeling meets gaming-simulation: A perspective to the future collaborations. Proceedings of 34th International Conference of ISAGA 2003

Duncan W (1996) A guide to the project management body of knowledge. PMI

Itami K, Nishida T, Nonaka I (2000) Dynamism of Ba and enterprise. Toyo Kiezai Sinpo Sya

Klabbers JHG (2003) Enhanching policy development through actor-based simulation. Proceedings of 34th International Conference of ISAGA 2003

Ministry of Public Management, Home Affairs, Posts and Telecommunications (2002) 2002 White paper on information and communications in Japan. pp 138–139

Minsky M (1986) The society of mind. Simon and Schuster, New York

Motzel E, Pannenbäcker O, Knöpfel H et al. (1999) ICB—IPMA competence baseline. IPMA/GPM—Eigenverlag, p 30

Ohara S (2001) Project management and Japanese qualification system. Proceedings of IPMC 2001, as a Keynote Speech at International Project Management Congress (IPMC 2001 Tokyo). A summary of two pages, pp 6–7, with its full text of 16 pages in CD-Rom Proceedings, November, Tokyo

Ohara S (2003) P2M—the Japanese version of complex project management for enterprise innovation in turbulent environment. 17th IPMA International Congress in Moscow, June 2003

Olve NG, Roy J, Wetter R (1999) Performance drivers. A practical guide to using the balanced scorecard. Wiley. Japanese Translation by Takeo Yoshikawa, pp 42–88

PMI (1999) The project management fact book. pp 42–43

Quinn JB, Zien KA, Baruch JJ (1997) Innovation explosion: using intellect and software to revolutionize growth strategies. Simon and Schuster Adult Publishing Group, pp 89–92

Scheer AW (1998) ARIS—business process frameworks. Springer, Berlin Heidelberg New York Tokyo, Japanese translation in 1999

Sherman H, Schultz R (1999) Open boundaries: creating business innovation through complexity. Santa Fe Center for Emergent Strategy, Perseus, pp 2–38

Taketomi T, Ohara S (2002) Project uncertainty and investment assessment by real option methodology. Quality Management Journal 53:30–37

Yoshikawa H, Yagiu T (1997) Abduction from engineering view. In: Gijutsuchi no Honsitsu (Essence of technological intellect). University of Tokyo Press, pp 135–158

28. Possibilities and Prospects of On-Line Games in Asia

Koichi Hosoi[1]

Introduction

This chapter presents a perspective of on-line gaming (networked commercial games), especially the situation and prospects in Asia. The worldwide number of paying users of on-line games for 2001–2002 was about 10 million, and it is possible to estimate a market size of about US $1 billion. However, this is a very conservative estimation. The entire game market, inclusive of packaged games, has been forecast to grow at a considerable pace into the future, and in particular, most research institutes are predicting that the on-line game market will expand considerably more rapidly than that of the game market as a whole.

For example, against the forecast of PricewaterhouseCoopers of the United States that the North American video game market, which was $7.8 billion in 2002, will grow to $13.5 billion, about 1.7 times its size, by the year 2007, Informa Publishing Group of the United Kingdom forecast that the on-line game market, which was $568 million worldwide in 2001, will grow to $5.648 billion, about ten times its size, by the year 2006.

Also, in the case of Korea, which is one of Asia's leading countries in on-line gaming, the total value of on-line game shipments has been growing fast: in 1998 it was only $2.5 million, in 1999 it was $16 million, in 2000 it was $100 million, and in 2002 it was $250 million. For Japan, packaged games are still the mainstream, but changes are also being seen in that market. According to the Digital Content Association of Japan, a research institute affiliated with the Japanese government, Japan's domestic market for packaged games in 2002 was about $4 billion, remaining at a year-on-year growth rate of 1.1 times. On the other hand, on-line games surged to about $55 million in sales, with a year-on-year growth rate of 4.2 times. The association has also forecast the 2003 network game market to be $170 million.

One assumes that there are a number of compound factors underlying such fast growth in on-line games, but excluding infrastructure aspects such as the

---

[1] Ritsumeikan University, Kyoto, Japan; hosoik@sps.ritsumei.ac.jp

spread of broadband, we can roughly sort them out into business model-related factors and factors related to the design of the game itself. In the case of the former, on-line games are generally more profitable than packaged games, and in the case of a hit game, profits are ensured over a long period of time, there are no losses from pirated versions unlike packaged games, and it is easy to develop systems that ensure receipt of payments. According to research by the Online Publishers Association of the United States, in 2001, US consumers paid a total of $675 million for on-line content, in 2002 the total was double that at $1.3 billion. In addition, a tendency has been observed for users to make the correct payments for on-line content.

With regard to factors related to the design of the game, it can be pointed out that, compared with packaged games, the percentage of traditional games such as Go and Mahjong in on-line games is high. Large entertainment firms, as well as Hollywood's film industry, are injecting large amounts of capital into on-line gaming, and games incorporating already well-established entertainment-related content are being created. This is tied to speculation and strategy of the leading manufacturers who maintain supremacy of the next generation game consoles, and is connected with the new development of a customer segment that has a wide range, going beyond the traditional packaged-game users.

Of course, the novelty of the business model and game design does not just give rise to a bright future for on-line gaming. Some intractable issues such as increases in development costs, the need to develop new relationships between users and manufacturers, etc, will also be taken up.

Status of On-Line Gaming in Asia

Figure 1 shows the transition in the Asian and United States game markets. The content of the calculation and the basis for the statistics in each country differ too much to mutually compare statistics; however, the market will admittedly expand rapidly in the main game-consuming countries, other than Japan, including the United States.

South Korea

South Korea is the most developed country regarding on-line games in the world. The industry developed from changes in national policy in 1998. Broadband services spread quickly, and 30 000 network cafes made the new industry. Except general ways to collect fees per month/day/hour, players can pay small (under $1) amounts by mobile phone. This creates a new style of games with a strong communication element, for example, Avatar Game. On-line games may be said to be only a tool of a highly efficient chat. In March 2002, more than half of the 27 million Internet users in South Korea—a country that promptly developed broadband due to the spread of ADSL—were experienced on-line gamers; the

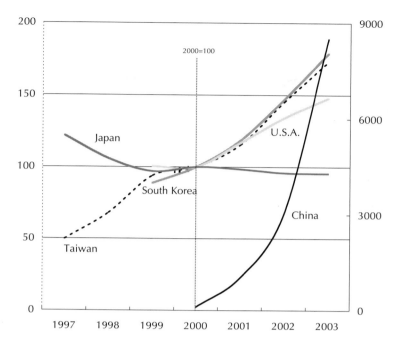

FIG. 1. Growing game markets of major countries. Refer to the *left axis* for all countries except China. Refer to the *right axis* for China

game market was estimated to be producing as much as $1.7 billion in revenue in 2003 (International Data Corporation 2003).

In addition, on-line games centered on MMORPG (massively multiplayer on-line role-playing game) have already created many correlative industries in South Korea. A typical example of this is the circulation market of merchandise related to the on-line games. Furthermore, some Internet auction sites, wherein various products related to on-line games have been bought and sold, have generated a turnover of $300 million. Moreover, for some of the free on-line games, a particular service exists wherein the player is able to buy items, clothes, arms, etc., worn by the character that the player manipulates, while playing the game with real money won in the game. In this business, the game users who buy not only items needed to win the game, such as arms and powers, but also items indirectly related to the game, such as customized externals of the character and/or the client software, have increased.

China

China is leading the explosive spread of MMORPG in Southeast Asia. The population of on-line players in China, as of 2003, is estimated to be 13 to 15 million people, most of whom have only been involved in on-line games for the past 2 years. In China, the explosive expansion of on-line games is a phenomenon not only in major cities such as Shanghai, Beijing, Hong Kong, and Chengdu, but also in small towns of provinces. It is predicted that within the next 3 years, this explosively expanding market will grow to three times its current size. In 2003, this market yielded revenue of approximately $300 million and is expected to yield $500 million in 2004. Shanda Network, the largest on-line game publisher in China, has issued 80 million ID in China and provides service for 700 000 people on-line simultaneously. The average fee of MMORPG is US $4.5 (35 RMB) per month, or 4 cents or less per hour with a prepaid card (China Internet Network Information Center 2003).

In China, pirated games prevented the industry from developing for a long time, although the Asian model of the network cafe has changed this situation considerably. A developer can identify individual players and collect reasonable fees from the players. The success of on-line gaming needs a real off-line community. The Net cafe has the environment that allows players to easily play with real friends. This helps expand the number of players and builds a strong player community.

There are two factors in the rapid growth of on-line games in South Korea and China. The first is that an existing packaged game industry barely existed. While a strong video game market did exist in Japan, the US, and Europe, it had not yet developed in Asia. There are two reasons for this, the first being that in Korea there was an import prohibition on all video game consoles made in Japan, and the second being that there was an interdiction on video game arcades in China. Thus, Internet games emerged from computer games as a new form of entertainment that exploded onto the market without warning and became extremely popular.

The second is the infrastructural factor of on-line games. There are three constituents in the infrastructure of on-line games: namely, the broadband environment, the payment system, and the Asian Internet cafe. As for the broadband environment, speed is not indispensable, but it is important that the telecommunications cost is low when considering that there is a wide range of on-line gamers in China who reside even outside the large coastal cities. As for the payment system, prepaid card is the main method of payment in China, whereas in South Korea, small-scale charging—made possible through the combination of cellular phones, fixed telephones, and resident registration numbers—has become the main form of payment. The use of credit cards, which is the main form of payment in the United States and Japan, is not suitable for small transactions, because all credit card transactions require a handling fee. The Asian Internet cafe is a significant factor in on-line gaming for the two countries. The Internet cafe is not only a terminal for on-line games but is also a form of infrastructure in which widespread users can train their computer skills.

Japan

Japan is completely lagging behind in on-line gaming. The entire gaming industry, including on-line games, is at a crossroads, and the Japanese domestic gaming industry is rapidly shrinking. Although the domestic market hit its peak in 1997, it had shrunk to about half that size by 2003. In addition, Japan is facing a worrisome decrease in international competitiveness, and the shares of Japanese companies in the American marketplace are continuing to shrink. In 2002, the shares in North America, which had been at 30%, fell below 20%. Moreover, there is extreme domestic competition with the mobile games of cellular phones, and the enterprise supplying materials for cellular phones has greatly increased its bottom line. Those rival enterprises have increased their bottom line because of services that they have created, rather than the games themselves, and have produced several services related to games combined with high-performance telephones.

In Japan, a major market of video game consoles has been established, so many on-line games appear as a combination of the "package model" and the "community model." The former is a business model based on the packaged game business and the latter is based on on-line game business. The number of MMORPG users in Japan currently under a pay service contract is 700 000 to 800 000 people, and only about 1.5 million people in total have participated in on-line gaming in Japan. Naturally, popular on-line game titles that have created large earnings do exist in Japan, but the market is still undeniably smaller than that of China and South Korea. In 2002, the on-line game market yielded revenue of approximately US $55 million (a 423% increase over the previous year), and the market of materials related to games used on cellular phones has yielded approximately $200 million (Digital Content Association of Japan 2003). Figure 2 shows an overview of the growing rates in the various game markets in Japan.

Business Model of On-Line Gaming

Design Features of On-Line Games

What can be understood from the situation in South Korea and China, where the market of on-line games was established before the market of packaged games, is that packaged games and on-line games are significantly different businesses. The success or failure of the on-line game industry depends not on the number of CD-ROM or DVD-ROM sales but on the number of users that maintain a long-term connection. In the on-line game business, the overall attractions are not only in the game's graphics, sound, and system but also in the user community (BBS, ML, SIG, etc.). In this sense, the on-line game industry resembles the service industry, because it obtains a profit when used for a long period. The on-line game industry has quite a different profit profile from that of the packaged game industry, which resembles the movie industry in that it will generate considerable marketing for the product, realizing profits in the short term.

The packaged game lacks the aspect of a charging model. To put it differently, the charging model must be included in the design of on-line gaming. The reason why on-line gaming in South Korea has succeeded in various ways is because a

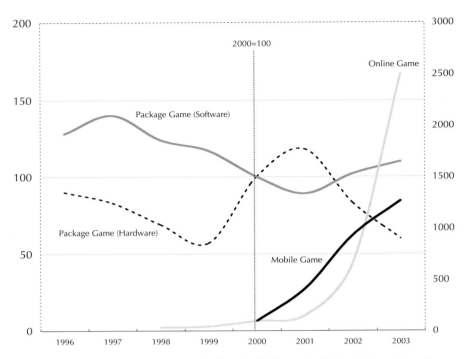

FIG. 2. Growth rates of Japanese game industries. Refer to the *left axis* for packaged games and the *right axis* for on-line games and mobile games

charging system has been built into the individual game design. Whenever new charging systems such as cellular phones and Internet cafes appear, they are incorporated into the game as the charging model. One reason why on-line games have not been successful in Japan is that the packaged game industry has switched to the on-line game industry with the packaged game business model. Therefore, it is necessary to fundamentally review the game design in consideration with the charging system of on-line gaming. Additionally, it is important to (1) charge users for providing them with added value generated by the community, and (2) proceed to create products that will have a long life, as well as creating horizontal industries of items and services derived from the long-term products created.

Moreover, MMORPG has had a strong influence on the gaming industry, and due to this strong influence, on-line games tend to be thought of as RPG (role-playing game). However, the number of ID in light or casual games has greatly increased in Japan, as well as in South Korea and China. The users of MMORPG are believed to have different preferences and budgets than the users of casual games, so when considering the design of an on-line game, it is important to develop MMORPG for the serious user differently from the casual games for the light user.

Business Aspects of On-Line Gaming

In Table 1, the production cost and profit ratio of an on-line game made by a major Japanese game manufacturer are compared with a packaged game for the same company. The numerical values are shown relative to those for the packaged game which are assumed to be 100. According to this information, the on-line game generates a larger profit, but the packaged game is still leading as a business product with respect to profit ratio. Furthermore, the on-line game is disadvantaged by the need of a running cost that is 120% of the production cost of the packaged game, which does not require a running cost. The development of the on-line game is very costly and requires considerable time. The running cost is also high, but the on-line game generates large revenue and profits. However, the on-line game has the characteristic that even if it becomes a success, the profit ratio will not be particularly high.

Promotional costs, employment costs, equipment costs (office, server, network, hosting, etc.), and the initial license fee are required for an initial investment, which is necessary when considering a concrete business frame. Running costs include marketing expenses, sales commissions (i.e., payment margins and sales incentives for the Internet cafe), employment costs, equipment costs, royalty payments, and so on. The business profit is what remains after the running costs are deducted from sales, but capital investment is difficult to judge. When open beta-testing is conducted, the number of users rapidly increases, and it is thus necessary to increase the capacity of the line and the server. However, in many cases, after the game begins to charge users, the number of users decreases. In other words, in consideration of the fluctuation of costs over time, there is a case wherein after charging users, the equipment reaches extreme excess in capacity.

Server technology and management expertise of the user community necessary for the production of on-line games and the necessary beta-testing process differ from the production of standalone games. In consideration of the above-

TABLE 1. Business considerations for package games and on-line games

	Package game	On-line game
Development cost	100	200
Development term	100	167
Retail price	100	100
Sales figures	100	100
Running cost	—	120[a]
Income	100	266
Profit	100	230
Profit rate	60%/2 years	44%/3.5 years

[a] The value of the running cost is compared with development cost of package game.

mentioned, the production of on-line games is not mere game making, as there are aspects of it that resemble city planning and real estate development businesses.

Conclusions and Perspective

The game industry started on a large scale about 20 years ago. It is a rare case historically that a player only plays with a computer. Traditional games have always been with real humans, so we can explain that gaming goes back to the traditional style. On-line games overcome the barriers of distance between users, and keep any required complexity and pliability via a computer. These make the new standard of value in the industry. In on-line games, gaming design and business models are often indivisibly related, because of network characteristics. Now the game industry is shifting from the package model to the community model. On-line gaming expands the meaning of a game as not only a work of art but also a service. Video games have been sold by the package by retailers; however, on-line games introduce different possibilities for distribution, download selling, prepaid cards, fee systems, and advertising models, etc. The critical difference between on-line game and packaged game is the importance of the "time" factor in business. The role of developer and publisher are not only in selling packages, but also in keeping quality by updating content. Game design should contain many features and expanded features are necessary to ensure that players do not tire of the game.

It is most important for successful on-line gaming to develop a player community. If many players play a game and join the community voluntarily, added value would come into existence. Players make their events, meeting in the game, and develop contents, websites, BBS, and mailing list, all based on the game. Players find new unexpected entertainment by themselves. Players are usually limited to using original content in the package games. However, a developer should recommend communities to players of the on-line game, because the number of players enhances value. Once developed, a game community provides benefits for a long time. Successful games are still in service and returning benefit, although some of these are over 5 years old and are showing their age. These phenomena occur in the console game, but not on-line. Developers have to plan the formation of a user community. Strong player communities may also become an ally to an enemy for a developer. Good reputation helps circulation between players, but bad reputation may subvert the game, and small problems tend to engulf the game. For example, if a cheater or a cracker increases his money drastically, heavy inflation in the game would happen out of developer management.

In a sense, the management of on-line games is like the management of the nation. Therefore, to change rules is similar to revising the law. Players will have the identity like people of the nation for the game and the developer must act as the Government. On-line games have the special feature that each country has a different type of community that is influenced by nationality. It is difficult to fix all characters of on-line games, because the industry is in a wave that is changing the whole world. We can, however, discuss how on-line games change our future with regard to life, business, culture, and politics (IGDA On-Line Game Committee 2003).

Acknowledgments. The author thanks the people listed below, who were speakers of the Plenary Session and related Parallel Session (On-line Game Design and Business): Kiyoshi Shin (IGDA, Tokyo), Jong-Hyun Wi (Chung-Ang University), Edward Z. Huang (Shanda Network Japan Office), Kenji Matsubara (KOEI Co., Ltd.), Taizo Son (BB Serve Inc.), Yoichi Wada (Square Enix Co., Ltd.), Rui Sato (CyberStep Inc.).

References

China Internet Network Information Center (2003) 12th Statistical Survey Report on the Internet Development in China, Beijing, China
Digital Content Association of Japan (2003) Digital Content White Paper 2003, Tokyo, Japan
International Data Corporation (2003) Korea Online Gaming Forecast 2002–2007, Massachusetts, USA
IGDA On-Line Game Committee (2003) On-line game white paper 2003. International Game Developers Association, San Francisco, USA

29. Information Technology Policy and Culture in France

Nagisa Yokoyama[1]

The Change to an Information Technology Policy

Since the United States announced the "Information Super-Highway" in 1993, information technology (IT) policy has become a priority for the peoples and nations of the world. By the end of 2002, the number of Internet users throughout the world had increased to over 665 million. Information and telecommunication systems are no longer the province of experts such as scientists and engineers but are now freely used by the general public. In this new environment, access to telecommunications infrastructure is indispensable for all people, especially in areas such as cultural and education policy, consumer protection, revision of the tax system, common law, and security measures.

In France, a variety of plans for "informatization" have now been put in place, because by the late 1990s there was an increasing awareness that France was far behind its northern European neighbors and the USA. However, once France had decided its policies, a government-oriented IT revolution was rapidly initiated and the IT industry grew significantly.

This chapter analyzes the key characteristics of the policy by retracing the steps taken to develop the information society in France.

Six Priority Areas to Create the Information Society— In the 1990s

In 1994 when France Telecom submitted their report the "Information Highway Service," the French government started to seriously address the problems of the information and communication technology (ICT) sector. Although the government chose to support 170 projects in the next year, in fact, it was not until Lionel Jospin became Prime Minister in 1997 that IT started being actively developed and encouraged by the French government.

In France a monochrome teletext system, Minitel, had already enjoyed widespread and popular use among companies and private households since the 1980s.

---

[1] Hjalmar Bergmansväg 78, 70359, Örebro Sweden; nagisa-yokoyama@hotmail.com

French people used this telecommunication system to routinely search and access information. Ironically it was the very popularity of the Minitel system that kept the French away from the Internet and the opportunity to fulfill the national desire to promote "France and French culture," and they then found themselves far behind other European countries in their presence on the Internet.

In January 1998, the government announced the Governmental Action Program for the Information Society (PAGSI) and focused on setting priorities in the following six areas: education, culture, the modernization of public services, enterprises and electronic trading, research and innovation, and the changes to the legal framework that were required.

Because informatization of the educational field was set as the first priority, the French government focused on and emphasized the importance of implementing an ICT policy in education. In the very same year as the announcement, Admifrance, the portal site for the French administrative body, was established and enabled companies and individuals to access information including a guide to citizen's rights and administrative procedures, articles on French law, advertisements for public tendering, the full text of white papers, and so on.[2]

In February 1999, Prime Minister Jospin himself made an announcement in an editorial entitled "France in the Information Society." The Prime Minister admitted that through the 1990s France had fallen behind in the information society and declared his determination to now strongly promote ICT policies as a nation and make up for this incomprehensible delay.

Elimination of the Digital Divide and Promotion of Research and Development—After 2000

In July 2000, Prime Minister Jospin chaired the Third Interministerial Committee for the Information Society (CISI). The committee firstly evaluated the progress of the PAGSI over the past 3 years. In the educational field, a top priority, it was confirmed that the access rate to the Internet in secondary schools was now among the highest in Europe. Informatization of the administration by distributing information equipment throughout the government and administrative institutions and wider public Internet access to government services was progressing well.

Also, for the purpose of closing the digital divide, 3 billion francs (450 million euros) was budgeted and 1 billion francs (150 million euros) was allocated for research and development expenses.

In order to eliminate the digital divide, the following ten targets were set by the government.

1. Establishing more than 7000 public spaces allowing access to the Internet over the next 3 years
2. Creating 4000 additional youth jobs as multimedia trainers

---

[2] Later, in order to respond more effectively to the needs of citizens and companies, the site was restructured and the new service named Service-Public started in September 2000.

3. Creating an "Internet and multimedia grade" for all pupils
4. Providing 1.2 million unemployed people with IT training sessions by 2002
5. Providing training centers for apprentices with IT equipment
6. Providing all student rooms with access to the Internet
7. Decreeing the unbundling of the local loop
8. Fostering gifts of multimedia equipment and digital material by companies to employees and associations
9. Developing gifts of multimedia equipment and digital material by the public sector to associations
10. Bridging the north/south digital divide

At the same time, further plans to create digital opportunities were drawn up for the future.

- Increasing the number of IT professionals
- Fostering research in IT with an extra one billion francs
- Speeding up the network for education and research
- Creation of a strategic Internet committee for IT

After the third meeting of CISI, a detailed policy on electronic government was announced and in the next year, the Strategic Internet Committee for Information Technologies, consisting of experts from industry and intellectuals from academia, was established.

In August 2001, the Minister for Administrative Reform declared that France had completed the first step to catch up with other countries on the road to an e-government, and, for the second step, the government started work on creating an on-line service for all administrative procedures. By March 2003, nearly 5400 public sites were open and the access rate to on-line administrative forms reached 84%. Compared with the past 6 months, a massive improvement can be seen.[3]

Moreover, in November 2002, the Plan RE/SO2007[4] (Pour une REpublique numérique dans la SOciété de l'information) was announced with three key points: (1) simplification and clarification of the existing regulations on the Internet; (2) democratization of Internet access for more people; and (3) a definition of the nation's role especially for electronic administration.

Lastly we look into the measures to promote the usage of ICT in educational institutions, which were announced in May 2003.[5] These measures intended to make it easier for the users of information equipment and services in the educational institutions to utilize the technology and included the following action points: support for primary schools where information equipment and services are not fully facilitated; lend information equipment to children who are sick and disabled; creation of a platform which pupils, teachers, and parents can use for communication and receiving information for the purpose of education; and security measures for the newly created academic communication network.

---

[3] As of September 2002, the number of public sites on the Internet was about 4880 with 74% of administrative forms online.
[4] http://www.internet.gouv.fr/francais/textesref/RESO2007.htm
[5] http://www.education.gouv.fr/actu/

The development of French ICT policy has been traced through this period and it is clear that France put an emphasis on two main topics: firstly government-oriented efforts for the elimination of the information gap by the promotion of ICT education and provision of enough facilities; secondly increase governmental support of research and development. It can be said that government intervention to increase informatization can solve the democratic issue by ensuring equal opportunities and that the information society has a significant political meaning.

The Information Society and the French Language

French Culture in the Information Society

When we keep in mind the government intervention to extend informatization in France and look at the details of its ICT policy, the relationship with "French culture" emerges.

Turning here again to the PAGSI released in 1998, the second priority "Culture" to encourage three areas: (1) creation support and development of a contents industry; (2) development of interactive contents which can be accessed by all; and (3) an international cooperation and development of francophonic community on the Internet. Simultaneously, a French language list of information and Internet-related terms, which compared with English words, was published in the *Journal officiel*.[6] We can glimpse here the French-style cultural policy, aiming to maintain and spread the country's language.

PAGSI's cultural policy encompassed the computerization of French cultural heritage and the expansion of cultural data on the Internet, for example, the national library, Bibliothèque nationale de France (BNF), is building an encyclopedic e-library by digitizing 100 000 texts, 250 000 images, as well as 90 000 videos. "Gallica," the Internet e-library enables access to 70 000 digital literary works, more than 80 000 images, and other items free of charge. In addition, in France there is a legal obligation to register all printed matter, publications, and other items with the national library (dépôt légal, Loi92–546, Art.1). The BNF multimedia department is responsible for storing multimedia and videos.

Moreover, in 1998, 22 million francs (3.4 million euros) of guaranteed funds was budgeted to nurture the culture industry, about 2.7 times the previous year's budget. It was clearly defined that publishing companies related to multimedia, service providers, and production companies were eligible to receive benefits from these funds. The main target of the fund was the film and audiovisual industries, and later cultural industries including multimedia, books, music, and theater were able to benefit. One reason for their inclusion was that the French multimedia industries, as well as film and animation industries, hold important positions in the world.

---

[6] Vocabulaire de l'informatique et de l'internet, *Journal officiel* du 16 mars 1999.

The culture industry is now at the center of the French economy. Among the rapidly growing multimedia industries, particularly striking is the development of the video game industry, which the government actively supports.

French journalist Louise Bastien pointed out,[7] however, that there are two challenges France has to deal with in order to keep its leading position in the future: firstly to widely introduce French culture by enabling worldwide access to French cultural heritage, and secondly to further energize creative activity by continuing to improve the already favorable environment for the development of multimedia and software manufacturers.

In July 2000 at the CISI meeting, France, which is active in the multilingual community within ICT society, budgeted substantial sums for professional education and research on the Internet. A 50 million-franc research budget was made available for public tendering to build a multilingual search engine, a mainly multimedia contents browser, and a search tool. More recently the Ministry of Culture and Communication also supported the design and spread of multilingual resources and the study of automatic and computer-supporting translations.

In order to maintain the "cultured nation," the French government has played a very active and leading role in creating a policy designed to promote French culture through a dynamic and financially well-supported information society.

The French Language on the Internet

Having successfully enabled worldwide access to French culture through the Web by a process of cultural digitization, this strategy allowed not only the development and dissemination of French but also the promotion of multilanguage use on the Internet.

Next, the expansion rate of French on the Internet will be presented with the aid of statistics.

Firstly, Table 1 shows the percentage of on-line population (native speakers) in each language zone. According to a survey by Global Reach, the population of French speakers who access the Internet is about 10% of English speakers.

When comparing the on-line populations of both languages, English at 35.6% and French at 3.7%, the gap is wide. In 2004, however, with the expected growth of French speakers with access to the Internet it is forecast the gap will close dramatically with English at 55% and French a close run 53%. On the other hand, compared with other languages—for example, in 2004 it is predicted German at 62%, Japanese at 70%, and Scandinavian languages at 81%—the ratio of on-line population in the French-speaking world is still low. Nevertheless, the statistics produced here are for the number of integrated regions where each language is spoken, therefore, the possibility of change is high if the statistics are examined country by country.

---

[7] *Label France* No.41, October 2000, French Ministry of Foreign Affairs.

TABLE 1. Number of people on-line in each language zone (native speakers)[8]

	Internet access (M)	Percentage of world online population	2004 (M)[a]	Total population (M)
English	262.3	35.6%	280	508
French	27.2	3.7%	41	77
German	51.6	7.0%	62	100
Scandinavian (total)	14.3	1.9%	16	19.7
Spanish	58.8	8.0%	70	350
Russian	18.5	2.5%	23	167
Japanese	69.7	9.5%	88	125
Total world	679.7		940	6330

[a] Estimated number for 2004.

TABLE 2. Chart of Web content, by language[9]

Language	Content
English	68.4%
Japanese	5.9%
German	5.8%
Chinese	3.9%
French	3.0%
Spanish	2.4%
Russian	1.9%
Italian	1.6%
Portuguese	1.4%
Korean	1.3%
Other	4.6%
Total Web pages:	313 B

Secondly, if we look at the ratio of the Web contents of each language, the pages written in English account for nearly 70% of the whole (Table 2), followed by Japanese and German with about 6% each, and the usage rate of French is only about 3%. In terms of the current French-speaking on-line population, this low 3% is understandable, but in order to achieve the government goal of strengthening French influence by using this new medium, further innovation will be needed.

The Government's Policy of Supporting the Video Game Industry

Through examining the French example of the government IT policy on culture, it has been clarified that the information society and culture are closely

[8] Global Reach, *Global Internet Statistics* September 2003 from Global Reach internet site, http://www.global-reach.biz/globstats/
[9] Global Reach, *Global Internet Statistics* as quoted by eMarketer.com, from Global Reach internet site, http://www.global-reach.biz/globstats/refs.php3

related. Considering the relation between the information society and culture, we cannot ignore the strategy of involving industry in supporting and nurturing them.

As mentioned earlier, as part of the French IT policy, the government actively supports both the cultural industries, which have already shown a growing presence in the world, and those who can be expected to succeed in the future.

Video Games as Culture

According to the report by the Ministry of Culture and Communication in July 2002, the video game industry is the sole culture industry in France that is internationally successful and comparable with the English-speaking world's top companies. Overall sales in France were 670 million euros (2001) and, although product sales figures are not yet comparable with Nintendo, Sony, and Microsoft, 24% of sales were of French products. According to government research, in the international video game market French products account for about 20% of sales.

However, even in the French video game industry that had developed so smoothly and rapidly by 2000, signs of recession could be seen and the number of industry bankruptcies exceeded the total bankruptcies of the previous 10 years. Even Infogrames, a leading player in the European games industry, announced a 60% reduction of employees in 2001.

Despite this recession, the video game industry has kept its position as the main industry in France. What lies behind this contradiction? In contrast to the flagging field of game creation, the sales of editing and production, equipment, and accessories have kept the industry's dominant position. The Ministry of Culture and Communication concluded that studio newcomers such as China, India, Russia, or the Czech Republic are all now actively participating in this strong French sector of game creation and are competing fiercely.

In the latter part of 2002, companies in the video game industry that were affected by the recession requested support from Prime Minister Jean-Pierre Raffarin. As a result, in 2003 they were given 6 million euros as support by the Multimedia Publication Support Fund (FAEM). In October 2002, the FAEM had already given special funds of 1.5 million euros to support 12 French game products. Nevertheless, the reduction of value-added tax (VAT),[10] which was requested at the same time, was refused. The Ministry's view was that video game products are a part of the "culture industry" but they are not considered as "oeuvres culturelles."

Video Games as a Strategic Sector in the Digital Society

In France, the multimedia sector, especially the video game industry, is carefully protected because it plays an important role to help French culture develop

---

[10] Currently, a 19.6% sales tax is imposed on video games and the industry requested a reduction of the rate to the same level as food (5.5%).

within the information society. Prime Minister Raffarin himself recognizes video games as the open public door to the Digital Republic (of France) and acknowledges its position as a strategic sector of French industry. In April 2003, he announced a platform of national support for the video game industry continuing on from the last autumn's RE/SO2007. These measures were presented at the inauguration of the video game hall in the Futuroscope science park[11] in Poitiers. They were based on ten proposals submitted by the Association of Multimedia Producers (APOM).

The main measures announced by the government were as follows.[12]

- Eligibility for the "Innovation Plan" (tax exemptions, etc.)
- Reinforcement of some projects including financial support by the National Research Promotion Agency (ANVAR) and multimedia organisations, as well as the creation of funds of specific support and of proximity investment dedicated to video games.
- Creation of a national school of the interactive media.

The reason why the French government supports the video game industry in this way is because the industry embodies creativity, and stands for innovation and excellence in France today. In fact, recently the French games industry has performed remarkably well and the sales figures of three French companies rank in the world top ten. French talent in the field of game design and conception has already been acknowledged throughout the world, and the country is proud of its excellent know-how and "French touch" label. Also, for children, computer games are now becoming an essential part of "culture." The government expects that France will hold its important position in ludic products and continue to encourage increasing numbers of people to use them. Moreover, computer games are not only used for leisure, but are also acknowledged for their effect on ludo-education.

Across the nation, the French government intervenes in the information society and makes every effort to maintain and develop its own culture by taking full advantage of government resources. This industry is a symbol of France's brilliance and is a key part of the strategy of informatization and cultural policy.

Conclusions

This study has examined the relation among France's IT policy, culture, and industry. It is clear that one of the characteristics of the French information society is that development has been mainly led by the government. In the back-

---

[11] Futuroscope is the general name for five zones consisting of a theme park and Technopole, which combines industry, education, and entertainment so as to encourage new industries.
[12] See the following site for a full text of the speech. http://www.premier-ministre.gouv.fr

ground there were strategies to support and nurture the industries needed to transmit French culture and the French language to the world.

In recent years the IT revolution has developed rapidly throughout the world and to introduce and manage information systems is enormously expensive. Even though the infrastructure, including a telephone network, had already developed before the 1990s in France, it is necessary, as for every country, to have a national strategy to allocate funds effectively: firstly the budget for informatization should be spent on the development of high-tech and user-friendly equipment; secondly the competitive market inside the country has to be encouraged; and finally but most importantly, there is the need to increase the international competitiveness of the software industry. These strategies resulted in the creation of an excellent information system at a lower cost.

From that perspective, French IT policy has met the nation's goal to protect and preserve the nation's culture and then develop and widely introduce it to the outside world.

Generally, France is said to be a conservative country, but this innovative and far-sighted policy will continue to be an effective strategy for the future. As pointed out in a variety of previous studies, the Minitel phenomenon, the government's centralized or vertical administrative structures and systems, and the anti-American attitude have all delayed the advent of the information society. However, at the present moment having plunged into the information society, France now actively studies new media including the Internet and makes full use of them as a means to transmit national information. Meanwhile, this new media also works to digitally save French historical literature, art works, and other items; therefore, state-of-the-art technology and cultural heritage are brilliantly and harmoniously blended.

Official Web Sites

Bibliothèque nationale de France <http://www.bnf.fr>
Internet.gouv.fr <http://www.internet.gouv.fr>
Legifrance <http://www.legifrance.gouv.fr>
Ministère de la jeunesse, de l'éducation nationale et de la recherche <http://www.education.gouv.fr>
Site du Premier ministre <http://www.premier-ministre.gouv.fr>

30. Agent-Based Simulation of Alliance of Automobile Enterprises

Shigemasa Suganuma[1], Van Nam Huynh[1],
Yoshiteru Nakamori[1], and Jian Chen[2]

Introduction

This article presents an extended model of landscape theory, called fuzzy landscape theory, and applies it to automobile industry. It is a way to simulate an agent-based model of how agents choose sides. There has been little research on how a company in the automobile industry decides what main shaft alliance to join. Increasing our understanding of the process would provide insights into the formation of automobile alliances.

Landscape theory provides a way of analyzing the many possible ways in which elements of a system, actors, can fit together. It can predict which configurations are most likely to occur, how much dissatisfaction with the outcomes is inevitable, and how the system will respond to changes in the relationship between the actors. Each of the actors try to change sides if it has more rapport with the other system. As applied to political, economic, and social problems, landscape theory can be used to analyze a wide variety of aggregation problems (Axelrod 1997).

In the next section, we present the basics of landscape theory, followed by a section on how the concept of the landscape has been extended by using the notion of a fuzzy partition. Then our concepts are applied to the case of the automobile industry. The final section illustrates our assumption model by estimating the choice of 12 automakers to join one of two alliances. We also consider how our assumption model could be applied to the Japanese auto industry.

Basics of Landscape Theory

This section briefly recalls key concepts from landscape theory. More detailed discussions of the theory, as well as its applications, are discussed by Axelrod (1997).

[1] Japan Advanced Institute of Science and Technology, Ishikawa 923-1292, Japan;
ssuga@jaist.ac.jp
[2] School of Economics and Management, Tsinghua University, Beijing, 100084, China

Landscape theory begins with a finite set of actors, denoted by A = $\{A_1, \ldots, A_n\}$. Each actor A_i has its own size $(s_i > 0)$ that reflects the importance of that actor to others. In addition, each pair of actors A_i and A_j has a propensity p_{ij} that is a measure of how willing the two actors are to be in the same coalition. For example, in the language of international alignments, the propensity number is positive and large if the two nations get along well together and negative if they have many sources of potential conflict. Furthermore, if one country has a source of conflict with another, then the second country typically has the same source of conflict with the first. Thus, the theory assumes that propensity is symmetric, that is $p_{ij} = p_{ji}$.

A configuration is defined as a partition of the set of actors. That is, each actor is placed into one and only one group. Given a configuration X, we then define the distance between any two actors A_i and A_j within X, denoted by $d_{ij}(X)$. For example, assuming that $X = \{X_j, \ldots, X_m\}$ is a configuration, then the simplest measure of distance can be defined as follows:

$$d_{ij}(X) = \begin{cases} 0 & if\ A_i, A_j \in X_k,\ for\ some\ k \\ 1 & otherwise \end{cases} \tag{1}$$

Using distance and propensity, the so-called frustration of an actor A_i is defined as the measurement of how poorly or how well a given configuration satisfies the propensities of a given actor to be near or far from each other actor. Formally, the frustration of an actor A_i in a configuration X is defined by

$$F_i(X) = \sum_{i \neq j} s_j p_{ij} d_{ij}(X) \tag{2}$$

where s_j is the size of A_j, p_{ij} is the propensity of A_i to be close to A_j, and $d_{ij}(X)$ is the distance between A_i and A_j in X.

Finally, the so-called energy, E, of an entire configuration X is now defined as the weighted sum of the frustrations of each actor in a configuration, where the weights are just the sizes of the actors. More precisely, the energy of a configuration X is as follows:

$$E(X) = \sum_i s_i F_i(X) \tag{3}$$

Similarly, the following equation defines the energy of a configuration in terms of sizes of the actors, their propensities to work together, and their distances in the configuration:

$$E(X) = \sum_{i,j} s_i s_j p_{ij} d_{ij}(X) \tag{4}$$

where the summation is over all ordered pairs of distinct actors.

The predicted configurations are based on the attempts of actors to minimize their frustrations based on their pairwise propensities to align with some actors and oppose others. These attempts lead to a local minimum in the energy landscape of the entire system.

Fuzzy Landscape Theory

In this section, we introduce an extension of landscape theory based on the notion of a fuzzy partition. It is worth noting that aggregation has been studied without landscapes as a descriptive problem in statistics, with the most commonly used technique being cluster analysis (Kaufman and Rousseeuw 1990). Under such an observation, the main idea of landscape theory is similar to that of clustering based on objective functions with the well-known c-means algorithms. This suggested that we formally restate landscape theory in terms of an optimized problem with constraints (Suganuma et al. 2003). Consequently, we were then able to extend the theory in a manner similar to that done in clustering (Ruspini 1969). On the other hand, it should also be noted that in landscape theory, the measure of distance in a configuration can be defined differently according to various applied situations. In previous studies (Kijima 2001a, 2001b; Iriuchijima 2000), the authors extended landscape theory by introducing another measure of distance. In our research, as mentioned above, we extended the theory by relaxing the notion of membership grades in the definition of a configuration. This is briefly recalled in the following. Let

- $A = \{A_1, \ldots, A_n\}$
  - A set of n actors and each A_i has its own size s_i, $i = 1, \ldots, n$,
- $[p_{ij}]_{n \times n}$
  - The symmetric matrix of propensities,
- $X = \{X_1, \ldots, X_m\}$
  - A configuration, where $1 < m < n$.

For any $A_i \in A$, $X_k \in X$, let us denote

$$u_{ik} := \mu_{X_k}(A_i) = \begin{cases} i & if \ A_i \in X_k \\ 0 & otherwise. \end{cases} \qquad (5)$$

where μ_{X_k} denotes the characteristic function of X_k.

It is easily seen that the measure of distance defined by Eq. 1 can be stated in terms of membership grades as follows:

$$d_{ij}(X) = \frac{1}{2} \sum_{k=1}^{m} (u_{ik} - u_{jk})^2 \qquad (6)$$

Substituting Eq. 6 into Eq. 4 yields the following expression of the energy of a configuration.

$$E(X) = \frac{1}{2} \sum_{i=1}^{n} \sum_{i \neq j=1}^{n} s_i s_j p_{ij} \sum_{k=1}^{m} (u_{ik} - u_{jk})^2 \qquad (7)$$

As mentioned in the preceding section, the problem is to find predicted configurations that are local minima in the entire system's energy landscape. Mathematically, the theory now aims at minimizing the objective function (Eq. 7) under the constraints of Eqs. 8–10 below.

$$1 < m < n; \quad u_{ik} \in \{0, 1\},$$
$$\text{For all } i \in \{1, \ldots, n\}, k \in \{1, \ldots, m\} \tag{8}$$

and

$$\sum_{i=1}^{n} u_{ik} > 0 \quad \text{for all } k \in \{1, \ldots, m\} \tag{9}$$

and

$$\sum_{k=1}^{m} u_{ik} = 1 \quad \text{for all } i \in \{1, \ldots, n\} \tag{10}$$

Under such a formulation, we can now extend the theory by relaxing the notion of a configuration into a fuzzy one. Then we aim at finding fuzzy configurations that minimize Eq. 7 subject to constraints.

$$\begin{cases} u_{ik} \in [0, 1], & \text{for all } i \in \{1, \ldots, n\}, k \in \{1, \ldots, m\} \\ \sum_{i=1}^{n} u_{ik} > 0 & \text{for all } k \in \{1, \ldots, m\} \\ \sum_{k=1}^{m} u_{ik} = 1 & \text{for all } i \in \{1, \ldots, n\} \end{cases} \tag{11}$$

Let us denote Eq. 12

$$\Gamma = \left\{ U = [u_{ik}]_{n \times m} \, \middle| \, u_{ik} \in [0, 1] \wedge \sum_{k=1}^{m} u_{ik} = 1 \wedge \sum_{i=1}^{n} u_{ik} > 0, \forall i, k \right\} \tag{12}$$

We also developed an algorithm for finding near-optimized solutions corresponding to predicted fuzzy configurations. In the algorithm, we utilized a genetic algorithm (GA) for generalizing configurations. We previously made two simulations with the proposed algorithm (Suganuma et al. 2003), one for the problem of the international alignment of World War II in Europe, and the other for the problem of coalition formation in standard-setting alliance in the case of UNIX operating system in the comparison to those results obtained by original landscape theory.

The algorithm proposed to solve the above optimized problem is described as follows:

Input:
The set of sizes of actors $\{s_1 \ldots, s_n\}$, the propensity matrix $[p_{ij}]_{n \times n}$
Output:
$U \in \Gamma$ that minimizes the energy function E.

1. Set $t = 0$, initiate the first configuration U_0 randomly, set a value for T.
2. Calculate the energy value for $U_0 = [u_{ik}^{(0)}]_{n \times m}$

$$\text{by} \quad E(U_0) = \frac{1}{2}\sum_{i=1}^{}\sum_{i \neq j=1}^{} s_i s_j p_{ij} \sum_{k=1}^{m} \left(u_{ik}^{(0)} - u_{jk}^{(0)}\right)^2$$

3. Set $t = t + 1$.
4. Use GA to generate the next configuration U_t from the preceding configuration.
5. Calculate the energy value $E(U_t)$.
6. While $|E(U_t) - E(U_{t-1})| \geq \varepsilon$ and $t \geq T$ do
   IF $E(U_t) < E(U_{t-1})$ Then go to step 3.
   Else set $t = t - 1$ go to step 3.

To illustrate the applicability of our approach and to test the proposed algorithm, we used the case of the automobile industry in Japan in the following simulation.

Application to Real Data

Following the lead of Daimler-Benz and Chrysler Corporation who attained joint management in 1998, the automakers in the world began to move to group their operations into larger units (see Fig. 1).

In the US automobile market, General Motors (GM), Ford, and Chrysler (now Daimler Chrysler) are well known as the "big three" and accounted for 69.4% of sales in 1999, down from 71.0% in 1998, and 71.7% in 1997. Their 1999 market shares (cars and trucks combined) are as follows: GM 29.5%, Ford 24.1%, and Chrysler 16.8% (Levy 2000, Culpan 2002). The big three's market share is gradually decreasing can be explained by the rise of Japanese makers, for example, Toyota, Honda, Nissan, Mazda, and Subaru (Minoguchi 2002).

FORD	
Ford	(USA)
Mazda	(Japan)
Volvo	(Sueden)
Mercury	(USA)
Lincoln	(USA)
LandRover	(England)
Jaguar	(England)
AstonMart	(England)

DAIMLER CHRYSLER	
Dodge	(USA)
Mercedes	(Germany)
Chrysler	(USA)
Jeep	(USA)
Smart	(Germany)
Plymouth	(USA)
Mitsubishi	(Japan)

GENERAL MOTORS	
Chevrolet	(USA)
OpelVauxh	(Europe)
Pontiac	(USA)
GMC	(USA)
Oldsmobile	(USA)
Saturn	(USA)
Cadillac	(USA)
Holden	(Australia)
Saab	(Sueden)
Isuzu	(Japan)
Buick	(USA)

PEUGEOT S.A	
Peugeot	(France)
Citroen	(France)

BMW	
BMW	(Germany)
Mini	(England)

TOYOTA	
Toyota	(Japan)
Daihatsu	(Japan)
Lexus	(Japan)

HONDA	
Honda	(Japan)
Acura	(Japan)

SUZUKI	
Suzuki	(Japan)
Maruti	(India)

HYUNDAI	
Hyundai	(South Korea)
Kia	(South Korea)

DAEWOO	
Daewoo	(South Korea)
Ssangyong	(South Korea)

RENAULT	
Renault	(France)
Nissan	(Japan)
Dacia	(Roumania)
Samsung	(South Korea)
Infiniti	(Japan)

FIAT	
Fiat	(Italy)
AlfaRomeo	(Italy)
Lancia	(Italy)
Ferrari	(Italy)
Maserati	(Italy)

VOLKSWAGEN	
Volkswagen	(Germany)
Audi	(Germany)
Seat	(Spain)
Skoda	(czech)
Bentley	(England)
Lamborghin	(Italy)
RollsRoyce	(England)

FIG. 1. The group of automobile enterprises

In the Japanese market, Toyota stands as the market leader with Honda in second position. Foreign automakers have experienced sluggish sales growth, with US manufacturers only gaining 3.1% (Maruka 1997). However, GM and Ford have taken a strategy by which expansion will be attained by tie-up. This tie-up includes joint management, a capital tie-up, buying over.

In this condition, ten domestic companies are formed which fall into six different types. To be more precise, it is as follows: General Motors partner group (Suzuki, Fuji, and Isuzu), Toyota partner group (Toyota, Daihatsu, and Hino), Ford partner group (Mazda), Daimler Chrysler partner group (Mitsubishi), Renault/Nissan partner group (Nissan), and a stand-alone company (Honda). Furthermore, these groups again can be roughly divided into two meta-groups, mainly GM-TOYOTA versus the others, in terms of technical supply (this information is taken from http://www.jama.or.jp). The behavior being predicted fit into the situations. (see Fig. 2)

In this research we study the formation of foreign-affiliated based alliances that were formed to increase the scale of expansion. Because these alliances must induce individual makers to join them in order to succeed, we concentrate on the incentives for makers to join such alliances. Our basic assumptions are that Japanese auto makers prefer to join such alliances in order to increase the probability of successfully promoting competitive power, and to avoid affiliation with Japanese rivals, especially close rivals, and thereby maximize benefits (Minoguchi

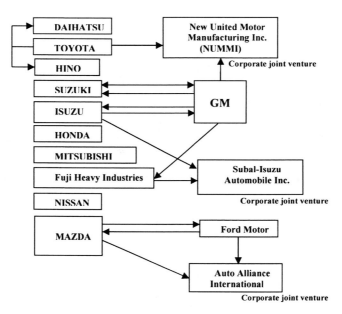

FIG. 2. The alliance of technical supply relationships

2002). By building on these premises, we define the parameter setting below. We analyze the effectiveness of our assumption by applying it to the year 2000 circumstances.

Parameter Setting

Parameters were identified for the 12 automobile enterprises that had the potential to play an important role in Japan. We first define s_j, p_{ij} and $d_{ij}(X)$ for any i, j and a configuration X.

In this case, we define the size s_j of an actor (i.e., a company) j by its production profile in the Japan automobile industry during 2000.

The calculation of propensities is carried out as follows: let i and j be two companies and suppose that

$$F_i = \{1, 2, \ldots, q, \ldots, m_i\} \text{ and } F_j = \{1, 2, \ldots, r, \ldots, m_j\}$$

are two sets of companies (capital partnership, supply from other company) co-operating with i and j, respectively. This means that i co-operates with m_i other companies while j cooperates with m_j other companies.

The total number of companies in this study is 12. For $r \in F_j$, we denote by $s_i(r)$ the attractiveness of r with respect to i, and $s_i(r)$ are calculated by

$$s_i(r) = \sum_{q=1}^{m_i} s_q(r) \tag{13}$$

where $s_q(r)$ indicates the relative importance of r with respect to q by taking into account their relation from establishment to the year 2000.

With n companies, there are $n(n-1)/2$ pairwise propensities. For $n = 12$, we have a total of 66 pairwise propensities.

Then, if there is capital partnership or supply between two companies, these factors count as +1 each for their propensity. However, if one company was not suitable for the other, the two companies count as −1 each for their propensity. These values are summed up. By these considerations we set

$$s_q(r) = \begin{cases} +1 & \text{if } r \text{ is able to be connected with } q \\ -1 & \text{if } r \text{ is unable to be connected with } q \end{cases} \tag{14}$$

Making use of these parameters, we now define the propensity of company i toward j by

$$p_{ij} = \sum_{r=1}^{m_j} s_i(r)/m_i \tag{15}$$

Table 1 lists the 12 companies considered as agents in this chapter. These agents are the ten Japanese automobile makers and two big US makers. The annual production of individual makers is shown (Japan Automobile Manufacturers Association, http://www.jama.or.jp). By using this data, we can also calculate propensity as shown by Table 2.

TABLE 1. Production profile in the automobile industry

Company	Annual production
1 General Motors	8 127 379
2 Ford	7 322 951
3 Toyota	5 954 723
4 Nissan	2 603 481
5 Honda	2 505 256
6 Mitsubishi	1 779 391
7 Suzuki	1 457 056
8 Mazda	925 876
9 Daihatsu	707 736
10 Fuji	581 035
11 Isuzu	476 952
12 Hino	36 000

TABLE 2. Matrix of propensity p_{ij}

	1	2	3	4	5	6	7	8	9	10	11	12
1 GM	1	−0.167	−0.167	−0.167	−0.167	−0.167	0.333	−0.167	−0.167	0	0.25	−0.167
2 Ford	−0.167	1	−0.167	−0.167	−0.167	−0.167	−0.167	0.417	−0.167	−0.167	−0.167	−0.167
3 Toyota	−0.167	−0.167	1	−0.167	−0.167	−0.167	−0.167	−0.167	0	−0.167	−0.167	0
4 Nissan	−0.167	−0.167	−0.167	1	−0.167	−0.167	−0.167	−0.167	−0.167	−0.167	−0.167	−0.167
5 Honda	−0.167	−0.167	−0.167	−0.167	1	−0.167	−0.167	−0.167	−0.167	−0.167	−0.167	−0.167
6 Mitsubishi	−0.167	−0.167	−0.167	−0.167	−0.167	1	−0.167	−0.167	−0.167	−0.167	−0.167	−0.167
7 Suzuki	0.333	−0.167	−0.167	−0.167	−0.167	−0.167	1	−0.167	−0.167	0	−0.167	−0.167
8 Mazda	−0.167	0.417	−0.167	−0.167	−0.167	−0.167	−0.167	1	−0.167	−0.167	−0.167	−0.167
9 Daihatsu	−0.167	−0.167	0	−0.167	−0.167	−0.167	−0.167	−0.167	1	−0.167	−0.167	−0.167
10 Fuji	0	−0.167	−0.167	−0.167	−0.167	−0.167	0	−0.167	−0.167	1	−0.167	−0.167
11 Isuzu	0.25	−0.167	−0.167	−0.167	−0.167	−0.167	−0.167	−0.167	−0.167	−0.167	1	−0.167
12 Hino	−0.167	−0.167	0	−0.167	−0.167	−0.167	−0.167	−0.167	−0.167	−0.167	−0.167	1

Simulation Results

Table 3 displays the results of the simulation, which include a configuration that is the actual alliance configuration. The configuration has two alliances. In configuration, all memberships are estimated correctly by comparing with the alliance of the technical supply relationships. There are $2^{11} = 2048$ possible alliance configurations of at most two alliances each. One configuration of alliance was Nash equilibrium. The equilibrium has the two following alliances. GM joins with Toyota, Suzuki, Daihatsu, Fuji, Isuzu, and Hino in the first alliance. On the other side, Ford, Nissan, Honda, Mitsubishi, and Mazda are grouped into another one. The configuration is the exact partnership of the actual alliance that is based on the technical supply relationships.

This match between empirical memberships and the predicted alliances in this illustration provides support for the fuzzy landscape approach. This result,

TABLE 3. Simulation results

Configuration			
Alignment 1		Alignment 2	
General Motors	0.999956572298	Ford	1.48E-05
Toyota	0.999953009369	Nissan	2.20E-04
Suzuki	0.999874549070	Honda	8.97E-05
Daihatsu	0.999947505175	Mitsubishi	1.05E-05
Fuji	0.999987753922	Mazda	1.22E-04
Isuzu	0.999974245258		
Hino	0.999981044967		

however, is open to question. At present, the propensity is specified only by capital partnership and supply data in this research. However, we think that it would be essential to consult domain experts to take other relationships among companies into the definition of propensity.

Conclusions

In this research, we have developed and illustrated an assumption model for predicting the membership of alliances among automakers that increase their scale of operation. We started with two assumptions: Japanese automakers prefer to join alliances to increase the probability of promoting the competitive power successfully, and to avoid collaborating with Japanese rivals, especially close rivals, in order to maximize its own benefits. We then defined the agents and their sizes, set the parameters, and discussed the result.

We illustrated the effectiveness of our methodology by applying it to the circumstances of the year 2000. Given a plausible set of assumptions concerning automaker size and propensity, we found a robust estimate of alliance configuration. The success indicates that the approach provides a practical method for suggesting which firms in an automobile industry will group together, by using capital partnership and supply data.

The simulation result shows that the proposed fuzzification of landscape theory allows us to analyze the flexible alignment. Using only manufacturer size and propensity, we estimated the probable alliance configurations. Further development of the model presented in this chapter should enhance the factors that determine alliance formation in other setting as is the case with the original theory.

References

Axelrod R (1997) The complexity of cooperation. Princeton University Press, Princeton, New Jersey

Culpan R (2002) Global business alliances: theory and practice. Quorum Books, Westport, CT, pp 105–142

Iriuchijima M (2000) Generalization of landscape theory and its application. Masters Thesis, Tokyo Institute of Technology

Kaufman L, Rousseeuw PJ (1990) Finding groups in data—an introduction to cluster analysis. New York, Wiley

Kijima K (2001a) Invitation to drama theory (in Japanese). Ohmsha, Tokyo, Japan, pp 58–63, pp 140–156

Kijima K (2001b) Generalized landscape theory: agent-based approach to alliance formations, Civil Aviation Industry. Journal of Systems Science and Complexity 14:113–123

Levy E (2000) Autos and auto parts. S&P Industry Survey 5

Maruka M (1997) Foreign carmakers fight for the share of Japan's market. Japan Times Weekly International Edition 37(4):14

Minoguchi T (2002) Understanding the automobile industry as well (in Japanese). Nippon Jitsugyo, Tokyo, Japan

Ruspini E (1969) A new approach to clustering. Information and Control 15:22–32

Suganuma S, Huynh V, Nakamori Y, et al (2003) A framework of fuzzy landscape theory with an application to alliance analysis. Journal of Systems Science and Complexity 16:1–12

Appendix: ISAGA 2003 Program

August 25 ───────────────────────────────────────

11:30–13:00 **ISAGA/JASAG Symposium 1: The Past, Present, and Future of JASAG**
Chairman: *Akira Sakamoto (Ochanomizu Univ.)*

The Past, Present, and Future of JASAG
Fumitoshi Kato (Keio Univ.) and Yusuke Arai (Tokai Univ.)

14:30–16:00 **ISAGA/JASAG Symposium 2: The Contribution of JASAG to S&G**
Chairman: *Fumitoshi Kato (Keio Univ.)*
Commentator: *Jan Klabbers (KMPC)*

The Contribution of JASAG to Simulation & Gaming I
Kiyoshi Arai (Chiba Institute of Tech.)

The Contribution of JASAG to Simulation & Gaming II
Tomio Kinoshita (Koshien Univ.)

The Contribution of JASAG to Simulation & Gaming III
Kinhide Mushakoji (Chubu Univ.)

16:20–18:00 **Opening Ceremony with JASAG Award**
Opening Address: Social Transformation and Politics in Japan
Tsutomu Hata (Former Prime Minister and Member of House of Representatives)

18:00–20:00 **Reception**

August 26 ───────────────────────────────────────

9:30–11:00 **Plenary 1: Social Contributions and Responsibilities of Simulation & Gaming 1**
Chairman: *Fumitoshi Kato (Keio Univ.)*

Toward a New Science of Simulation and Gaming: ISAGA and the Identity Problem of Simulation
and Gaming as an Academic Discipline
Rei Shiratori (Tokai Univ. & IPSJ)

Thoughts on the Retirement of Gaming-Simulation and Gamers
Cathy Greenblat (Rutgers Univ.)

11:30–13:00 **Plenary 2: Social Contributions and Responsibilities of Simulation & Gaming 2**
Chairman: *Shigehisa Tsuchiya (Chiba Institute of Tech.)*

Simulations and Social Responsibility: Why Should We Bother
Ivo Wenzler (Accenture)

From EN to INvironment: Simulation Games in Decision Making
Dmitri N. Kavtaradze (Moscow State Univ.)

14:00–15:30 _____

Utilization of Soft Computing Techniques to the Field of Simulation & Gaming 1
Chairman: *Norio Baba (Osaka Kyoiku Univ.)*

The Effects of the Insertion Timing of Commercial Breaks on a Loss of Attention
*Noriko Nagata (Kwansei Gakuin Univ.), Sanae H. Wake (Doshisha Women's College of Liberal Arts),
Mieko Ohsuga (Osaka Institute of Tech.) and Seiji Inokuchi (Hiroshima International Univ.)*

A Consideration on the Learning Behaviors of the Hierarchical Structure Learning Automata
Operating in the Nonstationary Multiteacher Environment: A Basic Research to Realize an
Effective Utilization of Artificial Neural Networks in the Nonstationary Environment
Norio Baba (Osaka Kyoiku Univ.) and Yoshio Mogami (Univ. of Tokushima)

Multiple Value Functions for a Computer Agent Interacting with Human
Yosuke Urushizaki (Fukui Univ.) and Naoyuki Kubota (Fukui Univ.)

Molecular Simulation Aiming at Life Simulation
Yuuki Komata (Hokkaido Univ.) and Mitsuo Wada (Hokkaido Univ.)

Actor-Oriented Approach to Simulation & Gaming
Chairman: *Kiyoshi Arai (Chiba Institute of Tech.)*

A New Horizon of Simulation and Gaming: Difficulties and Expectations of Facilitating Science, Technology and Practice
Kiyoshi Arai (Chiba Institute of Tech.)

Enhancing Policy Development Through Actor-Based Simulation
Jan Klabbers (KMPC)

Agent-Based Modeling Meets Gaming-Simulation: A Perspective to the Future Collaborations
Hiroshi Deguchi (Tokyo Institute of Tech.)

Structure-oriented Approach to Simulation & Gaming
Chairman: *Shigehisa Tsuchiya (Chiba Institute of Tech.)*

NEOS: New Employee Orientation Simulation
Richard Duke (Univ. of Michigan) and Jac Geurts

From Games to Policy Exercises: The Portfolio of 12 Simulations Within One Company's Transformational Change Initiative
Ivo Wenzler (Accenture)

Policy Exercise Creating Environment for Double-Loop Learning
Shigehisa Tsuchiya (Chiba Institute of Tech.)

16:00–17:30 _____

Computers, Games, and Interpersonal Relationships
Chairman: *Akiko Shibuya (Keio Univ.)*

The Influence of Video Game Use on Shyness: A Longitudinal Study of Secondary School Students
*Nobuko Ihori (Ochanomizu Univ.), Akira Sakamoto (Ochanomizu Univ.), Kurie Ide and Kumiko
Kobayashi (Ochanomizu Univ.)*

Idea Generation Aided a Computer Network: The Effect of an Evaluation System
*Rei Omi (Ochanomizu Univ.), Yumi Eto (Ochanomizu Univ.) and Akira Sakamoto (Ochanomizu
Univ.)*

Simulation and Gaming in Economics
Chairman: *Yoshihiro Nakajima (Osaka City Univ.)*

Power-Law Behaviors in Economical and Social Phenomena
Sasuke Miyazima (Chubu Univ.) and Keizo Yamamoto (Setsunan Univ.)

Investment Behavior of Electric Power Companies in Power Pool
Tatsuyuki Maitani (Kyoto Univ.), Hiroshi Takishita (Kyoto Univ.) and Tetsuo Tezuka (Kyoto Univ.)

Price Competition Between Middlemen: An Experimental Study
Kazuhito Ogawa (Kyoto Univ.), Kouhei Iyori (Kyoto Univ.) and Sobei H. Oda (Kyoto Univ.)

Simulation and Gaming in Politics and International Relations 1 (Election and Domestic Politics)
Chairman: *Rei Shiratori (Tokai Univ. & IPSJ)*

The Game of "Forming a Coalition Government"
Masayoshi Kuboya (Tokai Univ.) and Satoshi Kimura (Tokai Univ.)

The Artificial Politician Society: Modeling an Assembly in Silico
Katsuma Mitsutsuji (Univ. of Tokyo)

The Problem of Coordination
Jan-Erik Lane (The Univ. of Geneva) and Reinert Mæland (Lund Univ.)

Gaming Simulation of MUNICIPAL MERGERS: Its Development and Practical Application in the Classroom
Masami Ido (Akita Univ.), Kiyoshi Arai (Chiba Institute of Tech.) and Yukiharu Ishikawa (Akita Univ.)

Utilization of Soft Computing Techniques to the Field of Simulation & Gaming 2
Chairman: *Noriko Nagata (Kwansei Gakuin Univ.)*

Knowledge Extraction from Game Records by Using Probabilistic Model Based XCS
Hisashi Handa (Okayama Univ.)

Graininess Suppression Method for Transformation to the Digital Image from the Analog Image
Seiki Yashimori (Univ. of Tokushima), Yasue Mitsukura (Okayama Univ.), Sigeru Omatsu (Osaka Prefecture Univ.) and Koji Kita (Noritsu Co. Ltd.)

Development of a Intelligent Input Interface Using EMG for Mobile Terminal
Fumiaki Takeda (Kochi Univ. of Tech.) and Hironobu Sato (Kochi Univ. of Tech.)

Personal Identification Method Robust for Environmental Change
Hironori Takimoto (Univ. of Tokushima), Yasue Mitsukura (Okayama Univ.) and Norio Akamatsu (Univ. of Tokushima)

Intelligent Classification of Bill Money Using the LVQ Method
Sigeru Omatu (Osaka Prefecture Univ.)

A Theory of Gaming
Chairman: *Yeo Gee Kin (National Univ. of Singapore)*

Japanese Gaming Simulation 1941: A Historical Review
Arata Ichikawa (Ryutsu Keizai Univ.)

Scenarios in Simulation Games
Tse Min Lua (National Univ. of Singapore) and Yeo Gee Kin (National Univ. of Singapore)

A Business Game with Social Consequences
Joseph Wolfe (Experiential Adventures LLC)

Gaming Simulation for Risk Management
Chairman: *Hidehiko Kanegae (Ritsumeikan Univ.)*

Guaranties for Safety in Crisis Simulation
Jeannette Heldens (Univ. of Nijmegen), Bertruke Wein, Babette Pouwels and Ellen Hijmans

Emergency Headquarter Gaming for Training in Responding Earthquake Damage
Hideki Kaji (Keio Univ.), Katumi Matsumura (System Kagaku Kenkyujo), Tosiyuki Kaneda (Nagoya Institute of Tech.), Hidehiko Kanegai (Ritsumeikan Univ.), Kenichi Ishibashi (Keio Univ.), Mari Yahagi (Keio Univ.) and Jun Mihira (Keio Univ.)

A Tourist Management Game to Keep Stable Customers at Risk
Jungyoung Park (Ritsumeikan Univ.), Kyoung Bae. Ji (Ritsumeikan Univ.), Masahiro Shirotsuki (Ritsumeikan Univ.) and Hidehiko Kanegae (Ritsumeikan Univ.)

Agent Based Modeling Meets Gaming Simulation 1 (Fusion between Gaming and ABM)
Chairman: *Jan Klabbers (KMPC)*

Agent Based Modeling and Simulation Gaming for Exploring Institutional Change: Presentation of a Methodology
Stanislas Boissau (Wageningen Univ.)

Network Games with Human and Agents
Kouji Uchiyama (National Defense Academy), Akira Namatame (National Defense Academy) and Yuji Aruka (Chuo Univ.)

Analyzing BARNGA Gaming Simulation Using an Agent-Based Model
Yutaka I. Leon Suematsu (Kyoto Univ.), Keiki Takadama (Tokyo Institute of Tech.), Katsunori Shimohara (Kyoto Univ.), Osamu Katai (Kyoto Univ.) and Kiyoshi Arai (Chiba Institute of Tech.)

Identification of Player Types in Massively Multiplayer Online Games
Ruck Thawonnmas (Ritsumeikan Univ.), Ji-Yong Ho (Ritsumeikan Univ.) and Yoshitaka Matsumoto (Ritsumeikan Univ.)

Policy Exercise for Transition and Change 1
Chairman: *Shigehisa Tsuchiya (Chiba Institute of Tech.)*

Simulation Games in Organizational Change Processes
Marleen van de Westelaken (Univ. of Nijmegen) and Vincent Peters (Univ. of Nijmegen)

Openness: A Key to the Good Team Performance
Minako Fujiie (Tokyo Electric Power Company), S. Tsuchiya (Chiba Institute of Tech.), A. Tanabe (Aitel Corporation) and K. Sekimizu (Aitel Corporation)

Evaluating the Results of Simulation Games: Simulating the Simulation Game
Vincent Peters (Univ. of Nijmegen), Geert Vissers (Univ. of Nijmegen), Marleen van de Westelaken (Univ. of Nijmegen), Mario Kieft (Univ. of Nijmegen), Jeannette Heldens (Univ. of Nijmegen) and Babette Pouwels (Univ. of Nijmegen)

20:00–

The Demonstration of the Base Environment for Simulation and Gaming
Chairman: *Yoshihiko Suko (Keio Univ.)*

The Demonstration of the Base Environment for the Simulation & Gaming: Using Real Time Location Information and Profile Information
Yoshihiko Suko (Keio Univ.), Haruki Yokoyama (Keio Univ.), Shingo Yamada (Keio Univ.), Takashi Nagano (Keio Univ.), Yuzuru Takeuchi (Keio Univ.) and Fumitoshi Kato (Keio Univ.)

Simulation and Gaming in Politics and International Relations 4 (Coalition Game)
Chairman: *Masayoshi Kuboya (Tokai Univ.)*

Let's Play the Game of "Forming a Coalition Government"
Masayoshi Kuboya (Tokai Univ.) and Satoshi Kimura (Tokai Univ.)

Virtual Identity in Simulation and Gaming
Chairman: *Ohyama Keizo (Kumamoto Gakuen Univ.)*

Virtual Identity in Simulation and Gaming
Ohyama Keizo (Kumamoto Gakuen Univ.) and Shin'ichi Kabuki (Mejiro Univ.)

Comparing Two Forms of Group Decision Making: An Exercise in Analytical Hierarchical Process and Stakeholder Analysis
Chairman: *Nina McGarry (The George Washington Univ.)*

Comparing Two Forms of Group Decision Making: An Exercise in Analytical Hierarchical Process and Stakeholder Analysis
Nina McGarry (The George Washington Univ.) and Cynthia Knott

Policy Exercise for Transition and Change 3
Chairman: *Shigehisa Tsuchiya (Chiba Institute of Tech.)*

The Transfer Student: A Policy Exercise to Establish Symbiotic Relationships with the Local Community
Riho Yoshioka (Tokyo Electric Power Company), H. Sakai (Tokyo Electric Power Company), S. Tsuchiya (Chiba Institute of Tech.), A. Tanabe (Aitel Corporation) and D. Hyakushima (Chiba Institute of Tech.)

Understanding Yourself as a Facilitator of Simulations and Games
Chairman: *Elyssebeth Leigh (Univ. of Tech., Sydney)*

Understanding Yourself as a Facilitator of Simulations and Games
Elyssebeth Leigh (Univ. of Tech., Sydney) and Laraine Spindler (Univ. of Tech., Sydney)

August 27 ─────────────────────────────

9:30–11:00 **Plenary 3: Simulation & Gaming of P2M (Project and Program Management)**
Chairman: *Kiyoshi Arai (Chiba Institute of Tech.)*
Commentator: *Takao Terano (Tsukuba Univ.), Tametsugu Taketomi (PMCC) and Yoshikazu Goto (Ministry of Economy, Trade, and Industry)*

Enhancing Policy Development Through Actor-Based Simulation
Jan Klabbers (KMPC)

Complex Project Management and Gaming Simulation Methodology: Enriching Interfaces Between Mission and Performance
Shigenobu Ohara (Univ. of Tech., Sydney) and Kiyoshi Arai (Chiba Institute of Tech.)

11:30–13:00 **Plenary 4: Simulation and Gaming in Classrooms**
Chairman: *Akira Sakamoto (Ochanomizu Univ.)*
Commentator: *David Crookall (Univ. de Nice Sophia Antipolis)*

The Features and Role of Simulation Software in Classroom
Kanji Akahori (Tokyo Institute of Tech.)

Background and Current Status of Learning Games in the Field of Japanese School Education
Haruo Kamijo (The Quality Class Network)

14:00–15:30 ─────────────────────────────

Poster Presentation 1 (13:00–16:00)

Development of Simulation Code to Examine a Proper Group Decision Making
Masayori Ishikawa (Univ. of Tokyo), Nireka Adachi (Research Institute of Science and Tech. for Society) and Koichi Okamoto (Toyo Eiwa Univ.)

Conformity and Speech Order as Determinant Factors: Computer Simulation of Meetings
Nireka Adachi (Research Institute of Science and Tech. for Society), Masayori Ishikawa (Univ. of Tokyo) and Koichi Okamoto (Toyo Eiwa Univ.)

Instructional Technology for Developing and Making Use of Simulations and Games for Primary and Secondary Education 1
Chairman: *Toshiki Matsuda (Tokyo Institute of Tech.) and Natsuko Ishii (Tokyo Institute of Tech.)*

Alleviation of Language Anxiety Among Learners of Japanese Through Debate Activity
Mari Nishitani (Hitotsubashi Univ.) and Toshiki Matsuda (Tokyo Institute of Tech.)

Discovering New Relationships and Generalizations in Studied Mathematical Material with the Help of Computer Simulations
Gabriel Katz (Brandeis Univ.) and Vladimir Nodelman (Academic Institute of Tech.)

Instructional Activities Game: A Tool for Teacher Training and Research into Teaching
Toshiki Matsuda (Tokyo Institute of Tech.)

Gaming Materials for Planning ICT Integrated Lessons in Pre-service Teacher Training
Natsuko Ishii (Tokyo Institute of Tech.) and Toshiki Matsuda (Tokyo Institute of Tech.)

U-Mart: What We Have Learnt from the Virtual Market
Chairman: *Hiroyuki Matsui (Kyoto Univ.)*

The U-Mart System, an Artificial Futures Market Software and Its Usage for Education in Computer Science
Hajime Kita (Kyoto Univ.), Isao Ono (Univ. of Tokushima), Naoki Mori (Osaka Prefecture Univ.), Hiroshi Sato (National Defense Academy) and Hiroyuki Matsui (Kyoto Univ.)

Elementary Property of U-Mart found by Submitted Agents to "U-Mart International Experiment"
Yoshihiro Nakajima (Osaka City Univ.), Isao Ono (Univ. of Tokushima), Naoki Mori (Osaka Prefecture Univ.), Hiroyuki Matsui (Kyoto Univ.) and Hiroshi Sato (National Defense Academy)

A Report of U-Mart Experiments by Human Agents
Kazuhisa Taniguchi (Kinki Univ.), Yoshihiro Nakajima (Osaka City Univ.) and Fumihiko Hashimoto

Development and Analysis of Autonomously Trading Agents
Tomoharu Nakashima (Osaka Prefecture Univ.), Takanobu Ariyama (Osaka Prefecture Univ.) and Hisao Ishibuchi (Osaka Prefecture Univ.)

Facilitation in Simulation and Gaming
Chairman: *Fumitoshi Kato (Keio Univ.)*

Facilitation-in-Communication: A Study of Educational Gaming-Simulation
Fumitoshi Kato (Keio Univ.)

Personnel Development Through Gaming Simulation and Outdoor Training: Fundamental Principles, Similarities and Differences, Empirical Studies
Thomas Eberle (Univ. of Passau)

Group Size in Gaming Simulation: What Can We Learn from the Literature on Psychological Experiments and Gaming Simulations?
Mieko Nakamura (Ryutsu Keizai Univ.)

Unicrisis: An Experimental Learning Game for Leaders in British Universities
Edward Borodzicz (Univ. of Southampton)

Simulation and Gaming in Politics and International Relations 2 (International Relations)
Chairman: *Jan Erik-Lane (Univ. of Geneva)*

The Formation and the Change of National Identities in a Simulated Society Game
Hiroshi Yamaoka (Nagoya Univ.), Hiroki Takehashi (Nagoya Univ.) and Kaori Karasawa (Nagoya Univ.)

Modeling the International Economic Order: Absolute and Relative Gains
Kazutoshi Suzuki (Univ. of Tokyo)

Utilization of Soft Computing Techniques to the Field of Simulation & Gaming 3
Chairman: *Junzo Watada (Waseda Univ.)*

Wavelet Approach to Chaotic Forecasting of Stock Movement
Junzo Watada (Waseda Univ.) and Yoshiyuki Matsumoto

Face Extraction and Identification System Using Double Structure Neural Networks
Yasue Mitsukura (Okayama Univ.), Kesuke Mitsukura (Univ. of Tokushima), Minoru Fukumi (Univ. of Tokushima) and Shigeru Omatu (Osaka Prefecture Univ.)

Effective Utilizations of Soft Computing Techniques for the Design of Reliable Decision Support Systems Which Deal Stocks
Norio Baba (Osaka Kyoiku Univ.), W. Yaai (Osaka Kyoiku Univ.), Y. Sakatani (Osaka Kyoiku Univ.), T. Kawachi (Osaka Kyoiku Univ.), Xu Lina (Harbin Institute of Tech.) and D. Zhenglong (Harbin Institute of Tech.)

Digital Learning Software for Science in Classrooms
Chairman: *Kanji Akahori (Tokyo Institute of Tech.)*

Digital Learning Software for Science in Classrooms
Yoshiyuki Maeda (Japan Science and Tech. Corporation), Kazunori Terada (NHK ENTERPRISES 21, INC.), Chisato Funasaka (Media Art Co., Ltd.), Isamu Kawaishi (Total Media Development Institute Co., Ltd.), Kazunori Uryo (PKD Co., Ltd.) and Kanji Akahori (Tokyo Institute of Tech.)

Agent Based Modeling Meets Gaming Simulation 2 (Industry and Tech.)
Chairman: *Hiroshi Deguchi (Tokyo Institute of Tech.)*

Technological Efficiency and Organizational Inertia: An Agent-Based Simulation Model of the Emergence of Disruptive Technologies
Christian Buchta (Vienna Univ. of Economics and Business Administration), David Meyer (Vienna Univ. of Economics and Business Administration), Andreas Mild (Vienna Univ. of Economics and Business Administration), Alfred Taudes (Vienna Univ. of Economics and Business Administration) and Alexander Pfister (Vienna Univ. of Economics and Business Administration)

Evaluation of the Dealings Form in an Artificial Vegetables and Fruits Market II
Suguru Tsujioka (Shikoku Univ.) and Kohji Yamamoto (Shikoku Univ.)

Agent-Based Simulation on Alliance of Automobile Enterprises
Shigemasa Suganuma (Japan Advanced Institute of Science and Tech.), Yoshiteru Nakamori (Japan Advanced Institute of Science and Tech.), V.N. Huynh (Japan Advanced Institute of Science and Tech.) and Jian Chen (Tsinghua Univ.)

Hybrid-Gaming of Firm Strategy in High-Tech Industry: Human Agents and AI Agents Intermingled in A Simulation Model
Lee Hao (Kyoto Univ.) and Hiroshi Deguchi (Tokyo Institute of Tech.)

Simulation & Gaming of P2M (Project & Program Management) 1
Chairman: *Tametsugu Taketomi (PMCC)*

The Relevance of Case-Study Method in Business Management Curriculum: Evidences from India
K.B. Saji (Amrita Institute of Management)

Intelligent Enterprises Emerge in Japan by Program Management Thinking: A Japanese Knowledge Framework of Enterprise Innovation
Shigenobu Ohara (Univ. of Tech., Sydney)

Business Simulator Toward P2M Education
Takao Terano (Tsukuba Univ.)

Project and Program Management for Enterprise Innovation (P2M) and Program Management Application
Masayuki Ishikura (Project Management Professionals Certification Center) and Hironori Hayashi (Consultant, JRI)

Simulation and Gaming in Social Psychology
Chairman: *Junkichi Sugiura (Aichi Univ. of Education)*

Determinants of Cooperative Attitude to Prevent an Environmental Disorder: An Examination in the Simulated Society Game
Junko Toyosawa (Nagoya Univ.), Kaori Karasawa (Nagoya Univ.) and Nobuhiro Mitani (Nagoya Univ.)

The Effects of Guilt on Intergroup Relationship: An Examination in a Simulated Society Game
Nobuhiro Mitani (Nagoya Univ.), Kaori Karasawa (Nagoya Univ.) and Junko Toyosawa (Nagoya Univ.)

Producing Angry Programs
Shigeru Nakamaru (IOND Univ. Japan)

Subjective Dependence on Out-Group Resources and Cooperation with Out-Group Members: Research Using a Simulated Society Game and "Strategic Business Game"
Miyuki Mori (Ochanomizu Univ.), Murafumi Ono (Hitachi, Ltd.), Kouji Kitada (Mitsui Sumitomo Insurance Company, Limited), Takenori Yabukawa (West Japan Railway Company) and Hiroshi Nanami (Kwansei Gakuin Univ.)

16:00–17:30

Poster Presentation 2 (15:30–18:00)

The Effect of Resource and the Identification with the Super-Ordinate Group on Cooperative Behaviors
Hiroki Takehashi (Nagoya Univ.), Hiroshi Yamaoka (Nagoya Univ.) and Kaori Karasawa (Nagoya Univ.)

The Development of the Persuasion Game
Junkichi Sugiura (Aichi Univ. of Education)

The Effects of Guilt on Intergroup Relationship: An Examination in a Simulated Society Game
Nobuhiro Mitani (Nagoya Univ.), Kaori Karasawa (Nagoya Univ.) and Junko Toyosawa (Nagoya Univ.)

The Influence of Cyber-Friends on Loneliness and Social Anxiety: The Training Effects of "Natural" Simulation of Interpersonal Relationships
Reiko Ando (Ochanomizu Univ.), Akira Sakamoto (Ochanomizu Univ.), Kanae Suzuki (Univ. of Tsukuba) and Tsutako Mori (Konan Women's Univ.)

Instructional Technology for Developing and Making Use of Simulations and Games for Primary and Secondary Education 2
Chairman: *Toshiki Matsuda (Tokyo Institute of Tech.) and Natsuko Ishii (Tokyo Institute of Tech.)*

Educational Game to Train "The Informatical and Systematical Thinking" for "Information Study"
Rie Emoto (Tokyo Institute of Tech.) and Toshiki Matsuda (Tokyo Institute of Tech.)

Report Writing Simulator: A Tool for Training "Informatical and Systematical Thinking"
Mitsuyo Kuto (Japan Women's Univ.), Satoko Tsukiji (Kouen Women's Secondary School) and Toshiki Matsuda (Tokyo Institute of Tech.)

Simulation System for Training Judgment on Information Morals
Kazue Tamada (Tokyo Management College), Toshiki Matsuda (Tokyo Institute of Tech.) and Hiroshi Nakayama (Tokyo Denki Univ.)

Development of a Game for Engineering Ethics Education in Technical High School
Shinichi Endo (Technical High School attend to Tokyo Institute of Tech.) and Toshiki Matsuda (Tokyo Institute of Tech.)

How Simulated Experiences in Virtual Community Brings Social Contribution in Real Community: The Case of JNVC
Kikuko Harada (Center for Entrepreneurship Development)

Simulations in Economic Activity
Chairman: *Katsuyasu Fujita (Hokkaido Institute of Tech.)*

The Game of Technology Negotiations in IJVs: Experiences from India
K.B. Saji (Amrita Institute of Management)

Simulation Analysis of the Relationship Between Expenditure Dispersion Among Japanese Consumers and Economic Trends
Hisao Hirata (Tokyo Institute of Tech.), Hiromichi Mutoh (Japan Center for Economic Research), Nobuyuki Harada (Japan Center for Economic Research) and Kyoichi Kijima (Tokyo Institute of Tech.)

An Examination of the Social Consequences of Collusive Decision Making Practices in a Complex Business Game
Joseph Wolfe (Experiential Adventures LLC)

Simulation and Gaming in Politics and International Relations 3 (Political Education and Consciousness)
Chairman: *Rei Shiratori (Tokai Univ. & IPSJ)*

Re-creating the Immigrant Experience: An Interactive Simulation
David Rowland Grigg (Kaleidio Interactive Media Pty Ltd.)

Back to the Future and Future Perspective: What Do Students Learn from Simulation on the Past and the Future of International Relations?
Noboru Miyawaki (Matsuyama Univ.)

Utilization of Soft Computing Techniques to the Field of Simulation & Gaming 4
Chairman: *Sigeru Omatu (Osaka Prefecture Univ.)*

Utilization of Neural Networks & Genetic Algorithms in Order to Let Game Playing Much More Exciting
Norio Baba (Osaka Kyoiku Univ.) and Wang Shuqin (Osaka Kyoiku Univ.)

The Recognition Method of the EEG Feature Pattern Using the Factor Analysis
Shin-ichi Ito (Univ. of Tokushima), Yasue Mitsukura (Okayama Univ.), Norio Akamatsu (Univ. of Tokushima) and Rajiv Khosla (Univ. of La Trobe)

Learning Differently 1
Chairman: *Fumitoshi Kato (Keio Univ.)*

Teaching English to Children with Learning Difficulty
Akio Yamamoto (Gakushuin Boys' Senior High School), Akiko Okano (College of Clinical Welfare) and Noriko Tsuchiya (Tokyo Metropolitan School of Nursing)

Ethics in the ESP Classroom: A Case-Study Simulation
Mark Freiermuth (Univ. of Aizu)

Induction for International Students Within a UK Environment Using Interactive Teaching and Learning Methods
Helen Godfrey (Napier Univ.)

Agent Based Modeling Meets Gaming Simulation 3 (Business)
Chairman: *Takao Terano (Univ. of Tsukuba)*

A Simulation Analysis on Garbage Can Model by Using Colored-Petri Nets: For Evaluation on Procedure Design of Citizen Participation in Municipal Comprehensive Planning
Toshiyuki Kaneda (Nagoya Institute of Tech.)

Exploring Business Gaming Strategies by Learning Agents
Masato Kobayashi (Univ. of Tsukuba) and Takao Terano (Univ. of Tsukuba)

Business Simulator Development Cycle with Human and Computer-Players
Akemi Morikawa (Univ. of Tsukuba) and Takao Terano (Univ. of Tsukuba)

City Development Strategy
Vadim Chekalin (St. Petersburg State Univ.) and Elena Zarukina (St. Petersburg State Univ.)

Simulation & Gaming of P2M (Project & Program Management) 2
Chairman: *Shigenobu Ohara (PMCC)*

Uncertainty Evaluation for Program Cycle Management in P2M: Real Option Approach in Pharmaceutical R&D Model
Tametsugu Taketomi (PMCC)

Indian Economy and Enterprise Innovation: Adopting Programme Management (with Special Reference to the Tata Group)
Jiban K. Mukhopadhyay (Economic Adviser, Tata Group)

An Evaluation of Role-Playing Gaming on Reformation Toward Sustainable Rural Society: How to Awake a Regional Context in Citizens
Shinobu Kitani (Tohoku Univ.), K. Arai (Chiba Institute of Tech.), T. Hasebe (Tohoku Univ.), N. Nomura (Tohoku Univ.) and F. Nakano (Tohoku Univ.)

Policy Exercise for Transition and Change 2
Chairman: *Sigehisa Tsuchiya (Chiba Institute of Tech.)*

Search Conference: New Opportunities in Tourist Management of St. Petersburg
Tatiana Neshcheret (St. Petersburg State Tech. Univ.) and Larisa Taratina (St. Petersburg State Tech. Univ.)

System Dynamics Model for Scope Change Control
Sanjeev Nadkarni (Shailesh J Mehta School of Management, IIT-Bombay) and Karuna Jain (Shailesh J Mehta School of Management, IIT-Bombay)

E-Process Game Helps Governments Prepare for e-Government
Pieter van der Hijden (Sofos Consultancy)

20:00– ───

Instructional Technology for Developing and Making Use of Simulations and Games for Primary and Secondary Education 3
Chairman: *Akihiko Mitsuhashi (Sumida Junior High School) and Masato Nakagiri (Hida Senior High School)*

A Class for Increasing Self-Awareness of Fascism: The Simulation of a Fascist System
Masato Nakagiri (Hida Senior High School)

Let's Form a Company! A School Lesson Development with Simulation Method in Social Studies and Civics at Junior High School
Toshikazu Saegusa (Meguro dai-ni Junior High School)

Game Drawing Will Become A New Style of Gaming
Tsuyoshi Ajiro (Game Designer)

The Learning of Haiku on the Internet: The Haiku Game and Web KUKAI System for Children
Masaaki Sakaki (Japan Educational Publishing Co., Ltd.) and Mayumi Nishida (Shugakusha Co., Ltd.)

Hypothesis-Test Learning
Akihiko Mitsuhashi (Sumida Junior High School)

Search Conference as Feedback Tool
Chairman: *Nina Nemicheva (St. Petersburg State Tech. Univ.)*

Search Conference as Feedback Tool
Nina Nemicheva (St. Petersburg State Tech. Univ.) and Tatiana Neshcheret (St. Petersburg State Tech. Univ.)

Simulation and Gaming for Participatory Planning
Chairman: *Toshiyuki Kaneda (Nagoya Institute of Tech.)*

7-zones: Town Management Simulation
Yutaro Ito (Nagoya Institute of Tech.), Yuhi Inokuchi (Nagoya Institute of Tech.), Yuzuru Osakabe (Nagoya Institute of Tech.), Yoshihiro Nishimoto (Institute of Tech.) and Rim Meziani (Nagoya Institute of Tech.)

Simulation and Gaming in Politics and International Relations 5 (Simulation of International Relations)
Chairman: *Noboru Miyawaki (Matsuyama Univ.)*

Back to the Future and Future Perspective: What Do Students Learn from Simulation on the Past and the Future of International Relations?
Noboru Miyawaki (Matsuyama Univ.)

Simulation and Games for Standardization Managers Knowledge
Chairman: *Tatiana Kovaleva (International Management Institute of St. Petersburg)*

Simulation and Games for Standardization Managers Knowledge
Tatiana Kovaleva (International Management Institute of St. Petersburg)

Learning Differently 2
Chairman: *Joan Teach (Lullwater School)*

Colonizing a New World: From Social Studies to Social Skills Through Gaming
Joan Teach (Lullwater School)

Agent Based Modeling Meets Gaming Simulation 6 (Methodology & Society)
Chairman: *Kiyoshi Arai (Chiba Institute of Tech.)*

A Simulation of the Change of Public Attitude in a Social Space
Teruaki Ohnishi (The Wakasa Wan Energy Research Center)

Internal Dynamics and Multi-Agent Simulation
Takashi Sato (Japan Advanced Institute of Science and Tech.) and Takashi Hashimoto (Japan Advanced Institute of Science and Tech.)

Certification of Imitating Gaming and Non-gaming Products
July Mikhailovich Porkhovnik (St. Petersburg Univ. for Engineering and Economic) and A.I. Mihailuskin (St. Petersburg Univ. for Engineering and Economic)

Learning by Games, Games for Learning, and Learning Through Games
Chairman: *Masami Ido (Akita Univ.)*

Learning by Games, Games for Learning, and Learning Through Games
Masami Ido (Akita Univ.) and Haruo Kamijoh (The Quality Class Network)

Public Communication Games
Nobuyuki Sanai, Keiji Suzuki (Future Univ.-Hakodate) and Haruo Kamijo (The Quality Class Network)

Games for Learning Japanese as a Second/Foreign Language
Miyuki Ise, Mariko Suzuki and Haruo Kamijo (The Quality Class Network)

Games for Simulated School Settings
Masami Ido (Akita Univ.)

The Search & Rescue Game
Chairman: *Toshiko Kikkawa (Keio Univ.)*

The "Search & Rescue" Game
Toshiko Kikkawa (Keio Univ.), Haruo Hayashi (Kyoto Univ.), Katsuya Yamori (Nara Univ.), Tsuyoshi Ajiro (Game Designer), Reo Kimura (Kyoto Univ.), Satoru Sadohara (Yokohama National Univ.), Kei Horie (Earthquake Disaster Mitigation Research Center, National Research Institute for Earth Science and Disaster Prevention) and Mitsuhiro Higashida (Nippon Telegraph and Telephone West Corporation)

August 28 **ISAGA 2003's Open Day for the Public** ————————————————

10:30–11:00 **A Guide to Gaming: Principles and Practices**
Speaker: *Kiyoshi Arai (Chiba Institute of Tech.)*

11:00–12:30 ————————————————————————————————————

Learning Trust Through Multimedia Gaming
Gaming Director: *Arata Ichikawa (Ryutsu Keizai Univ.) and Akira Sakamoto (Ochanomizu Univ.)*

Teaching Economics with the Ideas of Experimental Economics
Facilitator: *Sobei H. Oda (Kyoto Sangyo Univ.)*

13:30–16:30 ————————————————————————————————————

Game for Teaching Environmental Problems
Facilitator: *Daisuke Sakamoto (Mitsubishi Research Institute, Inc.) and Hirotoshi Komoda (HISTORIA Institution)*

Cases of Educational Games
Facilitator: *Masami Ido (Akita Univ.) and Haruo Kamijo (The Quality Class Network)*

U-Mart 2003: A Virtual Futures Market Game
Game Director: *Hiroyuki Matsui (Kyoto Univ.)*

August 29

9:30–11:00 Plenary 5: Impact of Entertainment Games on Society
Chairman: *Arata Ichikawa (Ryutsu Keizai Univ.)*

Effects of Exposure to Violent Video Games
Craig Anderson (Iowa State Univ.)

The Impact of Electronic Games on Child and Youth Development
David Walsh (National Institute on Media and the Family)

11:30–13:00 Plenary 6: Possibility and Prospect of Online Game in Asia
Chairman: *Hosoi Koichi (Ritsumeikan Univ.)*

Possibility and Prospect of Online Game in Asia
Kiyoshi Shin (IGDA, Tokyo)

Possibility and Prospect of Online Game in Asia II
Jong-Hyun Wi (Chung-Ang Univ.)

Possibility and Prospect of Online Game in Asia I
Edward Z. Huang (Shanda Network Japan Office)

Possibility and Prospect of Online Game in Asia III
Kenji Matsubara (Koei Co., Ltd.)

Possibility and Prospect of Online Game in Asia IV
Son Taizo (BB Serve Inc.)

14:00–15:30

Online Game Business
Chairman: *Kiyoshi Shin (IGDA, Tokyo)*

Online Game Business 1
Son Taizo (BB Serve Inc.)

Online Game Business 2
Kenji Matsubara (Koei Co., Ltd.)

Online Game Business 3
Edward Z. Huang (Shanda Network Japan Office)

Bring Your Own Game: A Forum for "Students" of Gaming-Simulation 1
Chairman: *Fumitoshi Kato (Keio Univ.)*

Revealing What Is Hidden: An Environmental Treasure Hunt
Fiona French (London Metropolitan Univ.), D. Chapman (Univ. of East London), M. Kendal (London Metropolitan Univ.) and P. St. George (London Metropolitan Univ.)

Demonstration of "Content Cruising System"
Takaaki Ishida (Keio Univ.) and Shinichi Hisamatsu (Keio Univ.)

Development of Software Program for Predicting the Performance of Ultra-Micro Wind Turbine for Educational Use
Kentaro Namiki (Oyama National College of Tech.), Sumiyoshi Mita (Oyama National College of Tech.), Tairo Nomura (Saitama Univ.) and Toshiki Matsuda (Tokyo Institute of Tech.)

Peter F. Drucker's Thoughts and Gaming
Chairman: *Arata Ichikawa (Ryutsu Keizai Univ.)*

For the Knowledge Society: How to Involve Human Resources in Gaming
Arata Ichikawa (Ryutsu Keizai Univ.) and Mieko Nakamura (Ryutsu Keizai Univ.)

Policy Games for Strategic Management
Richard Duke (Univ. of Michigan) and Jac Geurts

Practicing Peter Drucker's Management Wisdom
Joseph Wolfe (Experiential Adventures LLC)

Social System Modeling
Chairman: *Yoshiteru Nakamori (Japan Advanced Institute of Science and Tech.)*

A Framework for Intelligent Indoor Navigation: Applicability for Gaming Simulation in Assumed Social Contexts
Kazuhiko Shibuya (Cyber Assist Research Center, National Institute of Advanced Industrial Science and Tech.)

Stochastic Dynamics of Social System Analysis
Hiroyuki Matsuura (National Graduate Institute for Policy Studies), M. Nakano (Univ. of Occupational and Environmental Health) and T. Nemoto (Tokyo Metropolitan College)

Design of an Agent-Based Gaming Simulation
Yuji Shinoda (Japan Advanced Institute of Science and Tech.) and Yoshiteru Nakamori (Japan Advanced Institute of Science and Tech.)

General Session
Chairman: *Toshiyuki Kaneda (Nagoya Institute of Tech.)*

Verification of Mental Influence in Man-Machine Interaction Based on Double-Bind Theory
Kazuo Ohnishi (Hannan Univ.) and Tatsuya Nomura (Hannan Univ.)

New Roles for Teachers in Edutainment Environment
Hanafizan Hussain (Multimedia Univ.) and Samsuri Hashim

Video Games and Violence
Chairman: *Akiko Shibuya (Keio Univ.)*

An Investigation of the Relationship Between Social Isolation, Self-esteem, Aggression, and Computer Game Play in Japanese Adolescents
Colwell John (De Montfort Univ.) and Makiko Kato (De Montfort Univ.)

Does Video Game Use Grow Children's Aggressiveness? Results from a Panel Study
Nobuko Ihori (Ochanomizu Univ.), Akira Sakamoto (Ochanomizu Univ.), Kumiko Kobayashi (Ochanomizu Univ.) and Fumika Kimura (Ochanomizu Univ.)

The Quantity and Context of Video Game Violence in Japan: Toward Creating an Ethical Standard
Akiko Shibuya (Keio Univ.) and Akira Sakamoto (Ochanomizu Univ.)

Agent Based Modeling Meets Gaming Simulation 4 (Environment & Education)
Chairman: *Keiko Zaima (Senshu Univ.)*

Agent-Based Simulation for Educational Policy Analysis
Atsuko Arai (Univ. of Tsukuba) and Takao Terano (Univ. of Tsukuba)

Environment Games with Strategic Agents
Shinji Tomita (National Defense Academy) and Akira Namatame (National Defense Academy)

Simulation of Thermostat Games among People by Coupling Agent-Based Model and Architectural Environment Model: Seeking Attitudes Suitable for Environmentally Symbiotic Society
Haruyuki Fujii (Tokyo Institute of Tech.) and Jun Tanimoto (Kyushu Univ.)

Agent-Based Simulation on the Diffusion of Green Products
Keiko Zaima (Senshu Univ.)

Environment Problems as Conflict and Cooperation from Simulation & Gaming 1
Chairman: *Susumu Ohnuma (Fuji Tokoha Univ.)*

Environmental Commons Game: Is Free Rider a "Bad Apple"?
Susumu Ohnuma (Fuji Tokoha Univ.)

Persuasive Communication on Environment Conscious Behavior
Junkichi Sugiura (Aichi Univ. of Education)

Do Resolutions of Environmental Problem Facilitate Global Identity in the North and the South Regions? Game-Simulations by SIMINSOC
Yumiko Taresawa (Nagoya Univ.)

Incongruence©: A Conflict Resolution Exercise
Richard Teach (DuPree College of Management, Georgia Tech.) and Robert Schwartz (Eastern Washington Univ.)

IT Policy and Game: International Comparison 1
Chairman: *Hiroshi Tokinoya (Tokai Univ.)*

Research and Development of the Game for the Simulation and Education in the United States
Seiji Moriya (Tokai Univ.)

IT Policy and Game: German Case
Yusuke Arai (Tokai Univ.)

Gaming and IT Policies: A Comparative View
Hiroshi Shiratori (Hosei Univ.)

16:00–17:30 ───

Poster Presentation 4

Applying Data Mining to Video Game Clustering Based on the Data of the Internet Survey
Tetsuya Onoda (Keio Univ.), Daiki Arai (Keio Univ.) and Yuka Nakano (Keio Univ.)

Online Game Design
Chairman: *Kiyoshi Shin (IGDA, Tokyo)*
Commentator: *Jong-Hyun Wi (Chung-Ang Univ.) and Kenji Matsubara (Koei Co., Ltd.)*

Online Game Design 1
Yoichi Wada (SQUARE ENIX Co., Ltd.)

Online Game Design 3
Rui Sato (CyberStep, Inc.)

Bring Your Own Game: A Forum for "Students" of Gaming-Simulation 2
Chairman: *Dmitri Kavtaradze (Moscow State Univ.)*

Green Bag: Set of Educational Simulation Games in Environmental Issues and Sustainable Development
Dmitri Kavtaradze (Moscow State Univ.)

Future Business Games for the Internet Age
Chairman: *Toshiro Kurozawa (Setsunan Univ.)*

The Effects of the Types of Companies in Decision Game Project
Katsuyasu Fujita (Hokkaido Inst. of Tech.) and Sadao Murahara (Musashi Inst. of Tech.)

Business Games Community on the Internet
Hiroaki Shirai (Yokohama National Univ.) and Motonari Tanabu (Yokohama National Univ.)

Computer Business Games: The Bridge Between Knowledge and Managerial Skills
Eugenijus Bagdonas (Kaunas Univ. of Tech.), Irena Patasiene (Kaunas Univ. of Tech.) and Vytautas Skvernys (Kaunas Univ. of Tech.)

Public Policy Game
Chairman: *Toshiyuki Kaneda (Nagoya Institute of Tech.)*

The Urban Network Game: A Simulation of the Future of Joint City Interests
Igor Mayer (Delft Univ.), Martijn Leijten (Delft Univ.), Linda Carton (Delft Univ.), Martin de Jong (Delft Univ.), Richard Scalzo (Erasmus Univ. Rotterdam), Ed Dammers (researcher at the Netherlands Institute for Spatial Research) and Femke Verwest (researcher at the Netherlands Institute for Spatial Research)

Developing "Playable Metagames" for Participatory Stakeholder Analysis
Pieter Bots (Delft Univ. of Tech.) and Leon M. Hermans (Delft Univ. of Tech.)

Public-Private Partnership to Develop Urban Freight Transport Policies: An Experiment on Cooperative Parcel Pick-Up System in Tokyo
Toshinori Nemoto (Hitotsubashi Univ.)

Simulation Analysis
Chairman: *Yoshiteru Nakamori (Japan Advanced Institute of Science and Tech.)*

Edutainment Content of Circus Acrobats Based on Dynamics
Suma Noji (Tokyo Institute of Tech.), Masayuki Nakajima (Tokyo Institute of Tech.) and Hiroki Takahashi (Tokyo Institute of Tech.)

Design of Simulator and Analysis for Biped Running Locomotion
Masahiko Isashi (Hokkaido Univ.), Kousuke Yamakita (Hokkaido Univ.), Kosei Ishimura (Hokkaido Univ.) and Mitsuo Wada (Hokkaido Univ.)

Analysis of Playing Style in Poker Game by Seven-Card-Stud Poker System
Chiharu Takahashi (Univ. of Tsukuba) and Takehisa Onisawa (Univ. of Tsukuba)

Simulation of Fish School Behavior in Fishpass with an Expanded Individual-Based Model
Masaaki Ishikawa (Tokyo Univ. of Fisheries), Fuxiang Hu (Tokyo Univ. of Fisheries) and Tadashi Tokai (Tokyo Univ. of Fisheries)

The Effects of Playing Video Games on Brain Activity
Chairman: *Kanae Suzuki (Univ. of Tsukuba) and Miho Tanaka (Ochanomizu Univ.)*

The Relationship Between Long-Term Playing of Video Games and Functions of the Prefrontal Cortex
Miho Tanaka (Ochanomizu Univ.), Kyoko Hirasawa (Tokyo Women's Medical Univ.), Kanae Suzuki (Univ. of Tsukuba), Akira Sakamoto (Ochanomizu Univ.) and Yukuo Konishi (Tokyo Women's Medical Univ.)

Relationship Between Long-Term Use of Video Games and Cognitive Abilities
Kanae Suzuki (Univ. of Tsukuba), Kyoko Hirasawa (Tokyo Women's Medical Univ.), Miho Tanaka (Ochanomizu Univ.), Akira Sakamoto (Ochanomizu Univ.) and Yukuo Konishi (Tokyo Women's Medical Univ.)

Frontal Deactivation in Video Game Players
Goh Matsuda (Univ. of Tokyo) and Kazuo Hiraki (Japan Science and Technology Corporation)

Agent Based Modeling Meets Gaming Simulation 5 (Economics)
Chairman: *Yoshihiro Nakajima (Osaka City Univ.)*

Experimental Economics Meets Agent-Based Finance: A Participatory Artificial Stock Market
Laszlo Gulyas (Computer and Automation Research Institute Hungarian Academy of Sciences), Balazs Adamcsek (AITIA Inc., Hungary) and Arpad Kiss (Lorand Eotvos Univ. and AITIA Inc., Hungary)

Common Information Controller in Minority Game
Keiji Suzuki (Future Univ.-Hakodate) and Keiji Miyanishi (Future Univ.-Hakodate)

A Model for Collusive Tendering Based on a Multi-Agent Approach
Jun Tanimoto (Kyushu Univ.) and Haruyuki Fujii (Tokyo Institute of Tech.)

U-Mart Project: New Research and Education Program for Market Mechanism
Hiroyuki Matsui (Kyoto Univ.), Kazuhisa Taniguchi (Kinki Univ.), Yasuhiro Nakajima (Osaka City Univ.), Isao Ono (Univ. of Tokushima), Hiroshi Sato (National Defense Academy), Naoki Mori (Osaka Prefecture Univ.), Hajime Kita (National Institution of Academic Degrees), Takao Terano (Tsukuba Univ.), Hiroshi Deguchi (Tokyo Institute of Tech.) and Yoshinori Shiozawa (Osaka City Univ.)

Environment Problems as Conflict and Cooperation from Simulation & Gaming 2
Chairman: *Willy Kriz (Univ. of Munich)*

Creating Effective Interactive Learning Environments and Social Contributions Through Gaming Simulation Design (Part I)
Willy Kriz (Univ. of Munich)

CRUZ DEL SUR: Creating Interactive Learning Environments and Social Contributions Through Gaming Simulation Design (Part II)
Matthias Puschert (Tech. Univ. and Ludwig-Maximilians-Univ. in Munich), Angelika Dufter-Weis (Tech. Univ. and Ludwig-Maximilians-Univ. in Munich) and Juliane Karl (Ludwig-Maximilians-Univ. in Munich)

Simulation of Flooding Conflict Game Between Cambodia and Vietnam in the Mekong River Basin
Hajime Tanji (Lab. of River and Coast, National Institute for Rural Engineering)

IT Policy and Game: International Comparison 2
Chairman: *Rei Shiratori (Tokai Univ. & IPSJ)*

Information Technology Policy and Culture in France
Nagisa Yokoyama

Russian IT Policy and Entering the WTO
Ryouichi Sato (Tokai Univ.) and Hiroyuki Fujimaki (Tokai Univ.)

Gaming and IT Policy: A Nepalese Perspective
Pravakar Adhikari (Tribhuvan Univ.)

18:00–20:00 **ISAGA Conference Dinner / Closing Ceremony**

Dinner Speech
Richard Duke (Univ. of Michigan)

Index